THE
ENCYCLOPEDIA
of
HERBS,
SPICES,
& FLAVORINGS

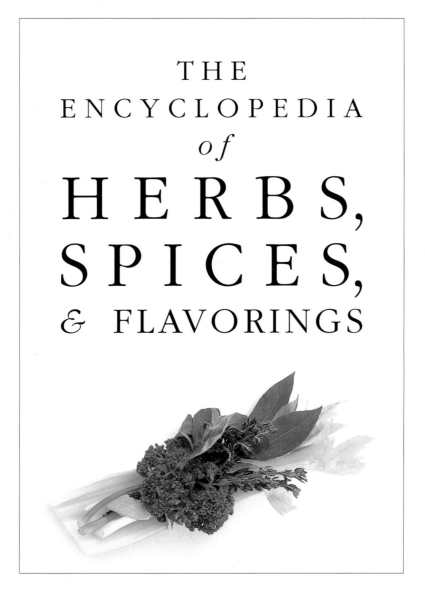

THE
ENCYCLOPEDIA
of
HERBS,
SPICES,
& FLAVORINGS

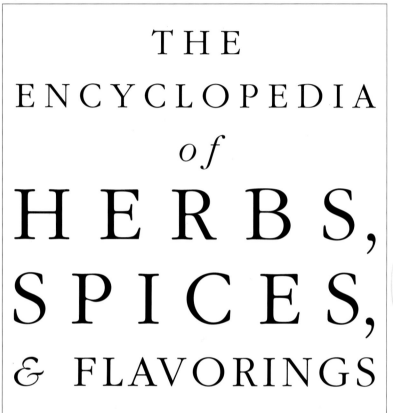

CONTRIBUTING EDITOR
ELISABETH LAMBERT ORTIZ

DK

DK PUBLISHING, INC

DK

A DK PUBLISHING BOOK

Created and Produced by
CARROLL & BROWN LTD
5 Lonsdale Road
London NW6 6RA

Editor **Laura Washburn**
Art Editor **Lisa Tai**
Photographer **David Murray**
Computer Operator **Debra Lelliott**
Production Controller **Lorraine Baird**

DK PUBLISHING, INC.
95 Madison Avenue
New York, NY 10016
http://www.dk.com

The Encyclopedia of herbs, spices, and flavorings/Elisabeth
Lambert Ortiz, contributing editor – 1st American ed.

8 10 9 7

First published in Great Britain in 1992
by Dorling Kindersley Limited
9 Henrietta Street, London WC2E 8PS

Includes index.
ISBN 1-56458-065-2
1. Herbs – Encyclopedias. 2. Spices – Encyclopedias. 3. Cookery
(Herbs) – Encyclopedias. I. Ortiz, Elisabeth Lambert.
TX406.ES4 1992
641.3'57 – dc20

Reproduced by Colourscan, Singapore
Printed and bound in Italy

FOREWORD

Since the art of cooking was developed, herbs have been used to enliven and enhance meals. The number of herbs is legion, and they may be used medicinally as well as in the kitchen. Herbs are always bracketed with spices, but the difference between the two is easily defined. Herbs are the leaves of fresh or dried plants, while spices are the aromatic parts: buds, fruit, berries, roots, or bark, usually dried, from plants that thrive in tropical regions. Their role in the kitchen is the same: to enhance the flavor of foods. Herbs, which are not confined to the tropics, are outdoor plants, although some can be grown indoors in sunny places. The categories can overlap because a plant can supply both a spice and an herb; for example, the aromatic seeds and dried ground form of coriander are known as "coriander" but the fresh leaves are usually called "cilantro." It is herbs and spices in combination that give the flavor and aromas that are a mingled sensation of smell and taste.

Herb cultivation and use has always been a peaceful enterprise. Spices, on the other hand, have upset and altered history, caused fortune or mishap, and have been prime movers in great events. The nations of Europe, especially Portugal, Spain, the Low Countries (Holland and Belgium), England, and France, became embroiled in colonial wars as a result of Columbus's search for a quick route to the Spice Islands. It was this search for spices that ended with Columbus discovering the Americas—an event with far-reaching consequences; he found not only a new world but new foods, including the capsicums (peppers) that greatly influenced world cooking and spread with astonishing rapidity over the globe.

Today, an ever-widening range of reliable seeds is available for sowing in home gardens, patio tubs, window boxes, or pots on ledges. In addition, more fresh herbs are on sale in supermarkets and specialty markets, as well as a wide variety of dried herbs, freeze-dried herbs, and packaged spice mixtures. The world of herbs, spices, and flavorings from faraway places, as well as the familiar ones of home, can add immeasurably to our gustatory pleasure, whether we are dining on family favorites or entertaining friends with new and exciting dishes. Our culinary horizons are expanded and our imaginations stirred. And travel away from home is more fulfilling when we have some knowledge of unfamiliar dishes and can choose with confidence from a menu in a foreign land. The flavors of the world are yours to discover, they are just waiting for you to try them, so accept their invitation—go and experiment, go and enjoy.

ELISABETH LAMBERT ORTIZ

CONTENTS

INTRODUCTION:
A WORLD OF FLAVORINGS

KITCHEN HERBS

Herbs, the fragrant plants that are used for seasoning dishes, were probably first cultivated thousands of years ago, before the dawn of civilization: perhaps their cultivation signaled the start of civilization itself. Records exist that testify to a very early knowledge of herb cultivation and use in Egypt, China, India, Arabia, Persia, and Greece, and the culinary use of herbs remains a firmly rooted tradition. Today herbs are more important and more accessible than ever ; they are cultivated on a small scale in private gardens, on a large scale for sale to supermarkets and grocery stores, and by chefs for use in their restaurant kitchens. Herbs are increasingly sold fresh, which is best, and dried stocks mean they are available year-round; many dried herbs happily retain their aroma. The extra advantage of herbs as garden plants is that they are easy to grow, for the most part undemanding of special soils and conditions. Attractive in the garden and on the plate, they improve the flavor of our food and are also good for us.

Borage

KITCHEN SPICES

Today all supermarkets and most small grocery stores have well-stocked spice shelves, offering a selection of seasonings from around the world. These spices are now all modestly priced, yet there was once a time when they were worth their weight in gold.

The Queen of Sheba brought spices, precious stones, and gold to King Solomon, proof that spices, with a temporary life, were rated as highly as enduring metals and gems. Aside from flavoring and preserving foods, spices played a considerable role in religion and an even greater role in medicine, and their role in politics was greater still. The spice trade virtually made the Dutch Empire and turned the small city-state of Venice into a great power.

Spice jars

Many spices originated in the Asian tropics: cinnamon, cloves, nutmeg, pepper, and gingerroot. The Americas contributed allspice, vanilla, and chilies; the Mediterranean countries provided cilantro, mustard, fennel, poppy seeds, and fenugreek; Europe's cooler regions brought forth caraway, dill, and juniper.

There was a time when spices were so precious that they were kept locked away in special boxes and an exuberant use of spices was an indication of the provider's wealth. Nowadays we look to spices to capture the exotic flavors of faraway places without ever leaving our own kitchens.

FLAVORS OF THE WORLD

The great dishes of the world's cuisines are characterized by specific combinations of herbs, spices and flavorings. These mixtures have developed over the centuries, influenced largely by the foodstuffs native to each region, the foodstuffs being determined by climate, soil, and local culture.

The scent of curry will instantly transport you to India, where the preferred spices are highly aromatic, with as many as ten used to flavor a single dish. Thai curries, although very hot, are more delicate with a far greater use of fresh herbs and it is more likely to be the aroma of lemongrass, Kaffir lime, and fresh cilantro leaves that evokes Thailand and its deliciously subtle cuisine. Chinese cooking is immensely diverse, yet it has a uniform characteristic flavor, a mingling of smell and taste that can evoke a whole country in our imagination. It may be the perfume of five-spice powder blended in soy sauce, or a stir-fry with black bean sauce, gingerroot, and garlic that is the trigger. The flavors of Indonesia are an intricate mixture of sweet and sour, with lemongrass, tamarind, Kaffir lime, chilies, and pungent dried shrimp combined. Soy sauce is also important in Japanese cooking—the most elegantly simple in the world—relying on the pure flavor of fresh seasonal ingredients. Although all these countries are in the Far East, their cuisines could not be more richly diverse.

North Africa uses many of the spices of Asia in ways that produce wholly different flavors. Europe uses spices more sparingly—mainly for pickling and baking—while in the Mediterranean, the use of herbs is predominant, with healthy doses of thyme, sage, bay, oregano, and rosemary. With a culinary history closely linked to Europe, North America uses herbs and spices in much the same way, although the Southwest is influenced by Mexico and the Pacific. The flavors of Mexico are hard to mistake; the aromas of baking corn tortillas and chilies roasting are characteristic of the region.

Chat masala

Highly spiced foods also are a feature of Central and South America and the Caribbean. Here, as in the rest of the world, the individual combinations of herbs, spices, and flavorings transform ordinary ingredients into culinary classics that can be enjoyed throughout the year, in the comfort of our own dining rooms.

VEGETABLE AND FRUIT FLAVORINGS

Vegetables and fruit are as important as their close relatives herbs and spices in turning our daily meals into sources of pleasure as well as sources of nutrition and so nourish both body and spirit. Mushrooms of many kinds, all with different flavors, are essential in an array of dishes from East to West. Life without the onion family would be a sorry thing because there is scarcely a savory dish that does not welcome one or other of the *Allium* genus, whether it be the onion, the delicate chive, or the robust garlic clove. Pungent roots like horseradish and wasabi add piquancy to foods as diverse as roast beef and raw fish. Olives bring with them the salty, sunny flavors of the Mediterranean, and it is hard to imagine how barren the culinary landscape would be without the tomato. From Mexico

comes chocolate, the royal drink of the Aztecs and the modern-day ingredient in sweets and desserts the world over. The citrus family—limes, lemons, oranges, and others—are infinitely useful in the kitchen; a few drops of their juices accent flavors of both savory and sweet dishes. They could well be called indispensable. Nuts are good just by themselves, and their texture and their varied flavors make them a welcome and often essential ingredient in sauces, snacks, main course dishes, and desserts.

Limes

EXTRACTS, ESSENCES, AND SWEETENERS

Natural extracts and essences bring a wonderful flavor into our cooking, conveniently bottled so that they will keep almost indefinitely. From Asia comes the soybean, and from around the world comes the variety of flavorful table condiments. For sweetness, the bees work hard, but we get the honey, and the sugar maple gives us the subtle flavor of its syrup. The fruits of summer are captured in purees, essences, and syrups, to bring the warmth and brightness of that season into our winter kitchens.

EDIBLE FLOWERS AND LEAVES

Flower gardens, as much as herb gardens, can be a valuable source of ingredients for the kitchen. Likewise, many plants have leaves that are not edible but do make valuable wrappings. Clambakes in New England and *curantos* in Chile would lose a great deal without the seaweed used in their preparation, and Japanese cooking would not be half as delectable if the seaweeds were taken away. Most flowers are used more for beauty than for flavor, though zucchini blossoms make a splendid soup and a fine first course when stuffed. Crystallized violets and rose petals are both beautiful to look at and delicious to eat—bringing the best of both worlds to the kitchen.

Salad with flowers

OILS, VINEGARS, AND DAIRY PRODUCTS

The fats—oil, butter, and cream—give food a rich and satisfying quality. Sour cream, buttermilk, and yogurt add a richness and tang to any dish, from soup to dessert. The acidic quality of vinegar is vital for both flavor and preserving. It is essential in vinaigrette, the classic salad dressing of French cuisine, and it adds the tartness that characterizes sweet-and-sour dishes.

SAUCES, PRESERVES, AND CONDIMENTS

All the good things of summer can be harvested and transformed into pickles, relishes, preserves, and chutneys, although nowadays modern agriculture and transport mean that many fruits and vegetables are available year-round. Many sauces can be made fresh whenever needed, making the winter table a very lavish one indeed. In addition, there are myriad commercial cooking and table sauces that can be used directly on cooked food or added during cooking. Sweet or savory, these sauces, preserves, and condiments enhance our meals and deserve a place on our kitchen shelves.

Pickles and relishes

COFFEE, TEA, AND SPICED DRINKS

Tea and coffee are both ancient drinks in their countries of origin: China and Ethiopia. Today they are both firmly established beverages in most countries of the world. Tisanes, or herb teas, have long been appreciated for their soothing and mildly medicinal properties, and they are gaining popularity as a flavorful and healthy alternative to coffee and tea. Fruit and vegetable juices, wines, spirits, and even yogurt are the perfect base for drinks, both hot and cold, to be flavored with herbs and spices.

Iced tea

FLAVORINGS AT HOME

Nothing quite equals the pleasure of going into the garden, or to the window box, and picking fresh herbs for the next meal. The flavor is incomparable and, beyond that, allows for last-minute decisions, improvisation, and even the possibility to improve an old favorite. As the summer moves inevitably to autumn, the crisp, cooler days are perfect for canning, preserving, and bottling the last of the season's fruit for the pantry or holiday gift giving. Any time of year, a gift from one kitchen to another is always welcome.

GROWING HERBS

Most culinary herbs are ideally suited to container growing, both indoors in pots on the windowsill and outside in tubs, window boxes, and hanging baskets. Not only does this result in extremely attractive additions to the garden environment, but it puts herbs immediately at hand for cooking.

Tubs and large pots can be conveniently placed near the back door or on the terrace or balcony; if space is really at a premium, small pots of herbs on a kitchen windowsill also work very well. With access to a bright window ledge, no cook has to be denied the authentic taste of fresh herbs for culinary creations.

A large tub will allow for a number of herbs in a relatively small area, but some attention to compatibility is necessary. Herbs such as rosemary, thyme, marjoram, and sage love a very sunny spot, whereas the mint family, chervil, and chives prefer filtered sunlight and a more moist atmosphere. Fussy herbs, such as basil, thrive indoors, where their needs can be monitored more easily. Invasive herbs, such as tarragon and mint, should be planted in separate pots so they do not encroach on other herbs.

A well-thought-out herb garden can enhance the landscape as much as it enhances the stockpot and salad bowl. With many green-, purple-, gold-, and silver-leaved herbs, as well as the many variegated types, there is an overwhelming choice for the home cook and gardener. The striking tricolor sage, with pink-tinged new growth, as well as the gold-green lemon thyme and the blue-green narrow-leaved rosemary column, among others, offer unlimited opportunities to design with form, color, and flavor.

Some herbs have beautiful flowers as well as flavorful leaves: borage, hyssop, rosemary, thyme, chives, mint, and sage, for example. In the kitchen, they can be used as last-minute garnishes for salads or cheese platters. In the garden, however, flowers will detract from the plant's ability to devote all of its flavor to the leaves, so prune them frequently.

Potted herbs

HOW TO PLANT

If only one plant is required, it is probably best to purchase a small herb from a specialist nursery or garden center and progressively transplant it into larger containers. For multiple plants, some herbs grow well from seed: tarragon, parsley, chives, or basil can all be sown directly into individual pots of potting soil. Place them in a warm spot and cover with plastic garbage bags until germination; then position them on the windowsill to grow to maturity.

In all instances, remember that the larger and deeper the pot, the more leaves the plant will be able to produce.

HERBS INDOORS

A vast array of clay and plastic pots are available for indoor planting. Because many herbs are native to the Mediterranean region, clay pots complement them visually while also allowing moisture to evaporate, which helps the roots breathe. Whatever the material you choose, always use containers with good drainage holes and add a few pieces of broken pot or a layer of gravel to prevent waterlogging. When potting, incorporate a half inch of horticultural sand two-thirds down from the edge of the pot, which will assist drainage and keep the soil from impacting and suffocating the roots.

Watering can

Herbs appreciate a moist atmosphere, particularly indoors. To increase humidity, stand the pots on a gravel bed in a saucer, if possible, with water not quite covering the gravel. The exception is basil, which tolerates moderate dryness.

Treat your herbs as you would wish to be treated; they will thrive in a comfortable environment: a stable temperature of 60–70°F (16–21°C), free from draughts. Water regularly, but err on the dry side. When in doubt, touch the soil; if it feels dry, the herb requires watering. Always use lukewarm water, not cold. Windows can reduce the available light substantially, so turn the pots regularly to expose all parts of the plant to some sun. Herbs such as marjoram, oregano, thyme, and basil require full sun to thrive. Chives, parsley, chervil, and mint prefer less direct sun and a cooler position.

Remember to pinch out the growing tips of the herbs to encourage a bushier plant. If the herb is used regularly for cooking, this natural pruning will be adequate for a long supply.

HERBS OUTDOORS

Wooden half-barrels, old basins, chimney pots, and the myriad of terra-cotta and clay pots are all suitable for herb

Hanging basket

growing. The final choice depends entirely on personal taste and space available. However, wood or clay does seem to set off herbs to their best advantage.

Several herbs grown together in one large tub often seem to do better than plants that are grown in individual pots. For balconies or patios, this creates an instant herb garden that is both decorative and useful. Try a combination of annuals, such as sweet basil, dill, and summer savory, surrounding a central, taller herb such as rosemary or bay. Fill in any gaps with lemon thyme, marjoram, and purple sage.

Some herbs are not compatible. Fennel should not be mixed with caraway, dill, or cilantro, and parsley does not do well with mint.

Another idea, if space is limited, is to fill a large strawberry pot with a different herb for each opening, thus creating an unusual focal point for the terrace. This type of container does need careful monitoring because it tends to require more watering than conventional tubs.

If herbs are in single pots, remember that the bigger the pot, the better the leaf production. Raise large tubs and pots off the ground by balancing them on two pieces of wood; this frees the drainage hole and prevents waterlogging. Invasive herbs, such as tarragon and the mints, are more suited to individual planting. These smaller pots look very attractive in groups, which also encourages the more humid environment that they appreciate and thrive in.

Hanging baskets are an attractive way to display low-growing and compact herbs. Exposure to the wind can be a problem because they may

have little shelter from other plants and nearby structures. Sturdy herbs, such as various thymes, curly-leaf parsley, prostrate rosemary, and nasturtiums, are most suitable.

CARE AND MAINTENANCE

All container plants need careful monitoring. Check topsoil daily and water as required. Bear in mind that smaller tubs and pots dry out quicker. When watering, try to maintain an even moistness throughout, not wet in parts and parched elsewhere.

Pinch out the growing tips to encourage full, bushy plants, particularly sage, which tends to become untidy.

Watch out for the usual garden pests, such as aphids, slugs, and caterpillars, as these can decimate plants in a very short time. An environmentally-friendly method of controlling the onslaught is to spray with a diluted detergent at the first indications. Be sure to wash any treated herbs thoroughly before using in foods.

In the autumn, resite tubs and pots that are in exposed parts of the garden to more sheltered areas and mulch the roots well with organic matter. In extremely cold snaps, wrap a handful of straw around the top growth of perennial herbs, such as bay and rosemary, with a layer of plastic garbage bags as insulation until the worst is over. Individual pots can be wintered in an unheated greenhouse or conservatory.

Strawberry pot with herbs

HARVESTING HERBS

Having successfully grown the various herbs on the windowsill or in the garden, there are a few principles that should be observed when it comes to harvesttime.

Different parts of the herb are gathered at different times and in a variety of ways. It is advisable to use a shallow, flat-bottomed container so that the herbs can be placed in a single layer, which prevents damage by bruising.

Obviously, with roots and bulbs, such as garlic, the entire plant is forfeited at the end of the season, but annual leafy herbs, such as basil, can be successfully maintained in the garden until late autumn by careful picking and pruning of leaves. It is very important to take into account the type, size, and age of the plant. Perennial herbs, such as sage, thyme, and rosemary, should not be weakened by severe pruning or overstripping of the leaves before winter sets in, particularly if the plant is small, or quite young, or only just recently established.

When harvesting any plant, in the garden or indoors in pots, do not take more than a maximum of 10 percent of the growth otherwise the shock effect can be detrimental. Careful harvesting of all leafy perennial herbs results in more vigorous leaf production and healthier plants.

LEAVES

These can be picked throughout the year, particularly from herbs such as rosemary, thyme, parsley, chives, and chervil. The flavor is best just before the herb flowers. Try to pick the young leaves from the parent plant in the morning, when the dew has evaporated. Discard any imperfect leaves or those damaged by insects. Handle as little as possible, because bruising or crushing the leaves releases the volatile oils, thereby reducing the flavor.

FLOWERS AND BULBS

Herb flowers—chives, marigolds, borage, and chamomile—should be picked carefully when they are fully open. Lavender is best when the flowers have just begun to open. In all cases, avoid old, damaged, or wilted specimens. Place in an open container, uncovered, until needed and do not harvest too far in advance. Harvest bulbs, such as garlic, in late summer, when the leaves start to die off.

SEEDS

When the seed heads and pods have formed, keep a close eye on their progress, since timing is all-important to their harvest. There should be no green coloring on the seeds, and the pods, if any, should be very dry. If there is a risk of scattering, as with fennel, carefully cut off the entire stalk holding the seeds and invert into a paper bag or over a container.

Place the seeds or seed heads in a warm, well-ventilated room for a few days to dry thoroughly. As they dry, the seeds will drop into the bag or container, so there will be no waste. It is a good idea to label the seed container when harvesting begins, to avoid identification problems later. Store the dried seeds in a dark, airtight glass jar. If they are required for next year's planting, store them in a cool, dry place until needed.

Basket for harvesting herbs

DRYING HERBS

For centuries cooks have endeavored to maintain good supplies of herbs year-round. Originally this was achieved by drying or by infusing in oils and vinegars. Nowadays, with greatly improved methods of transportation, there is an extended season for fresh herbs and these traditional techniques are often overlooked. This is a disadvantage to the modern cook since these preserving methods extend the flavoring potential of both herbs and spices.

To retain most of the flavor and color of the herb, speed is vital, as is the freshness of the herbs at harvest.

DRYING

This is one of the most popular methods of preservation, and in some cases it actually improves the flavor of the herb, especially with bay leaves. Brush off any loose soil from the leaves and dust with a soft pastry brush or similar implement; washing is necessary only if the leaves are very gritty. The easiest procedure is to hang the herbs in small, loose bunches from a rack in a warm room. The temperature should not exceed 86°F (30°C) or the essential oils will evaporate.

Drying rack

Do not let leaves become so dry that they disintegrate into a powder when touched. Also, despite the attractive appearance of herbs hanging in bunches, try to avoid drying them in the kitchen, which is often full of condensation from cooking. To prevent dust from settling on the bunches, place a paper bag over the herbs, leaving the bottom of the bag open to the air.

When the leaves are crisp and dry, after about a week (but this depends on the thickness of the leaf and the warmth of the room), they are ready for storage. Strip the leaves whole from the stems and place in a jar, without crushing them. After a day, check for condensation inside the jar; this is a sign leaves are not yet dry enough. If condensation is present, remove the leaves for further drying; otherwise the batch will spoil. For small quantities, make an herb-drying rack by covering an oven shelf, or a simple wooden frame, with fine wire mesh; place the herbs on top of the rack in a single layer. Leave in a warm place, as before, checking periodically on the progress of the drying herbs.

It is not advisable to dry herbs in the oven, however low the temperature, because this treatment does seem to diminish the flavor.

Microwave ovens, however, are useful for drying herbs. Place a single layer of herbs on a paper towel and cook on full power. Time will depend on quantity and oven wattage; see manufacturer's instructions for best results. After about 1 minute, turn the herbs and continue cooking until dry.

Bundles of herbs for drying

15

PRESERVING AND STORING

Storage jars

Dried herbs should be stored in airtight dark glass or pottery jars. Clear glass containers should be stored inside kitchen cabinets. Light and exposure to air and moisture makes the herbs deteriorate more quickly, which is why it is important to use well-sealed containers and keep them in a dark place.

Freezing is another effective means of extending the availability of herbs, especially dill, fennel, basil, and parsley. Clean the herbs as appropriate and seal in small quantities—about 2–3 tablespoons—in freezer bags. Freeze alone or in favorite combinations, such as the traditional bouquet garni (see page 55) or a tomato sauce seasoning with oregano, thyme, and parsley. Label clearly and choose a large, rigid container for an assortment of frozen herb bags. This prevents having to empty the entire freezer searching for the individual items. It also prevents damage to the frozen herbs.

Another method, which also makes it easier to flavor individual dishes, involves ice-cube trays. Finely chop the herbs, half-fill each cube compartment with the chopped herbs, and fill with water. Freeze, then remove the cubes and place meal-size quantities into freezer bags, or store in a large, rigid container for easy access.

To regain the taste of summer herbs in the winter, look to oils, vinegars, and butters as a means of preserving.

Herb-infused vinegars are made by bruising the herbs slightly, placing them in a clean glass jar, and pouring over warmed vinegar. Good-quality wine and sherry vinegars work best for flavor; light-colored vinegars are the most attractive because the herbs can be seen. Do not use a metal container, such as one of untreated aluminum, which reacts to the acid in the vinegar, imparting a metallic taste. Leave to infuse for about 3 weeks, stirring daily. Taste at the end of the period. If it is not strong enough, discard the infused herbs and add fresh ones, then leave for another week or so.

Herbs for freezing

Strain the vinegar to remove the old herbs. If desired, transfer to a decorative bottle and add a fresh sprig of the herb for decoration and identification. Use only caps and seals that have plastic linings with vinegar; an old vinegar bottle is the perfect choice, cleaned of course. Some flavorful vinegar and herb combinations include cider vinegar with applemint, red-wine vinegar with garlic and rosemary, and white-wine vinegar with tarragon, summer savory, and thyme.

The method is the same for herb-infused oils. The less strongly flavored oils, such as sunflower and safflower, are generally suitable, since the herb taste is more prominent. However, olive oil, with a flavor reminiscent of the Mediterranean area, makes a wonderful partner for the earthy flavor of many herbs and spices. When using garlic as well, remove the cloves after a couple of days because garlic tends to overpower the other herbs. Prolific summer herbs, such as basil, can be enjoyed throughout the winter by preserving them in the form of paste. Place the whole leaves in a blender or food processor with a few tablespoons of lemon juice, some cloves of garlic, and olive oil just to cover. Process until thoroughly mixed. Transfer to a clean jar with an airtight lid and refrigerate, or freeze in ice-cube trays.

Peaches in alcohol

Basil oil

EDIBLE GIFTS

The bounty of an herb garden can be kept for home use, or it can be used as a source of innumerable edible gifts. Likewise, store-bought herbs, spices, and other ingredients can be pressed into service for an array of flavorful offerings that are as satisfying to make as to give.

The first step in preparing edible gifts is to find suitable containers. A collection of glass jars will prove most useful; just be sure to remove all traces of the labels. Usually a long soak in hot soapy water will suffice, and any remaining bits of glue and paper can be removed with steel wool or even nail polish remover. It is best to compile an assortment of jars, being sure there is a good supply of plastic-lined lids, because foods containing vinegar should not come in contact with metal lids. Also, take into consideration the size of the jar. Wide-mouth jars are best for preserving fruit in alcohol (see page 253), while small jars are best for herb and spice sugar mixtures (see page 195) or flavored mustards (see page 66). Baby food jars are a handy, uniform size for an assortment of gifts, such as chutneys and relishes (see page 254). Wine, vinegar, fruit juice, and mineral water bottles can be used for fruit syrups (see page 204), plum sauce (see page 250) or homemade ginger beer (see page 277). If the caps cannot be reused, secondhand bottles can be corked (see page 233).

Ceramic jars or handmade pottery flasks are ideal for packaging seasoned salt mixtures (see page 104) or herb and spice mixtures (see Index) that do not need a large container but do require an airtight, dark one.

Decorative jars

Airtight cookie tins can house a large number of gingerbread men (see page 109), English toffee wrapped in cellophane (see page 197), or fruit jellies in paper cases (see page 205).

Alternatively, any gift that goes in a box can also be presented in an attractive basket on top of colorful shredded cellophane and secured with a sheet of plastic wrap that is taped to the bottom.

Labels also play an important role, not only as decoration and identification but to indicate a use-by date wherever necessary.

A calligraphy pen filled with black or colored ink is best for pretty lettering, or sheets of rub-off type can be purchased in stationery stores, although this can prove time-consuming. A simple solution for the amateur artist is to type out the labels on a typewriter and then trace over the letters with a black pen. This gives an unusually attractive handwritten effect.

Once the goods have been bottled and labeled, all that is required is a bit of embellishment. Ribbons and fabric swatches are easy to obtain, and they can be used separately or together. Use similar colors and textures or mix and match for a more dramatic effect. Dried flowers and herbs can be tied up in bunches or tucked into the ribbons, or the jars can be wrapped in colored tissue paper and tied with metallic string that has been beaded. The country associated with the food is also a good guideline for presentation. For example, a green- or ocher-colored earthenware jar is most appropriate when filled with *herbes de Provence* (see page 51), while warm reds and golds would be best for wrapping an Indian chutney.

Herb and spice decorations

KITCHEN
HERBS

CHIVES

HOW TO STORE
Stems: Refrigerate in an
airtight container, or freeze
in ice-cube trays.

HOW TO DRY
Suspend from heads on
wire mesh for use in
arrangements or as garnish.

R ich in vitamins A and C, chives are a member of the
onion family. Indeed, their flavor is reminiscent of
onion, but more delicate because they contain less
sulfur. When finely snipped, their bright green color
makes them an attractive as well as flavorful addition to
dishes. They are one of the classic *fines herbes* (see page
24) along with parsley, tarragon, and chervil, and they
marry well with egg dishes, like omelets, and with egg-
based sauces. Long cooking diminishes their flavor, so it
is best to add them to dishes at the last minute. Chive
flowers can be sprinkled into salads for added eye-
appeal and flavor. A handful of chopped chives is the
perfect finish for just about any salad, soup, or sauce,
adding to the taste as well as the presentation.

*Flowers are light purple with a
delicate chive flavor*

*Fresh stems are
long, hollow and
grasslike, with a
bright green
color*

Chinese chives
*(Allium tuberosum)
have gray stems that
are wider and
flatter*

TASTES GOOD WITH/IN

Stems: Eggs, salads, cream
cheese, sauces, soups.
Flowers: Salads.

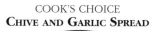

COOK'S CHOICE
CHIVE AND GARLIC SPREAD

Serves 2–3

*¹/₂ cup (125 g) low fat cream
cheese, softened*

2 tbsp mayonnaise

1 garlic clove, crushed

2 tbsp snipped chives

Salt

Freshly ground black pepper

In a bowl, whisk together the
cheese, mayonnaise, garlic,
and chives. Add salt and
pepper to taste. Scrape into a
serving bowl and smooth the
surface with the back of a
spoon. Refrigerate for at least
30 minutes before serving.

COOKING TIPS
Add at the last minute
because long cooking
destroys their flavor. For
chopping *stems*, a pair of
scissors is the best tool. Use
flowers for salads and
garnishes.

DILL

FORMS
Leaves: Fresh and dried
Seeds: Whole and ground

HOW TO STORE
Fresh leaves: Can be kept in a plastic bag in the refrigerator. To freeze, chop finely, mix with water, and freeze in ice-cube trays. *Dried leaves and seeds*: Keep in airtight jars in a cool, dark place.

HOW TO DRY
Hang bunches in a warm, dry, well-ventilated place.

Seeds *are tiny, flat, and oval*

Dried leaves *are a dark green color*

Chopped fresh dill

COOKING TIPS
For best flavor, use *fresh leaves*. Cooking diminishes the flavor of fresh dill, so add just before serving. *Dried leaves* do not retain much flavor, so use generously.

For the ancient Romans, dill was a symbol of vitality; for the Greeks, it was a remedy for the hiccups. In the Middle Ages, it was believed to be a protection against witchcraft, although, in fact, dill was an ingredient in many magic potions. In the kitchen, dill is prized both for its seeds and its leaves, and each has its own distinctive taste. Both forms are widely used in the cuisines of Scandinavia, Germany, and Central and Eastern Europe. In addition to culinary use, dill seeds are also known for their soothing digestive properties.

Fresh leaves are aromatic, feathery, and green in color

Leaves: Mild cheeses such as cream cheese or cottage cheese, omelets, seafood, mustard-based sauces, cold soups, stuffed grape leaves, herring, salmon, potato salads, cucumber, veal, green beans.
Seeds: Breads, braised cabbage, meat stews, rice, cooked root vegetables.

COOK'S CHOICE
DILL PICKLES

Makes 10 pickles

About 10 pickling cucumbers, scrubbed clean
1 bunch fresh dill
5 tbsp (75 g) coarse sea salt
1 tsp dill seeds
1/2 cup (125 ml) white-wine vinegar
1 tsp black peppercorns
1 tbsp pickling spice (see page 75)

Put the cucumbers and fresh dill in a 1½-quart (2-liter) sterilized, clamp-top jar. In a saucepan, combine 5 cups (1.25 liters) of water with the salt, dill seeds, vinegar, peppercorns, and pickling spice. Bring to a boil over high heat for 3 minutes. Leave to cool. Pour the cooled mixture over the cucumbers; if there is too much liquid, be sure to add all the spices to the cucumbers and discard any remaining liquid. Seal the jar and store in a cool, dark place for 3 weeks before serving. Refrigerate after opening.

OTHER NAMES
Garden angelica, wild angelica, European angelica, Japanese angelica

FORMS
Stems: Crystallized *Leaves:* Fresh, crystallized, and dried *Seeds:* Fresh and dried

HOW TO STORE
Crystallized stems: Wrap in aluminum foil and store in a cool, dry place; do not refrigerate.
Dried leaves: Strip from the stems and store in airtight glass bottles away from light and moisture.
Seeds: If fresh, dry in a warm place before storing.

HOW TO DRY
Collect the *leaves* before the plant begins to flower, then hang them in a warm, dry, well-ventilated place.

COOKING TIPS
If the *crystallized stems* are somewhat dry and brittle, soak them briefly in warm water to soften, then pat dry with paper towels.

Stems are hollow, thick, and ridged and should be cut early in the season for crystallizing

Fresh stems

ANGELICA

Although best known in the form of crystallized stems used as decoration on cakes and desserts, all parts of this strongly aromatic plant can be eaten. The fresh leaves can be added to tart fruit dishes, such as stewed rhubarb or gooseberries, where they will help to reduce acidity and their sweetness will minimize the need for sugar. Young shoots can be blanched and added to salads, and all parts of the plant, fresh or crystallized, can be used to imbue homemade jellies and jams with a delicate flavor. Angelica can be used in fruit syrups (see page 204) to make a pleasant summertime drink, or enhance a salad of winter fruits. The dried leaves, when infused as a tisane, are said to calm the nerves and remedy indigestion. The dried seeds can be added, along with the stems, to flavor spirits such as gin, vodka, or vermouth. In some countries, the stems and roots are boiled and served as a vegetable.

The leaves are large and bright green with serrated edges and a sweet, pungent smell

(see page 204)

TASTES GOOD WITH/IN
Fresh leaves: Vegetable salads, custards, tart fruit such as rhubarb and plums, court bouillon for poached seafood.

COOK'S CHOICE
CRYSTALLIZED ANGELICA

Makes 12 oz (350 g)

12 oz (350 g) fresh young angelica leaves and stems
1 cup (250 g) sugar
Superfine sugar for coating

Separate the leaves from the stems and cut stems and leaf stems into pieces about 5 in (12 cm) long. Place in a heat-proof bowl. In a saucepan, combine the sugar with 1¼ cups (300 ml) water and bring to the boil. Pour the boiling syrup over the angelica—there should be enough to cover it generously. Let it stand in a cool place for at least 24 hours. Transfer the angelica and syrup to a saucepan and bring to a boil. Simmer until the stems and leaves turn bright green. Drain and cool completely, then coat with sugar.

Crystallizing fresh angelica
After cooking and cooling, the stems and leaves are rolled in superfine sugar to coat. Then spread the crystallized pieces out on a cake rack and allow to dry thoroughly. If you don't intend on using right away, store in an airtight container.

CHERVIL

OTHER NAMES
Garden chervil

FORMS
Leaves: Fresh and dried

AFFINITY WITH OTHER HERBS/SPICES
Saffron, tarragon, parsley

HOW TO STORE
Leaves are best when used fresh but they can be kept in a plastic bag in the refrigerator. Although much of the flavor is lost, chervil can be dried and stored in an airtight jar.

HOW TO DRY
Spread the *leaves* on wire racks and dry in a cool, well-ventilated place, away from light. When dry, strip the leaves and crumble.

COOKING TIPS
To retain the delicate flavor, add *leaves* at the end of cooking time.

Chopped fresh leaves *can be sprinkled over dishes just before serving*

Dried leaves *have little flavor so add generously*

C hervil is a hardy annual that grows wild in damp, shady spots. Chervil is one of the first herbs to appear in spring, it is easy to grow, and prefers a cool, moist climate. One of the *fines herbes* (see page 24), it is essential in French cooking, often supplanting parsley, which it does resemble although the leaves are more feathery, and the flavor is reminiscent of anise. Chervil is used much like parsley, but it is very delicate; long cooking or high temperatures should be avoided. It is at its best when sprinkled over a salad just before serving.

Sprigs are delicate and fernlike, with a bright green color

TASTES GOOD WITH/IN

Poached fish and shellfish, cream-based soups, omelets and scrambled eggs, chicken, delicate butter sauces, cream cheeses, glazed vegetables such as carrots, smoked fish, and green salads.

COOK'S CHOICE
CREAM OF CHICKEN SOUP WITH CHERVIL

Serves 6

1 large potato, peeled
2 tbsp unsalted butter
2 oz (60 g) fresh chervil sprigs, chopped
6 cups (1.5 liters) chicken stock
1¼ cups (60 ml) whipping cream
Salt
Freshly ground black pepper
Chervil sprigs for garnish

Place the potato in a saucepan of cold water and bring to a boil. When cooked, drain, chop coarsely, and set aside. Heat the butter in a saucepan, add the chervil, cover, and cook over very low heat for 5 minutes. Stir in the chicken stock and simmer for 10 minutes. Pour into a food processor, add the potato, and mix until smooth. Return to the saucepan and stir in the cream. Season to taste and cook until heated through. Garnish with chervil sprigs.

Whole fresh leaves *are a flavorful garnish for both hot and cold dishes*

TARRAGON

OTHER NAMES
French tarragon, true tarragon

FORMS
Leaves: Fresh and dried

HOW TO STORE
Fresh leaves: Can be stored in a plastic bag in the refrigerator, frozen in ice cube trays, or preserved in white-wine vinegar or oil and packed in sealed, sterilized jars.
Dried leaves: Should be kept in a cool, preferably dark place, in airtight containers.

HOW TO DRY
Dry in a warm, well-ventilated place. Strip *leaves* from stems before storing.

Tarragon Vinegar
White-wine vinegar flavored with tarragon is a useful and flavorful condiment. Use in salad dressings, or to deglaze skillets (see page 249). Place a large sprig in a sterilized bottle or glass jar, bring the vinegar to a boil, and pour in enough to cover. Seal and store away from light.

Tarragon, with its subtle and sophisticated flavor, is an essential herb in French cuisine. Native to Siberia, it became a common culinary herb throughout Europe by the fifteenth century. The Latin name, meaning "little dragon," derives from the medieval belief that it was an antidote for the bites of venomous animals. Wine vinegar perfumed with tarragon is a classic, while the reverse—tarragon leaves preserved in vinegar—is a delicious and practical use for abundant plants. Fresh or preserved leaves can be mixed with cream cheese, or pureed with cream and used for canapés. There are two closely related forms of this valuable culinary herb: French, or "true" tarragon, and Russian tarragon. Because of its delicate anise-like flavor, French tarragon is the preferable type, although it is harder to cultivate because it seldom sets viable seed. Russian tarragon grows easily from seed but has a slightly bitter, more pungent flavor.

TASTES GOOD WITH/IN
Many classic French sauces, such as *béarnaise* or *tartare*, with *oeufs en gelée* (eggs in aspic), omelets, poached fish, mushrooms, poultry, especially chicken, mustard sauces, and salad dressings.

COOKING TIPS
Tarragon has a flavor that, although subtle, diffuses quickly through dishes, so it must be used sparingly. Tarragon butter is simple to make and can be stored in the freezer. For each 2 tbsp softened butter, add 1 tsp finely chopped tarragon, 1 tsp fresh lemon juice, and salt to taste.

FINES HERBES

This is a traditional French blend of four subtle herbs: parsley, chervil, chives, and tarragon. Finely chopped and used fresh, it brings an aromatic bouquet to simple green salads, and the delicate flavors marry well with egg dishes—especially omelets—and poached chicken and fish. Heat diminishes the taste, so it is best to add this seasoning at the end of the cooking time or sprinkle on for a delicious garnish.

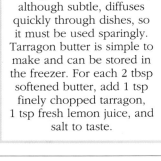

Dried fines herbes
Mix together equal quantities of parsley, chives, tarragon, and chervil.

Fresh fines herbes
With a sharp knife, chop equal amounts of each of the four herbs and combine.

Tarragon

Parsley

Chervil

Chives

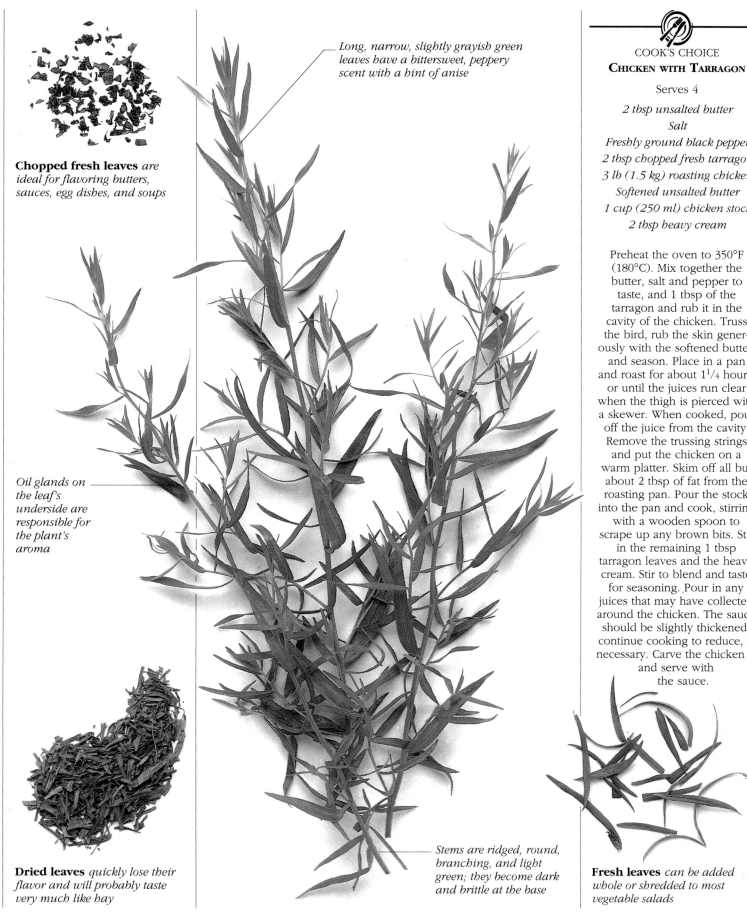

Chopped fresh leaves *are ideal for flavoring butters, sauces, egg dishes, and soups*

Long, narrow, slightly grayish green leaves have a bittersweet, peppery scent with a hint of anise

Oil glands on the leaf's underside are responsible for the plant's aroma

Dried leaves *quickly lose their flavor and will probably taste very much like hay*

Stems are ridged, round, branching, and light green; they become dark and brittle at the base

COOK'S CHOICE
CHICKEN WITH TARRAGON

Serves 4

2 tbsp unsalted butter
Salt
Freshly ground black pepper
2 tbsp chopped fresh tarragon
3 lb (1.5 kg) roasting chicken
Softened unsalted butter
1 cup (250 ml) chicken stock
2 tbsp heavy cream

Preheat the oven to 350°F (180°C). Mix together the butter, salt and pepper to taste, and 1 tbsp of the tarragon and rub it in the cavity of the chicken. Truss the bird, rub the skin generously with the softened butter, and season. Place in a pan and roast for about 1¼ hours, or until the juices run clear when the thigh is pierced with a skewer. When cooked, pour off the juice from the cavity. Remove the trussing strings and put the chicken on a warm platter. Skim off all but about 2 tbsp of fat from the roasting pan. Pour the stock into the pan and cook, stirring with a wooden spoon to scrape up any brown bits. Stir in the remaining 1 tbsp tarragon leaves and the heavy cream. Stir to blend and taste for seasoning. Pour in any juices that may have collected around the chicken. The sauce should be slightly thickened; continue cooking to reduce, if necessary. Carve the chicken and serve with the sauce.

Fresh leaves *can be added whole or shredded to most vegetable salads*

BORAGE

HOW TO STORE
Fresh leaves: These wilt too
rapidly for successful
storage.
Dried leaves: In airtight
containers.

HOW TO DRY
Remove *leaves* immediately
after picking. Dry on wire
racks in a well-ventilated
place free from humidity.

COOKING TIPS
Always chop the *leaves*
before using because they
have a disagreeable texture.
When using *flowers* for a
dressed salad, add at the
last moment because the
dressing will discolor the
flowers and make them
wilt. For *crystallized
flowers,* brush the petals
with a solution of gum
arabic and rose water, dip
in sugar and dry on wire
racks (see page 211).

Borage flowers *are bright
purple and star shaped with
distinctive black stamen tips*

orage came originally from the Middle East and
now grows wild in Mediterranean countries. It is a
very large, pretty plant, with velvety gray-green leaves
and beautiful, star-shaped, vivid purple flowers; it is said
to lift the spirits, banish melancholy, and give courage. It
is a favorite of bees, because the flowers are filled with
nectar. Although its use in the kitchen is limited, the
leaves give a refreshing cucumberlike flavor to drinks
and salads. In China, the leaves are stuffed and rolled
like grape leaves, while the Germans add the large
leaves to stews and court bouillons. It is a traditional
part of the Pimm's No. 1, a gin-based drink that was
created about 100 years ago by the proprietor of Pimm's
London restaurant. For a more elaborate garnish,
crystallized flowers can be used.

*Flowers can be
scattered over
salads*

*The gray-green leaves are
wide and oval, with a
fuzzy texture*

COOK'S CHOICE
BORAGE SOUP

Serves 4

2 tbsp unsalted butter
1 medium onion, finely chopped
3 cups (750 ml) chicken stock
*4 oz (125 g) young borage
leaves, chopped*
*1 lb (500 g) potatoes, peeled and
sliced*
3/4 cup (175 ml) light cream
Salt
Freshly ground black pepper
*Chopped borage leaves for
garnish (optional)*

Heat the butter in a large,
heavy saucepan and cook the
onion over moderate heat until
soft but not browned. Stir in
the stock, borage, and potatoes. Simmer gently, covered,
until the potatoes are very soft.
Pour the soup through a fine
sieve set over a bowl. Return
the liquid to the saucepan and
transfer the solids to a food
processor to puree. Return the
mixture to the saucepan, taste
for seasoning, and pipe or stir
in cream. Heat until warmed
through; sprinkle with the
chopped borage, if desired,
and serve. This soup can also
be served chilled.

TANSY

OTHER NAMES
Cow bitters, bitter buttons

FORMS
Leaves: Fresh

HOW TO STORE
Tansy is best used fresh but it can be kept briefly in a plastic bag in the refrigerator, or chopped and frozen in ice-cube trays.

HOW TO DRY
Leaves: Hang in a dark, warm, well-ventilated place.

COOKING TIPS
Chop *fresh leaves* finely to use in stews, but use only in small amounts.

Tansy is a hardy perennial herb native to Europe. With its yellow buttonlike clusters of flowers and fernlike leaves it makes a decorative garden plant. The Greeks and Romans regarded it as a symbol of immortality, while in Tudor England the dried leaves were placed in beds and closets to repel insects and vermin. In the seventeenth century, tansy tea was regarded as a stimulating tonic. It was once widely used for its internal cleansing and purifying properties, although this is now considered dangerous. Tansy is also one of the bitter herbs of the Jewish Passover. Because of its bitter flavor, culinary uses for tansy are limited, although it has been a traditional ingredient in many cakes and puddings. A "tansy" can also refer to a dessert made with tansy leaves, served at Easter, and young leaves and shoots can be used in salads, omelets, and stuffings.

Flowers are used for yellow dyes

Fresh leaves are aromatic, toothed, fernlike, and dark green, with a bitter taste

Whole leaves *can be rubbed onto meat before grilling to impart flavor without bitterness*

TASTES GOOD WITH/IN
Leaves: When finely chopped, add sparingly to salads, omelets, custards, cakes, or ground meat for savory pie fillings.

COOK'S CHOICE
TANSY CUSTARD

Serves 6

Butter for custard cups
2 oz (60 g) fresh young tansy leaves, coarsely chopped
3 cups (750 ml) light cream
4 large eggs, lightly beaten
1/4 cup (50 g) superfine sugar
Pinch of salt
1/8 tsp freshly grated nutmeg
1/3 cup (50 g) blanched almonds, ground

Preheat the oven to 350°F (180°C); butter six custard cups. Make the tansy juice: put the tansy leaves into a food processor and reduce to a puree, using a little water if necessary. Scrape the puree into a sieve set over a bowl. Press down hard with a wooden spoon to extract the juice (about 1 tbsp). Set aside. Pour the cream into a small saucepan and scald. Set aside. In a bowl, combine the eggs, sugar, salt, nutmeg, and almonds. Mix in the tansy juice a little at a time, to taste. Stir in the cream and pour into the custard cups. Set in a pan of hot water and bake, 30-40 minutes, or until a knife inserted into the center comes out clean. (Do not let the water boil during baking.) When cool, unmold and serve.

Chopped fresh leaves *can be added to stuffing mixtures*

27

CORIANDER/ CILANTRO

HOW TO STORE
Fresh leaves: Fresh cilantro does not keep well and the flavor of dried is not comparable. Store wrapped in paper towels in a plastic bag, or place stem-ends in a glass filled with water in the refrigerator; remove leaves as they wilt or discolor. Do not remove the roots or rinse the herb until ready to use.
To freeze, finely chop the leaves, place in ice-cube trays and add water to fill.
Seeds: Keep in airtight containers in a cool place away from light.

Native to Southern Europe as well as the Middle and Far East, this ancient annual herb, a member of the carrot family, is one of the most popular herbs in cuisines around the world. Coriander is a pretty plant, with white, pink, or pale mauve flowers and delicate light green leaves, a little like flat-leaf parsley. Bunches of the fresh herb are available in some supermarkets and gourmet stores, and seeds are always on spice shelves.

All parts of the plant are used, and each has its own distinct flavor. The leaves have a faint overtone of anise, and the seeds are vaguely reminiscent of orange peel.

The root is widely used in Thai curries and other Southeast Asian dishes, and it tastes like an intensified version of the leaves. One of the bitter herbs eaten at Passover, coriander is mentioned in the Bible, and seeds were found in the tombs of the pharaohs. The leaves are favored in cuisines throughout the Middle East, Spain, Portugal, and Mexico. In Northern Europe, where the seeds have always been more popular than the leaves, seeds are used for flavoring gin or as an ingredient in pickling spices. But it is on the Indian subcontinent that leaves and seeds are exploited fully, both being essential ingredients in curries. Throughout the book, the word "cilantro" indicates the fresh leaves and "coriander" is used for the seeds and ground form.

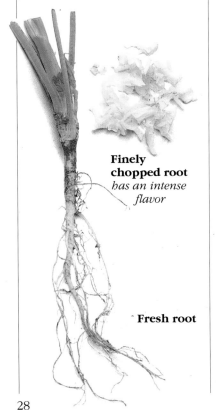

Finely chopped root *has an intense flavor*

Fresh root

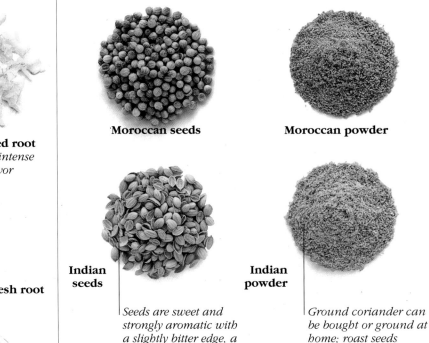

Moroccan seeds

Moroccan powder

Indian seeds

Indian powder

Seeds are sweet and strongly aromatic with a slightly bitter edge, a bit like orange peel

Ground coriander can be bought or ground at home; roast seeds before grinding

COOKING TIPS
Fresh leaves produce the best flavor when added to the dish at the very last minute. Chop the *roots* finely and add to curries or stews for a more intense flavor. Keep the *seeds* whole until needed because they quickly lose flavor. Roast lightly before crushing or grinding with a mortar and pestle.

COOK'S CHOICE
GUACAMOLE

Serves 2–4

1 large ripe avocado
1 medium tomato, peeled and chopped
1 small white onion, finely chopped
1 small fresh hot green chili, seeded and chopped (optional)
2 tbsp chopped fresh cilantro
1 tbsp lemon juice
2–3 tbsp light cream (optional)
Salt
Freshly ground black pepper

Cut the avocado in half and remove the pit. Holding one avocado half in the palm of your hand, mash the flesh with a fork, then scoop it out into a bowl. Repeat with the other half. (It should retain some texture.) Add the tomato, onion, chili if using, cilantro, and lemon juice and stir to blend. Add the cream if using. Taste for seasoning. Serve as a dip with crudités or tortilla chips, or as an accompaniment to grilled meats.

COOK'S CHOICE
COLD BRAISED CELERY WITH CORIANDER SEEDS

Serves 4

*4 medium celery stalks, trimmed
and cut into 6-in (15 cm) pieces*

Salt

3 tbsp unsalted butter

*3 scallions, white and green
parts, chopped*

1 1/2 cups (350 ml) chicken stock

1 tbsp coriander seeds, crushed

2 tbsp lemon juice

*Fresh cilantro sprigs
for garnish*

Blanch the celery pieces in
boiling salted water for
2 minutes. Drain and set aside.
Melt the butter in a skillet,
preferably nonstick, add the
scallions and cook over low
heat until soft. Add the celery,
pour in the stock, and season
to taste. Cover and cook over
low heat for 15 minutes. Add
the coriander seeds and lemon
juice and continue cooking
until the celery is tender, 15
minutes more. If there is more
than about 1/2 cup
(125 ml) liquid, remove the
celery and reduce over high
heat. Combine the celery and
liquid in a shallow dish, cover
with plastic wrap, and leave to
cool in the liquid. Drain, and
serve chilled or at room
temperature, garnished with
the sprigs of fresh cilantro.

*White or pale pink
flowers appear in
early summer*

*Lower leaves are
broad and finely
scalloped; their
taste is preferable
to the upper leaves*

*Fresh green leaves look a bit like
flat-leaf parsley, but cilantro can
always be identified by its
distinctive aroma*

Chopped fresh leaves *are
widely used in Mexican and
Tex-Mex cooking where they are
combined with chilies and
added to salsas, guacamole, and
seasoned rice dishes*

Fresh leaves *make an attractive garnish but they should be
used sparingly with delicate
ingredients because their taste
easily dominates others*

LEMONGRASS

OTHER NAMES
Takrai (Thailand), *sereh*
(Indonesia)

FORMS
Whole stalk: Fresh, dried,
and ground

HOW TO STORE
Fresh: In plastic bags in the
refrigerator, or freeze.
Dried: Keep in airtight
containers in a cool place,
or refrigerate but protect
from humidity.
Ground: In an airtight jar
kept in a cool, dark place.

COOKING TIPS
Use *fresh stalk* whole or
chopped. Bruise stem to
release flavor. Use only
lower 4–6 in (10–15 cm),
discarding upper fibrous
part (see below). Soak
dried stalks in hot water
before use. When substituting, 1 teaspoon *ground* is
roughly equivalent to
one stalk.

Common in the tropics of Southeast Asia, although also widely grown in many parts of the world including India, Africa, Australia, South America, and parts of the United States, lemongrass is characterized by a strong citrus flavor. Prominent in the cuisines of Thailand and Vietnam, it is not always easy to find in Western markets. If it is unavailable, substitute lemon peel with a tiny amount of fresh grated gingerroot.

Lemongrass has long spear-shaped leaves and a bulbous base that is fibrous and woody

TASTES GOOD WITH/IN
Curries, soups, stews, and
casseroles, particularly
those made with chicken
and seafood.

COOK'S CHOICE
**HOT AND SOUR SHRIMP
SOUP**

Serves 4

5 cups (1.2 liters) chicken stock

*4 scallions, white and green
parts, chopped*

2 tbsp chopped fresh cilantro

*1 small fresh hot green chili,
seeded and chopped*

*3 lemongrass stalks, cut into
1-in (2.5 cm) pieces*

1 tbsp nam pla (Asian fish sauce)

Salt

*1-in (2.5 cm) piece lime or
lemon peel*

2 tbsp lime or lemon juice

1 lb (500 g) shrimp

*Chopped scallions and cilantro
for garnish*

In a saucepan, combine all the ingredients, except the shrimp. Bring to a simmer, cover, and cook over low heat for 20 minutes to blend the flavors. Strain and discard the solids. Return the liquid to the saucepan, add the shrimp, and cook until the shrimp are just heated through, 1–2 minutes. Pour into a soup tureen, garnish with the chopped scallions and cilantro, and serve.

Ground stalks *can be
added directly to the dish*

Dried shredded stalks
*must be soaked in hot
water before using*

**Chopped fresh
stalks**

FENNEL

This hardy perennial, native to Southern Europe, has been used as an herb, spice, and vegetable for thousands of years. Popular with the Romans and Greeks, it was also known in ancient China, India, and Egypt. All over Europe it was, and still is, widely used with fresh and cured fish. Several varieties exist, but wild or common fennel, grown primarily in Central Europe and Russia, has the most bitter taste. Florence fennel, an annual plant, is grown for its bulbous stalk bases and also for the young stems that are cooked and eaten as a vegetable. Florence fennel leaves taste of anise and are not bitter, making them a pleasant addition to dishes both raw and cooked. Florence fennel is smaller than common fennel, although both forms have blue-green feathery leaves and bear attractive bright yellow flowers that last through the summer.

OTHER NAMES
Wild fennel, Roman fennel, Florence fennel, *finocchio*

FORMS
Leaves: Fresh and dried
Stems: Fresh and dried
Seeds: Dried

AFFINITY WITH OTHER HERBS/SPICES
Parsley, oregano, sage, thyme, chili

HOW TO STORE
Fresh leaves: Keep in a plastic bag in the refrigerator, or chop finely and freeze in ice-cube trays. They can also be infused in olive oil or wine vinegar. *Dried stems and seeds:* Keep in airtight containers in a cool, dark place.

Seeds *are small, aromatic, flat ovals with yellow ridges*

Feathery blue-green leaves are similar to dill in appearance, but not in taste

COOKING TIPS
Use *fresh leaves* in a bouquet garni to flavor fish dishes. With a mortar and pestle, lightly crush *seeds* to release their flavor. For Indian dishes, roast before use. The seeds can also be sprouted and added to green salads.

TASTES GOOD WITH/IN

Whole fresh leaves: Baked or grilled seafood, court bouillons. *Chopped fresh leaves:* Mayonnaise, sauces, stuffings, soups, vinaigrette dressing, vegetable and seafood salads, pork. *Seeds:* Breads, crackers, sausages, spicy meat mixtures, curries, cabbage dishes, and apple pie.

COOK'S CHOICE
SEA BASS WITH FENNEL
Serves 4–6

5 lb (2 kg) sea bass, scaled, gutted, and rinsed
Salt
Freshly ground black pepper
10 stems fresh or dried fennel
Olive oil
4 tbsp anise-flavored liqueur, such as Pernod (optional)

Preheat oven to 350°F (180°C). Season the fish with salt and pepper and stuff the cavity with 2 fennel stems. Brush the fish with oil, then brush a baking dish with oil. Arrange the remaining fennel stems in the dish, lay the fish on top, and bake until the flesh feels firm to the touch, 30–40 minutes. If using anise-flavored liqueur, transfer the baking dish to a work surface. Warm the liqueur, pour it over the fish, and ignite. When the flames die out, transfer the fish to a warmed platter and serve immediately or separate the fillets and serve on warmed, individual plates.

Chopped fresh leaves *can be sprinkled over soups or salads as a garnish*

HYSSOP

This is an herb of great antiquity. Frequently mentioned in the Bible from Moses to John the Baptist, it was also venerated by the Arabs. The ancient Greeks boiled it with rue and honey and used it as a cough remedy. Much used as a medicinal herb in the past, hyssop is also used to flavor liqueurs, such as the French Chartreuse. The flavor is rather bitter, with a trace of mint, and some herbalists even find an overtone of rue. In the kitchen, it can be added to soups and stews, and a few fresh leaves will enliven a salad. Hyssop is also used in tisanes, and when infused in a sugar syrup (see page 196), it can be added to fruit desserts. A fragrant plant in the garden, it attracts both bees and butterflies and has been said to discourage the cabbage butterfly from damaging the vegetable patch.

FORMS
Leaves: Fresh and dried
Flowers: Fresh

HOW TO STORE
Fresh leaves and flowers: In tightly sealed plastic bags kept in the refrigerator. *Dried leaves:* Keep in airtight containers in a cool, dark place.

HOW TO DRY
Hang in warm, dark, well-ventilated place.

COOKING TIPS
Hyssop flowers from June to October and the tiny buds can be sprinkled over a salad of mixed lettuce and sliced hard-boiled eggs. Use chopped fresh *leaves* in green salads.
Do not use both leaves and flowers in the same dish as the stronger flavor of the leaves will dominate that of the delicate flowers.

Flowers are generally purple but may be pink or white

Chopped fresh leaves

Fresh leaves *have a slightly bitter, slightly minty flavor*

Leaves are aromatic, pointed, and narrow

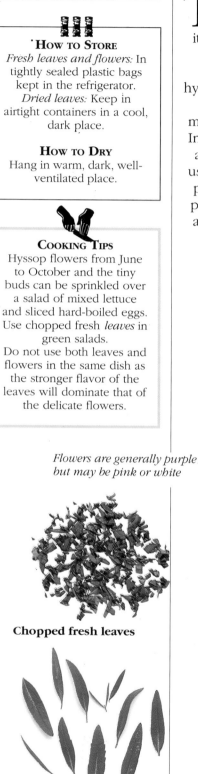

TASTES GOOD WITH/IN

Dried leaves: Soups, stews, herbal teas. *Fresh leaves:* Soft cheeses such as goat cheese and cottage cheese, flavored butters, sandwiches, sauces, dips, hot or cold pasta dishes. *Flowers:* Green salads.

COOK'S CHOICE
GLAZED CARROTS WITH HYSSOP

Serves 4

1 lb (500 g) young carrots, peeled and thinly sliced
1 cup (250 ml) chicken stock
1 tbsp clear honey
1 tbsp unsalted butter
Salt
Freshly ground white pepper
1 tbsp finely chopped fresh hyssop leaves

In a saucepan, combine the carrots, stock, honey, butter, and salt and pepper to taste. Bring to a simmer over medium heat. Cover and cook over low heat until the carrots are tender and the liquid is a syrupy glaze, about 20 minutes. Toss the carrots with the hyssop and serve immediately.

BAY

OTHER NAMES
Sweet bay, sweet laurel

FORMS
Leaves: Fresh and dried

HOW TO STORE
Fresh leaves: Should be used immediately, although they will keep for a few days in a plastic bag in the refrigerator.
Dried leaves: Keep in an airtight container in a cool, dark place.

HOW TO DRY
Hang in a dry, dark, well-ventilated place. Once dried, remove *leaves* from stems before storing.

COOKING TIPS
The strong, spicy flavor of bay intensifies with drying; however, *old leaves* lose their flavor and should be discarded. *Fresh leaves* have a slightly bitter flavor, which dissipates if left for a few days to wilt. *Whole leaves* release more flavor when shredded or chopped. Remove whole leaves before serving.

The bay tree may have come originally from Asia Minor but it has been in the Mediterranean region for so long that it is thought of as a native. A small tree with glossy dark green leaves, it can reach a considerable height but is often grown in tubs and pruned into attractive round shapes. It has waxy, creamy blossoms much loved by bees. In ancient Greece and Rome, bay leaves were used to make the crowns of laurel worn by victors in battle or sports contests. Poets were also honored with a wreath of bay leaves and were hailed as poets laureate, which is a term still in use today.
In the kitchen, the bay leaf is indispensable. It seems to go in and with almost everything: from savory meat and fish dishes, to pasta sauces and even sweet dishes such as custard. Cuisines the world over make use of this most versatile and flavorful herb. Bay is one of the vital ingredients of a bouquet garni (see page 55) and, in a pinch, a single bay leaf is flavorful enough to act as a substitute for the whole bundle.

TASTES GOOD WITH/IN
Bouquet garni, soups, meat and poultry dishes, pasta sauces, fish dishes, and even some desserts.

COOK'S CHOICE
POTATOES WITH BAY LEAVES

Serves 4–6

Olive oil
2 lb (1 kg) potatoes, peeled and cut into ¹/₂-in (1.5 cm) slices
2 large garlic cloves, chopped
4 large bay leaves
Salt
Freshly ground black pepper
2 cups (450 ml) chicken stock

Brush a shallow, flameproof casserole with olive oil. Make a layer of half the potatoes, garlic, and bay leaves. Season with salt and pepper to taste and drizzle with 2 tbsp olive oil. Repeat with the remaining potatoes, garlic, bay leaves, 2 tbsp olive oil, and salt and pepper. Pour in the chicken stock, bring to a simmer, and cook, covered, over low heat until the potatoes are tender and the liquid is absorbed, 25–30 minutes. If any liquid remains, pour it off. Discard the bay leaves before serving.

Fresh leaves should be glossy and unblemished

Dried bay leaves *can be used either whole or crumbled*

Fresh bay leaves *should be shredded before use*

LOVAGE

OTHER NAMES
Love parsley, garden lovage, Italian lovage

FORMS
Leaves: Fresh, dried, crystallized *Seeds:* Dried *Stems:* Fresh, crystallized

HOW TO STORE
Dried leaves and seeds: Keep in airtight containers in a cool, dark place. *Fresh leaves:* Can be frozen whole in ice-cube trays.

HOW TO DRY
Hang in a dry, well-ventilated place away from light. Separate *leaves* from *stems* before storing.

Seeds *are small, brown, and aromatic*

Leaves are large, toothed, and glossy green with a strong celerylike flavor

COOKING TIPS
Use lovage sparingly because the flavor can be overwhelming if used too lavishly. Tender *young leaves* can be added raw to salads, while *old leaves* can be used in soups, stocks, stews, and with soft cheeses. *Stems* can be crystallized, or they can be chopped and added to soups and stews. The stems can also be steamed, but must be peeled or scraped before cooking. *Crystallized leaves* can be used for decoration. *Seeds* can be sprinkled on salads.

Lovage is a tall perennial herb with hollow stems and serrated green leaves that resemble celery. A fast-growing plant, it is one of the earliest herbs to appear in the garden at the beginning of spring, and the flowers come out as pale yellow umbels. The seeds, roots, and leaves were widely used by the ancient Greeks and Romans, but these uses have been lost for the most part. Lovage tastes very strongly of celery, but unlike celery, it does stand up well to long cooking, so only a few leaves or chopped young stems are needed to flavor a slow-simmering stew or soup. Its leaves and stems can be crystallized and used like angelica for cake decoration. In parts of Czechoslovakia and Italy, the roots are peeled to remove the bitter skin, cooked, and served as a vegetable.

Top leaves are smaller and contain less stalk than those lower down

Stems are hollow and ridged

TASTES GOOD WITH/IN
Soups, salads, stuffings, stews, and meat dishes.

COOK'S CHOICE
LOVAGE SOUP WITH TOMATO AND APPLE

Serves 4–6

4 tbsp unsalted butter

1 medium onion, finely chopped

1 lb (500 g) tomatoes, peeled, seeded and chopped

4 large cooking apples, peeled, cored, and chopped

4 oz (125 g) lovage leaves, coarsely chopped

4¹/2 cups (1 liter) chicken stock

Salt

Freshly ground black pepper

Finely chopped lovage leaves or yogurt for garnish

In a saucepan, combine the butter and and cook onion over low heat until soft. Add the tomatoes, apples, and lovage leaves and cook for 2–3 minutes, stirring occasionally. Pour in the chicken stock, bring to a boil, cover, lower the heat and simmer for 30 minutes. Puree in batches in a food processor until smooth. Place a sieve over a clean saucepan and pour the soup through. Season to taste and heat through. This soup is delicious hot or cold. If serving hot, garnish with fresh lovage and serve immediately. For a cold soup, refrigerate until sufficiently chilled, then serve in bowls, each one topped with a dollop of yogurt.

Dried leaves *retain their strong flavor*

LEMON BALM

OTHER NAMES
Balm gentle, balm mint, sweet balm, melissa, bee herb

FORMS
Leaves: Fresh and dried

HOW TO STORE
Fresh leaves: Best to use fresh, but may be stored in plastic bags in the refrigerator for a few days.
Dried leaves: Keep in an airtight container in a cool, dark place, but the flavor lessens with time.

HOW TO DRY
Use the second crop of *leaves* because they are smaller; hang in a warm, dark, well-ventilated place.

COOKING TIPS
Prefer *fresh* over *dried*. Add chopped fresh leaves to a fruit salad. Infuse *fresh* or *dried leaves* for a refreshing and relaxing tea.

Chopped fresh leaves
will add zest to sweet or savory dishes

Fresh leaves

Lemon balm enhances a wide variety of dishes, and most cooks will agree that any dish using lemon juice will be improved by the addition of a few balm leaves. It is a pretty plant in the garden or in a tub, with fragrant, attractive white flowers, although they should be cut back if the leaves are needed in the kitchen. *Melissa* derives from the Greek for "honeybee," and lemon balm, with heart-shaped, crinkled, and serrated leaves, attracts bees with its sweet, lemon-scented perfume. The plant almost certainly originated in the Middle East but spread quickly to the Mediterranean, where it has been cultivated for more than 2,000 years. Lemon balm is the basis of the cordial *eau des Carmes* and is used in various liqueurs. It makes a delicious addition to all kinds of stewed fruits.

Leaves are light green, deeply veined with jagged edges, and have an aroma of lemon with a trace of mint

TASTES GOOD WITH/IN
Egg dishes, especially omelets; herbal teas; milk infused for drinking or custards; salads; soups; casseroles, especially those made with game birds, white-wine punches.

COOK'S CHOICE
MELISSA WINE PUNCH

Makes 3 quarts (3 liters)

1 lb (500 g) peaches, preferably white peaches, peeled, pitted, and pureed
Sugar
4 oz (125 g) fresh lemon balm leaves, coarsely chopped
3 quarts (3 liters) medium-dry white wine, chilled
A few fresh lemon balm sprigs for garnish

Put the pureed peaches in a small bowl and add sugar to taste. Add the lemon balm leaves and 2¹/₂ cups (600 ml) of the wine. Stir to blend. Leave to macerate in the refrigerator for at least 2 hours. When ready to serve, strain, discarding the lemon balm. Pour into a punch bowl and stir in the remainder of the wine. Garnish with fresh lemon balm sprigs and serve.

MINT

FORMS
Leaves: Fresh and dried

AFFINITY WITH OTHER HERBS/SPICES
Parsley, cilantro, chili, cardamom, basil

HOW TO STORE
Fresh leaves: All the mints are best used fresh and should be stored only briefly, in plastic bags in the refrigerator. They may be frozen in ice-cube trays.
Dried leaves: Should be kept in an airtight container in a cool, dark place.

The many varieties of mint can be used in both sweet and savory dishes, and there are many recipes that feature mints of all kinds. The great number of species of this perennial herb leads to confusion, although fortunately there are several whose flavor does not differ widely, and they can be used interchangeably. Spearmint is the preferred type for mint sauce or mint jelly to accompany lamb, and it is equally good with new potatoes, peas, and carrots. Spearmint is also used for the tea that is such a favorite in North Africa and the Middle East and for the mint julep from Kentucky, made with Kentucky bourbon and fresh mint leaves, and served in a special silver cup. In the West, peppermint is rarely found in savory dishes, but is used to flavor cordials, liqueurs, candy, and desserts. Lemon mint has too potent a flavor to be of much use in cooking, although sometimes it is used in drinks.

TASTES GOOD WITH/IN
Fresh and dried: Herb tea, soups, salads, sauces, plain meats, fish, poultry, stews, sweet dishes, chocolate-covered candies and lemon-based desserts such as mousses and tarts.

COOKING TIPS
Though *fresh* mint is usually preferred, *dried* mint can be used in Middle Eastern dishes, especially for cheese pastry fillings, yogurt dressings and sauces, grain- and bread-based salads, and in stuffings for vegetables such as eggplants, bell peppers and tomatoes.

The variegated dappled cream and pale green leaves are known for their fruity flavor

The most widely known and used of the mints has leaves that are closely set, toothed and bright green

Leaves are hairy and bright green

Pineapple mint

Red raripila spearmint *is characterized by pointed, dark green leaves, dark stems and purple flowers; it has a sweet minty flavor*

Apple mint *has rounded wooly leaves full of the flavor of apples and is sweeter and more mellow than other varieties*

Moroccan spearmint

MINT VARIETIES

CRYSTALLIZED MINT

Crystallized mint leaves make attractive decorations for cakes and pastries, especially when used with crystallized violets, rose petals (see page 211), or angelica. They can also be served instead of traditional mints with after-dinner coffee.

Gather the best and largest leaves and inspect carefully for blemishes. In a shallow bowl, dissolve 2 oz (60 g) gum arabic (also known as *edible gum*) in 1¼ cups (300 ml) water. Have ready a bowl of superfine sugar and a pastry brush. Using the pastry brush, thoroughly paint each side of the mint leaves with the gum solution to coat completely. Dip the leaves into the sugar to cover both sides, shaking gently to remove the excess. For a strong mint flavor, let the leaves remain submerged in the sugar for several hours or sprinkle a few drops of peppermint oil over the sugar-coated leaves. Spread the leaves out to dry on a wire cake rack. Allow to dry for 24 hours, then turn and dry the other side for another 24 hours. When both sides are dry, pack the leaves into airtight containers and store in a cool place away from light.

Dried leaves *can be used in certain sauces, although fresh are preferred, and are ideal for creating soothing teas*

Chopped fresh leaves

With more than 600 known varieties of mint, there are quite a number with distinct flavors and scents. The two most common flavorings used in cooking are spearmint and peppermint. The spearmint bought at any supermarket may well be the Moroccan variety shown. The easily cultivated red raripila variety has a strong flavor and is recognizable by its red stems. For a milder spearmint flavor, any variety of the apple mints can be used. With their distinctive scents, apple mint and its variegated relative, pineapple mint, are attractive and useful herbs to have in the garden. Peppermint is always easily recognized by its strong aroma; it is most often used in the form of peppermint oil for flavoring candies or chocolates. Basil mint, so named for its similarity in appearance to basil, has a very pleasant lemon scent and is delicious when stirred into cake or cookie batters.

Look for bright green, unblemished leaves and a fresh, minty fragrance

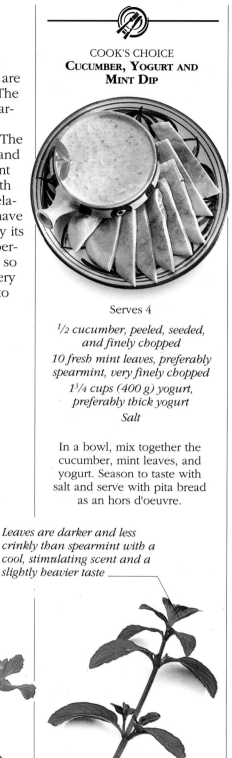

Leaves are darker and less crinkly than spearmint with a cool, stimulating scent and a slightly heavier taste

Basil mint

Black peppermint

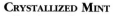

COOK'S CHOICE
CUCUMBER, YOGURT AND MINT DIP

Serves 4

½ cucumber, peeled, seeded, and finely chopped
10 fresh mint leaves, preferably spearmint, very finely chopped
1¾ cups (400 g) yogurt, preferably thick yogurt
Salt

In a bowl, mix together the cucumber, mint leaves, and yogurt. Season to taste with salt and serve with pita bread as an hors d'oeuvre.

BEE BALM

OTHER NAMES
Wild bergamot, horse mint

FORMS
Flowers: Fresh and crystallized
Leaves: Fresh and dried

HOW TO STORE
Fresh flowers and leaves: Can be kept for a short time in a plastic bag in the refrigerator.
Dried leaves: Should be kept in airtight containers in a cool, dark place.
Crystallized flowers: Should be wrapped in foil and kept in a cool place.

HOW TO DRY
Pick *leaves* when young, preferably in spring or summer, as flowers form. Hang to dry in a warm, well-ventilated place.

COOKING TIPS
Both *fresh leaves* and *flowers,* gently torn apart or coarsely chopped, add greatly to green salads. Try *fresh leaves* in recipes calling for fresh mint.

A member of the mint family, bee balm is native to North America. Its genus name, *Monarda,* derives from the Spanish physician, Nicholas Monardes, who first discovered and described it. The North American Oswego Indians made an herb tea from the leaves. At the time of the Boston Tea Party, settlers called it Oswego tea and drank it instead of tea imported from Britain. The young leaves can be used sparingly in salads or stuffings. The flowers make a colorful garnish, either fresh or crystallized. Two other plants are sometimes confused with bee balm: eau de cologne mint and bergamot orange. The latter is a small citrus plant with a sweet perfume that is grown in southern Italy, but both of these are quite separate from the herb.

Flower head clusters are shaggy, tubular, and scarlet

Leaves are toothed and oval shaped with red veins

A pretty plant with red pin-cushion flowers that are sweet tasting, full of nectar, and a favorite of bees—hence the name bee balm

Stem is hairy, hard, ridged, and square in shape

Whole leaves
One of these can be added to a cup of fresh China tea to reproduce the flavor of Earl Grey.

TASTES GOOD WITH/IN

Salads, herb teas, summer drinks, vegetable dishes, stews, poultry, and meats, especially pork.

COOK'S CHOICE
BEE BALM SAUCE FOR PORK

Makes about 1 cup (250 ml)

2 tbsp unsalted butter
1 medium onion, finely chopped
1 tbsp all-purpose flour
1 cup (250 ml) chicken stock
1 tbsp lemon juice
Salt
Freshly ground black pepper
1 tbsp finely chopped fresh bergamot leaves

Heat the butter in a small saucepan, add the onion and cook until it is soft. Add the flour and cook, stirring with a wooden spoon, for about 2 minutes. Gradually stir in the chicken stock and cook until the sauce is smooth and thickened. Stir in the lemon juice and season to taste with salt and pepper. Add the bee balm leaves and cook for 2 minutes more. Transfer to a gravy boat and serve hot, with roast pork.

Chopped fresh leaves
These can be added in judicious amounts to stuffings and salads.

SWEET CICELY

OTHER NAMES
Spanish chervil, anise root, European sweet chervil

AFFINITY WITH OTHER HERBS/SPICES
Bay leaf, mint, lemon balm

HOW TO STORE
Fresh leaves: Can be kept in sealed plastic bags in the vegetable compartment of the refrigerator. To freeze, chop, place in ice-cube trays and add water to fill.

COOKING TIPS
Sweet cicely is a useful sugar substitute. Use it to add sweetness to fruit desserts and drinks, and as a pleasant alternative to sugar for sweetening cream or yogurt. It will enhance the flavor of any herb with which it is used.

Chopped fresh leaves
These can be sprinkled into drinks or whipped into cream to add sweetness and a delicate anise taste. Make a tea from the leaves to help cure indigestion.

Sweet cicely, a perennial herb native to the mountains of the Savoy region of France, owes its charming name to its fernlike, pale green leaves that have a sugary taste. An attractive plant, its kitchen use is fairly limited although its natural sweetness can be put to good use. It will reduce the need for added sugar when cooked with sour fruit such as rhubarb and gooseberries. The seeds are the most flavorful part, tasting strongly of anise or licorice. Chopped unripe seeds can be used in salads or creamy desserts; whole ripe seeds can be used like cloves. Sweet cicely does have a place in the garden not just for its fragrance but because of its persistence. It is one of the first herbs to appear in spring and one of the last to go in the fall. Boiled sweet cicely roots were once served as a salad, dressed with oil and vinegar.

Unripe seeds are green and are used chopped

Ripe seeds are glossy brown and are used whole

Clusters of white flowers are soon followed by seeds

The stems are hollow, the leaves fernlike

TASTES GOOD WITH/IN
Any sweet dish, especially those made with fruit, whipped cream, rice pudding, bouquet garni, soups, stews; fresh leaves are particularly nice in mixed green salads.

COOK'S CHOICE
FRUIT AND WINE COOLER
Makes about 8 servings

2 cups (500 ml) orange juice
1 cup (250 ml) lemon juice
1 bottle dry red wine
2 tsp finely chopped fresh sweet cicely

Combine all the ingredients in a large glass jug. Stir to mix and refrigerate until ready to serve. Put 2–3 ice cubes into each 1-cup (250 ml) goblet and pour in the wine cooler.

BASIL

B asil is one of the most important of the culinary herbs. The Greek name for it means "king," which shows how highly it has been regarded throughout the ages. There are many types of basil, which vary in size, color, and flavor, and all can be used for culinary purposes. Purple ruffle and dark opal are two of the more unusual but useful varieties. Basil goes with almost everything, but it has a special affinity with tomatoes. Freshly torn basil leaves are delicious on a salad of sliced tomatoes, lightly seasoned with salt and freshly ground pepper and drizzled with a fruity extra-virgin olive oil, accompanied by crusty bread. Perhaps the greatest basil dish is pesto—an Italian sauce of basil, garlic, cheese, and pine nut—which turns spaghetti into a feast, although it can also be used as a marinade. Bottled pesto can be bought during the months when it is too cold for basil to grow, which is certainly better than having no basil at all. Italian cooks, however, preserve their prolific basil crops by filling a jar with the leaves, lightly salting them, topping up the jar with olive oil, closing it tightly, and storing it in the refrigerator.

OTHER NAMES
Sweet basil

FORMS
Leaves: Fresh and dried

AFFINITY WITH OTHER HERBS/SPICES
Parsley, rosemary, oregano, thyme, sage, saffron

HOW TO STORE
Fresh leaves: Can be kept briefly in plastic bags in the refrigerator, preserved in olive oil or vinegar, or frozen. To freeze, leaves should be pureed with a little water and put into ice-cube trays. When frozen, the cubes can be stored in the freezer in plastic bags.
Dried leaves: Keep in airtight containers at room temperature away from light and heat.

TASTES GOOD WITH/IN
Tomatoes, spaghetti sauces such as pesto, with fish, especially red mullet, mushroom dishes, soups, stews, salads, chicken, egg and rice dishes, and mixed with other herbs.

Dried basil *does not have the same flavor as fresh; a more minty taste predominates*

Fresh torn leaves

Chiffonade strips
Evenly cut shreds of basil leaves make a delightful soup garnish.

Whole fresh leaves

Flowers are creamy white or purple-tinged

The young leaves at the top of the plant are sweetest

Pestle, pesto, and pistou
Italian pesto, known as **pistou** *in France, is best made with a mortar and pestle.*

Sweet basil

Look for soft, green, unbruised leaves with a strong scent

COOK'S CHOICE
FRESH SPAGHETTI WITH PESTO

Serves 2–4

2 oz (60 g) fresh basil leaves
2–4 garlic cloves, or to taste
1 oz (30 g) pine nuts
4 tbsp extra-virgin olive oil
4 tbsp freshly grated Parmesan cheese
Salt
1 lb (500 g) fresh spaghetti

Combine the basil, garlic, and pine nuts in a food processor and reduce to a puree. With the machine running, slowly add the oil, pouring in a steady stream. When the mixture is well emulsified, add the cheese and process briefly. Scrape out into a bowl, taste for seasoning, and add a little salt if necessary. Cook the spaghetti in a large pot of boiling salted water. Drain, transfer to a bowl and toss with the pesto. Serve hot or at room temperature.

Greek basil
This has tiny green leaves with a good flavor and is a compact garden plant.

Purple ruffle basil
This is one of the red varieties that is attractive as a garnish and can be used in place of its green cousins.

Leaves are crinkly with attractive ruffled edges

Leaves are toothed with a good medium flavor

Dark opal basil
Widely available as a garden plant, this has a more spicy, gingerlike flavor.

COOKING TIPS
Fresh leaves are better torn than cut when used for salads; add at the last minute because vinegar-based dressings will diminish the fresh taste. Sprinkle over salads, pastas, egg dishes, and tomato-based sauces. Pound with butter, ground black pepper, and freshly grated lemon peel for an excellent accompaniment to grilled steak, chicken, or seafood.

41

MARJORAM AND OREGANO

OTHER NAMES
Sweet marjoram, knotted marjoram, pot marjoram, common marjoram, wild marjoram, *rigani*

FORMS
Leaves: Fresh and dried

HOW TO STORE
Fresh leaves: Can be kept in a plastic bag in the refrigerator or frozen. To freeze, mix finely chopped leaves with a little water in ice-cube trays. Store frozen cubes in the freezer in plastic bags until needed.
Dried leaves: Should be stored in airtight containers in a cool, dark place.

HOW TO DRY
Tie stems together and hang in a warm, well-ventilated place.

These two perennial herbs are so closely related that they do not need to be classified separately. The name *oregano* derives from the Greek for "joy of the mountains," which is where the wild varieties of this herb thrive. They are similar in appearance, with small, soft, sometimes mottled green leaves and small white or pink flowers that form clusters. Marjoram has a more delicate flavor and is a gentler herb than oregano, which is actually a wild variety of marjoram and has a more potent flavor. These herbs are native to the Mediterranean region, appearing in many French and Italian dishes, especially tomato-based sauces. The more robust flavor of oregano is the quintessential pizza flavoring, and it is also a favorite herb in Greece. It is one of the ingredients of commercial chili powder. There are many more wild species, most of which grow in Greece, where they are all called by one name, *rigani*. These are more strongly flavored and coarser than either ordinary marjoram or oregano.

TASTES GOOD WITH/IN

Oil and vinegar salad dressings, fresh or canned anchovies, Italian and Greek dishes, poultry, game, seafood, soups, beans, eggplants, pasta, grilled meats, tomato-based sauces.

COOKING TIPS
The powerful flavor of *oregano* comes through very well when *dried*, but *marjoram*, which is more delicate, is best added *fresh* at the end of cooking.

Can be infused as an aromatic tea

Chopped fresh marjoram *can be added to salads and butter sauces for fish*

Leaves will turn golden when grown in full sun

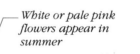
White or pale pink flowers appear in summer

A compact, bushy plant with small, dark green leaves

Golden curly marjoram

Fresh marjoram

Dried marjoram

Gold splash marjoram

A hardy perennial, the flavor of oregano varies, depending on climate and soil

Golden marjoram

Oregano

CORN SOUP WITH FRESH MARJORAM

Serves 4

12 oz (350 g) frozen whole corn kernels, defrosted
4¹/₂ cups (1 liter) chicken stock
1 oz (30 g) fresh marjoram, finely chopped
Salt
Freshly ground black pepper
Marjoram sprigs for garnish

Puree the corn in a food processor with a little of the chicken stock, then force the mixture through a sieve. Combine the corn puree with the remaining chicken stock in a saucepan, cover, and simmer for 5 minutes. Stir in the marjoram, season to taste with salt and pepper, and simmer for 5 minutes longer. Garnish with marjoram sprigs and serve in soup bowls.

An attractive garnish, this is created by placing several leaves on top of each other and cutting them into thin lengthwise strips

Oregano chiffonade

Dried oregano *retains its original flavor well and is good used in sauces, stews, and soups, particularly those with a tomato base*

43

PARSLEY

FORMS
Leaves: Fresh and dried

HOW TO STORE
Fresh leaves: Keep in a plastic bag in the refrigerator or sprinkle with water and wrap in paper towels. For maximum freshness, put cut ends in cold water.
Dried leaves: Keep in an airtight container away from light and moisture.

COOKING TIPS
When available, use *flat-leaf parsley* as the flavor is much better than that of *curly parsley.*

Persillade
This is a mixture of finely chopped parsley leaves and garlic that is sautéed and added at the last minute to numerous dishes such as broiled lamb or beef steaks, fried fish, chicken, or vegetables.

Gremolada
This is a Milanese flavoring mixture consisting of sautéed orange and lemon zest, finely chopped garlic, and parsley. Traditionally, gremolada is sprinkled over osso buco just before serving, although it can be used to enhance any braised meat dish. It should always be added at the last minute.

This popular herb, originally from Southern Europe, is now grown in all of the world's temperate regions. There are two main types—curly and flat-leaf. Both types are a rich source of vitamins and minerals. Flat-leaf parsley, with its dark green foliage, is best for cooking as it is more flavorful and stands up better to heat. The curly variety is ideal for garnishing a wide variety of dishes. Although less flavorful, it does keep well when refrigerated. A sprinkling of finely chopped parsley, added just before serving, provides color and gives a fresh flavor to sauces, salads, or buttered new potatoes. The stems and leaves should be used in bouquet garni (see page 55), and the leaves are essential to the classic seasoning mixtures persillade and gremolada.

Deep-fried sprigs of whole parsley are delicious partnering seafood or broiled meats. Hamburg parsley is used not as an herb, but for its root, which has a flavor that is rather like a mixture of celery root and parsley. Sold as parsley root, it is very pleasant when boiled and added to mashed potatoes.

Look for bright green, unblemished leaves

Flat-leaf parsley

TASTES GOOD WITH/IN

Omelets, salads, stews, vegetables, soups, eggs, sauces, rice and pasta dishes, fish, shellfish, any meat and poultry, mixed with soft cheeses such as ricotta or cottage cheese.

COOK'S CHOICE
ZUCCHINI AND PARSLEY FRITTATA

Serves 2–3

2 tbsp unsalted butter
1 tbsp olive oil
1 small onion, finely chopped
½ lb (250 g) zucchini, trimmed and chopped
½ lb (250 g) tomatoes, peeled, seeded and chopped
3 tbsp finely chopped flat-leaf parsley
Salt
Freshly ground black pepper
4 large eggs
Curly parsley sprigs for garnish

Heat the butter and oil in a nonstick skillet and sauté the onion until it is golden and tender. Add the zucchini, tomatoes, parsley and salt and pepper to taste. Cook over low heat until the zucchini is tender, about 8 minutes. Break the eggs into a bowl and beat them lightly; season lightly. Pour over the zucchini mixture, stirring with a wooden spoon to mix. Turn the heat to very low and cook until the eggs have set. Run the pan under the broiler to brown the top, if liked. Slide out of the pan and serve hot. Garnish with parsley.

Chopped fresh leaves *can be used as a garnish*

BURNET

FORMS
Leaves: Fresh and dried

HOW TO STORE
Fresh leaves: These wilt easily, so they should be kept in a plastic bag and refrigerated as quickly as possible after picking. They can be frozen, finely chopped, in ice-cube trays.
Dried leaves: Keep in an airtight container in a cool, dark place. This herb does not dry well, but it can be grown year-round for use fresh.

COOKING TIPS
Old leaves of burnet tend to be tough and should be avoided. *Young leaves* are more tender but wilt rather quickly, so use while still fresh to best savor their pleasant cucumber taste.

A delicate-looking, pretty plant with reddish pink flowers, salad burnet is nonetheless hardy enough to produce green leaves throughout most winters. A perennial herb, it is native to Europe. A very popular herb in Elizabethan England, it has fallen out of use in most places, although it can still be found in some French or Italian dishes. Burnet is useful in salads and sauces, where its delicate, cucumberlike flavor adds freshness. This herb should not be confused with great burnet (*Sanguisorba officinalis*), which is similar in appearance. Great burnet was once known as bloodwort because it was believed to be useful in stopping wounds from bleeding. Yet another plant is called burnet; this is burnet saxifrage *(Pimpinella saxifraga),* which is not a burnet at all but a member of the parsley family.

Chopped leaves

The lacy, fine-toothed leaves are on long, graceful stems and have a faint cucumberlike scent

TASTES GOOD WITH/IN

Fresh sprigs: White-wine coolers, cold poached chicken, seafood, green salads, as a flavoring for vinegar, cold soups.

COOK'S CHOICE
BURNET SAUCE FOR POACHED FISH

Serves 4

1 3/4 cups (450 ml) fish stock made with white wine

1 tbsp red-wine vinegar

2 oz (60 g) young burnet leaves, finely chopped

4 tbsp unsalted butter, chilled and cubed

2 lb (1 kg) boneless, skinless, poached fish fillets, such as sole

Pour the fish stock into a saucepan and reduce to half its volume over high heat. Reduce the heat, stir in the vinegar and burnet leaves, and simmer for a further 2–3 minutes. Lower the heat and beat the butter into the liquid, a piece at a time, to obtain a creamy sauce. Taste for seasoning. Do not allow the sauce to boil or it will separate. Pour over the fish and serve with plain rice.

Young leaves
are more tender and best suited to salads

ROSEMARY

FORMS
Leaves: Fresh, dried
Sprigs: Fresh *Flowers:* Fresh

HOW TO STORE
Fresh sprigs: Keep for
several days in a plastic bag
in the refrigerator, or place
stem ends in water.
Dried leaves: Keep in an
airtight container in a cool
place away from light.

HOW TO DRY
Hang *fresh sprigs* to dry in a
warm, dry place. Be sure to
strip off *leaves* before
storing.

COOKING TIPS
To release the flavor of
dried leaves, crush them
just before using.
The needlelike form and
tough texture of *fresh leaves*
can be unpleasant when
encountered in a finished
dish. It is best to chop them
very finely or crush in a
mortar and pestle before
use. Alternatively, use
whole sprigs to infuse long-
cooking dishes with flavor
and remove before serving.
Sprinkle *flowers* over salads
or use as a garnish.

Herb skewers
*Rosemary stems stripped of
their leaves can be used to
thread vegetables or tender
cuts of meat for broiling.*

The name of this lovely aromatic herb, with its
needlelike leaves and delicate light blue flowers,
is derived from Latin and means "dew of the sea." This is
appropriate because the plant is indigenous to the
Mediterranean area, where it thrives in the calcium-rich
soil, the dry climate, and the salty sea spray.

It has a strong flavor that is pungent but undeniably
pleasant. In Italy, it is the preferred herb with veal,
poultry, or lamb dishes, especially those simmered with
wine, olive oil, and garlic. Other Mediterranean countries
do use it, although less lavishly, while in Northern
Europe, it often finds its way into sausage mixtures. This
versatile herb tastes good with strongly flavored vegetables, jams and jellies, and even wine punches. It should
always be paired with lamb; a sprig placed on a roasting
leg lends the meat an incomparable flavor.

*The thin, dark green,
needlelike leaves are very
aromatic with a crisp,
woodsy perfume*

TASTES GOOD WITH/IN
Meat dishes, especially lamb
and pork, chicken, tomato-
based sauces, breads,
stuffed vegetables, pizza,
potato gratins, apple jelly.

COOK'S CHOICE
BEETS WITH ROSEMARY
Serves 4

*12 small beets, with tops
Salt
2 rosemary sprigs
3 tbsp unsalted butter
Freshly ground black pepper*

Place the beets in a saucepan.
Add water to cover and salt,
then simmer, covered, until
the beets are tender, 30–45
minutes depending on the size
and age of the vegetable.
When cool, peel and slice.
Strip the leaves from the
rosemary sprigs and chop
finely. In a saucepan, toss the
sliced beets with the rosemary,
butter, and salt and pepper to
taste for 2–3 minutes just to
blend all the flavors; do not let
the butter brown. Serve
immediately.

Fresh leaves *can be tied up in
a square of cheesecloth to make
them easier to remove*

Chopped fresh leaves *can be
used to add flavor to sauces,
stews, and marinades*

SORREL

HOW TO STORE
Fresh leaves: Can be kept briefly in plastic bags in the refrigerator. Sorrel does not dry well, but it can be frozen successfully.

COOKING TIPS
Sorrel's high acidity causes it to discolor when it is cooked in iron pots, or when it is chopped with other than stainless-steel knives.

Sorrel Chiffonade
A chiffonade is an attractive and flavorful way to diffuse sorrel through a dish. To proceed, wash the sorrel and pat dry. Trim the stems and then stack the leaves. Roll up the leaves tightly, then slice thinly crosswise (see above). Use the chiffonade as is, or make a puree: Combine 8 oz (250 g) sorrel chiffonade with 2 tbsp butter in a small saucepan and cook over low heat, stirring often, until the leaves have melted into a puree, about 10 minutes. Serve with poached fish.

Garden sorrel and French sorrel are two of several allied species cultivated for use as green vegetables or herbs. The slightly less acidic French sorrel, *Rumex scutatus,* is preferred by cooks. Another member of the group, *Rumex patienta,* known also as *spinach dock,* is of lesser culinary importance. All of the sorrels, whose name derives from the Teutonic word for "sour," are very ancient herbs. They were used in pharaonic Egypt, and they are still employed in modern Egyptian cooking. The ancient Greeks and Romans used the acidity of sorrel to aid digestion and offset the effects of rich food. Sorrel has always been popular throughout Europe, especially in France, where it still enjoys its greatest popularity, most notably in sorrel soup and *saumon à l'oseille,* or salmon with sorrel sauce. The leaves are a very rich source of potassium and vitamins A and C. Sorrel is very easily pureed, making it the ideal base for an excellent sauce to accompany poached fish or eggs. Because of its acidity, it acts as a meat tenderizer and can be wrapped around cubes of tough meat before stewing or braising.

Garden sorrel has large green, lance-shaped leaves with a broad base

Young shoots are less acidic and ideal for use in salads and sandwiches

TASTES GOOD WITH/IN
Mixed green salads, sandwiches, cream-based sauces, soups, omelets, quiches and other egg dishes, soft cheeses, especially goat cheese, veal, pork, fish.

COOK'S CHOICE
VEAL STEW WITH SORREL
Serves 6

2 tbsp vegetable oil
2 tbsp unsalted butter
2 lb (1 kg) boneless veal , cut into 1¹/₂-in (4 cm) cubes
2 medium onions, finely chopped
8 oz (250 g) mushrooms, sliced
1 cup (250 ml) dry white wine
1 cup (250 ml) chicken stock
Bouquet garni (see page 55)
Salt
Freshly ground black pepper
Sorrel chiffonade (see left)

Heat the oìl and butter in a skillet, add the veal, and sauté over low heat until golden. Transfer to a casserole. Sauté the onions and mushrooms in the same skillet until they are tender. Add to the casserole with the wine, stock, bouquet garni, and salt and pepper to taste. Cover and simmer until the veal is tender, about 1¹/₂ hours. Transfer the veal cubes to a serving dish. Remove the bouquet garni. Reduce the cooking liquid by half, stir in the sorrel chiffonade, and heat through. Pour over the veal and serve with rice.

Finely chopped leaves

SAGE

Sage, a universal flavoring herb, is a native of the North Mediterranean coast. A medium-sized perennial shrub, it is very aromatic with blue or lilac flowers that appear at the end of spring. Sage is one of many herbs not restricted to culinary use; in the past it was believed to have healing qualities and was used medicinally for a long time before it found its way into the kitchen. Greeks, Romans, and Arabs all used sage for its curative powers, as a general tonic, and for snakebites; in the Middle Ages it was considered a cure-all. Just when its use in the kitchen overtook its use in the sickroom is not clear, but it has certainly kept its place in cooking for several centuries. The Italians use it in meat dishes, particularly with calves' liver and veal, the Germans add sage to eel dishes, and in France, it is cooked with pork, veal, and some charcuterie. In many countries, especially Greece, sage tea is popular. In the Middle East, sage is added to salads, and many cooks use it for flavoring fresh sausages, in the traditional stuffing for pork, turkey, or goose, and mix it with cheese. It is one of the few herbs whose flavor strengthens when it is dried, and since it has a powerful flavor, the dried and ground versions should be added discreetly.

Dried sage *is more powerful than its fresh form and should be used sparingly*

Leaves are long and narrow with a pungent flavor

Garden sage has thick, downy gray-green leaves

Broad-leaf garden sage

Narrow-leaf garden sage

Chopped fresh leaves *are a flavorful addition to pasta sauces and stuffings*

Whole leaves *can be threaded on kabobs*

COOKING TIPS

This is a strongly flavored herb with overtones of camphor and should be used with discretion. It is good with fatty meats because it aids digestion. *Fresh leaves* are milder in flavor than the *dried* version and can be added more freely. The pretty gray-green *leaves* can be used whole in many dishes. Very small young *leaves* are mild enough to be used in a green salad, provided that they are shredded into small bits beforehand. Thread sage *leaves* between pieces of meat or vegetables when preparing kabobs.

A half-hardy variety, the leaves are green, splashed with pink, and have white margins

Tricolor sage

Sage varieties
Purple leaf, purple variegated, and gold variegated sage make an attractive garden trio and can be used like common gray-green sage in the kitchen.

When mature, the leaves are soft and deep purple

Purple sage

Plant contains both green and yellow leaves

Golden sage

COOK'S CHOICE
SALTIMBOCCA

Serves 4

8 small veal scallops

8 small slices dry-cured ham, preferably prosciutto

8 large, fresh young sage leaves

Freshly ground black pepper

1 tbsp olive oil

3 tbsp unsalted butter

3/4 cup (175 ml) marsala or port

With a meat mallet or rolling pin, pound the scallops until thin. Lay a slice of ham and a sage leaf on top of each scallop. Season with pepper, then roll up to enclose the filling; secure with a toothpick or kitchen string. Heat the oil and butter in a skillet and sauté the rolls over moderate heat until they are browned all over. Pour in the marsala or port and bring to a simmer. Cover and cook over low heat for 10–15 minutes. Serve hot, with buttered pasta.

Adding the sage
Center the ham and sage leaf on the meat, then roll up.

SAVORY

FORMS
Leaves: Fresh and dried

AFFINITY WITH OTHER HERBS/SPICES
Rosemary, thyme, sage, fennel, bay leaf

HOW TO STORE
Fresh leaves: Keep in a plastic bag in the refrigerator, or chop finely and freeze in ice-cube trays. *Dried leaves:* These retain their flavor for a considerable time if kept in airtight containers, away from light.

HOW TO DRY
For best results, summer and winter savory *leaves* should be harvested just before the plant flowers. Hang in a dark, warm, well-ventilated place.

There are two varieties of this herb, one annual and one perennial. Both come from the Mediterranean and are attractive for gardeners and cooks. They have a strong, slightly peppery taste thought by some to be reminiscent of thyme. In very early times, the Romans made a sauce of vinegar and summer savory, very much like the mint sauce of today. All beans and peas are greatly enhanced by this herb with which they have a particular affinity, and sausages, stuffings, and herb mixtures often contain savory. Winter savory, an evergreen, is a shrublike plant, growing up to 12 in (30 cm) high, with glossy, bright green leaves and pinkish flowers. The flavor is stronger, sharper, and spicier than that of summer savory. The latter grows much higher, to about 18 in (45 cm) tall, and has narrow, dark green leaves and lilac flowers. Summer and winter savory are commonly grown alongside each other.

TASTES GOOD WITH/IN
Legumes, especially lentils and white beans, cooked vegetable salads, broiled veal and pork, poultry, rabbit, soups, horseradish sauce, cucumbers, stuffings and charcuterie, goat cheese, tomato-based sauces, marinades, fish, especially trout.

COOKING TIPS
Savory is useful for those on a salt-restricted diet because the *leaves* have a strong flavor. Use summer savory with fresh beans and winter savory with dried ones. For a more subtle savory flavor, infuse wine vinegar with *fresh sprigs* and use in dressings for salads containing fresh or dried beans. Add savory to stuffing mixtures for roast poultry.

Winter savory is a hardy perennial with narrow green leaves and a strong, spicy flavor

Pale purple or white flowers bloom from midsummer to autumn

Leaves are sharp-tipped and shiny on upper surface

Chopped fresh leaves *are an excellent addition to horseradish sauce*

Dried leaves *keep their flavor well*

Winter savory *has a less-pleasing texture than that of the annual variety*

Whole fresh leaves

COOK'S CHOICE

GREEN BEANS WITH SUMMER SAVORY

Serves 4–6

2 lb (1 kg) fresh young green beans, trimmed

Salt

4 tbsp unsalted butter

2 tbsp finely chopped fresh summer savory leaves

Freshly ground black pepper

Place the beans in a large saucepan of briskly boiling water. Add salt and continue to boil beans over high heat, uncovered, for 8–10 minutes, depending on the age and freshness of the beans. They should be tender but still crisp. Drain, rinse under cold running water, drain again, and return to the saucepan. Add the butter and savory. Season with pepper to taste and a little salt if necessary. Cook for 1–2 minutes and serve hot.

Summer savory, an annual, is intensely aromatic and bears small white or lilac flowers in late summer

Leaves are slightly larger and more rounded than those of winter savory; they are dotted with oil glands

Stems are pale purple and slightly downy

Summer savory *has an aroma reminiscent of both mint and thyme; one or two chopped leaves are effective when added to salads, cheese dishes, and herb mixtures*

HERBES DE PROVENCE

This a mixture of the herbs that flourish in the hills of southern France during the hot summer months. Used in handfuls when fresh, they can also be dried for use until the next season. Herbes de Provence is a useful addition to any dish from the Mediterranean region and is especially good in stews, with baked tomatoes or roast chicken, added to pizza toppings, or sprinkled over kabobs before broiling.

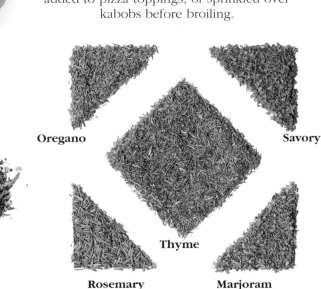

Oregano

Savory

Thyme

Rosemary

Marjoram

Traditional terracotta jars *are ideal for storing this herb mixture until a fresh supply can be gathered*

THYME

There are believed to be about 100 species of thyme, but for most culinary purposes three are sufficient. Used extensively in ancient Greece, this herb may well have been employed in the Mediterranean region even earlier. It is one of the great culinary herbs of European cuisine; lacking thyme, a bouquet garni becomes a less valuable flavoring ingredient. Few are the dishes that cannot be improved by thyme. Its amiable and positive flavor blends well with many other herbs, especially rosemary, enhancing them without ever overpowering them when combined in the stockpot. Thyme is an herb that aids the digestion of fatty foods and it is therefore useful in dishes of mutton, pork, duck, or goose. Wild French thyme, *serpolet,* grows profusely in Provence and gives the cooking of that region much of its distinctive flavor. Lemon thyme has an attractive citrus perfume and makes an excellent herb tea. All the thymes are wonderfully aromatic and are to be encouraged in the garden—or failing a garden, in window boxes, balcony planters or pots on kitchen counters.

TASTES GOOD WITH/IN
Any slowly cooked dish, especially stews and soups, sautéed or baked vegetables, tomato-based sauces, stuffings, roast poultry, broiled or roasted meat, breads, sauces.
Lemon thyme: Can be used sparingly with fish and chicken, and in some fresh fruit desserts.

Chopped fresh leaves *are much more pungent than dried. If using in place of dried leaves in a recipe, add more sparingly*

Dried leaves *retain their aroma and flavor well*

Variegated varieties can be used wherever ordinary thyme is called for, but they are more difficult to grow

Leaves are aromatic, pointed, oval, and green; they are covered in fine hairs

Garden thyme bears pale lilac blooms in summer and has a woody stem

Fresh leaves *are useful in just about any savory dish*

Variegated thyme   **Garden thyme**

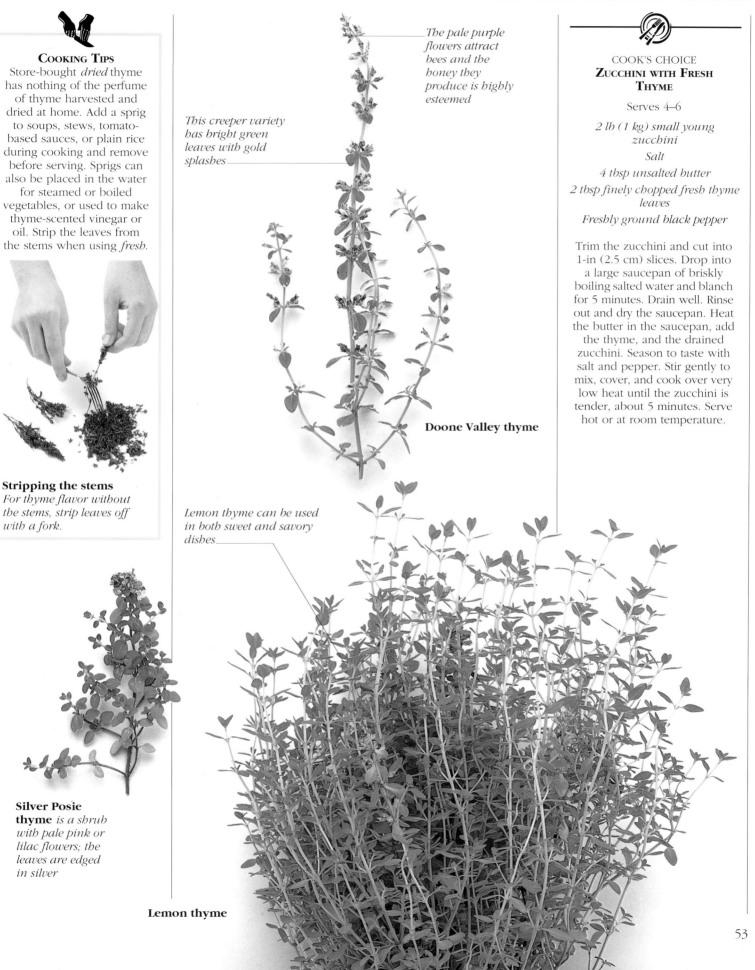

COOKING TIPS

Store-bought *dried* thyme has nothing of the perfume of thyme harvested and dried at home. Add a sprig to soups, stews, tomato-based sauces, or plain rice during cooking and remove before serving. Sprigs can also be placed in the water for steamed or boiled vegetables, or used to make thyme-scented vinegar or oil. Strip the leaves from the stems when using *fresh.*

Stripping the stems
For thyme flavor without the stems, strip leaves off with a fork.

The pale purple flowers attract bees and the honey they produce is highly esteemed

This creeper variety has bright green leaves with gold splashes

Doone Valley thyme

Lemon thyme can be used in both sweet and savory dishes

Silver Posie thyme *is a shrub with pale pink or lilac flowers; the leaves are edged in silver*

Lemon thyme

COOK'S CHOICE
ZUCCHINI WITH FRESH THYME

Serves 4–6

2 lb (1 kg) small young zucchini

Salt

4 tbsp unsalted butter

2 tbsp finely chopped fresh thyme leaves

Freshly ground black pepper

Trim the zucchini and cut into 1-in (2.5 cm) slices. Drop into a large saucepan of briskly boiling salted water and blanch for 5 minutes. Drain well. Rinse out and dry the saucepan. Heat the butter in the saucepan, add the thyme, and the drained zucchini. Season to taste with salt and pepper. Stir gently to mix, cover, and cook over very low heat until the zucchini is tender, about 5 minutes. Serve hot or at room temperature.

LEMON VERBENA

OTHER NAMES
Lemon-scented verbena

FORMS
Leaves: Fresh and dried

HOW TO STORE
Fresh leaves: Keep in tightly sealed plastic bags in the refrigerator.
Dried leaves: Keep in airtight containers in a cool, dark place.

COOKING TIPS
Fresh leaves can be added to fruit salads, but use sparingly because the flavor can be reminiscent of lemon-scented cosmetics.

L emon verbena is a small deciduous shrub that grows not higher than 15 ft (4.5 meters) high in warm climates and far less in cooler ones. The leaves are strongly perfumed, filling the air with their scent of lemons. The plant is native to Chile and was brought to Europe by the Spaniards, where it was first put to use scenting soaps and cosmetics. The light green leaves are long and pointed with little mauve flowers that appear in clusters at the ends of the branches. Use as a substitute for lemongrass in Asian recipes because the lemon flavor is very pronounced. It should not be confused with vervain, although they are both members of the same botanical family.

TASTES GOOD WITH/IN
Fresh fruit drinks, especially those made with peaches or strawberries; herb teas made with licorice or mint; fruit salads, and infused in custard-based dessert sauces.

COOK'S CHOICE
LEMON VERBENA RICE PUDDING

Serves 4–6

8 oz (250 g) short-grain rice
$1/2$ tsp salt
2 cups (500 ml) milk
2–3 fresh lemon verbena leaves
$1/2$ cup (125 g) sugar
1 tbsp unsalted butter
4 large egg yolks, lightly beaten
Fresh lemon verbena leaves for garnish

In a saucepan, combine the rice, 2 cups (500 ml) water and the salt. Bring to a boil and cook, uncovered, over moderate heat until the rice has absorbed all the water, about 10 minutes. In another saucepan, scald the milk and pour it over the rice, stirring to mix. Bury the verbena leaves in the rice and cook, uncovered, over very low heat, stirring gently from time to time until the milk is almost absorbed. Remove and discard the verbena leaves. Add the sugar, butter, and egg yolks and continue to cook, stirring from time to time, until the sugar, butter, and eggs have been absorbed and the mixture is creamy. Pour the pudding into a serving dish, cool, then refrigerate to chill. Serve garnished with lemon verbena leaves.

Leaves are long, pointed, and rough textured with a strong lemon scent; they grow in groups of three on the branch

Fresh leaves *taken from the top of the plant can be chopped and added to fruit or vegetable salads*

Chopped fresh leaves

54

HERB BUNDLES

Certain herbs and foods have an affinity with each other: rosemary with lamb, sage with pork and veal, fennel with fish, and basil with tomatoes. There are also combinations of herbs that marry particularly well. These range from a few fresh sprigs tied together, to a simple bouquet garni, to more elaborate mixtures that are used to flavor soups, stews, sauces, and many other dishes. Fresh herbs can be tied in bundles with string; dried herbs should be tied in a cheesecloth bag. Always remove the bundles at the end of cooking time.

For example, for long-cooking poultry dishes, combine a celery stalk with a sprig each of parsley, thyme, marjoram, tarragon, and a bay leaf, and tie in a cheese-cloth bag; for game birds add six juniper berries. With lamb, tie together sprigs of rosemary, thyme, savory, mint, and parsley; for beef stews, add orange peel and remove the mint. Add sprigs of fresh sage, thyme, and marjoram to pork, or use the dried forms of these herbs and tie in a cheesecloth bag. Seafood is best with dill, tarragon, and lemon zest.

FRESH BOUQUET GARNI

Bouquet garni is the French term for a bundle of herbs. Indispensable in the kitchen, the classic combination calls for 3 sprigs of parsley, 1 small sprig of thyme, and 1 small bay leaf. It can be enclosed in an aromatic vegetable wrapping; a celery stalk or the green part of a leek are the most common. When creating these bundles, be sure to use herbs that complement one another; remember that bay leaf is potent and parsley is mild. Size depends only on the volume of the dish; a small bouquet garni will be lost in a big pot of soup and a large one may overpower a small pan of sauce.

Use a piece of string to secure when the herb stalks are sufficiently long

Traditional bouquet garni
The classic combination of three parsley sprigs, 1 bay leaf, and 1 sprig of thyme can be altered to suit the make-up of the dish. This is a larger than average arrangement.

Bouquet garni with a celery stalk, a twist of orange peel, and oregano

Thyme

Mixed dried herbs can be tied in a square of cheesecloth

Cheesecloth bags

Bay

Parsley

DRIED BOUQUET GARNI

A bouquet garni made of dried bay, parsley, and thyme can either be store-bought or made at home. Mix together equal quantities of the herbs and place in a square of cheesecloth. Tie the cheesecloth with kitchen string or cotton thread. The bag should be removed at the end of cooking time. Homemade dried bouquet garni make excellent presents, and the choice of herbs can be varied to suit different types of dishes.

Tea bag-style bouquet garni

KITCHEN
SPICES

GALANGAL

Both the galangals are closely related members of the gingerroot family, *Zingiberaceae,* and are vital in the cooking of Southeast Asia. Greater galangal *(Alpinia galanga),* which is native to Indonesia, has large spicy roots that are knobby like gingerroot, with a tawny or pale creamy colored skin. With its gingerlike flavor, galangal is much used in the cuisine of Thailand, where it almost replaces gingerroot as a spice. The lesser galangal *(Alpinia officinarum)* is used more as a vegetable than a spice in Southeast Asia, and is peeled or shredded before being added to curries or stews. In China, it is used mostly for medicinal purposes. *Kempferia galangal* is another type, rarely available in the West. Once widely used in European cooking, it is still used in liqueurs and bitters. In the Middle Ages, galangal was called *galingale* in England, a name also used for the roots of sedge.

TASTES GOOD WITH/IN
Curries, soups and stews, chicken, seafood, especially shrimp, coconut-based sauces, lamb.

COOKING TIPS
If galangal is not available, substitute fresh grated gingerroot, halving the amount. The flavor will be more pungent and less aromatic.

COOK'S CHOICE
SOUTHEAST ASIAN-STYLE CHICKEN

Serves 2–4

6 large garlic cloves, crushed
1 tbsp ground black peppercorns
2 tbsp ground galangal, or 1 tbsp grated gingerroot
1/2 tsp salt or to taste
8 chicken thighs
Oil for deep-frying

In a bowl, mix together the garlic, peppercorns, galangal or gingerroot, and salt. Rub the mixture into the chicken thighs, put into a bowl, cover, and refrigerate for 3–4 hours to marinate. Pour enough oil into a frying pan to reach a depth of 2 in (5 cm). Heat to 375°F (190°C) on a frying thermometer or until hot but not smoking. Add the chicken thighs and fry until golden brown and cooked through. Drain on paper towels and serve with rice.

Similar to gingerroot rhizomes, with a peppery, gingerlike flavor

Greater galangal

Fresh slices

Dried slices

Kempferia galangal

Ground galangal

CELERY SEED

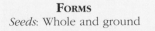

Celery was developed in the seventeenth century from smallage, or wild celery, found in the salt marshes of Europe. There are three main types: white, green, and turnip-rooted celery. The latter is called celery root, or celeriac, and is cooked as a vegetable or eaten raw in salads. Celery seeds are tiny and brown in color; they taste strongly of the vegetable and are aromatic and slightly bitter. The flavor is pleasant though, and the slight bitterness enhances other flavors. They are sometimes used where celery itself would not be appropriate, such as kneaded into bread doughs or sprinkled on crackers. They can be used whole, tossed in salads or over cooked vegetables just before serving, or they can be ground and added to cooked dishes. Celery seasoning is salt flavored with ground celery seeds and other herbs, and is a useful addition to many dishes such as soups, stews, and salad dressings—almost anywhere an aromatic salt is needed.

The tiny seeds are brown with lighter ridges and have a slightly bitter taste

Whole seeds

Celery ribs

Celery seasoning is especially good when sprinkled on meats before grilling

TASTES GOOD WITH/IN

Soups, sauces, stews, fish, breads, crackers, tomato juice, relishes, pickles, chutneys, egg dishes, especially omelets, salad dressings.

COOK'S CHOICE
POACHED CUCUMBERS WITH CELERY SEED

Serves 6

2 lb (1 kg) cucumbers, peeled and cut widthwise into 1-in (2.5 cm) slices
Chicken stock or water
1–2 tbsp unsalted butter
2 tsp finely ground celery seed
2–3 tbsp heavy cream (optional)

In a saucepan, combine the cucumber slices with enough chicken stock or water to barely cover. Bring to a simmer and cook, covered, over low heat until the cucumbers are tender, about 5 minutes. Drain thoroughly and return to the saucepan. Melt the butter in a small saucepan and stir in the ground celery seed; add the cream if using. Pour the mixture over the cucumbers and toss gently. Transfer to a warmed serving dish and serve hot as a vegetable. (The celery seed may be left whole.)

ANNATTO

OTHER NAMES
Achiote, bija, bijol, roucou, lipstick tree

FORMS
Seeds: Whole and ground

HOW TO STORE
Seeds: In airtight containers, kept in a cool, dark place. If brick red in color, they will keep indefinitely; avoid brownish seeds.

COOKING TIPS
Color rather than flavor is annatto's main role in the kitchen, however, oil that has been colored and gently imbued with annatto is a valuable ingredient in the cooking of the Caribbean. To make annatto oil, heat 1 cup (250 ml) grapeseed oil in a small saucepan. Add 2 oz (60 g) annatto seeds and cook, stirring, until the oil turns a deep orange color, about 2–5 minutes; timing depends on the potency of the seeds. Once the color is rich and deep, remove the pan from the heat. Cool, strain, and store the oil in a glass container in the refrigerator; it will keep indefinitely.

The annatto tree is an extremely attractive small flowering tree of the *Bixaceae* family that grows throughout the Caribbean, Mexico, and Central and South America. It bears large pink flowers that look like wild roses. However, it is the dye from the pulp that surrounds the fifty or so seeds inside the heart-shaped, prickly scarlet fruits that makes the tree commercially important. The warlike Carib Indians used the dye to paint their bodies, and it was also used by the ancient Mayans in Guatemala. Annatto is exploited to its fullest in the cooking of the Caribbean and Latin America, being used primarily as a coloring although also as a gentle flavoring. It is an ingredient in the spicy sauce that is served over the Jamaican national dish of ackee and salt cod. In Mexico, annatto seeds are ground with other herbs and spices, among them cumin and oregano, for a seasoning mixture that has a fragrant and flowery taste. Annatto was introduced to the Philippines by the Spaniards, and it has since become an important ingredient in many dishes. In Europe, annatto is used to color many cheeses, including Muenster, Livarot, Leicester, and Red Cheshire. Annatto has a great many names, which vary from island to island and country to country.

Annatto oil

Seeds

TASTES GOOD WITH/IN
Legumes, grains, rice, poultry, fish, especially salt cod, pork, beef and lamb stews, soups, okra, pumpkin, bell peppers, onions, tomatoes, curries, spice mixtures, shellfish, especially shrimp, chili sauces, egg dishes, sweet potatoes, plantains.

COOK'S CHOICE
PILAF RICE
Serves 4–6

1 1/2 cups (275 g) long-grain rice
4 tbsp annatto oil (see left)
2 1/2 cups (600 ml) chicken stock
Salt

Rinse and drain the rice. Heat the oil in a pan. Add the rice, stir, and cook until translucent, about 2 minutes. Add the stock and salt to taste. Bring to a boil, then simmer, covered, until the liquid is absorbed, about 20 minutes. Let stand 10 minutes. Fluff with a fork before serving. This goes well with spicy chicken dishes.

The seeds are extracted from the pods

SASSAFRAS

It was Louisiana's Choctaw Indians who were the first users of sassafras, a handsome tree of the laurel family native to North America. It grows to a considerable height and can reach nearly 90 ft (27 meters). The tree is aromatic with yellow-green flowers and dark blue fruits with red stalks. It has bright green leaves of three different shapes, all of which appear on the same tree. In the past, sassafras leaves and bark were used to make tea, to flavor medicines and, combined with other ingredients, to make a cordial. Its principal use today is as filé powder, which is obtained from the dried ground leaves of the tree. The powder is used as a thickening agent in gumbo, a dish that is a cross between soup and stew, most popular in the southern United States. Gumbos are the result of the meshing of American Indian, French, Spanish, and African cuisines. The name "gumbo" probably derives from an African Bantu word for okra, *gombo*, which arrived in the area via the French Caribbean; the two ingredients are easily confused since okra is also used as a thickening agent. If very young, tender leaves are available, they make a pleasant addition to green salads.

COOK'S CHOICE
SHRIMP AND CRAB GUMBO

Serves 6

4 tbsp vegetable oil

1 medium onion, finely chopped

4 scallions, chopped

4 celery stalks, chopped

1 medium green pepper, seeded and chopped

3 tbsp all-purpose flour

Salt

1 lb (500 g) cooked, shelled shrimp

1 lb (500 g) cooked crabmeat, picked over to remove any shell and cartilage

$1/2$ tsp chili sauce

4 tsp chopped flat-leaf parsley

1 tbsp filé powder

In a saucepan, combine the oil, onion, scallions, celery, and green pepper, and sauté until soft. Sift in the flour and cook for 2–3 minutes; do not brown. Gradually stir in 9 cups (2 liters) water; season to taste. Bring to a simmer and cook, covered, for 15 minutes. Add the shrimp and crabmeat and cook just long enough to heat them through. Stir in the chili sauce and the parsley; taste for seasoning. Remove from the heat and stir in the filé powder, blending thoroughly. Serve with plain rice.

Ground bark

Dried bark

Ground leaves (filé powder)

OTHER NAMES
Black mustard, brown
mustard, white mustard,
yellow mustard

FORMS
Seeds: Dry, whole, oil
Prepared: Strong, mild,
and flavored

HOW TO STORE
Seeds: In airtight containers
in a cool, dry place.
Prepared: In airtight jars in
the refrigerator.

COOKING TIPS
For strongest flavor, mix
dry mustard with cold
water and let it stand 10–30
minutes before using.
Japanese mustard is always
mixed with boiling water,
covered, and allowed to
stand before use. In
cooking, add mustard
toward the end and heat
gently. For stews, dry
mustard can be added to
the oil in which onions
and/or garlic is sautéed.
When making mayonnaise,
always use a *prepared
mustard* such as Dijon,
never a dry mustard.

MUSTARD

The name *mustard* derives from the Latin *mustum ardens,* or "burning must." The spice was so named because, as the seeds were pounded with unfermented grape juice, or must, their pungent qualities developed, hence "burning." All mustards, and they are legion, derive from three members of the cabbage family, two of them closely related. The close relatives are *nigra,* or black mustard, which can grow as tall as 7 ft (2 meters), and *juncea,* or brown mustard. Both plants bear small round seeds, although brown mustard has largely replaced the black type because its smaller size makes it easier to harvest. These mustards have the strongest flavor; black mustard in particular is prized for the distinctive taste it lends to the cuisines of India. The third mustard, *alba,* or white mustard, is native to the Mediterranean region and bears large yellowish seeds. This is the mustard that is grown with garden cress for salads, and it is the least pungent. White mustard is used extensively in the production of American prepared mustards, occasionally in English mustards, but not at all in Dijon mustards.

TASTES GOOD WITH/IN

Dry: Soups, stews. *Strong
prepared:* Sauces for
poultry, roasts, cold meats,
charcuterie, mayonnaise,
salad dressings.
Mild prepared: Sauces, fish
dishes, especially salmon
and herring.

SPROUTING SEEDS
White mustard sprouts,
Brassica alba, are usually
grown with garden cress,
Lepidium sativum, to
produce a crisp and slightly
peppery salad herb.
Growing these seeds
together became popular in
Victorian England, when
gardeners used earthen-
ware cones that were
grooved to hold the seeds.
Mustard can be grown from
seed on a thin layer of soil
in small trays, on a piece of
damp cloth, or even on
cotton batting. Kept moist,
the sprouts should be ready
to eat in about two weeks,
or when they are about
2 in (5 cm) high. If grown
with cress, plant the cress
3–4 days after the mustard
because it germinates more
quickly. Use the delicate
shoots in salads, sand-
wiches, or as a garnish.

*The pale, sandy-brown or
yellow seeds of the white
form are the largest kind*

*Strong and pungent
in flavor but smaller
in size than white*

White seeds

Black seeds

*Bitter, hot and
aromatic, brown
seeds are more
commonly
grown than
black and used
in place of them*

Brown seeds

Dry mustard

*The bright yellow
color of a
prepared mustard
is usually due to
the addition of
turmeric*

Prepared mustard *is
the most commonly used
form of the spice,
particularly in its use as
a condiment*

MAKING MUSTARD SAUCE

The fiery flavor of mustard is best savored when used uncooked. While a dollop on a platter of cold meats is often the only required seasoning, some dishes call for a more elaborate treatment. Many cold sauces, such as vinaigrette, mayonnaise, or the dill sauce shown here, are flavored with mustard. All of these sauces will go well with vegetable salads, but this dill sauce is particularly suited to gravlax (see page 102).

1 Dissolve 1–2 tbsp sugar in 1¹/₂ tbsp white-wine vinegar. Gradually whisk in ¹/₂ cup (125 ml) extra-virgin olive oil until well blended.

2 Add 6 tbsp Dijon mustard, 2–3 sprigs chopped fresh dill, and freshly ground white pepper to taste. Whisk to blend.

PREPARED MUSTARD

This condiment is a long-standing tradition in many cuisines around the world. It has been on the tables of the ancient Egyptians, Greeks, and Romans, and Pope John XXII was said to have appointed a private mustard maker to the palace in Avignon to ensure the quality of the papal jars. During the eighteenth century, when mustard came into fashion, there were at least ninety-three varieties available for consumption. The manufacturing process has also been handed down through the ages. In modern factories, as in the Middle Ages, the seeds are blended and then left to macerate in a liquid: grape juice, grape must, wine, vinegar, cider, or water. Finally, the seeds are ground to a fine paste. The temperature must never exceed 104°F (40°C) during manufacture or the volatile oils in the seeds, which are the source of the flavor, will evaporate. The culinary usage of prepared mustard has also changed little through the ages. It can be used to accompany cold meats, as an ingredient in cold sauces, or it can be added to hot dishes at the end of cooking time. As a condiment, this fiery mixture has universal appeal and there is a mustard flavor to fit every occasion.

STORING MUSTARD

Prepared mustard can be kept up to one year before it loses strength, but as soon as the jar is opened, the flavor begins to deteriorate and it is best used quickly. The shape of the traditional mustard pot, with a small neck, evolved because it was easier to seal and it prevented a large surface area from coming into contact with the air, keeping it fresh longer.

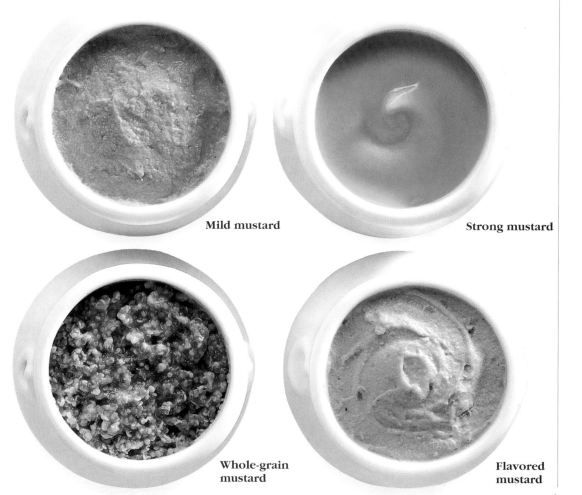

Mild mustard

Strong mustard

Whole-grain mustard

Flavored mustard

MILD AND STRONG MUSTARD

WHOLE-GRAIN MUSTARD

Whole-grain mustards are mild Dijon mustards made of partly crushed and partly ground brown seeds blended with vinegar and spices. The most well-known type is *moutarde de Meaux*, identified by its attractive stoneware jar with a red wax seal. English mustard was much like this before sifting and straining were introduced; nowadays both crunchy and smooth mustards are popular. Whole-grain mustard is relatively mild in taste because the hull is not totally removed.

Although there is an astonishing range of mustards, there are two basic types: mild and strong. The seed determines the difference between the two. For mild mustard, the seed coat, or hull, is left on, completely or partially; for strong mustard, it is sifted out. The most popular strong mustard is Dijon. Mild prepared mustards contain a higher percentage of the hull and not less than 20 percent dry mustard powder. Bordeaux, Beaujolais, and whole-grain mustards are the most commonly available mild types. American mustards are made from the milder, ground white mustard seeds, blended with vinegar, sugar, spices, and often turmeric, which is the source of the characteristic yellow color. German mustards are generally dark and smooth, made from a blend of black or brown dry mustard and vinegar, and vary in strength.

COOK'S CHOICE
MUSTARD CREAM SAUCE

Makes about ³/₄ cup (175 ml)

4 tbsp unsalted butter
¹/₂ cup (125 ml) heavy cream
1 tsp lemon juice, or to taste
Salt
Freshly ground black pepper
1–2 tsp whole-grain mustard
2–3 tbsp snipped fresh chives

Melt the butter in a shallow saucepan over moderate heat. When foaming, pour in the cream. Bring to a boil and allow to cook until slightly thickened, about 5 minutes. Add the lemon juice, salt and pepper; stir in the mustard. Taste for seasoning. Remove from the heat and stir in the chives. Serve immediately with broiled fish, meat, or poultry. If it cannot be brought to the table immediately, put the sauce into a bowl and place it on a rack over a pan of simmering water. It can be kept warm for about 15 minutes but cannot be kept further than this or reheated.

Dijon mustard

Bordeaux mustard

German mustard

American mustard

Beaujolais mustard

Sweet mustard

FLAVORED MUSTARD

FLAVORINGS FOR PREPARED MUSTARDS

Commercially prepared flavored mustards are now widely available. A delicious condiment for cold meats, fish, and poultry, they can also be used in recipes that call for ordinary prepared mustard, as long as the flavors marry. These mustards can also be made at home for a fraction of the cost. Use about 2 tsp fresh herbs, or other flavoring, for every ¹/₂ cup (125 g) mustard and let stand at least 10 minutes before using. For stronger flavors, adjust to taste. Mix with yogurt or sour cream for a quick and delicious sauce for steamed vegetables or cold poached seafood.

Flavored mustards are prepared mustards that are enhanced by the addition of an herb, spice, or other flavoring. There are many flavored mustards on the market. They can be gently imbued with delicate herbs such as basil, tarragon, chives, or mint; with spicier ingredients such as green peppercorns, chilies, cumin, or ginger; or with fruits such as lemon, lime, or berries. Some manufacturers are very inventive. *Moutarde aux quatre fruits* is a French four-fruit mustard that is flavored with summer fruits and beets. In England, mustard is often flavored with honey, malt whisky, or real ale. Despite its name, the Italian *mostarda di Cremona*, which combines a variety of candied fruit in a sweet mustard syrup, is more like a chutney than a mustard.

Chilies

Lemon

Green peppercorns

Mint

Many-flavored mustards
Mustard is a good base on which to build a custom flavoring. Herbs, spices, vegetables, and fruit are among the many additions that can be combined with it.

Herb mustard

Fruit mustard

Horseradish mustard

Lemon mustard

Chili mustard

COOK'S CHOICE
SALMON WITH LEMON MUSTARD SAUCE

Serves 4

4 salmon steaks, weighing about 6 oz (175 g) each
Juice of 1 large lemon
Juice of 1 large orange
4 tbsp unsalted butter
Salt
¹/₂ cup (125 ml) heavy cream
Freshly ground black pepper
1 tbsp lemon-flavored Dijon mustard
Chopped fresh parsley for garnish (optional)

Rinse the salmon and pat dry. Place in a shallow dish and pour over the lemon and orange juices. Cover with plastic wrap and refrigerate for about 1 hour to marinate; turn occasionally. Remove the fish from the marinade and pat dry with paper towels; reserve the marinade. Heat the butter in a large nonstick skillet. When foaming, add the salmon, sprinkle with salt and cook for 2 minutes, turn, salt, and cook the other side for another 2 minutes. Total cooking time depends on the thickness of the steaks; cook longer if necessary. Transfer the salmon steaks to a dish and keep warm. Add the marinade to the same nonstick pan and bring to a boil. Cook until reduced by two-thirds. Add the cream and continue reducing, 2–3 minutes. Season with pepper and stir in the mustard. Pour the sauce over the salmon, garnish with the parsley if using, and serve immediately with plain rice.

DRY MUSTARD

Developed in the early eighteenth century, dry mustard powder was obtained from black and white mustard seeds that were ground together. The blend was then sifted to produce a smooth powder, and this mixture replaced the milder, grainy type used at the time. The technique for producing dry mustard has changed little since then; nowadays wheat flour is added to the seeds, as well as turmeric for color, and some sugar, salt, and spices. Dry mustard also acts as a preservative and is often included in pickle and chutney recipes. Even hotter than dry mustard is the spicy Chinese mustard called *gai* made from the brown mustard seed. The hottest of all mustards is the Japanese *karashi* used in soy dipping sauces and, in very small quantities, to accompany Japanese dishes. Use both sparingly because they are very potent.

Once in its powdered form, mustard must be mixed with water to develop its pungent flavor

Dry mustard powder

Chili mustard powder

Peppercorn mustard powder

Whole-grain mustard powder with mint

Chive mustard powder

COOK'S CHOICE
CAJUN MUSTARD

Makes about ¹/₂ cup (125 ml)

2 oz (60 g) dry mustard
1 tbsp flour or cornstarch
3 tbsp white-wine vinegar
1 tbsp honey
1 garlic clove, finely chopped
1 tbsp hot red pepper flakes
1 tsp dried oregano
1 tsp ground cumin
1 tsp dried thyme
1 tsp coarse black pepper
1 tsp paprika

Combine the dry mustard and flour. Gradually stir in ¹/₄ cup (60 ml) cold water and leave to stand for 15 minutes. Stir in the remaining ingredients and mix thoroughly.

COOK'S CHOICE
HONEY MUSTARD

Makes about ¹/₂ cup (125 ml)

2 oz (60 g) dry mustard
1 tbsp flour or cornstarch
2 tbsp cider vinegar
1 tbsp brandy
1 tbsp honey

Combine the dry mustard and flour. Gradually stir in ¹/₄ cup (60 ml) cold water and let stand for 15 minutes. Add the remaining ingredients and mix thoroughly.

FLAVORING DRY MUSTARD

Dry mustard can be flavored with the same variety of herbs and spices as prepared mustard. Crushed chilies and cracked or ground black or white peppercorns lend a very strong flavor, while dried herbs such as basil, mint, or tarragon add a "cool" contrast to the pungency of the mustard. The zest of a lemon, lime, or orange can be grated into a small quantity of dry mustard; even grated fresh gingerroot or horseradish can be used. If combining very strong flavors, mix a little flour or cornstarch into the dry mustard before diluting with water.

CHILI

DRYING CHILIES

Fully mature red or yellow chilies are most suitable for drying. Place them on racks that allow air to circulate underneath, but turn them frequently to prevent mold from developing. Alternatively, they can be strung. Using a needle and heavy thread, puncture each chili at the top, just below the stem, and string. Hang in a warm, dry place, where they will dry in about a week.

PREPARING CHILIES

Fresh and dried chilies should be handled with care. Capsaicin (see right) can be painful if it gets on skin or into the eyes or nose. Wear rubber gloves when handling, and afterward, wash hands and all surfaces that came into contact with the chilies. If your hands get a chili "burn," it can sometimes be remedied by rinsing in a mild bleach solution, which renders the capsaicin water-soluble.

Peppers, sweet and hot, are members of *Solanaceae,* a vast assemblage of plants to which potato, tomato, and eggplant also belong. They were first cultivated in the Valley of Mexico in North America about 9,000 years ago. Their name in Nahuatl, the language of the region, was *chilli,* and this term was applied to all members of the genus. All chilies fall into the genus of *Capsicum* and most of the readily available ones belong to the *annuum* species. Despite their antiquity, the capsicums (peppers) remained one of the most well-kept secrets of the New World until Columbus introduced them to Europe at the end of the 1400s. That was the first leg of the capsicum's long journey around the cuisines of the world. The Portuguese then took them to the East Indies, Asia, and Africa. During the Ottoman invasions of the sixteenth century, Europeans rediscovered chilies, and the circle was completed when they were taken back to the Americas by European immigrants in the 1600s. There are hundreds of chili varieties—over 150 in Mexico alone—ranging in pungency from sweet to fiery hot. Chilies are rich in vitamin C, an extra bonus to their mouth-tingling flavor. Used in cuisines around the world, chilies spice up many savory dishes and are quite frequently made into "hot sauces." Thailand has its hot sauce, *nam prik,* Indonesia has a relish, *sambal,* which uses both sweet peppers and hot chilies (see page 69), Mexico has its *salsas,* and Tunisians make the fiery *harissa,* which is also found in Algeria and Morocco (see page 71). In Mexican cuisine and the cooking of the American Southwest, chilies are commonly used as a main ingredient.

Dried chilies

Crushed chilies

Fresh unripe chili

Fresh ripe chili

THE HEAT SCALE

Chilies contain capsaicin, which is the source of their fiery flavor. It is an oily substance, not water-soluble, which can be painful when it comes in contact with the eyes or other sensitive areas.
The heat of a chili is measured in Scoville units. The mildest chilies, such as sweet banana chilies, have a rating of 0 because they contain no heat. The hottest chili, the habanero, ranges from 100,000 to 300,000 Scoville units.

COOKING TIPS

• The longer a chili is cooked, the hotter the flavor. Simmering results in a dish that is hot overall; stir-frying adds flavor and a bit of spice.
• Small pieces of chopped chili provide a uniform hotness, but larger pieces can be more easily separated from a dish.
• To reduce their heat, soak fresh or dried chilies in a solution of 3 parts mild wine vinegar to 1 part salt for 1 hour.

Seeds are hot and are usually removed before cooking

Ribs also contain capsaicin, the source of a chili's heat; remove before use

Skin is usually removed; the distinctive flavor is found inside the meat

FRESH CHILIES

COOK'S CHOICE
CHILES RELLENOS

Serves 6

6 large green chili peppers, such as poblanos, with stems

1 lb (500 g) mozzarella or mild cheddar cheese, cut into sticks

2 eggs, separated

Salt

Oil for frying

Sifted flour for coating

Tomato sauce (see page 171)

Remove the skins from the chilies (see page 69), taking care not to break off the stems. Make a lengthwise slit and remove the seeds. Place the cheese inside the peppers; secure the slit and any minor tears with toothpicks. Place the egg whites in a bowl and add a pinch of salt. Beat until they hold stiff peaks. Lightly beat the egg yolks, then fold into the whites. Heat the oil in a large, heavy skillet. When hot, lightly coat the peppers in flour, dip into the egg mixture, and place in the hot oil. Cook until browned on one side, then turn and brown the other side. Transfer to paper towels to drain. If necessary, cook the chilies in batches. Place the sauce in another large, shallow pan and heat until warm. Add the drained, cooked chilies and cook just long enough to heat through. Serve immediately with boiled rice.

I n the cooking of Mexico and the southwestern United States, it is traditional to use only fresh chilies for certain dishes and dried for others. Generally, it is the small, hot chilies that are used fresh. Jalapeños, serranos, poblanos, Anaheims, and banana chilies are among the most common. They can be pickled and served on their own; milder varieties can be added to fresh sauces or *salsas*. Usually they require peeling (see page 69) before being added to a dish. Shapes and sizes vary, as do levels of pungency. Jalapeños and banana chilies, sometimes called *Hungarian wax peppers*, are medium-hot and juicy. Poblanos are also medium-hot, although the flesh is less juicy, while serranos are strong, hot, and less juicy. It is the seeds and ribs that contain the capsaicin, and the flesh that carries the distinctive flavor of each variety. For this reason, substituting one chili for another is a delicate task.

COOKING TIPS

• When using whole for stuffing, cut out stem end. Remove seeds and ribs with a spoon. Or, slit along one side, stuff, secure with a toothpick and bake.
• To lessen heat, remove the seeds and ribs, which are the hottest parts. The skins of fresh chilies are best removed before use (see page 69).

Fresh chilies should be firm and smooth, to make removal of the skins easier

Habanero chilies

Serrano chilies

Anaheim chili

Hot green chilies

Bullet chilies

COOK'S CHOICE

INDONESIAN GREEN PEPPER SAMBAL

Serves 4

1 tbsp vegetable oil

2 medium green peppers, seeded, deribbed, and diced

2 small fresh green chilies, seeded and finely chopped

1 medium onion, finely chopped

3 large garlic cloves, chopped

1 tbsp sugar

2 tbsp lime juice

1 tbsp nam pla (Asian fish sauce), or soy sauce

Salt

Heat the oil in a skillet. Add the peppers, chilies, onion, and garlic and cook, stirring constantly, until soft, about 3 minutes. Add the sugar, lime juice, and fish sauce and simmer over low heat, stirring occasionally, for 5 minutes. Taste for seasoning and salt, if necessary. Transfer to a bowl to cool. Serve immediately or cover and refrigerate for up to 3 days.

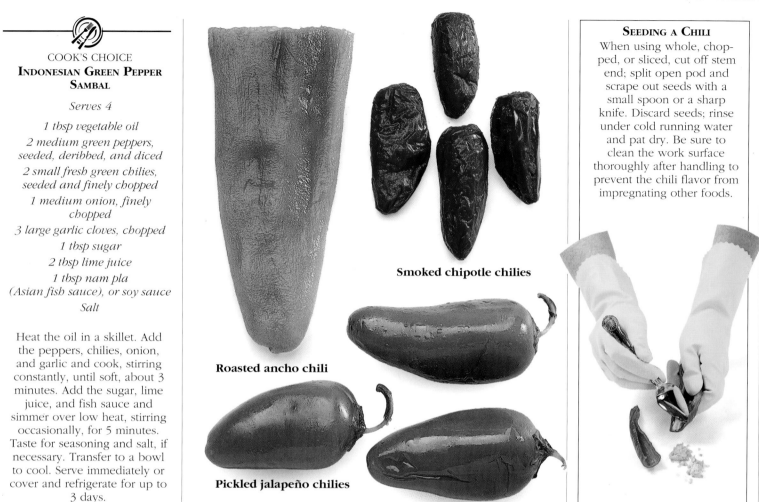

Smoked chipotle chilies

Roasted ancho chili

Pickled jalapeño chilies

SEEDING A CHILI

When using whole, chopped, or sliced, cut off stem end; split open pod and scrape out seeds with a small spoon or a sharp knife. Discard seeds; rinse under cold running water and pat dry. Be sure to clean the work surface thoroughly after handling to prevent the chili flavor from impregnating other foods.

PEELING CHILIES

Most fresh chilies have a thick skin that needs to be removed before cooking. Unless a recipe specifies a method, any of the illustrated ones can be used, or for thick-meated chilies, try a vegetable peeler. When cooking fresh and dried chilies, watch cooking stages carefully. Do not let them burn because the fumes from burning chilies can irritate the eyes and nose. After cooking, peel away the skin with gloved fingers under running water or "sweat."

Charring
When only a couple of chilies need to be prepared, this is a quick and easy method, though due caution must be taken. Hold the chili over a gas flame or electric burner with tongs. Turn frequently until all sides are blistered and blackened.

Roasting
Preheat the oven to 400°F (200°C). Rub the chilies with oil (wear rubber gloves), then place on an oven rack. Roast, turning occasionally, until soft and charred on all sides.

Frying
Heat vegetable oil in a heavy-bottomed saucepan. Dip chilies into hot oil and submerge completely for 5 seconds. Remove and cool before handling.

Sweating chilies
Place hot, roasted chilies in a plastic bag or wrap in a damp cloth and allow to sweat for 5–10 minutes, or until skin slips away easily. Remove any clinging skin with gloved fingertips or a small, sharp paring knife.

DRIED CHILIES

AFFINITY WITH OTHER HERBS/SPICES

Cilantro, basil, ginger, oregano, cinnamon, black pepper, cumin, fennel, flat-leaf parsley

COOKING TIPS

• To bring out the most intense flavor, larger varieties should be dry-roasted (see below).
• In recipes that require the chilies to be pureed, they are best soaked beforehand to soften. Wearing rubber gloves, tear the chilies into pieces and soak in hot water for 1 hour.
• A pair of scissors is often the best utensil for chopping dried chilies. Always be sure to clean the scissors thoroughly after use to rid them of all traces of spicy capsaicin.
• For a more complex flavor, combine several different varieties of dried chilies and grind together to a fine powder. Use wherever ground chili is required.

Dry-Roasting

Heat a dry cast-iron or nonstick skillet. When hot, add the chilies and press with a wooden spatula to sear. Remove from the heat as soon as they begin to plump and soften, only a few minutes, depending on the size of the chili. Do not allow the chilies to undergo any color change or become crisp.

As a rule, large dried chilies tend to be milder than small ones, although there are always exceptions. Dried chilies are a useful ingredient to have on hand because they have a fairly long shelf life if stored properly. When choosing dried chilies, suppleness is a sign of freshness; larger chilies tend to stay supple longer than small ones. Always buy in clear plastic packaging that allows a view of the contents. Don't be dismayed if chilies are dusty: this does not reflect age but the state of the packing house. Simply wipe gently before use with a soft, dry cloth. A wide variety of chilies are available dried. Ancho chilies are dried poblanos; the freshest ones smell vaguely of prunes. Guajillos are medium-hot dried chilies that are rarely available fresh, and pasillas are somewhat hotter.

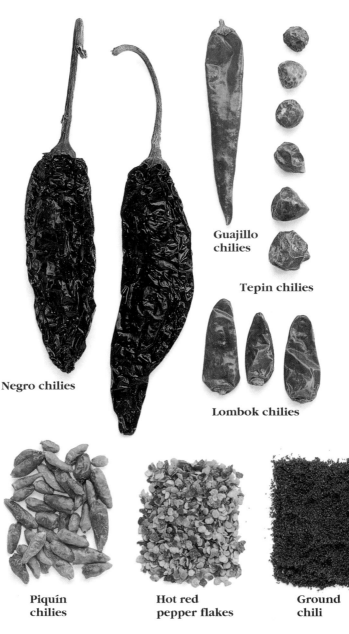

Guajillo chilies

Tepin chilies

Negro chilies

Lombok chilies

Piquín chilies

Hot red pepper flakes

Ground chili

HOW TO STORE

Whole: Should be kept in a tightly sealed plastic bag in the refrigerator.
Ground: Keep in airtight containers in a cool, dark place.

COOK'S CHOICE
MEXICAN BEANS WITH CHORIZO AND CHILIES

Serves 6

1 lb (500 g) dried black or pinto beans, soaked overnight

1 tbsp lard or oil

1 medium onion, chopped

8 oz (250 g) chorizo sausage, thickly sliced

2 poblano chilies, roasted, peeled, seeded, and chopped (or 2 ancho chilies, ground)

2 tomatoes, peeled, cored, seeded, and chopped

Salt

Chopped fresh cilantro for garnish

Place the beans in a saucepan with 8½ cups (2 liters) cold water to cover. Bring to a boil and simmer until tender, 1–2 hours; set aside. In a large skillet, heat the lard or oil. Add the onion, chorizo, and chilies and cook until golden brown, 5–10 minutes. Add the beans with their liquid and the tomatoes. Season to taste and simmer, uncovered, for 30 minutes. Sprinkle with the cilantro and serve.

Ancho chili

COOK'S CHOICE
HARISSA

Makes ¼ cup (60 g)

2 oz (60 g) dried red chilies
2 garlic cloves
Salt
2 tsp coriander seeds
1½ tsp ground cumin
1 tsp caraway seeds
1 tsp crumbled dried mint
Extra-virgin olive oil

Seed the chilies and tear into pieces. Soak in warm water until soft, about 20 minutes. Drain and pound with a mortar and pestle or use a food processor. Crush the garlic with a little salt. Blend all the dry ingredients into a paste. Stir in 2 tbsp oil. Transfer to a jar, cover with a layer of oil, and refrigerate. This will keep for up to 6 weeks. Use as a marinade for grilled chicken, lamb, or fish, as a table condiment, or with North African dishes such as couscous.

Chilies

Harissa

Garlic

Salt

Mint

Cumin

Coriander seeds

GROUND CHILIES

Many commonly available chili powders are blends of a number of spices and seasonings, although almost all dried chilies can be ground and used as a pure powder. For a homemade mixture, experiment with herbs and spices.

String fresh chilies to dry, then crush in a spice grinder for homemade ground chili

Commercial chili powders
In addition to ground dried chilies, powders can contain garlic, onion, cumin, oregano, allspice, salt, and other spices. Not to be used in place of ground chilies, these powders are often used to season chili con carne.

Ground cayenne
Ground from small red chili peppers of the Capsicum frutescens *variety, cayenne has been used to spice up the dishes of many countries. It is about as spicy as other dried ground chilies and is sometimes used as a table condiment.*

Hot red pepper flakes
A fiery seasoning, this spice can be purchased or made at home from dried chilies. It is more traditional to crush in a mortar, although fumes and chili dust can irritate eyes and nose. An electric spice grinder is best.

PAPRIKA

The sweet peppers that are dried and ground for paprika have a complex history. The plant originated in the southernmost tip of Mexico, was taken to Spain and Morocco by the Spanish, and then found its way to Hungary, where it became naturalized and an essential ingredient in local cuisine. The thick-fleshed peppers are as broad as they are long and similar to other members of their large family, and are excellent sources of vitamin C. Whole fresh peppers can be difficult to find, but with their slightly piquant flavor, they make excellent peppers for stuffing. Ground paprika lends an appealing flavor to foods as well as a beautiful deep-red color. Spain has a similar pepper, called *pimientó*. It is a pointed, heart-shaped fruit that is used to make *pimentón*, a spice similar to paprika. In its fresh form, it is most familiar as the red stuffing inside green Spanish cocktail olives.

Color can vary from bright red to light pink; flavor can range from sweet to fiercely hot

Spanish pimentón

Fresh pepper

Hungarian paprika

AJOWAN

OTHER NAMES
Ajwain, bishop's weed, *omam, omum*

FORMS
Seeds: Whole and ground

HOW TO STORE
If kept in an airtight container in a cool, dark place, this spice will keep indefinitely.

COOKING TIPS
Use in rich pastry hors d'oeuvres or crackers and with legumes to minimize flatulence. Because it gives food a very strong flavor of thyme, it should be used sparingly.

Native to Southern India, ajowan is closely related to caraway and cumin, although it tastes strongly of thyme. The seeds look similar to large celery seeds, and the taste, in addition to the thymelike flavor, is hot and bitter. The plant, which also flourishes in Egypt, Iran, Pakistan, and Afghanistan, is pretty, and resembles wild parsley. It has seeds that range from light brown to red in color. It is also cultivated for its essential oil, thymol, which is used as a germicide and an antiseptic as well as for culinary purposes. Like many spices used in Indian cooking, it serves a dual purpose: alongside flavor, it has medicinal properties that help to control problems of digestion such as flatulence. Thus, for reasons of both flavor and practicality, its natural affinity is with starchy foods and legumes.

TASTES GOOD WITH/IN
Pickles, Indian breads, Indian snack mixes of nuts and dry beans, pastry, root vegetables and legumes.

COOK'S CHOICE
SPICY BROWN LENTILS
Serves 4

8 oz (250 g) brown lentils
2 tbsp vegetable oil
1 medium onion, finely chopped
1 garlic clove, chopped
1/4 tsp ground ajowan seeds, or to taste
1/4 tsp cayenne pepper, or to taste
Salt

Combine the lentils and 2 cups (450 ml) water in a saucepan and soak for about 1 hour. Heat the oil in a skillet and sauté the onion until soft. Add the garlic and sauté for 30 seconds. Scrape the contents of the skillet into the saucepan and add the ajowan, cayenne, and salt to taste. Bring to a simmer over moderate heat. Cover and cook until the lentils are tender and the liquid is absorbed, about 1–1 1/2 hours. Serve hot.

The crushed seeds are highly aromatic

Ground ajowan

Seeds *are similar to large celery seeds, with a strong, pungent flavor of thyme*

Nan

Indian breads *such as nan, pakora, and paratha, are made with ajowan; this imparts a thymelike flavor to the dough*

Pakora

73

CARAWAY

HOW TO STORE
Seeds: Both dried and
ground should be stored in
airtight containers and kept
well away from light.
Leaves and taproots: Store
briefly in plastic bags in the
refrigerator.

COOKING TIPS
Seeds enhance the flavor of
many vegetables; they are
especially delicious when
tossed with boiled, buttered
new potatoes or cabbage.
Taproots can be boiled or
baked and eaten as a
vegetable.

Caraway has been used as a spice for about 5,000 years; there is evidence of its culinary use in the Stone Age. Originally from the countries of temperate Asia, including Iran and Turkey, it has since spread widely in North America and Europe. Its name comes from the ancient Arabic, *karawya*, by which it is still known in the region. A biennial plant, caraway grows up to 2 ft (60 cm) in height with feathery leaves and creamy white flowers. It was once popular in English cooking; seed cake is a very old favorite in Great Britain and Shakespeare's Falstaff is invited to partake of "a pippin and a dish of caraways." Later, during the reign of Queen Victoria, use of the seeds was revived, in keeping with the fashion for things German. Nowadays, caraway is most popular in Austrian and German cooking, where it is used to flavor breads and pastries; in other countries, its use is limited. Its kitchen contribution is greatest when it is used sparingly. Medicinally, it serves as an aid to digestion; the seeds are chewed after a meal, or can be infused and served as a tisane.

Ground caraway

Fresh leaves *are feathery with a mild flavor*

Dried seeds *are dark brown with light brown ridges and have an aromatic and spicy flavor*

TASTES GOOD WITH/IN
Young leaves: Finely
chopped, add to salad, as a
garnish, or to any dish
where parsley would be
used. *Seeds:* Cakes, breads,
vegetables, especially
potatoes, cabbage, carrots
and mushrooms, sausages,
rich meats such as pork,
duck, and goose.

COOK'S CHOICE
SEED CAKE

Makes one 9 in (23 cm) cake

*Butter and flour for preparing
the pan*
1 cup (225 g) unsalted butter
*1 cup plus 2 tbsp (225 g)
superfine sugar*
4 eggs
*1 3/4 cups (225 g) all-purpose
flour*
1/2 tsp salt
1 tsp baking powder
1 tsp vanilla extract
1 tbsp caraway seeds

Preheat the oven to 350°F (180°C). Grease and flour a 9-in (23 cm) cake pan. In a bowl, cream together the butter and sugar until light and fluffy. Add the eggs, one by one, beating well after each addition. Sift the flour, salt, and baking powder together and add to the butter mixture, blending thoroughly. Stir in the vanilla and caraway seeds and pour the batter into the prepared pan. Bake until the cake is golden and pulls away from the sides of the pan, about 50 minutes. Let the cake stand for 10 minutes before removing it from the pan. Place on a cake rack to cool. Serve plain or frost with buttercream (see page 197).

SPICE MIXTURES

In the past, a kitchen cabinet full of exotic spices was a symbol of wealth, and spice mixtures were a lavish mark of prestige. Nowadays, with spices so readily available, cooks tend to prefer individual spices and mixtures have fallen from favor. However, some traditional European blends survive: *quatre-épices*, mixed or pudding spice, and pickling spice. In India and Asia, spice mixtures such as curry powder retain their importance, and there are some, often based on chilies, that are prevalent in the Americas. Middle-Eastern and North African blends are also well known.

PICKLING SPICE

This is a mixture used when making pickled fruits and vegetables, chutneys and spiced vinegar. The proportions of the spices vary, and so do the spices used—this is a representative recipe. Fennel seed could also be included, and a pinch of freshly grated nutmeg could replace the mace.

Combine 1 tablespoon each whole black peppercorns, yellow mustard seeds, hot red pepper flakes, allspice berries, dill seed, and crushed mace. To this, add 1 crushed 2-in (5 cm) cinnamon stick, 2 crumbled bay leaves, 1 teaspoon whole cloves, and 2 tablespoons ground ginger. Use in pickle-making brines, or tie in a small square of cheesecloth and remove after pickling.

MIXED SPICE

From the 1600s onward, cookbooks began to list spices separately with each individual recipe, rather than as basic mixtures at the front, but a few popular blends are still in use. This traditional English blend of spices, also called *pudding spice*, is used to flavor steamed puddings. Like all mixtures, the proportions and the ingredients vary according to personal taste.

Grind together 1 tablespoon coriander seeds, 1 crushed 2-in (5 cm) cinnamon stick, 1 teaspoon allspice berries, and 1 teaspoon whole cloves. Stir in 1 tablespoon freshly grated nutmeg and 2 teaspoons ground ginger. Store in an airtight container and keep in a cool place away from light.

QUATRE-ÉPICES

A French spice mixture, the name means "four spices." It is much used in the preparation of French charcuterie and to a lesser extent in slowly cooked meat and poultry dishes. The composition varies but is generally based on black peppercorns, nutmeg, cloves, and ginger. Allspice and cinnamon are sometimes substituted for other spices in the blend.

In a spice grinder or coffee mill, grind 1 heaped tablespoon black peppercorns and 2 teaspoons whole cloves. Combine with 2 teaspoons freshly grated nutmeg and 1 teaspoon ground ginger. Store in an airtight container and keep in a cool place away from light.

CASSIA

OTHER NAMES
Chinese cinnamon, false cinnamon

FORMS
Dried: Peeled, rolled bark, ground, leaves, buds

HOW TO STORE
In airtight glass containers kept in a cool, dark place.

COOKING TIPS
Ground cassia turns stale quite quickly, so make sure it is stored properly, away from light. Use in any recipe where cinnamon is called for because the flavor is almost, if not quite, identical; use slightly less cassia than cinnamon because the taste is stronger.

Although closely related to cinnamon and often confused with it, cassia originated in Burma—a long way from cinnamon's birthplace in Sri Lanka. Cultivated extensively in Southern China and Indonesia, cassia is one of the oldest of the spices. It was used in China as far back as 2500 B.C. and it reached Europe by the old spice routes from the East. Indeed, most cinnamon and cassia still comes from the Orient. Like cassia, cinnamon comes from the bark of an evergreen laurel tree. The bark is peeled from thin branches that are dried in the sun to form "quills," or cassia sticks. Cassia quills are larger and coarser than cinnamon quills, and their flavor is sweet and aromatic, although it has been described as a coarser species of cinnamon. The leaves also have a cassia flavor and they can be used as a flavoring like bay leaves. The buds, which look a little like cloves, are useful where a slight cinnamon flavor is needed. Cassia is one of the traditional ingredients in Chinese five-spice mixture, and it is less expensive than cinnamon, which makes it a popular substitute.

TASTES GOOD WITH/IN
Curries, pickles, especially pickled beets, relishes, tomato ketchup, rhubarb, and baked goods.

COOK'S CHOICE
CASSIA TOAST

Serves 4

Day-old bread, cut into 8 slices
6–8 tbsp unsalted butter, at room temperature
4 tbsp sugar
1 1/2 tsp ground cassia, or to taste

Preheat the broiler. Butter the bread generously and cut it into triangles or halves. Combine the sugar and cassia and sprinkle over the bread. Broil just until the sugar melts; serve the toast hot.

Cassia has a sweet, strong flavor reminiscent of cinnamon

Cassia toast

Cassia bark

Cassia buds

Ground cassia *is dark and ruddy with a warm aroma*

CINNAMON

FORMS
Dried: Rolled sticks, quillings, ground

HOW TO STORE
In airtight containers kept in a cool, dark place.

COOKING TIP
A pinch of *ground* cinnamon will enhance most meat stews, especially those made with lamb. It is also good in stuffings for duck or goose, or in any stuffing made with dried fruit such as apricots or prunes. Cinnamon *sticks* are useful for flavoring hot drinks such as mulled wine, hot chocolate, and coffee.

This delicately fragrant, slightly sweet spice is native to Sri Lanka, although it is now grown in most hot, wet tropical regions. One of the oldest known spices, cinnamon is mentioned in the Bible and in Sanskrit manuscripts. The first mention of cinnamon comes from ancient China, where it was known as *kwei*. From very early times, there has been a confusion between cassia and cinnamon. Today, most of the cinnamon sold in the United States is actually cassia, while the cinnamon sold in Britain comes from Sri Lanka and is considered to be true cinnamon. Cinnamon comes from a small, laurellike evergreen tree. The spice itself is the bark, peeled from thin branches. Then, the outer bark is peeled away, and the inner bark is rolled up into a quill about 1 in (2.5 cm) in diameter. While the use of cinnamon in most European countries is limited to sweets, in the Middle East it is commonly added to meat stews, especially those made with lamb. It is also combined with dried fruit for poultry or pork stuffings and is delicious on buttered acorn squash or sweet potatoes.

TASTES GOOD WITH/IN
Cakes, puddings, cookies, and breads, meat and game stews, vegetables, stewed fruit, and curries.

COOK'S CHOICE
CINNAMON CUSTARD SAUCE

Makes 2 cups (500 ml)

1½ cups (375 ml) milk
½ cup (125 ml) light cream
1 cinnamon stick
5 egg yolks
4 tbsp sugar

Place the milk, cream, and cinnamon in a saucepan and bring to a boil. Off the heat, leave to infuse for at least 15 minutes. In a large bowl, whisk together the yolks and sugar until thick and lemon colored. If necessary, reheat the milk and cream. Pour the hot liquid into the yolk mixture, stirring constantly. Return to the saucepan and place over low heat. Cook gently to thicken, stirring constantly with a wooden spoon. The sauce is done when a finger drawn across the back of the spoon leaves a mark. Strain into a clean bowl. Cover and refrigerate until needed. This custard sauce can be served with steamed puddings, cakes, or pies, especially those made with apples.

Cinnamon bark

Cinnamon can be used to flavor many dishes, both sweet and savory

Cinnamon sticks

Cinnamon quillings

Ground cinnamon

SAFFRON

OTHER NAMES
Hay saffron, saffron crocus

FORMS
Dried: Threads, ground

HOW TO STORE
In airtight containers kept away from light. For best results, buy in small quantities because saffron quickly loses its flavor.

COOKING TIPS
To bring out the strongest saffron color and flavor, grind *threads* in a small ceramic mortar. Transfer the ground saffron to the dish and rinse the mortar and pestle in the cooking liquid so as not to lose any of the saffron. When adding *threads* to dishes with very little liquid, it is best to soak the saffron first in tepid water and add toward the end of cooking. *Ground* saffron can be added directly to dishes.

Over a quarter of a million crocus flowers must be harvested to obtain one pound of saffron, and the three stigmas from each crocus must be collected by hand, which explains why saffron is the single most expensive spice. Fortunately, very little saffron is needed in most dishes, sometimes as little as a pinch. Saffron has been used in cooking since the tenth century B.C. It was a great favorite of the Phoenician traders, who took it with them wherever they went. It is cultivated in a number of Mediterranean countries, although Spain is the main producer. Some authorities believe it was the Phoenicians who introduced saffron to Spain, and later to Cornwall in England, where they traded it for tin. Saffron buns are still made in both of these areas, a legacy, no doubt, from this trade. Pungent, with a beautiful yellow color, saffron is indispensable in a number of dishes, such as bouillabaisse and paella, and saffron bread is a traditional part of the Swedish Christmas feast. It is used also in liqueurs, the best known being Chartreuse. Saffron threads are preferable to the ground form because the latter can easily be adulterated. The spice should not be confused with meadow saffron, *(Colchicum autumnale),* which is poisonous.

TASTES GOOD WITH/IN

Fish dishes, especially those with garlic, such as French bouillabaisse, Spanish zarsuela and paella, poultry and beef stews, tomato-based sauces, sweet breads and cookies.

COOK'S CHOICE
MONKFISH WITH SAFFRON SAUCE

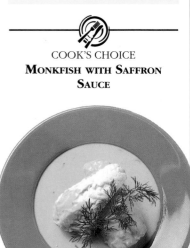

Serves 6

2 lb (1 kg) monkfish fillets, cut into 2-in (5 cm) pieces
Salt
Freshly ground black pepper
1 cup (250 ml) dry white wine
¹/₂ cup (125 ml) fish stock
¹/₂ cup (125 ml) heavy cream
4 tbsp chilled unsalted butter, cut into pieces
¹/₂ tsp saffron threads, ground

Place the fish in a deep skillet and season to taste. Add the wine and stock and bring to a simmer. Cover and cook gently until the fish is cooked through, 7–10 minutes. Remove the fish and keep warm. Add the cream to the liquid in the pan. Whisk in the butter, bit by bit; do not boil. Stir in the saffron. Add the fish with any juices that may have collected and warm before serving.

Ground saffron

Threads are wiry and about 1 in (2.5 cm) long

To impart an even saffron yellow color, soak threads before using

Saffron threads *are a rich, red-orange; the deeper the color, the better the quality*

CUMIN

FORMS
Seeds: Whole and ground

HOW TO STORE
In airtight containers away from light.

COOKING TIPS
It is best to use *whole seeds* and grind in a mortar just before use because the flavorful oil escapes rapidly after grinding. Dry-roasting the seeds before grinding enhances their warm flavor. Unless a strong cumin flavor is sought, use sparingly because this spice is potent and will dominate most others.

Garam masala *is a traditional spice mixture from Northern India, most often combining cumin with coriander seeds, cardamom, black peppercorns, cloves, mace, bay leaf, and cinnamon*

An annual, originally from the East, cumin has been grown in India, Egypt, Arabia, and the Mediterranean countries from very early times. It is grown even more widely today, needing only a warm, equable climate to flourish. The spice comes from the seed of this plant, which grows to about 1 ft (30 cm) high and has flowers that range in color from mauve or rose pink to white. In ancient Rome, cumin was used as a substitute for black peppercorns, and it was also ground into a paste for spreading on bread. The essential oil extracted from cumin is used by the perfume industry, and it was once believed to have medicinal properties. According to Roman scholar Pliny, his students used it to encourage their pallor and feign exhaustion. Because of its resemblance to caraway, these spices are often confused. Likewise, black cumin is sometimes confused with nigella. However, cumin's distinctive warm flavor is unique and makes a valuable contribution to many dishes. Cumin will evoke Indian and Mexican cuisines, since it is a vital flavoring in both; it is also used extensively in North Africa and in the Middle East.

Cumin seeds

Ground cumin

Black cumin seeds

Ground black cumin

TASTES GOOD WITH/IN

Pickles, cabbage, Mexican dishes, especially those from the Yucatán, chili, North African dishes such as couscous, Indian dishes such as curries, meat stews, some cheeses, sausages, tomato-based sauces, stuffing mixtures.

COOK'S CHOICE
SPICY PORK STEW

Serves 6

1 large onion, chopped
2 garlic cloves, chopped
1/2 tsp salt
1/2 tsp cumin seeds, ground
1/4 tsp black peppercorns, ground
3 lb (1.5 kg) lean boneless pork, cut into 2-in (5 cm) cubes
4 1/2 cups (1 liter) lamb stock or water
4 oz (125 g) hulled pumpkin seeds, finely ground
1 tbsp lemon juice

In a heavy flameproof casserole, combine all the ingredients except the pumpkin seeds and lemon juice. Simmer, covered, over low heat until the pork is tender, about 2 hours. Add the pumpkin seeds and simmer until the liquid is thickened, about 5 minutes. Taste for seasoning and add salt if necessary; stir in the lemon juice and serve immediately with boiled rice.

TURMERIC

A handsome perennial with large lilylike leaves and yellow flowers, turmeric is a member of the ginger family and, like ginger, it is the underground rhizome of the plant. Turmeric has been cultivated for over 2,000 years in India, China, and the Middle East and is now grown in all the tropical regions of the world. It is thought to be one of the ancient Persian yellow spices that were associated with sun worship. Although sometimes available fresh, turmeric is most often sold dried and ground. It adds a warm, mild aroma and distinctive yellow color to foods. It is essential to curry powders, and it is also used to flavor many Indian vegetarian dishes. In both India and China, turmeric is used as a dye for cloth, and in India as a mild digestive and a remedy for liver ailments.

COOKING TIPS
Although lacking in the exquisitely aromatic flavor of saffron, turmeric can be used as a substitute. The taste will be more mild and musky, but the color will be a brilliant golden-yellow. It can also be used as a substitute for annatto (see page 60) which is also yellow, and for the less well-known Peruvian spice, *palillo*, which imparts a bright sunshine-yellow color to food.

A colorful spice
The plant is known for its brilliant golden yellow color, which has long been exploited for dye-making purposes.

Fresh turmeric *has a brownish skin with bright orange flesh*

Dried turmeric

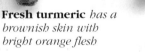

Ground turmeric

COOK'S CHOICE
CHICKEN WITH TURMERIC

Serves 4

2 tbsp corn or peanut oil
1 medium onion, finely chopped
1 garlic clove, finely chopped
1 tsp ground turmeric
3 lb (1.5 kg) chicken, cut into serving pieces
Salt
Freshly ground black pepper
2 cups (500 ml) chicken stock
2 tbsp lemon juice
Flat-leaf parsley for garnish

In a large casserole, combine the oil and onion and cook over low heat until soft, about 5 minutes. Add the garlic and cook 2 minutes longer. Stir in the turmeric. Raise the heat, add the chicken, and cook until browned. Season to taste and add the chicken stock. Bring to a simmer, cover, and cook over very low heat until the chicken is tender, about 45 minutes. Stir in the lemon juice. Remove the chicken. Reduce the sauce over brisk heat to thicken slightly. Pour over the chicken. Garnish with parsley and serve with basmati and wild rice.

CURRY POWDERS

Although curry powders are associated with the cuisines of India, the word *curry* was actually coined by British colonials in India. Curries are savory dishes of meat, fish, or vegetables served in a hot and spicy sauce. Each sauce may be based on a different blend of spices, mixed according to personal taste. These blends, known as *masalas*, are intricate mixtures of ground or whole spices, which may be mild or strong. There is no one specific blend, and they are based on the spices native to India: turmeric, ginger, pepper, coriander, cumin and chilies. Some masalas may include all these spices and more, such as cloves, cinnamon, and nutmeg; others may use only two or three spices. In general, the spices are dry-roasted in a skillet before grinding to enhance their flavor. While most curry blends are thought of as dry mixtures, there are, in fact, many that are pastes.

POUDRE DE COLOMBO

This is an example of a spice blend used in the curries of the West Indies. In the nineteenth century, Ceylonese immigrant workers brought their cooking to the region, and it soon became popular with the inhabitants. Taking their name from Colombo, the capital of Sri Lanka, *colombos* are fiery stews made with pork, chicken, goat, or tropical vegetables. White wine, stock, coconut milk, and even rum can be added for the sauce.

Peel and crush 3 garlic cloves; seed and finely chop 2 fresh chilies (see page 69), and place in a small bowl. Combine ¹/₂ teaspoon ground turmeric, ¹/₂ teaspoon ground coriander and 1 teaspoon dry mustard and blend. Add to the garlic mixture and blend thoroughly. Stored in an airtight container in the refrigerator, this will keep for 4–6 weeks.

BASIC CURRY POWDER

Spice blending is essential for Indian cooking and the hundreds of mixtures used throughout the subcontinent reflect its different regions, dishes, and cooks' temperaments. This recipe is simply a blueprint; for a more aromatic and less spicy mixture, reduce the number of chilies and add 1 teaspoon of ground cinnamon and a few ground cloves. Use dry, or blend with lukewarm water to make a paste.

Combine 6 dried red chilies, 2 tablespoons coriander seeds, ¹/₂ teaspoon mustard seeds, 1 teaspoon black peppercorns, and 1 teaspoon fenugreek seeds in a heavy, cast-iron skillet. Roast over medium heat until dark, taking care not to burn. Leave to cool, then grind to a powder with a mortar and pestle. Blend in ¹/₂ teaspoon ground ginger and ¹/₂ teaspoon ground turmeric. Store in an airtight jar, kept in a cool, dark place for up to 3 months.

Although called a powder, this powerful mixture is, in fact, a paste

THAI RED CURRY PASTE

Thai curries tend to be fiery. They are often served with Oriental-style noodles or salads that serve to balance the heat of chilies. *Trasi* is a firm paste made from fermented shrimp. It is sometimes known as *blachan* and can be bought from Oriental grocers. This paste is best used with beef.

Heat a skillet, combine 1 teaspoon cumin and 1 tablespoon coriander seeds and dry-roast, 2–3 minutes. Cool. With a mortar and pestle, grind to a powder together with 1 teaspoon black peppercorns. Add 3 chopped shallots, 2 crushed garlic cloves and 2 chopped lemongrass stalks, and grind to a smooth paste. Seed and chop 10 dried red chilies, and add to mix, along with 1 tablespoon ground galangal, 2 teaspoons grated lime zest, a small piece of trasi and salt to taste. Store in an airtight container in the refrigerator for 2–3 days.

CARDAMOM

FORMS
Dried: Pods, loose seeds, ground seeds

HOW TO STORE
In airtight containers kept in a cool, dry place.

COOKING TIPS
Loose and *ground seeds* lose flavor quickly so it is best to buy whole *pods*. Discard the papery pods before grinding the seeds. Avoid brown cardamoms which are not true cardamoms and have a flavor reminiscent of camphor.

Loose seeds and ground cardamom lose their flavor quickly, so it is best to buy whole pods and grind at home

This is a spice of great antiquity used first by the early Egyptians and then by the ancient Greeks and Romans. It came into Europe by way of the old caravan routes, and after saffron and vanilla, it is the third most expensive spice. Cardamom is used most extensively in India and the Middle East, although it is an ingredient in the cakes and pastries of Germany, Russia, and Scandinavia. In the United States and France, the essential oil is used in perfumery. The plant grows profusely on the Malabar Coast of India, while another variety grows in Sri Lanka, Mexico, and Guatemala. A member of the ginger family, it is a tall perennial shrub with lance-shaped leaves and short flowering stems.

After flowering, the stems carry small green seed capsules that must be harvested by hand; these capsules can contain up to 20 aromatic seeds. Green cardamom pods are the most common, and white pods are simply green ones that have been bleached. Brown cardamom pods are not true cardamom but a related variety. The flavor and texture are not as delicate as those of the green variety, in fact they are rather unpleasant. For best results, the highly aromatic seeds should be taken from green or white pods only just before use.

TASTES GOOD WITH/IN

Cakes, pastries, liqueurs, coffee, curries, pilafs, pickles, pickled herrings, meat dishes, punches, spiced wines, custards, and fruit dishes.

GRAINS OF PARADISE
Grains of paradise, or Melegueta pepper, is a spice related to cardamom. The tiny grains have a hot and peppery taste. The aroma, however, is very similar to that of cardamom.

Seeds

Green cardamom pods

Ground cardamom

White cardamom pods

Brown cardamom pods

COOKING WITH CARDAMOM

The strong, almost lemony flavor of cardamom enhances both savory and sweet dishes. Cardamom is a constant ingredient in Indian cooking, essential in pilafs and curries, especially those from North India and Pakistan, and in creamy dessert dishes such as *kulfi*, a rich pistachio- and almond-flavored ice cream. Used extensively throughout the Middle East, cardamom is a frequent flavoring especially in the many sweetmeats and sweet pastries of the region. In both the Middle East and North Africa, cardamom is used to mellow the flavor of the traditionally strong, bitter coffee, while other African countries prefer it in tea. Its digestive properties have made it popular as an after-dinner infusion, and it acts as a breath freshener when chewed. In Northern European countries, cardamom is associated with warmth, and it is often added to warm winter punches and mulled wines. In Germany, it is added to some charcuterie preparations, and in Scandinavia cardamom finds its way into spice buns, breads, and pastries. Cardamom marries well with fruit: use when poaching pears, baking apples, or add ground cardamom to a fruit salad. Delicious ice cream can be made by infusing the hot cream or milk with bruised cardamom pods.

CARDAMOM DRINKS

An after-dinner infusion of cardamom pods is not only refreshing and flavorful, but an aid to digestion as well. In the Middle East, strong black espresso-type coffee is often flavored with ground cardamom. To prepare an infusion, add 12 whole crushed pods to 6 ¾ cups (1.5 liters) boiling water. Add a strip of orange peel and leave to infuse for 10 minutes. Add 2–3 tablespoons tea leaves. Infuse as desired, strain, and serve with hot milk and sugar.

Green cardamom pods

Cardamom tea

Cardamom-flavored coffee

COOK'S CHOICE
FRUIT SALAD WITH CARDAMOM

Serves 4

2 tbsp sugar
½ cup (125 ml) orange juice
½ tsp ground cardamom
2 oranges, segmented or sliced (see page 172)
1 apple, diced
1 pear, diced
2 bananas, sliced
2 plums, diced
Assorted soft fruit for garnish such as grapes, cherries, blueberries, and raspberries
Fresh mint for garnish

In a small saucepan, combine the sugar and ½ cup (125 ml) water over medium heat. Simmer until the sugar is dissolved. Leave to cool. Add the orange juice and cardamom. Combine the oranges, apple, pear, bananas, and plums in a glass bowl and pour over the cardamom mixture. Chill for at least 30 minutes, garnish with the soft fruit and mint, and serve.

CLOVES

FORMS
Buds: Dried, whole, and ground

HOW TO STORE
Keep in airtight containers in a cool, dark place.

COOKING TIPS
Use a clove-studded onion to flavor chicken stock. Add a clove to the bouquet garni used for long-cooking meat dishes such as daubes or pot-au-feu.

Place a clove in with the standard parsley, bay leaf, and thyme before securing the bag

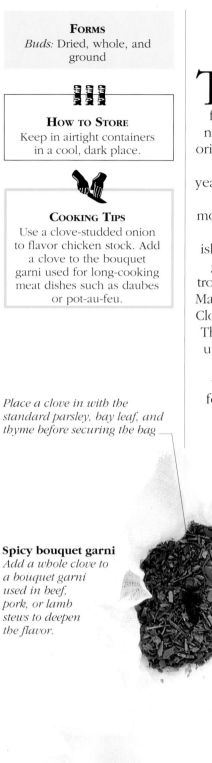

Spicy bouquet garni
Add a whole clove to a bouquet garni used in beef, pork, or lamb stews to deepen the flavor.

Bouquet garni

The name for this spice comes from the Latin *clavus*, meaning a nail. Indeed, these dried, unopened flower buds of the evergreen clove tree do resemble nails. Cloves have a long and fascinating history. They originated in the Moluccas, or Spice Islands, in Southeast Asia, and were used by Chinese cooks hundreds of years before the Christian era. When the Western nations sought spices, it was the Dutch who established a monopoly in the islands after driving out the Portuguese in 1605. They restricted cultivation of cloves to one island, but by 1770 the French had succeeded in smuggling seeds to Mauritius. The trees flourish only in a tropical maritime climate and are now grown in Indonesia, Madagascar, Tanzania, Sri Lanka, Malaysia, and Grenada. Cloves have a warm, strongly aromatic perfume and flavor. They can be quite bitter on their own, making them an uncommon spice in everyday cooking, but the heat of cooking tempers their flavor. No kitchen should be without a jar of cloves. This spice is essential to many festive cakes and cookies, and a clove-studded onion will add depth of flavor to broths for boiled meats.

Whole cloves

Clove-studded onion

COOK'S CHOICE
BAKED HAM WITH CLOVES

Serves 4

2–3 tbsp soft brown sugar
1 tsp Dijon mustard
4 tbsp milk or apple juice
3 lb (1.5 kg) whole cooked ham
Whole cloves for studding

Preheat the oven to 350°F (180°C). In a bowl, combine the sugar, mustard, and milk or apple juice, and stir to blend. Trim all but a 1/2-in (1 cm) layer of fat from the ham. Score the fat in a diamond pattern. Spread the sugar mixture over the ham, pressing well into the fat. Insert a clove in the crossed point of each diamond. Place the ham in a shallow roasting pan. Bake for 30 minutes, basting frequently; take care that the glaze does not scorch. Serve hot, with mustard and baked potatoes, or cold, accompanied by spiced fruits, chutneys, and salad.

Ground cloves

ASAFOETIDA

COOKING TIPS
When adding to dishes, use *ground* in minute quantities. Rub a broiler rack lightly with a piece of asafoetida before cooking meats.

There is no concealing the fact that asafoetida, the resinous substance from two species of the giant fennel, has a dreadful stink. The repellent smell is caused by sulfur compounds present in the resin, which fortunately, disappear with cooking. A much-used seasoning in Asian cuisine, asafoetida is especially popular for flavoring Indian vegetarian dishes. The larger species, *Ferula asafoetida,* can grow as high as 12 ft (3.5 meters), while *Ferula narthex* reaches only 8 ft (2.5 meters). The plants are native to Afghanistan and Iran, and the leaves and stems are still eaten as a vegetable in these countries. The ancient Romans used the resin medicinally as well as for flavoring sauces and wine. Ground asafoetida is the most convenient form to buy; in order to appreciate the strong flavor, use in minute quantities. A tiny pinch is the right amount to use for any dish. The culinary plant should not be confused with *Ferula communis,* which is often grown as a foliage plant and called *giant common fennel.* This is unrelated to garden fennel and is poisonous. Many other plants of the genus *Ferula* are believed to have medicinal properties and are used in Chinese herbal remedies.

Ground asafoetida

Chat masala *is an Indian spice blend made with ground asafoetida, mint, ginger, ajowan, cayenne, black salt, mango powder, cumin, and dried pomegranate seeds*

TASTES GOOD WITH/IN
Fish, salt fish, vegetables and all legume dishes. In very small quantities: chutneys, pickles, sauces.

COOK'S CHOICE
RICE WITH PINE NUTS AND MUSHROOMS

Serves 4

4 tbsp unsalted butter
4 oz (125 g) mushrooms, sliced
Salt
Freshly ground black pepper
1 oz (30 g) pine nuts
1 ²/₃ cups (250 g) long-grain rice, cooked
Small pinch of asafoetida
2 tbsp finely chopped parsley

The Romans stored asafoetida in jars with pine nuts and used a few crushed nuts to flavor dishes. This version of risotto is a modern-day setting for this ancient and pungent spice. Melt the butter in a skillet, add the mushrooms and cook them over moderate heat until they are lightly browned. Season to taste. In a small skillet, roast the pine nuts, shaking the pan until they are very lightly browned, 2–3 minutes. If necessary, reheat the rice to warm through. Fold the mushrooms, pine nuts, asafoetida, and parsley into the rice and taste for seasoning. Serve immediately.

Compound
Specialty shops often sell asafoetida in this packaged form.

STAR ANISE

OTHER NAMES
Chinese anise, badian anise

FORMS
Dried: Whole, broken, ground, and seeds

HOW TO STORE
This spice will stay fresh indefinitely if stored in an airtight container and kept away from light.

COOKING TIPS
For a spicy-sweet flavor, place a small piece in the cavity of a chicken or duck before roasting or braising or add to pork, chicken, or duck stews.

Star anise is the star-shaped fruit of a small evergreen tree native to China. The tree, which grows to a height of about 26 ft (8 meters), does not bear fruit until it is about 6 years old, but it can continue to bear fruit for up to one century. Its yellow flowers are followed by brown fruit that opens, when ripe, into star shapes. Each point of the star contains a shiny brown seed that is less aromatic than the pod. Star anise is much used in Chinese and Vietnamese cooking, and it is an essential ingredient in Chinese five-spice powder. It is believed that an English sailor brought this spice to Europe at the end of the sixteenth century, but it has never been widely used as a culinary spice. It is similar in flavor to anise because it contains the same essential oil, anethole, but is slightly stronger. Medicinally, it is a stimulant and a diuretic, and an infusion is thought to relieve a sore throat. The essential oil is used to flavor liqueurs such as anisette.

TASTE GOOD WITH/IN
Oriental-style dishes, especially pork, duck, and chicken, stir-fried vegetables, long-simmered dishes also flavored with soy sauce, fish and shellfish dishes, and pumpkin.

COOK'S CHOICE
ORIENTAL-STYLE CHICKEN WINGS

Serves 4

16 chicken wings
4 tbsp dry sherry
1 cup (250 ml) chicken stock or water
2 tbsp soy sauce
1 star anise, broken
Salt

Place the chicken wings in a casserole and pour the sherry over them. Let them stand for 30 minutes, turning from time to time. Add the stock or water, soy sauce, star anise, and season to taste. Bring to a simmer and cook, covered, over moderate heat until tender, about 45 minutes. Taste for seasoning. Serve as an appetizer, or with boiled rice as a main course.

Seeds

Whole star anise

Broken star anise

Ground star anise

Five-spice powder *is a blend of star anise, fagara, cassia, fennel seeds, and cloves that is used throughout China and Vietnam*

JUNIPER

The fruit of a small evergreen shrub, juniper berries are purplish in color when ripe and ready to pick. Too pungent to be eaten fresh, the flavor of the dried berry is aromatic and spicy with a slight overtone of pine. For culinary use, the berries must be crushed to release their full flavor. In cooking, juniper is used primarily with game, where its powerful flavor marries well with the equally powerful flavor of venison, wild boar and squab. The potency of the berries varies by region, with juniper from Southern Europe being the most flavorful. Juniper is essential as a flavoring for gin and other liqueurs popular in Holland, Belgium, and Germany. In folklore, both the tree and its berries are associated with protection and safekeeping. The Holy Family is said to have sheltered under the branches of a juniper tree when fleeing from King Herod, the Romans believed the tree protected them, and there are countless legends in which the juniper tree serves as a guardian.

FORMS
Berries: Fresh and dried

HOW TO STORE
Dried berries: Keep in an airtight container in a cool, dark place.

COOKING TIPS
Always crush lightly before using to release the flavor. Freshly *dried* berries have the most intense flavor, but this fades quickly; buy in small quantities and do not store for more than six months. Apple jelly flavored with juniper goes well with lamb and game.

Juniper berries grow on the branches of this evergreen shrub

Fresh berries

Dried berries

TASTES GOOD WITH/IN

Marinades for meat or game, infused in sauces, stuffings, pot roasts, pâtés, sausages, cabbage.

COOK'S CHOICE
VENISON STEAKS WITH JUNIPER SAUCE

Serves 4

4 tbsp unsalted butter
2 tbsp all-purpose flour
2 cups (500 ml) beef stock
1/2 cup (125 ml) dry Madeira, such as Sercial
2 tsp ground juniper berries
Salt
Freshly ground black pepper
2 tbsp oil
4 venison tenderloin steaks, about 4 oz (125 g) each

Melt 3 tbsp of the butter in a saucepan. Stir in the flour and cook over very low heat for 2–3 minutes, stirring constantly. Off the heat, gradually stir in the beef stock until smooth. Stir in the Madeira and return to the heat. Add the juniper and continue to cook, stirring, until the mixture is slightly thickened, about 5 minutes. Season to taste; keep warm. In a skillet, combine the remaining 1 tbsp butter and the oil over high heat, add the venison and cook, about 6 minutes for medium-rare. Season to taste, transfer to warmed dinner plates, pour over the sauce and serve with buttered vegetables.

MACE AND NUTMEG

FORMS
Mace: Whole, ground
Nutmeg: Whole, ground

AFFINITY WITH OTHER HERBS/SPICES
Cardamon, cinnamon, cloves, ginger, pepper

HOW TO STORE
Whole and ground: In jars in a cool, dark place, *ground mace* keeps better than most ground spices.

TASTES GOOD WITH/IN

Mace: Cakes, puddings, custards, desserts, soufflés, sauces, soups, poultry, fish.
Nutmeg: Baked or stewed fruit, custards, eggnog, punches, sauces, especially onion sauce and bread sauce, pasta, vegetables, especially spinach.

COOKING TIPS
Add freshly grated nutmeg at the end of cooking because heat diminishes the flavor. Boil vegetables such as cabbage, potato or cauliflower, mash with butter, salt and pepper, and stir in a pinch of freshly grated nutmeg.

Records of the use of mace and nutmeg go back to the first century A.D. when the Roman writer Pliny described a tree bearing a nut with two separate flavors. Indeed, these two spices are distinct yet inseparable. The nutmeg is the hard kernel of the fruit of an evergreen tree native to the Moluccas, or Spice Islands. The fruit is split open to reveal the seed—nutmeg—which is wrapped in a bright red lacy covering—mace. Relatively unknown to the ancient civilizations of the West, both nutmeg and mace had long been used in India. The Arabs were the first to import these spices to the Western world and it was not long before they were precious and sought after. Nutmeg was often carried in special containers of silver or wood, and the grater was attached, so the spice could always be on hand.

The nutmeg is surrounded by a lacy covering, or aril, which is mace

Nutmeg is oval-shaped with a wrinkled exterior and lies within the shell of the seed

Whole nutmeg

Ground nutmeg
Available pre-packaged, it is always better to grind your own supply as needed because it soon loses flavor.

Traditional graters *have a storage compartment so that freshly grated nutmeg is always on hand*

COOKING WITH MACE AND NUTMEG

FUSILLI WITH MUSHROOMS AND NUTMEG

Serves 4

4 tbsp unsalted butter
2 medium onions, finely chopped
2 lb (1 kg) mushrooms, sliced
¼ tsp ground nutmeg
Salt
Freshly ground black pepper
1 cup (250 ml) heavy cream
1 lb (500 g) fusilli pasta
Freshly grated Parmesan cheese for serving

Heat the butter in a large, heavy saucepan, add the onions, and cook over moderate heat until they are softened. Add the mushrooms and cook until they have given up all their liquid. Add the nutmeg and season to taste. Add the cream and cook just long enough to heat the mixture through. Cook the fusilli according to package directions. Drain thoroughly. In a large bowl, toss together the pasta and sauce until blended. Serve immediately, with the Parmesan. This sauce is suitable for any type of pasta.

Essential oil
Primarily used for nonculinary purposes, a drop or two of nutmeg oil added to hot drinks at bedtime increases their sedative effects.

In the kitchen, these are versatile spices with uses in both sweet and savory dishes. Nutmeg has a warm flavor and an affinity for rich foods; this is not entirely a coincidence since it is also an aid to digestion. In Italy, it is used to great effect in many filled pastas, either mixed with the stuffing or grated on top at the last minute. It is essential in *béchamel* sauce and many charcuterie mixtures. The flavor of mace—a combination of cinnamon and pepper—is similar to that of nutmeg, although much more subtle.

Mace blades
The color of the blades is often a clue to the derivation of the spice. Orange-red blades tend to be Indonesian; orange-yellow blades are more likely to come from Grenada.

The two forms of mace
Mace is impossible to grate and most home-ground mace is coarse in texture because it is difficult to grind finely. Use a coffee grinder in preference to a mortar and pestle.

Ground mace

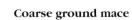

Coarse ground mace

NUTMEG CAKE WITH LEMON-MACE SAUCE

Serves 6

Butter for preparing the pan
2 cups (250 g) all-purpose flour
¾ cup (150 g) superfine sugar
1 cup (200 g) brown sugar
1 cup (250 g) unsalted butter, at room temperature
1 tsp baking soda
1 tsp grated nutmeg
1 egg
1 cup (250 ml) sour cream
3 oz (90 g) chopped walnuts
7 ½ tbsp honey
Salt
1½ tbsp cornstarch
2 tbsp lemon juice
1 tsp grated lemon zest
2 tbsp unsalted butter
Pinch of ground mace

Preheat the oven to 350°F (180°C); butter a 9-in (23 cm) cake pan. In a bowl, sift together the flour, superfine sugar, and brown sugar. Add the butter and cut with a pastry blender until it forms coarse crumbs. (Alternatively, blend in a food processor.) Press half of this mixture into the cake pan. To the remaining half, add the soda, nutmeg, egg, and sour cream and mix to blend. Pour this on top of the crumbs in the pan and sprinkle with the walnuts. Place in the oven and bake until the sides of the cake come away from the pan, 30–40 minutes. Cool slightly in the pan placed on a cake rack, then turn out.
For the sauce, combine the honey and a pinch of salt in a saucepan and heat gently to melt. Dissolve the cornstarch in the lemon juice and add to the honey, along with 1 cup (250 ml) water. Bring gently to a boil, stirring constantly, until thick. Boil for 1 minute. Remove from the heat and stir in the lemon zest, butter, and mace. Slice the cake while warm and serve immediately with the sauce.

NIGELLA

Panch phoran *is an Indian spice mixture that combines the seeds of cumin, fennel, mustard, fenugreek, and nigella; it is used to flavor legumes and vegetables*

The pretty plant love-in-a-mist, with feathery foliage and attractive blue flowers, is a very close relative of nigella, and the two are often called by the same name. It is nigella, however, whose edible seeds are used in cooking. The culinary nigella plant is native to western Asia, the Middle East and southern Europe, though today it is grown primarily in India, where it is used extensively in the cuisine of all regions. It is a familiar ingredient in the many spice mixtures of the area and is frequently found sprinkled on breads, including those of Turkey and other Middle-Eastern countries. A hardy annual growing to about 2 ft (60 cm) in height, its seeds must be gathered before they are ripe; otherwise the pods will burst and the seeds will be lost. They are very small and black in color with a lightly aromatic, peppery flavor, and look rather like onion seeds, with which they are often confused. This spice seems to attract confusion; in France it is sometimes, inaccurately, called *quatre-épices* (see page 75) and in India *kala jeeras*, which is black cumin (see page 79). It can be purchased in speciality grocery stores under its Indian name, *kalonji*.

Nigella seeds

Ground nigella

Nigella seeds can be ground using a pepper mill for use in the kitchen or at the table

TASTES GOOD WITH/IN
Vegetables, legumes, breads, yogurt, cottage cheese, salads, especially cucumber and yogurt salad, lamb and poultry casseroles, pickles, chutneys.

COOK'S CHOICE
SPICY CUCUMBER SALAD

Serves 2–4

1 cucumber, finely diced
Salt
1 cup (250 g) thick yogurt, preferably Greek yogurt
1/2 tsp nigella seeds
1 tbsp finely chopped fresh mint leaves
Crisp lettuce leaves for garnish

Place the cucumber in a shallow bowl and season to taste. Add the yogurt, nigella, and mint and toss to blend. Serve lightly chilled, on plates garnished with lettuce leaves. If preparing in advance, do not toss with the yogurt, nigella, and mint until ready to serve or the cucumber will dilute the dressing.

POPPY SEEDS

FORMS
Seeds: Whole and ground

HOW TO STORE
In airtight containers kept in
a cool, dark place.

COOKING TIPS
Use poppy seed oil when a
very light, delicate oil is
needed for a salad dressing.
Known as *huile d'oeillette* in
France, it must be from the
first cold-pressing which
produces a clear, odorless
oil with a slight almond
flavor. Further pressings
produce an oil that is used
in artist's paints, soaps, and
ointments. It is important
not to confuse the oil from
an artist's supply shop with
the culinary oil.
The nutty flavor of the *seeds*
is improved if lightly
toasted before use.

This spice is the seed of the opium poppy, whose botanical name means "sleep-bearing." Native to the Middle East, this large annual plant has handsome pink, white, or lilac flowers. The minute slate-blue, kidney-shaped seeds have a nutty flavor and a crunchy texture. The spice consists of the ripe seeds, while the medicinal derivatives—opium, morphine, and codeine—come from alkaloids in the sap of unripe seed pods. The ripe seeds are used widely in the cooking and baking of central and northern Europe, the Middle East, India, and some areas of North America. Most of the seeds in Europe are the slate-blue variety, but there are also yellow seeds used in India and brown seeds used in Turkey. Opium was valued for its medicinal properties by the ancient Egyptians, and was not an abused narcotic until the 1800s, when opium smoking became fashionable, especially in China and among many artists and writers. As a precaution, many countries prohibit cultivation of the opium poppy without a permit.

TASTES GOOD WITH/IN

Breads, crackers, cakes,
pastries, salads, especially
coleslaw, cream-based
dressings, curries, sauces
for meat and fish, egg
noodles, or sprinkled on
vegetables as a garnish.

COOK'S CHOICE
POPPY SEED FILLING

Makes about 1½ cups (350 g)

*½ cup plus 2 tbsp (125 g)
sugar*
½ cup (125 ml) milk or water
¾ cup (125 g) poppy seeds
*⅓ cup (75 g) raisins, coarsely
chopped*
2 tbsp clear honey
Grated zest of 1 lemon

In a small saucepan, combine
the sugar and milk or water,
and bring to a simmer over
moderate heat. Cook, stirring
constantly, for 5 minutes. Add
the poppy seeds, raisins,
honey, and lemon zest, bring
to a simmer, and cook for
3 minutes longer, stirring
constantly. The mixture should
be thick. Cool before using as
a filling for cakes and pastries.

Brown seeds *are
usually Turkish in
origin*

Slate-blue seeds *are
most common in
Europe*

Yellow seeds

**Poppy seed
paste** *is
made from
roasted,
ground poppy
seeds mixed
with poppy
seed oil and
is used in a
variety of
Turkish
dishes and
pastries*

Ground poppy seeds

Ripe seed head *has a
ribbed outer casing and is
crowned with a stigma;
inside are several
chambers containing
hundreds of seeds*

ALLSPICE

OTHER NAMES
Jamaica pepper, myrtle pepper

FORMS
Berries: Whole, ground

HOW TO STORE
In airtight containers kept in a cool, dark place.

COOKING TIPS
An all-around spice, this enhances the flavors of most other spices.
Add to pickles, savory preserves, or chutneys, or use to impart a warm flavor to baked goods or mulled drinks. Add *whole* berries to the pepper mill.

Although allspice is a native of the New World, unknown elsewhere until it was introduced into Europe by the Spaniards in the sixteenth century, it is now used in cuisines the world over. One of the myrtles, the tree is handsome and very aromatic. It grows to a considerable height and has small white flowers. Allspice berries are the size of large peppercorns; they are green when unripe, at which time they are harvested and sun-dried. They turn brown when dry and are then ready for use. The name "allspice" describes its flavor, which is a combination of nutmeg, cinnamon, and cloves with slight peppery overtones. The best berries come from Jamaica, which produces most of the world's supply. The cultivated trees grow in what is called an *allspice walk*, and when they are flowering the air is filled with perfume from the aromatic bark, leaves, flowers, and later, the berries. The West Indian Arawak and Carib tribes used allspice, and it is more than likely that it was used in Aztec and Mayan kitchens. For the best flavor, grind a few berries in a mortar and pestle; the taste will be fresher than the preground spice.

TASTES GOOD WITH/IN

Pickling spice mixtures, marinades for fish, shellfish, meats, game and poultry, all charcuterie, especially ham, vegetables, rice, cakes, pies, puddings, relishes, and chutneys.

COOK'S CHOICE
SHRIMP WITH ALLSPICE
Serves 4

4 $^{1}/_{2}$ cups (1 liter) beer

$^{1}/_{2}$ tsp salt

1 tsp lightly crushed allspice berries

1 lb (500 g) large, frozen, cooked shrimp, defrosted

In a large saucepan, combine the beer, salt, and allspice berries and bring to a simmer. Cover and simmer for 5 minutes. Remove from the heat. Add the shrimps and leave to infuse in the liquid as it cools. Drain and serve as an hors d'oeuvre or as a first course with a tomato coulis or a vinaigrette dressing.

A pepper mill *can be used in place of a mortar and pestle when a fresh supply of the ground spice is required*

Ground allspice

Allspice is a versatile spice that can be used in both sweet and savory dishes, but it is best to grind berries as needed rather than buy the ground version

Allspice and peppercorns
For a flavorful pepper alternative, combine equal amounts of allspice with dried green, black, and white peppercorns.

Whole allspice berries *are pea sized and have a roughly textured surface*

ANISE

One of the oldest spices, anise is a botanical relative of dill, fennel, caraway, and cumin. The plant grows to a height of about 2 ft (60 cm) with leaves similar to cilantro and clusters of yellow-white flowers. Native to the Middle East, it is now grown in southern Russia, Turkey, India, and many parts of Europe, where it is a popular spice for flavoring alcoholic drinks. Ouzo is a favorite anise aperitif in Greece, while arrack is the drink of the eastern Mediterranean countries. Anisette, an anise-flavored liqueur, is widely popular, especially in Spain, both as a drink and in cooking. In France, *pastis* is the catch-all name for the many brands of anise-flavored drinks quite popular in cafés in the south, where they are served in glasses over ice with a pitcher of water. Pastis is also used in cooking, most often added to fish soups or snail butter, but lobster and other seafoods are also greatly enhanced by the flavor of anise. An infusion of aniseeds sweetened with honey can be drunk to aid digestion.

OTHER NAMES
Aniseed, sweet cumin

FORMS
Seeds: Dried *Leaves*: Fresh

HOW TO STORE
Leaves: Can be stored, briefly, in plastic bags in the refrigerator.
Seeds: Keep in airtight containers in a cool, dark place. Do not keep too long; the flavor does not persist over long periods, even when correctly stored.

Small creamy-white flowers appear in summer followed by seeds

Pale brown, ribbed, and fuzzy, the seeds are the most flavorful part of the plant

Aniseeds

Anise-flavored drinks
such as Pernod, Ricard, and Sambuco are popular as aperitifs; they can also be used to great effect in cooking

Ground anise *loses its flavor and aroma rapidly, so buy in small quantities or grind whole seeds with a mortar and pestle*

TASTES GOOD WITH/IN

Sweets, cakes, cookies, breads, fish and shellfish, tomato-based sauces, vegetable dishes, sweet and savory mixtures with nuts and dried fruit, especially figs and chestnuts.

COOKING TIPS
For the best flavor, the *seeds* should always be bought whole, not ground, in small quantities for grinding as needed; the seeds are easily ground in a mortar. Young *leaves* can be added, sparingly, to green salads, cooked vegetables, fish soups or stews, and fruit salads.

COOK'S CHOICE
ANISE FRITTERS

Makes 10–12 fritters

1 tbsp sugar
1/4 tsp salt
2 tbsp aniseeds
1 1/2 cups (175 g) all-purpose flour, sifted
1 large egg
Oil for deep frying
Sugar for coating

In a large saucepan, combine 1 cup (250 ml) water with the sugar, salt, and aniseeds and bring to a boil. Add the flour all at once and beat with a wooden spoon until smooth. Off the heat, add the egg and beat until thoroughly incorporated. In a deep-fat fryer, heat the oil to 375°F (190°C) on a frying thermometer. Force the mixture through a pastry bag fitted with a large tip (or use a large funnel) and fry in long strips in the oil until golden. Drain on paper towels, cut into 3-in (7.5 cm) pieces, and coat with sugar while still warm. Serve immediately.

PEPPER

FORMS
Fresh: Whole *Dried:* Whole,
crushed, ground
Processed: Pickled whole

HOW TO STORE

Dried: Black and white
peppercorns should be
kept in a cool, dark place
in an airtight container.
Ground: Should also be
stored in an airtight
container away from light,
although the keeping time
of ground spices is generally shorter than that of
whole. *Fresh:* Can be kept
in an airtight container in
the refrigerator.
Processed: In cans and jars,
will keep indefinitely.

Invaluable in the kitchen, pepper is quite rightly
known as the king of spices. This spice, which plays
an important role in cuisines the world over, is the berry
of the plant *Piper nigrum.* India is the world's foremost
producer, but it is also cultivated in Indonesia, Malaysia,
and Brazil. Pepper production accounts for one-quarter
of the global spice trade, with the U.S. being the single
largest importer. Records of its use go back as far as the
fourth century B.C., when its Sanskrit name was *pippali.*
Like salt, it was a precious spice, and its value was
increased by the Roman Empire's demand. The Arabs
grew rich furnishing the Romans with pepper, and
ancient Roman grocers often blended juniper berries in
with peppercorns to stretch the product and increase
their profits. There was even a time when pepper was
worth its weight in gold. Pepper probably changed the
course of history, being the single most important factor
in the European search for sea routes to the East. This
quest for pepper dominated the spice trade for centuries;
without it, the colonial empires of modern history might
not have existed. The glorious past of this simple berry
may have long since faded, but for the cook, pepper
remains a vital and ever-present spice.

COOKING TIPS

The *ground* form of pepper
fades in a relatively short
period of time, so it is best
to use *whole* peppercorns
and grind as needed.
Always pepper at the end
of cooking for maximum
flavor. Because ground
pepper quickly loses its
flavor in long-cooking
dishes, use whole pepper-
corns tied in a cheesecloth
bag for easy removal. Take
care when cooking dishes,
such as peppered steak,
which require a great deal
of pepper to be cooked
over a high heat. The effect
is similar to that of chili,
and the pepper smoke will
irritate the nose, eyes, and
respiratory tract. Be sure
the kitchen is properly
ventilated before proceeding with the dish.

Black peppercorns *are
green fruits that have been
sun-dried after fermenting*

*The green
berries can be
added to
duck dishes
and
creamy
sauces*

White peppercorns *are
the dried insides of ripe
berries with the outer skin
rubbed off*

Ground black pepper

*Pepper
berries are
harvested
from their
vines in
spring and
summer*

**Fresh unripe
peppercorns**

Ground white pepper

Fresh green pepper-corns *can be difficult to obtain; crush lightly for soups, stews, butters, and sauces*

Mixed peppercorns *are especially attractive in glass pepper mills for use at the table*

Dried green pepper-corns *can be rehydrated to use in stocks, soups, or casseroles; crush before using dry*

Pink peppercorns *should be used sparingly; their flavor is less delicate, but their color will enhance any finished dish*

Pickled green peppercorns *should be rinsed before using in pâtés, flavored butters, or sauces*

TYPES OF PEPPER

The pepper plant is native to the equatorial forests of India and the berries from the Malabar Coast are held to be the finest. It is a perennial vine that takes about 8 years to reach maturity, and in good conditions it will continue to fruit for up to 20 years. Green peppercorns are harvested while still unripe. Their flavor is milder and fruitier, but not entirely without spice. Sun-dried green peppercorns are more commonly known as black peppercorns. For white pepper, the same berries are left on the plant until fully ripe and red in color. They are then soaked and peeled to expose the inner white corns, which are then dried. The flavor is slightly less piquant than that of black pepper. Tree-ripened red peppercorns are rarely found outside their country of origin. The almost ripe, soft pink berries of a South American tree, *Schinus terebinthifolius*, are known as pink peppercorns, although they are not a true pepper. They have a slightly resinous flavor and their culinary value is primarily visual; they offer a stunning contrast when combined with whole green, black, and white peppercorns. Use sparingly because pink peppercorns can be toxic in great quantity.

FAGARA
Unrelated to pepper, fagara is the dried berry of a Chinese variety of a small prickly ash tree. Also known as Szechwan pepper, these berries have a spicy, woody aroma with a tingly taste. Fagara is essential in Chinese five-spice powder, along with star anise, cloves, fennel, and cassia. Before use, the berries should be dry-roasted in a cast-iron skillet, until smoking, then ground.

SANSHO
Sometimes called Japanese pepper, this spice is not a true pepper. It is a table spice, usually sprinkled on cooked foods, and it is available only ground. Another use for sansho is in *shichimi*, or Japanese seven-spice mixture, which combines sansho, seaweed, chili, orange peel, poppy seeds, and white and black sesame seeds. This is often sprinkled over noodles or into soups.

95

PIPER NIGRUM

BLACK AND WHITE PEPPER

There are many different types of black and white peppercorns with varying flavors; much depends on where they are grown. Singapore black pepper, grown on the Malay Peninsula, has a particular taste due to the local method of drying. The rather large berries are spread to dry on suspended mats with an herb fire smoldering beneath. The smoke both dries and flavors the berries, resulting in one of the most aromatic peppers available. Alleppey and Tellicherry peppers are both grown on the Malabar coast of India. These have a flavor that is clean, aromatic, and slightly less pungent than other black peppers. White pepper from Livorno, in Italy, is a fine pepper that is produced in limited quantities. Decorticated white pepper is a very high-grade pepper manufactured in England. Especially large, fragrant berries are imported, and after soaking, several layers are removed as opposed to the single layer that comes off for ordinary white pepper. This results in white pepper with a refined flavor.

ASIAN PEPPERS

The unripe berry of the *Piper cubeba*, cubeb, or tailed pepper, is native to the Indonesian islands, mainly Java. A popular spice up until the 1600s, it is now virtually unknown in the West. Its original purpose was medicinal, mainly as a treatment for respiratory problems, and it was widely used in the East before Arab spice traders introduced it to the West. The spice is a feature of Indonesian cuisine, lending a distinctive taste more akin to allspice than pepper. It can be used in the North African spice mixture, *ras-el-hanout* (see page 210) for a more authentic flavor. Long pepper, *Piper longum*, is another related species of pepper that is seldom available in the West. The unripe dried berry is used mainly in parts of India and Indonesia, where it is added whole to curries and pickles.

MIGNONETTE PEPPER

This is a roughly ground mixture of black and white peppercorns widely used in France, both in cooking and as a table seasoning. It has the advantage of being a visually appealing mix of black and white peppercorns, as well as a mix of the two flavors. The recipe is simply equal parts of black and white peppercorns, coarsely ground, which is best achieved with a mortar and pestle. The mixture can be used in any recipe that calls for ordinary crushed black peppercorns, but it is especially nice for pepper steaks. If a pepper mill is used, the result is more finely ground and can be used interchangeably with black pepper. The addition of a few allspice berries gives the blend a hint of clove, cinnamon, and nutmeg. Finely ground mignonette is also available and is sometimes called *poivre gris*, or gray pepper.

White peppercorns come from ripe red berries that are soaked after harvesting to facilitate removal of the red skin; these have the advantage of being less visible in delicate sauces

Black peppercorns are obtained from unripe green berries that are left to ferment for several days before drying; the flavor is pungent and aromatic

96

COOKING WITH PEPPER

From East to West, pepper is appreciated for its warm aroma and spicy flavor, which adds depth and balance to many dishes. It lends vigor to meats such as pork and beef, picks up the delicate flavor of eggs, and enhances the subtle flavor of seafood. Whole peppercorns are as much a delight to the eye as to the palate; slices of black-specked peppered salami are much more appetizing than plain, and uniform liver pâtés get a lift from the addition of pretty green peppercorns. Apicius, the Roman author of the first cookbook, recommended adding pepper to enliven the flavor of dull boiled foods, and also to enhance the flavor of some sweet dishes. Indeed, pepper still finds its way into sweet fruit preparations, especially those made with pears or strawberries. Green peppercorns can be stirred into mayonnaise for seafood or egg salads or added to simple cream-based sauces served with pan-fried meats, such as duck breast or veal. They also feature in many charcuterie items. White peppercorns are hotter than black, but they lack perfume and flavor. Use alone when a peppery flavor is desired but black specks are not, for example, in white or cream sauces, egg dishes, light cream soups, savory custards, or mayonnaise. The best way to use pepper remains the age-old standard: a few turns of the mill just before serving.

PEPPER MILL

The ideal storage method, a pepper mill is also an attractive way to serve pepper at the table. The setting can be adjusted from coarse to fine, to accommodate the type of food or recipe. Choose a sturdy mill with a strong metal grinding apparatus; plastic grinders are not as effective, nor as durable. Use peppercorns alone, in combination, or mixed with other whole spices.

Black peppercorns

Coriander seeds

Allspice

Cardamom

Berber spice mixture

Ginger

Chilies

Ajowan

Cinnamon

SUMAC

HOW TO STORE
Keep in an airtight container away from light. The flavor stays intact for several months in the *whole* berry, although it fades more quickly in the *ground* form.

COOKING TIPS
Seeds can be soaked in water. Use 3 ¹/₂ oz (100 g) seeds for 1 ¹/₂ cups (350 ml) water and soak for 30 minutes. Strain through a cheesecloth-lined sieve and squeeze to extract the flavor. Use liquid in dressings or marinades.

With leaves that turn a beautiful red in fall, sumac is a highly decorative bush. It grows wild throughout the Middle East, and while gardeners in the West regard it solely as ornamental, cooks from Lebanon, Syria, Turkey, and Iran esteem the spikes of bright red berries it bears. The berries are a deep, brick-red when dried, and are used, whole or ground, in a large number of dishes. They have a fruity sourness and were used by the Romans before lemons reached Europe. The berries have a pleasantly sour and rather astringent flavor, but without the sharpness of either vinegar or lemon juice. Mixed with yogurt and herbs, they make a light and refreshing sauce. The Lebanese and Syrians sprinkle sumac on fish; the Iraqis and Turks add it to salads; and the Iranians and Georgians season kebabs with it. Now an uncommon spice in European cooking, sumac can be bought, usually ground, from stores that stock Middle Eastern products. Several other members of the sumac family, prevalent in North America, are poisonous. These include poison sumac (poison dogwood) and the various poison ivies and poison oaks, which produce an oil that causes intense skin irration.

TASTES GOOD WITH/IN

Seafood, vegetable salads, stuffings, rice, legumes, poultry, and mixed meat dishes such as meat balls, kabobs and stews.

COOK'S CHOICE
ONION SALAD

Serves 4

1 large sweet onion, about 8 oz (250 g), thinly sliced
Salt
1 tsp ground sumac

Place the onion in a bowl with ice water to cover and let stand for 15 minutes. Drain thoroughly and pat dry. In a salad bowl, combine the onion, salt to taste, and sumac, and toss to blend. Let stand for 15 minutes. Serve immediately or refrigerate until needed.

Sumac berries *are not uniform in color; they can vary from brick to brown- or purple-red depending on their origin*

Ground sumac *will keep its flavor for several weeks if kept in an airtight jar*

Sumac seeds *are small and brown and found in the middle of the berries*

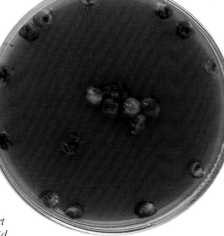

Soaking berries
If berries are used whole, they must be cracked and then soaked in water for 20 minutes. Next they are pressed well to extract all the juice, which can then be used as part of the cooking liquid.

Zahtar *is a Middle Eastern spice blend combining sumac, roasted sesame seeds, and ground thyme*

This aromatic mixture can be sprinkled on meat balls or vegetables; mixed with olive oil, it can be brushed over bread before baking

SESAME SEEDS

HOW TO STORE
Keep in airtight containers in a cool, dark place.

COOKING TIPS
The somewhat bland flavor of the *seeds* can be enhanced by dry-roasting in a skillet before use. Use roasted sesame seeds as a garnish for dishes flavored with sesame oil. For example, parboil vegetables, such as green beans, sauté in a little sesame oil, and sprinkle with roasted sesame seeds.

There is some confusion over the origin of the sesame plant. Some authorities say it originated in Africa, others say India. It has been known and used in China for about 2,000 years but is still regarded as a foreign plant. A tall, straight-growing annual, it has deeply veined, ovate leaves and white or pink flowers. There are several varieties—white, brown or black—which burst out of the seed capsules when they are ripe. Because of this tendency to scatter, sesame seeds destined for the spice rack are harvested while still green, unripe, and neatly contained within the pod. The seed, although small, is quite rich, containing 50 percent oil that is extracted for culinary use. With a versatile nutty flavor, sesame is popular in many countries and with many types of food, both sweet and savory. A paste made from untoasted white seeds, known as *tahini*, is used in Middle Eastern cooking; while a similar paste made from toasted seeds is used in Asia. Another Middle Eastern sesame seed product, halvah, is sweet, and a variation of this is made in India.

White seeds

Tahini *is a thick paste made from ground sesame seeds; it is most often added to sauces and dips that accompany Middle Eastern-style kabobs and pita bread sandwiches, and it can be used to flavor vegetable and fruit dishes*

Brown seeds

Black seeds

Halvah

Sesame oil

TASTES GOOD WITH/IN

Bread, rolls, cakes and cookies, vegetables, especially green beans, rice, meat, noodles.

COOK'S CHOICE
COLD SESAME NOODLES
Serves 4

3 tbsp soy sauce
3 tbsp rice vinegar
1 tsp sugar
3 tbsp Asian sesame paste
3 tbsp sesame oil
1 tsp chili oil, or to taste
1 tbsp freshly grated gingerroot
Salt
1 lb (500 g) Oriental noodles
3–4 tbsp roasted sesame seeds
Chopped scallions for garnish

In a large bowl, combine the soy sauce, vinegar, and sugar and stir to dissolve. Add the sesame paste, sesame oil, chili oil, and gingerroot and stir to blend. Bring a large pan of water to a boil; add salt then the noodles, and cook until just tender. (Cooking time depends on the type of noodle; follow package directions.) Drain the noodles, add to the sesame sauce, and toss to coat the noodles. Serve chilled or at room temperature. Sprinkle with the roasted sesame seeds and scallions before serving.

SALT

HOW TO STORE

All salt should be stored in a dry place to prevent it from solidifying or caking; under proper conditions it will keep indefinitely. Do not store salt in silver saltshakers or saltcellars because the chlorine in the salt reacts with the silver, causing a green discoloration. A traditional saltcellar that keeps out light is the most convenient method for keeping salt fresh and dry, and the most attractive way of keeping it handy in the kitchen.

Few are the recipes that do not include salt. It is an essential ingredient both in simple everyday cooking, and in the finest of *haute cuisine*. The role of salt is threefold: It seasons food, it preserves food and it provides sodium and chlorine, which are nutrients necessary to the body's fluid balance and muscle and nerve activity. Always a highly prized commodity, it was once commonly taxed by governments—just as alcohol and tobacco are taxed today—and this provided a reliable source of revenue. We read in the Old Testament that precious salt was used as an offering to God, and the Romans valued it so highly that their soldiers were given a salt allowance. The English word *salary* is derived from the Latin *salarium*, or "salt money." A certain amount of controversy surrounds the culinary uses of salt. Research has revealed a link between high levels of salt consumption and high blood pressure, increasing the risk of stroke and heart disease. While a diet high in processed foods makes salt intake difficult to control, if used moderately with fresh ingredients, salt can be a healthy source of nutrients.

COOKING TIP

When cooking in a microwave oven, salt can toughen meat and "burn" vegetables, so season after microwaving.

MONOSODIUM GLUTAMATE

Most commonly known as MSG, monosodium glutamate is the sodium salt of glutamic acid, which is an amino acid also found in mushrooms. MSG has no flavor of its own, but it does enhance the flavor of other foods. Originally extracted from seaweed or wheat gluten, it was first discovered in the Orient, where it remains a popular flavor enhancer. While MSG cannot be tasted, its presence can be felt by those who are sensitive to it; unpleasant sensations of pressure behind the eyes and forehead are often provoked. The largest concentrations of glutamic acid occurring naturally in the body are found in nervous tissue, so it is thought that the symptoms of MSG syndrome are merely a temporary excess of the acid. But this theory has not been confirmed. MSG is used extensively in the cuisines of Japan, China, and Vietnam.

Coarse salt

Fine salt

Black salt, *also called sanchal, adds its rich flavor to many dishes from Northern India*

Monosodium glutamate

SALT FROM THE EARTH

Sodium chloride, or salt, is present in the Earth and has been since its formation. Rock salt occurs in underground deposits as seams of impacted salt. The salt is extracted, boiled down, and crystallized to varying degrees of fineness. At its best, many regard it as the finest flavored of all salts, although there are those who claim sea salt to be superior; this debate is surely a matter of taste. Coarse or crystal rock salt can be used in the kitchen or on the table, although it is usually placed in a saltshaker for table use. Table salt is finely ground rock salt, and it is the most widely used type. It can also contain magnesium carbonate or other chemical anticaking agents to provide an easy flow. Because of these additives, table salt is considered the least flavorful by discerning cooks. "Rock salt" refers to freezing salt for ice cream machines and is inedible.

Refined table salt *is often treated to make it more free-flowing*

Crystal rock salt *is mined only from deposits safe for human consumption*

Coarse rock salt *can be used for curing foods; rubbing meats and fish with it is an ancient technique*

Fine sea salt *dissolves quickly and is most suitable for table use*

English sea salt *should be used sparingly because it is very flavorful*

French sea salt *gets its color from the minerals in the sea floor*

SALT FROM THE SEA

All of the world's salt deposits are of marine origin; salt mines are simply markers for the areas where water once flowed. Sea salt is obtained either naturally by sun and wind evaporation or artificially from water evaporation pans. Unlike rock salt, it contains only 34 percent sodium chloride and is rich in trace elements. There are several types available. English sea salt comes primarily from Essex. It has a very "salty" taste and can be distinguished by its flake form. Brittany sea salt from France has a gray color characteristic of the sea floor beneath the salt marshes. With a delicate flavor, it is an exceptional salt for both kitchen and table. *Fleur de sel,* which translates literally as "flower of salt," from the salt marshes in Guérande is very rare. It is said to form only when the wind blows from the east. It is harvested manually, using traditional wooden scoops, from June to September.

COOKING WITH SALT

Salt is a basic flavor. In fact, "saltiness" is one of the four categories that make up the range of flavors discernible by human taste buds. And while salt is undoubtedly the most common kitchen ingredient, it is also the most easily abused; a pinch too much or too little can make or break the taste of a dish. The most important thing to remember when using salt is that it is not added as a flavoring in its own right, but as an enhancement to the overall flavor of the dish. This is why a lack of it results in bland food; salt is the background against which other flavors are displayed. When salt is added to a dish depends on many factors. Since salt raises the boiling point of water, it should be added after a boil to reduce cooking time. Consider the way in which salt interacts with ingredients. Salt draws moisture out of food; therefore, do not add prior to cooking beef, for example, as it will drain away the flavorful juices. Sometimes, however, this effect is desirable. For example, when sautéing onions to soften but not to brown, the addition of salt at the beginning draws the moisture out of the onions and into the pan. This little bit of added humidity lessens the harshness of the heat, allowing the onions to cook without browning. Always bear in mind the salt content of the other ingredients in a dish; foods such as cheese, bacon, and ham are already salty. Mastering the use of salt in cooking is the mark of a great chef and it takes a great deal of experience to develop a sense for the proper dose.

DRAWING OUT BITTERNESS

Vegetables such as cucumbers or eggplants are often salted prior to preparation to draw out their bitter juices. This process is called degorging, from the French *dégorger*, to draw out. However, there are many cooks who feel that degorging detracts from natural flavors, and frown upon this practice. Much depends on the quality of the vegetables and personal taste. Slice the vegetables thinly, arrange in a colander or sieve and sprinkle with salt. Weight the vegetables if necessary and leave for about 30 minutes or until the juices appear. Rinse thoroughly and dry if sautéing.

COOKING TIPS

• In sweet mixtures, salt helps to develop flavor; this is why most batters and doughs often call for a pinch of salt.
• Salt balances the action of yeast and is an integral part of bread making. Thus, follow recipes exactly as the ingredients are calculated carefully and quantities of yeast must be adjusted in low- or no-salt breads.
• A pinch of salt can be added to lightly beaten egg whites when preparing meringues; the salt "relaxes" the protein, making it easier to whisk the whites into stiff peaks.
• Always salt the water for boiling vegetables; this enhances their natural flavor and diminishes the need to add salt at the table. Also, salting at this stage prevents the nutritious mineral salts present in the vegetables from dissolving into the cooking water.

SALT AS A COOKING AGENT

Gravlax, a traditional Swedish dish, is an example of a simple dry-salted dish that can be prepared at home. Serve with rye or whole-grain bread and mayonnaise flavored with chopped fresh dill or mustard-dill sauce (see page 63).

Be sure to choose very fresh salmon and ensure that constant refrigeration is maintained. Signs of poorly salted salmon are salt crystals on the surface, discoloration, and a stringy texture. Do not keep longer than two days.

1 Grind together 6 tbsp salt, 6 tbsp sugar, and 2 tbsp black peppercorns in a mortar and pestle.

2 Sprinkle half the mixture evenly over one fillet of a 2-lb (1-kg) salmon. Cover with a layer of chopped fresh dill.

3 Cover the dill with the remaining salt mixture and place the second salmon fillet on top so that the skin side is uppermost.

4 Wrap in plastic wrap and weight with a heavy pan or kitchen weights. Place in the coldest part of the refrigerator for 24–36 hours.

Serves 6

8 oz (250 g) salt cod fillets
2 tbsp cornstarch
2 cups (500 ml) milk
6 tbsp unsalted butter
1 medium onion, grated
2 medium tomatoes, peeled,
seeded, and chopped
2 tbsp capers, drained
Salt
Freshly ground black pepper
Unsalted butter for ramekins
6 eggs
Freshly grated Parmesan
cheese

One day before preparing the dish, soak the cod in cold water to cover for at least 12 hours, changing the water several times. Drain and rinse the fish. Place in a saucepan and add cold water to cover. Bring just to a simmer over moderate heat, cover and remove from the heat. Leave for 10 minutes, or until the fish flakes easily when tested with a fork. Drain, remove the bones and skin, flake the fish and set aside. In a bowl, mix the cornstarch with a little of the milk until blended. Add the remaining milk and pour into a saucepan. Add 1 tbsp butter and cook, stirring, over moderate heat until the mixture is smooth and lightly thickened. In another saucepan, melt the remaining 5 tbsp butter. Add the onion and cook until soft, about 3 minutes. Add the tomatoes and cook until the mixture is thick. Stir in the milk mixture and the capers. Fold in the cod and add a little salt if necessary. Season generously with pepper. Preheat the oven to 400°F (200°C). Butter six small ramekins and break 1 egg into each. Pour the cod mixture over the eggs and sprinkle each ramekin with Parmesan cheese. Bake until the egg is set and the top is browned, about 8 minutes. Serve immediately with crusty bread.

PRESERVING WITH SALT

Salted anchovies   **Preserved lemons**

Before every kitchen was equipped with a refrigerator, salt was one of the principal means of food preservation. The ancient Romans were the first to use this method, salting olives, seafood, and cheese; and while less popular, preservation with salt is still widely used today. Salt preserves by acting on the bacteria present in foods. By drawing out the moisture, salt limits the humid environment that fosters these microorganisms. In some cases, salt inhibits bacterial growth; in others, it stops it entirely. Saltpeter is not sodium chloride, but a potassium salt, potassium nitrate. It is used in small quantities with salt in the preservation of meat and fish, and it is saltpeter that gives many of these foods their characteristic pink color.

Makes about 10–12 lemons

About 3 lb (1.5 kg) untreated
lemons
6 oz (175 g) coarse salt

Cut the lemons into quarters without slicing all the way through; they should remain attached at the stem ends. Sprinkle the salt inside the lemons, on the flesh. Place the lemons in a sterilized clamp-top jar, push them down and weight. Store in a cool, dark place for about 1 month. The peel and the fruit can be used together, whole or chopped, and served with Middle Eastern rice, meat, or fish dishes. The juice can be used as a flavoring for grain or vegetable salads.

COOKING TIPS
Add sparingly when reducing because salt does not evaporate and the flavor can become too concentrated. Do not salt meat before cooking; the salt draws out all the flavorful juices, but fish fillets will benefit from a bit of salt during refrigeration prior to cooking.

DRY-SALTING AND BRINING

Rubbing coarse salt over the surface of food prior to storage is known as *dry-salting*. Brining, which involves soaking ingredients in a salt solution, is the method most often used for large cuts of meat or fish. The methods are equally effective, but brining is best suited to bulky ingredients, because dry-salting does not penetrate deeply enough to hamper bacterial growth. For very large cuts of meat, the brining solution is often injected into the center as a safeguard.

Sauerkraut
Widely used in the cuisines of Eastern Europe, this is the classic example of an ingredient preserved by brining.

Prosciutto
This is the Italian version of salt-cured ham. There are other types, but this is the most widely available.

HERB AND SPICE SALTS

A variety of flavored salts is a useful addition to any kitchen cupboard. Many commercial seasoning blends are available; sometimes they are labeled as "salt" although they may also be labeled as "seasoning." These seasoning mixtures contain varying quantities of salt, and sometimes none at all, so always check before using to avoid oversalting. When prepared at home, herb and spice salt mixtures can add a new dimension to an old standard or spice up an otherwise ordinary dish. Celery salt with tomato juice is classic, but flavored salts have many uses: rub into meat or fish before cooking, use to season vegetables and sauces, dust over homemade potato chips or add to cream cheese for a simple canapé spread. If making in large batches to keep on hand, use free-running table salt. Seasoned salts are also used in many Asian cuisines. *Gomashio* is a Japanese blend of black sesame seeds and salt. To prepare, allow three parts black sesame seeds to one part coarse salt. Dry-roast the seeds, cool, and then pound together in a mortar and pestle. A similar Chinese spiced salt mixture consists of equal parts of dry-roasted fagara (see page 95) and coarse salt pounded together.

1 Combine all the ingredients in a mortar and crush with a pestle until combined.

2 Spoon into airtight containers for storage.

Garlic salt *can be bought or made in a mortar by pounding a garlic clove with a few tablespoons of salt*

Celery salt

Seasoned salts
Homemade seasoned salts are ideal for sprinkling over meat, poultry, and fish before broiling.

Herb salt

TAMARIND

HOW TO STORE
In plastic bags kept in a cool place or in the refrigerator.

COOKING TIPS
It is worth searching for tamarind *concentrate*, which is a sticky dark paste without seeds or fibrous, broken pods. This is the most convenient form because only a small amount is ever needed for most dishes. Alternatively, soak the *fresh* pulp in water for a souring agent that can be used like vinegar and lemon juice. Pour ¹/₂ cup (125 ml) hot water over 7 peeled pods and leave for 30 minutes. Strain into a bowl, cover and refrigerate. Keep for up to 1 week.

The exact origin of the tamarind tree is not known. The tree may have originated in tropical East Africa or in southern Asia. It has been cultivated in India for many centuries and was probably introduced into Europe in the fifteenth century. The Spanish conquistadores took it to the West Indies and Mexico in the 1600s, and it has remained a popular ingredient in the cuisines of the islands and the South American mainland. An evergreen with light green, oval leaves, it has red-veined yellow flowers that ripen into dark brown pods. Tamarind is characterized by a sour, fruity flavor and a pleasant aroma. It is useful where a gentle sourness is needed, and it so enhances the flavor of fish and poultry dishes. Although its primary importance is in the kitchen, both red and yellow dyes are derived from the leaves. It is also used in many commercial products, most notably in Worcestershire sauce.

TASTES GOOD WITH/IN

Indian curries, fruit drinks, vegetable stews, desserts, jams and jellies, hot-and-sour soup, chutneys, rice, lentils, seafood, especially shrimp, meat and chicken dishes.

COOK'S CHOICE
TAMARIND WATER

Makes 13 cups (3 liters)

4 oz (125 g) tamarind concentrate
13 cups (3 liters) cold water
Sugar

Combine the tamarind concentrate with water in a pitcher and let stand in a cool place for about 4 hours or until the pulp has softened. Stir from time to time. Strain through a fine sieve and sweeten to taste. Serve chilled. Alternatively, reduce the amount of soaking water and serve the drink over ice cubes.

The brown pods can reach a length of 4 in (10 cm) and are picked when fully ripe and cracked

The shells are brittle and house a fleshy pulp, which can contain as many as ten seeds

Tamarind pods

Tamarind seeds

Tamarind block

Tamarind concentrate

FENUGREEK

FORMS
Seeds: Fresh sprouted, dried, whole, crushed
Leaves: Dried, fresh

HOW TO STORE
Keep in airtight containers in a cool, dark place.

COOKING TIPS
Fenugreek is so strongly aromatic that the whole plant gives off a spicy odor. The *seeds*, however, are very disagreeable and bitter in their raw state, and they should always be lightly roasted before use. A heavy iron skillet is ideal for dry-roasting the seeds, which then have a pleasant aroma and flavor.

A sturdy annual whose Latin name means "Greek hay," fenugreek is native to western Asia, although it has been cultivated in Mediterranean regions since ancient times. Although this spice is associated primarily with Indian cuisine, it has been used in the West for medicinal purposes and as cattle fodder. The ancient Egyptians used a paste made from ground fenugreek that was plastered on the body to reduce fever; today it is used in the manufacture of some oral contraceptives. In cooking, the seeds must be dry-roasted before use to remove their bitter flavor, although overroasting will leave them just as unpleasant. Ground fenugreek is an essential ingredient in curry powders and is also used for pickling. In parts of Africa, the seeds are soaked and prepared like legumes. The seeds can also be sprouted and added to green salads, where they add a crunchy texture and a slightly bitter flavor.

Golden-brown with a deep furrow on one side, they are smooth and hard

Fenugreek seeds

Ground fenugreek

Crushed fenugreek

Fresh leaves *have few culinary uses but sprouted leaves can be tossed into salads and the plant can be eaten as a vegetable*

Hard to grind, fenugreek seeds are best pounded in a mortar after dry-roasting

Dried leaves *known also as methi, are often combined with root vegetables in Indian and Middle Eastern dishes*

TASTES GOOD WITH/IN
Seeds: Indian curries of all kinds, Egyptian and Ethiopian breads, Berber spice mix (see page 97), stews and to coat fried foods. *Sprouted seeds:* Salads. *Dried leaves:* Boiled root vegetables.

COOK'S CHOICE
POTATOES WITH FENUGREEK

Serves 4

1 lb (500 g) new potatoes
Salt
5 tbsp unsalted butter
6 oz (175 g) fresh fenugreek leaves, finely chopped, or 2 tbsp dried fenugreek leaves
$1/2$ tsp curry powder
$1/2$ tsp mango powder (optional)
Freshly ground black pepper

Cook the potatoes in boiling salted water until just tender, 10–15 minutes. Drain and pat dry. Melt the butter in a large pan. Add the potatoes and fenugreek leaves and cook gently until golden, 5–10 minutes. Sprinkle on the curry and mango powder if using, and cook for 5 minutes longer; stir often for an even golden brown color. Season to taste. Serve either hot or at room temperature.

HOW TO STORE

Whole beans: Can be stored in glass jars with tightly fitting lids, kept in a cool, dark place.
Liquid extract: This is best stored in an airtight container in a cool, dark place, or it can be refrigerated.

Beans *are dark brown, narrow, long, wrinkled, waxy, and supple*

The flesh gives off a rich, mellow, perfumed tobaccolike aroma

COOKING TIPS

Vanilla is expensive, but it is best to buy *whole beans* because as they are more flavorful and can be used sparingly; they can also be used more than once. After splitting a whole bean to scrape out the seeds for use in a recipe, leave the bean to dry for several days. Place the dried bean in a sealed jar of sugar. Keep topped up with fresh sugar, which will take on the delicate vanilla aroma; add more beans to maintain a steady supply of flavor. Alternatively, split the beans, extract the seeds, place them in a bowl, and pour over some boiling milk. Sweeten to taste and allow the mixture to stand for 15 minutes. Use in rice puddings or in any sweet recipe calling for milk.

VANILLA

The bean of a climbing orchid, vanilla originated in southern Mexico. When the Spaniards conquered Mexico, the Aztecs were already flavoring their hot chocolate with vanilla, a practice the world has since copied. It was the Aztecs who developed the technique of curing the beans by repeatedly sweating and drying them to develop the white crystalline vanillin, without which the beans have no flavor. The best pods are supple but tough, dark brown in color, and covered with a frosting of aromatic crystals. Because it is an expensive spice, there is a great deal of false vanilla on the market, much of it chemical. Synthetic vanilla can be recognized by its coarse aroma and unpleasant aftertaste.

The best vanilla comes from the state of Veracruz in Mexico and, where it grows, the air is richly scented. It is also grown in Madagascar, Central America, Puerto Rico, Réunion, and other areas with a suitable climate.

Vanilla beans *should be plump and tender; avoid those that are brittle and dry*

Vanilla sugar

Vanilla extract *is very concentrated and should be used sparingly*

TASTES GOOD WITH/IN

Chocolate, coffee, puddings, custards, ice cream, fruit desserts; in small quantities, with savory dishes such as those made with veal and lobster.

COOK'S CHOICE
VANILLA GRANOLA

Makes about 2 lb (1 kg)

3 cups (250 g) rolled oats
2 1/2 cups (250 g) barley flakes
1 cup (125 g) slivered almonds
1/2 cup (60 g) whole-wheat flour
1 cup (125 g) chopped dried apricots
1 vanilla bean, split
1/2 cup (125 ml) honey
1/2 cup (125 ml) sunflower oil

Preheat the oven to 375°F (190°C). Combine the oats, barley, almonds, flour, and apricots. Scrape out the vanilla seeds. Whisk together the vanilla seeds, honey, oil, and 1/2 cup (125 ml) water. Stir in the dry ingredients. Spread in a pan and bake, stirring often, until golden, 30–45 minutes. Cool. Place in an airtight jar; add the vanilla pod. Leave for 1 week before using.

Split beans with seeds

GINGER

HOW TO STORE
Fresh: Rhizomes are best refrigerated, wrapped in paper towels, in tightly closed plastic bags, where they will keep for several weeks.
Dried: Should be stored in airtight containers kept in a cool, dark place.
Pickled: Should be refrigerated in its container.
Preserved: Should be stored in its container and kept in a cool, dark place.

The underground rhizome of an attractive flowering plant, gingerroot is used extensively in the cuisines of Asia, where it is second in importance only to salt. It has been cultivated in tropical Asia for over 3,000 years, although its exact origins are unknown. Gingerroot was also used in the Middle East and southern Europe well before Roman times. The Portuguese introduced it into Africa, the Spanish took it to the West Indies, and by the 1500s, the Spaniards had a flourishing Jamaican ginger trade with continental Europe. With a clean, fresh, spicy flavor, gingerroot is appreciated in many dishes both sweet and savory, although it is in the Orient that it is used to its full potential. There are many forms: fresh, dried, pickled, preserved in syrup, and crystallized. In Chinese cuisine, fresh is preferred to the dried, for both flavor and texture. Chopped, crushed, or sliced into matchsticks, it is used to season innumerable meat, fish, and vegetable dishes. Pink pickled ginger, called *gari* in Japan, is the familiar condiment for sushi. The Japanese also have a special tool, an *oroshigane*, which is reserved for grating fresh gingerroot.

TASTES GOOD WITH/IN
Curries, soy sauce, meat and poultry stews, chutneys and pickles, vegetables, soups, fish and cheese dishes, stewed and baked fruit, cakes, puddings, cookies, sweet breads, drinks, and mulled wine.

COOKING TIPS
Always have some *fresh* gingerroot in the refrigerator and buy a fine grater of the kind (sold in Japanese shops) made especially for grating it. Grate the gingerroot and squeeze out the juice, which will lift any fish or shellfish dish out of the ordinary. Add to soups, marinades, and stews, especially those made with beef, just before serving.

Fresh grated gingerroot
With a sharp knife, peel away the rough outer skin only as far as the flesh to be grated.

Knobbly, branched, and off-white or buff-colored, the rhizome should feel firm

Fresh ginger

Mainly used for desserts and other sweet dishes, it imparts a rich and warming flavor

Dried ginger

Ground ginger

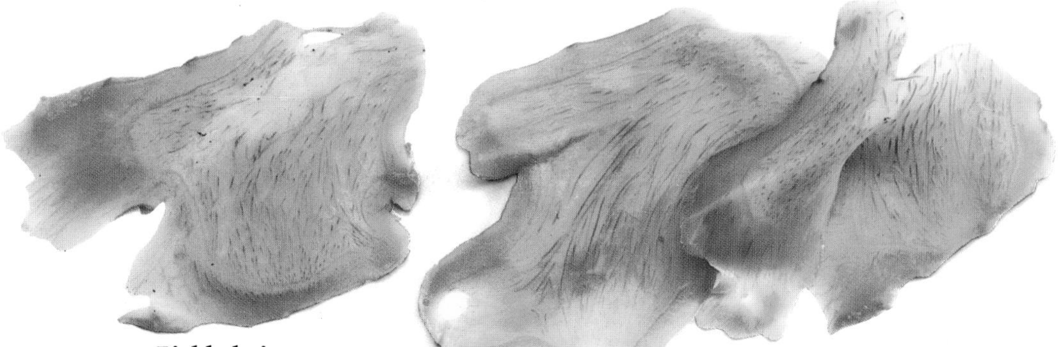

Pickled ginger

Preserved ginger

Crystallized ginger

CRYSTALLIZING GINGER

Peel and thinly slice 1 lb (500 g) fresh gingerroot. Place in a saucepan, add water to cover, and cook gently until tender, about 30 minutes. Drain. Weigh and place in a saucepan with an equal amount of sugar and 3 tbsp water. Bring to a boil, stirring often, until the ginger is transparent and the liquid is almost evaporated. Reduce the heat and cook, stirring constantly, until almost dry. Toss in sugar to coat. Store in an airtight jar for up to 3 months.

COOKING WITH GINGER

The uses for ginger in the Western kitchen are many. It adds a clean, fresh bite to seafood, picks up the flavor of dull foods, and cuts the fattiness of rich meats such as duck or pork. In marinades, ginger has an affinity for citrus fruit, garlic, soy sauce, and onions. When choosing fresh rhizomes, weight and firm flesh are a sign of freshness. Length is a sign of maturity, and mature rhizomes will be hotter and more fibrous. For grated gingerroot, the fibers are not problematic although they can be when slicing. Fresh gingerroot will keep for about 1 week in a cool place. In the refrigerator, it will keep for a few weeks wrapped in paper towels to absorb moisture and placed inside a plastic bag. Dried ground ginger tastes nothing like fresh, and the two are not interchangeable in recipes; ground ginger is best in sweet dishes such as breads, cookies, and puddings. It also has a wonderful affinity for baked rhubarb and apples.

COOK'S CHOICE
GINGERBREAD COOKIES

Makes about 30–40 cookies

7 ¹/₂ tbsp honey

¹/₃ cup (75 g) packed brown sugar

2 tbsp unsalted butter

3 cups (375 g) all-purpose flour, sifted

2 tsp ground ginger

Pinch of ground cinnamon

Pinch of ground cloves

Pinch of ground cardamom

1 egg yolk

1 tsp baking soda

In a pan, combine the honey, sugar, and butter over low heat and stir to dissolve. Leave to cool. Preheat the oven to 325°F (160°C). In a bowl, combine two-thirds of the flour, the spices, the egg yolk and the honey mixture. Dissolve the baking soda in 1 tbsp tepid water and add to the mixture. Knead in the remaining flour, as needed, to obtain a firm dough. Roll out ¹/₂ in (1 cm) thick and cut out shapes. Place on a greased baking sheet and bake for 10–12 minutes.

Gingerbread cookie

FLAVORS
OF THE
WORLD

THE MIDDLE EAST

Just as the Middle East has always been a melting pot of different cultures, so is its cuisine a rich mix of flavors. It is a combination of gleaming fruit and vegetables eaten almost straight from the fields and long-stewing, slow-baking dishes featuring lamb, yogurt, beans, and spices, mopped up either by rice or by the region's characteristic flat disks of bread. To walk down any Middle Eastern street at dusk is to breathe in the scent of gently barbecuing meat, with different fragrances vying for attention like traders in the *souk*, or marketplace.

In the many countries that make up the area known as the Middle East—Egypt, Syria, Iran, Iraq, Lebanon, Jordan, Saudi Arabia, Yemen, Kuwait, and Israel—the style of cooking is not affected by fashion or new fads. A deeper-rooted respect for traditional values is mirrored in dishes that have a history stretching back many centuries, to the time when they were devised by Persian princes, Palestinian farmers, or bedouin nomads scratching a living from the desert.

TRADITIONAL INGREDIENTS

Allspice*
Basil*
Bulgur
Caraway*
Cardamom*
Cassia*
Chick-peas
Chilies*
Cilantro/Coriander
Cinnamon*
Cloves*
Cumin*
Dill*
Eggplants
Fennel*
Fenugreek*
Figs
Garlic*
Gingerroot*
Honey*
Lemon*
Marjoram*
Mint*
Olives*
Orange-flower water*
Parsley*
Phyllo pastry
Pine nuts
Pomegranates
Rosemary*
Saffron*
Sesame seeds*
Sumac*
Tahini*
Thyme*
Turmeric*
Yogurt*
Zahtar*
Zhug

(*see Index)

INFLUENCES

It was in the Fertile Crescent, formed by Iraq, the Levant, and Egypt, that humans first became farmers rather than hunters, some 12,000 years ago. Wheat, barley, pistachio nuts, pomegranates, and figs flourished alongside flocks of sheep and goats. And while the Middle East influenced the rest of the world's eating habits, the rest of the world has had little effect in return. All the main culinary influences and traditions have come from countries or empires that are or were found within the region.

Around A.D. 700, invading Arabs flooded out from what is now Saudi Arabia, bringing with them the gospel of Muhammad and a desert diet in which goat's or sheep's milk was substituted for water and nuts and dates for fresh vegetables and fruits. By the tenth century, when Baghdad had become the administrative, cultural, and culinary center of this empire, a more sophisticated court cuisine evolved. This essentially set the style for Middle Eastern food, marrying more simple Arab dishes with more complex Persian creations (using rice, fresh fruits, duck, and almonds) as well as the many Oriental spices—cumin, cardamom, cilantro, fenugreek, turmeric, and gingerroot—which Arab traders were transporting to all corners of their sprawling empire.

Four centuries later, the luxury-loving sultans of Turkey's Ottoman Empire added new layers to this already very colorful confection of foods. They introduced sweet, sticky pastries, such as honey-drenched *baklava* and *kadaïf*, as well as the thick, sweet coffee that is still popular today. This is ground from a mixture high in mocha beans (named after the Yemeni port Al Mokha), flavored with ground cardamom pods and is drunk from small cups, in vast quantities, throughout the region.

FLAVORINGS

In the prolific use of spices, Middle Eastern chefs come second only to their Indian counterparts in enthusiasm. Among the most commonly used are aniseed, caraway, clove, cilantro, cumin, gingerroot, nutmeg, sesame seed, and allspice. Likewise, the markets of the Middle East are thick with the scent of kitchen herbs: basil, cilantro, dill, fennel, marjoram, mint, parsley, rosemary, sage, and thyme. In addition, each country has its own preferred seasoning blend. *Zahtar*, for example, is a blend of powdered marjoram leaves, thyme, roasted sesame seeds, and the sour red berries of the sumac tree, and it is widely used in Jordan. *Zhug* is a fiery Yemeni paste made of ground cardamom, cumin, garlic, and chilies, which is often added to soups and stews for extra bite.

Tahini paste, made from oil and sesame seeds, forms an integral part of many dips and dishes. Nuts feature prominently in Middle Eastern cooking; almonds are

favored in Iran, pine nuts in the Levant, and walnuts and hazelnuts in Iraq. Olives and olive oil are to be found in every domestic kitchen, as are jars of pickled vegetables, called *torshi*; the most well known is made from turnips, colored pink with beets.

The smoky flavor of charcoal grilling is imparted to meats, poultry, and fish. For sweets and desserts, honey is often used in place of sugar, and many are also delicately imbued with the perfume of orange-flower and rose water.

OTHER INGREDIENTS

Lamb is the dominant meat, due largely to the predominance of the Muslim and Jewish religions, which forbid the eating of pork. Lamb is often cubed and barbecued over charcoal (*kebabs*) or minced with herbs and spices and turned into meatballs (*koftas*) or stewed with spices and then yogurt for the bedouin dish, *laban ummo*. Lamb also forms the basis of the Iranian national dish *chelow kebab*, in which lamb kabobs are served on a bed of crusted rice and accompanied by a generous portion of butter and raw egg yolk. Goat and camel meat are also widely eaten across the Middle East, as is chicken, which, along with turkey, is the main source of meat in Israel.

Whereas a meal without meat is conceivable, a meal without bread is unthinkable. Most Arab bread is made from wheat that has been lightly leavened and shaped to a hollow flat round, forming a pocket that is perfect for stuffing. Cracked wheat, *bulgur*, is served as either a bread accompaniment or a substitute. Rice is used in the same way. It was introduced to the area by the Persians, who had adopted it from their Indian neighbors. Rice with cardamoms, cloves, cumin, and cassia is still an Iranian specialty (*polo*).

Eggplants are commonly used, as a guest in stews and as a host for stuffings of rice, meat, and nuts, or simply sliced, salted, and fried. Zucchini, okra, olives, grape leaves, cucumbers, and tomatoes come close behind. Brown fava beans, seasoned with garlic, onion, lemon juice, and cumin, form the Egyptian national dish, *ful medames,* which is eaten and enjoyed throughout the country, in luxury restaurants, at roadside stands, and even on the breakfast table.

Fish tends to decrease in importance away from the various Middle Eastern coastlines, where fresh-caught mullet, swordfish, and sardines are often barbecued, after being marinated in olive oil, lemon juice, and onion. Gefilte fish—white fish fillets minced with eggs, bread crumbs, and onions—is an Israeli favorite.

MEALS

Early morning in the Middle East sees a bustle of activity outside most bakeries, as people come to buy still-warm bread for their breakfast, to eat with eggs, fresh fruit and vegetables, honey, nuts, and yogurt.

Coffee is drunk throughout the day, at home, at work, in restaurants and coffeehouses that also provide a bubbling hookah, or water pipe. Only in Iran is black tea, usually taken with large sugar lumps, a more popular drink than coffee.

Lunchtime brings with it a selection of small dishes, known collectively as *mezze*, usually featuring pita bread in abundance with hummus, yogurt, *rissoles*, tabbouleh, assorted vegetable salads, stuffed grape leaves, taramasalata, and a variety of dips.

The evening meal is generally the largest of the day. In traditional households, it is eaten in two shifts; first the men, then the women and children. Before eating, a jug filled with soapy water is passed around, and all diners wash their hands before their first mouthful. The food is served in communal dishes, and it is customary to eat with the fingers—preferably just the thumb and first two fingers, though all five are allowed for more fiddly foods. To show that they have finished, satisfied diners lean back and lick their fingers. Sweet pastries or puddings are not usually served after a meal, except when entertaining.

The Arab tradition of hospitality pervades the households of the Middle East. Shame is attached to the host who does not extend a surfeit of food toward the guest, and equally to the guest who does not pay fulsome tribute to his host.

Many culinary customs are dictated by religion. For example, alcohol is forbidden by the Koran. Nevertheless, some fine wines are made in Lebanon, as well as in Egypt and Israel.

MENU GUIDE

Tabbouleh
A salad of chopped parsley, tomatoes, onions, bulgur, lemon juice, and olive oil

Hummus bi Tahina
Pureed chick-peas blended with tahini

Moutabal
Smoked, pureed eggplants with tahini

Felafel (Israel)
Ground deep-fried chick-pea balls, served in pita bread

Ful Medames (Egypt)
Brown fava beans tossed in a cold dressing of lemon, garlic, cumin, onion, and oil

Kibbeh
(Syria and Lebanon)
Ground meat, bulgur, and onions, usually deep-fried

Labaneya (Egypt)
Spinach soup with yogurt

Sambousek (Lebanon)
Phyllo pastries filled with meat, onion, and pine nuts

Kofta Mabrouma (Syria)
Baked rolls of ground meat with a filling of pine nuts

Samak Masguf (Iraq)
Barbecued fish with a tomato and curry sauce

Khouzi (Saudi Arabia)
Whole roast lamb

Faisanjan (Iran)
Duck or chicken in walnut sauce flavored with pomegranate juice

Khoresh (Iran)
Lamb in thick sweet-and-sour sauce

Kadaïf
Shredded pastry dough cake stuffed with honey syrup and chopped nuts

Ma'amoul
(Syria and Lebanon)
Nut- or date-filled pastries

GREECE AND TURKEY

From the whitewashed walls and blue skies of the Greek islands to the bare plains and citadel towns of eastern Turkey is a distance of some 700 miles (1100 km). It is a journey that crosses not only the Aegean Sea, but also from a Christian land to a Muslim, from Europe to Asia. Centuries of differences divide the two nations, and yet in their cooking they are united. They have one thing in common: a hot, often harsh climate, making for land that does not yield readily to the plow. Not here the lush meadows of Northern Europe, but dry, baking hillsides on which flourish not tall pines but hardy, hunched olive trees and herds of goats. The cuisine reflects the landscape: a rugged peasant fare of bread, tomatoes, olives and eggplants, enlivened by barbecued meat and, in Turkey, by skillful deployment of spices. A few European dishes have found their way into Greece, and Russian influence is apparent in Turkey's Black Sea region, but by and large this is a cuisine that has its gaze very firmly fixed toward the East.

TRADITIONAL INGREDIENTS

Allspice*
Bulgur wheat
Chicken
Chick-peas
Chilies*
Cinnamon*
Cumin*
Dill*
Eggplants
Fennel*
Feta cheese
Figs
Garlic*
Grape leaves*
Grapes
Honey*
Lamb
Lemons*
Marjoram*
Mint*
Octopus
Olive oil*
Olives*
Onions*
Oregano*
Parsley*
Peppers
Phyllo pastry
Pine nuts
Pistachios*
Pita bread
Rice
Rose water*
Saffron*
Sardines
Spinach
Sunflower seeds
Tomatoes*
Watermelon
White beans
Yogurt*

(*see Index)

INFLUENCES

As far back as the fifth century B.C., Greece had a reputation for cooking every bit as distinguished as it enjoyed in the fields of art, politics, and literature. The early Greek writers Philoxenus and Archestratus wrote whole treatises on the art of cooking. We know from them and others that bread, goat cheese, wine, olives, beans, fish, fruit, honey, and pine nuts formed the basis of an early Athenian's diet. Five centuries later, when Greek power had waned, it was still every Roman nobleman's ambition to employ a Greek chef in his household.

The greatest outside influence on Greek cooking came with the invasion of the Ottoman Turks in the fifteenth century. Previous occupation by the Venetians had introduced pasta to the region, but the Turks came bearing an altogether spicier, fruitier cuisine, heavily influenced by Persian cooking, but also comprising a variety of dishes devised by the court chefs of the Ottoman capital Constantinople (modern-day Istanbul). These were rich mélanges of eggplants, tomatoes, olive oil, and meats, along with syrupy candies that bore luxurious, at times lascivious, names such as "girl's breasts" and "ladies' navels."

For nearly four centuries, the Ottoman sultans ruled Greece, and throughout this period the two nations' cuisines became inextricably intertwined. Today, many dishes share not only the same ingredients but also the same names.

FLAVORINGS

Green and fruity-tasting olive oil lies at the heart of most Turkish and Greek cuisine. It serves as a dressing, a marinade, a flavoring, and a cooking medium.

Garlic is another flavoring that is intrinsic to both regions; combined with olive oil, it forms the basis for the Greek sauce *skorthalia* and its Turkish counterpart *tarator* (with the addition of walnuts); both sauces are used to accompany otherwise plainly cooked fish and vegetables.

Lemon is another constantly recurring flavor; its sharpness is used to balance the richness of olive oil in the two savory dips that are synonymous with this area and which even share the same name in both languages: *hummus* (olive oil, sesame seed paste, pureed chick-peas, and lemon juice) and *taramasalata* (pureed smoked cod roe, olive oil, and lemon juice).

In Greece, lemon juice is an almost mandatory ingredient in salad dressings; along with eggs, it forms the principal ingredient of the Greek sauce *avgolemono*, used to flavor soups and stews, and to bring zest to fish and vegetable dishes.

Herbs such as dill, mint, parsley, marjoram, and oregano flourish in the temperate Greek climate, while spices are more a Turkish phenomenon. Most commonly used are allspice, cinnamon, and cumin, which are mixed in with ground meat to make *kofta* or *rissoles*. These, like many Turkish dishes, have a distinctive, spicy-sweet character.

OTHER INGREDIENTS

Patterns of meat consumption are dictated by both cultural and geographical factors. In Muslim Turkey, for example, eating pork is forbidden on religious grounds; in Christian Greece it tends to be eaten only on festival and feast days. As for beef, the general lack of green pastures makes the raising of cattle impractical. Lamb is therefore the prevailing meat, and it forms the starting point for large numbers of Greek and Turkish dishes.

Both countries have long coastlines, and their seas harbor rich supplies of fish and seafood. Shrimp, lobster, red mullet, and tuna are often served, plainly broiled or barbecued, with a light seasoning of oil and lemon juice; squid and octopus are stewed in a red wine and tomato sauce or deep-fried in batter (as are whitebait and cuttlefish).

The most common vegetables of the region are eggplants, tomatoes, onions, peppers, white beans, olives, and grape leaves. The bulbous-shaped, purplish-black eggplant loves olive oil and soaks it up like blotting paper; eggplants are simmered, stewed, or deep-fried, or they are stuffed with tomatoes, garlic, peppers, onions, and herbs as in the famous Turkish dish *imam bayildi*, which means "the priest fainted" (from pleasure, tradition has it).

Flattened, oval-shaped, lightly leavened pita bread is the staple of both countries, and is usually served warm. A popular variation in Turkey is *semit*, a crisp ring of white bread covered in sesame seeds.

Wafer-thin, flaky phyllo pastry is used in both countries to make baklava, a popular dessert filled with nuts and spices and drenched in honey syrup. Phyllo pastry also forms the outer casing for the many different Turkish *boreks*, pastry parcels filled with mixtures of melted cheese, spinach, or minced meat.

Rice is used mainly for stuffing vegetables, but it also forms the basis for the Turkish *pilafs*—dishes in which the rice is cooked along with the other ingredients: chicken, ground lamb, green peppers, tomatoes, and even plain roasted wheat grain. In southeastern Turkey, cracked wheat (bulgur) is used instead of rice.

Goat and sheep yogurt are found everywhere. Combined with thick Greek honey, they become a popular dessert; diluted with ice water and salt, they become the refreshing Turkish drink *ayran*. The other most common dairy product is cheese, eaten in melted form in both countries, but more commonly in solid form in Greece; no Greek salad is complete without some crumbled chunks of feta, goat cheese.

MEALS

The Greeks generally eat three meals a day: first, a light breakfast of bread, goat cheese, olives, and tomatoes, then at midday their main meal, and in the evening a lighter collection of snacks.

The Turks, on the other hand, favor four visits to the table, with two main meals (breakfast and dinner) and two lighter snacks (at lunchtime and last thing at night).

In both countries, a selection of appetizers (*mezze*) usually forms the bulk of the lighter meals. These may be as simple or complicated as required, ranging from cubes of salty goat cheese, slices of tomato drizzled with olive oil, and a bowl of plump black olives, to selections of savory dips, stuffed vegetables, oil-soaked large white beans, and spicy meatballs. In Turkey, soup (*chorba*) will often be the starter for a main meal, even at breakfast.

Strong Turkish coffee (known as Greek coffee in Greece) is always served at the end of the meal. In Greece, guests may also be offered preserved fruits or spoonfuls of sweet jam dissolved in water. Other sweets include *baklava* and *kadaïf*, syrup-soaked pastries filled with rich mixtures of honey and nuts.

The instinct of extending hospitality toward strangers is deeply ingrained in both the Turks and the Greeks. In remote rural areas, travelers are likely to be invited not just to have dinner but also to stay the night in a local family's home. Failure to accept can result in deep offense.

In traditional Turkish homes, food is eaten with the fingers; only the thumb, the index and the middle finger are used, and damp washcloths sprinkled with toilet water are passed around frequently.

In the restaurants of both countries, meals are taken at a leisurely pace, and diners are usually invited into the kitchens to inspect the food before making their choice.

MENU GUIDE

Mezze
A selection of hot and cold appetizers

Hummus
Chick-peas pureed with olive oil and lemon juice

Taramasalata
Cod roe blended with olive oil and lemon juice

Tzatziki (Greece)
Çaçik (Turkey)
Yogurt with cucumber, mint, and garlic

Borek (Turkey)
Pastries stuffed with spinach, cheese, or ground meat

Fasoulia (Turkey)
Beans cooked in tomato sauce

Skorthalia (Greece)
Tarator (Turkey)
Creamy garlic paste

Avgolemono Soup (Greece)
Chicken soup with rice, eggs, and lemon juice

Imam Bayildi (Turkey)
Eggplant stuffed with onion, tomatoes, and garlic

Kleftico (Greece)
Slow-roasted lamb on the bone flavored with spices

Moussaka (Greece)
Layers of baked vegetables and ground lamb covered in a light cheese sauce

Chicken Guvech (Turkey)
Chicken cooked with green peppers, onions, and tomatoes

Gharithes Yiouvetsi (Turkey)
Shrimp baked in a special tomato sauce with feta cheese

Pilaf (Turkey)
Rice cooked with meat, vegetables, or bulgur

Halvah (Turkey)
Hard, cookielike fudge, made with nuts

Rahat Loukoum (Turkey)
Turkish delight

EUROPE

E urope is the world's dairy. On no other continent are milk, butter, and cheese produced so plentifully and used so prolifically. And together with onions, bread, and potatoes, they make up the superstructure of European cooking, at the pinnacle of which stand the rich varieties of meat and fish that prosper in this largely temperate zone. The focal point of any European meal is the main course, be it a roast leg of lamb, a bubbling beef stew, or a tureen of steaming seafood; appetizers and desserts play a secondary role. While there is much diversity, the three-course-meal pattern prevails, as does the use of knives, forks, and spoons. Trade, wars, and migration have consistently blurred the region's physical and political boundaries, but throughout the process the different European peoples have largely succeeded in preserving their own languages, their own cultures—and their own foods.

TRADITIONAL INGREDIENTS

Asparagus
Bay leaf*
Beets
Butter*
Cabbage
Caraway*
Cherries
Chocolate*
Cinnamon*
Cream*
Dill*
Dried fish*
Game
Garlic*
Herring
Mushrooms*
Mustard*
Nutmeg*
Olive oil*
Onions*
Parsley*
Pasta
Peppers
Potatoes
Rabbit
Sage*
Sausage
Smoked fish
Tarragon*
Thyme*
Tomatoes*
Variety meats
Vinegar*
Wine
Yogurt*

(*see Index)

MEDITERRANEAN EUROPE

United by a common, near-landlocked sea, the countries that comprise Mediterranean Europe—Spain, Portugal, Italy, and Southern France—have for many centuries enjoyed a circular interchange of trade, people, and foods. Merchants have always plied these waters, beginning with the Phoenicians, then the Greeks, the Romans, the Venetians, and countless others. Although they use largely the same ingredients, all the Mediterranean countries have retained their own clearly defined cuisines. Pasta remains inviolably Italian, sherry and ham Spanish, port and spicy sausages Portuguese, and wine and herbs French.

With such a long coastline, fish and seafood play a key role. By contrast, beef cattle like neither the high summer temperatures nor the lack of lush pastures; Mediterranean cooking thus tends to revolve around the hardy pig and chicken.

Rarely does a meal in the Mediterranean pass without olive oil having played a part. Sprinkled with vinegar over fresh green salad, quickly fried with silvery sardines, or long-stewed with meat and tomatoes, olive oil spreads its fruity, delicate flavor throughout the region's food. Add some sunshine and you have the unmistakable aroma that characterizes dishes from this region.

More often than not, olive oil works in partnership with garlic, suffusing dishes with a flavor that varies in strength from lightly perfumed to fiercely pungent. Garlic also forms the principal ingredient (along with eggs and olive oil) of the French mayonnaise *aïoli*, which in Spain becomes *alioli*, minus the eggs but plus herbs. In Italy they eat pasta with nothing but garlic and olive oil (*aglio e olio*), and in Portugal chefs pack garlic cloves into *açorda de alhos*, a substantial bread soup.

Alcohol is often used to flavor Mediterranean dishes: the wine bottle is never far from the French or Italian cook's grasp, while Spanish and Portuguese chefs tend to use sherry more often.

Herbs are widely used in French and Italian cooking, principally basil, tarragon, parsley, sage, thyme, marjoram, and bay leaves. The pounding of basil, Parmesan cheese, pine nuts, and olive oil produces a tasty, concentrated paste called *pesto* in Italy (used as a sauce for pasta) and *pistou* in France, where it lends its individual personality to a vegetable and vermicelli soup (*soupe au pistou*). In Spain, parsley has a higher profile than elsewhere in the Mediterranean, forming the principal ingredient of *salsa verde*, the piquant green sauce (with olive oil, garlic, and shallots) that accompanies boiled meat or fish dishes. The Portuguese have a fondness for fresh cilantro in their soups, fish stews, and vegetable dishes.

Many Mediterranean dishes contain saffron, either in thin, silky threads or (more commonly) in powder form. It appears in the French seafood soup *bouillabaisse*, in Italian *risotto alla milanese,* and in Spanish *paella*, spreading aroma and a yellow hue. However, the cuisines of Spain and Portugal place more emphasis on spices than do those of France and Italy, with the most popular being paprika, chilies, cinnamon, nutmeg, cloves, and saffron.

Garlic

Pork is the most common meat of the region, and from it comes cured ham, popular throughout the Mediterranean. This is ham that has been salted, then hung and dried for several months; it is served in near-translucent slices. In Italy, the most famous kind is prosciutto, in France it is *jambon de Bayonne* (slightly smoked). The Spanish version is *jamon serrano* and the Portuguese *presunto*. Numerous varieties of pork sausage are also to be found.

From the sea comes a host of ingredients: red mullet, anchovies, sardines, sea bass, hake, sole, monkfish, mussels, scallops, squid, cuttlefish, lobster, spiny lobster, clams, and shrimp. Fish stews are prevalent throughout the region: *brodetto* (Italy), *caldeirada* (Portugal), *zarzuela de pescado* (Spain), and bouillabaisse (France).

As well as being a primary ingredient, fish is used as flavoring. A tuna mayonnaise sauce accompanies cold slices of poached veal in the Italian dish *vitello tonnato*. Likewise, anchovies are pounded into a paste with olive oil and garlic, to become the tangy fish sauce called *anchoïade* in France and *bagna cauda* in Italy.

A visit to any Mediterranean market demonstrates the region's abundance of fresh vegetables. Tomatoes are the basis of the well-known Spanish soup gazpacho, enhanced with raw peppers and cucumber. Onions contribute much to Mediterranean cuisine; chopped and lightly sautéed in olive oil, they are called *refogado* in Spain and *sofrito* in Portugal, and act as a base for many stews and sauces.

Bread is the automatic accompaniment to any meal, be it the French baguette or the Italian olive oil-based *ciabatta*. Rice is most common in Spain and Italy. For Italian risottos, the native Arborio rice is laboriously stirred in simmering stock, often with small pieces of meat, fish, or vegetables, until the liquid is absorbed and the rice cooked to a soft consistency. The paella dishes of Spain are similar, though usually on a larger scale. Portuguese cuisine has rice dishes similar to those of Spain while rice often accompanies the daubes (stews) of Southern France.

In Italy there are supposedly 200 different shapes and types of pasta, the country's celebrated staple. Pasta is made from durum wheat and comes in many forms: long, thin straws (*spaghetti*), flat noodles (*tagliatelle*), and squat tubes (*rigatoni*), among many other configurations. Popular sauces for pasta dishes include Bolognese (ground beef, onions, tomatoes, wine and herbs), carbonara (eggs, cream, and bacon) and vongole (clams). Other unique Italian staples include the much-loved pizza.

In Italy, egg yolks whisked with sugar and marsala and served warm is *zabaglione*. In France, it is called *sabayon*. The *flan* (baked caramel custard) is probably one of Spain's most popular dessert offerings.

As well as a wide variety of eating cheeses, France and Italy boast a large range of cooking cheeses. Most notable of these is Italy's hard, pungent Parmesan, often sprinkled on pasta dishes, and the softer, chewier *mozzarella*, which is a frequent topping for pizzas made outside Italy. The most widely eaten Spanish cheese is the firm-textured manchego, while *queijo da serra*, made from ewe's milk, is the most popular Portuguese cheese.

French olives

MENU GUIDE

Tortilla Española
Spanish omelet

Caldo Verde (Portugal)
Cabbage and potato soup

Vitello Tonnato (Italy)
Cold veal in a tuna sauce

Mejillones en Salsa Verde
(Spain)
Mussels in green parsley sauce

Riñones al Jerez (Spain)
Kidneys in sherry sauce

Lomo a la Naranja (Spain)
Loin of pork with oranges

Osso Buco (Italy)
Braised veal shin

Calamares en su Tinta
(Spain)
Squid cooked in its own ink

Brandade de Morue
(France)
*Salt-cod puree with olive oil
and croutons*

Risotto alla Milanese (Italy)
Creamy rice with saffron

**Arroz de Bacalhau com
Coentros** (Portugal)
Salt cod with cilantro

**Chanfana à moda da
Bairrada** (Portugal)
Kid or lamb in red wine

Daube de Boeuf Provençale
(France)
*Long-simmered beef stew with
wine, herbs, and garlic*

Granita all' Arancia (Italy)
Orange ice

Tiramisù (Italy)
*Cake layers or ladyfingers with
mascarpone and marsala*

Flan de Huevos (Spain)
Sweet egg custard

Clafoutis aux Cerises
(France)
*Cherries baked in a custard
batter*

Arroz Doce (Portugal)
Rice pudding

THE BRITISH ISLES

Britain has absorbed many culinary influences over the centuries. Early invaders included the Romans, from whose festive bread, *siminellus,* descends the Easter Simnel cake (with almond paste and dried fruit); the Vikings brought with them a fondness for pickled and smoked fish, and the Normans for dairy products. In addition, the British have always been great travelers and traders, with a love of spices and condiments. The influence of the British presence in India can still be seen, for example, in chutneys and pickles, as well as in the breakfast dish kedgeree (rice, fish, eggs, and spices, from the Indian dish *khichri*) and mulligatawny soup (spicy meat and vegetable broth). Peasant cooking remains a strong tradition, with one-pot dishes such as Lancashire hotpot (lamb), Welsh *cawl* (bacon and beef or lamb), and Irish stew (mutton). Suet figures prominently as either an extra (beef stew and dumplings) or a more substantial savory (steak and kidney pudding) or sweet (spotted dick, jam roly-poly) pudding. Roasts are very British, especially when served with roast potatoes and Yorkshire pudding (batter baked in hot beef fat). Sauces include horseradish sauce for beef, mint sauce for lamb, and applesauce for pork.
Fish has always been popular, whether fish and chips or regional dishes such as the Cornish stargazey pie (mackerel under pastry crust with the heads visible around the edges), as well as shellfish such as oysters, mussels, and cockles. Afternoon tea is an institution, with sweet breads (scones, crumpets, and muffins) spread with homemade preserves and sometimes cream, and cakes such as Bakewell tart, Eccles cakes, gingerbread, and flapjacks.

NORTHERN EUROPE

A characteristic of most North European nations is that they have not been subjected to the same deluge of invasions as the more southerly parts of Europe. They have invaded one another, but unlike Italy (invaded by Ottoman Turks) and Spain (occupied by North African Moors), which have been substantially influenced by the cooking of their invaders, Northern European cuisine has remained relatively insular.

Amid the different national cuisines, two distinct styles stand out. The first belongs to mainland Europe, covering northern France, Belgium, Holland, Germany, Austria, and Switzerland. This can be categorized as a predominantly meat-based diet, with emphasis on the taste of the basic ingredients rather than on added flavorings. The second style belongs to Scandinavia, a lighter, predominantly fish-based cuisine that is similarly concerned with the freshness and quality of raw materials.

In mainland Northern Europe, the moderate climate and generally fertile land provide an environment ideal for the raising of beef and dairy cattle, as well as sheep and pigs. Historically, meat has always been of sufficiently good quality not to need great embellishment from spices and herbs. More problematic has been the storage of meat after slaughter, which is why the predominant tastes—salting, marinating, and smoking—are all methods of prolonging storage as well.

After salt and pepper, the most common condiment is mustard, a blending of mustard seeds, vinegar, water, and salt, with the optional addition of herbs and spices. Particularly popular in Germany, along with horseradish (*Meerrettich*), mustard is used to accompany the vast range of Northern European charcuterie. In northern France, herbs are an important flavoring; the combination of bay leaf, thyme, and parsley, known as bouquet garni, is the flavor base for many stocks and stews. Tarragon is seen as the natural partner of chicken, and it features frequently in French mustards and vinegars.

Meats of all kinds are eaten throughout mainland Northern Europe: beef, rabbit, and chicken are common; duck, lamb, and game birds are enjoyed mainly in Germany and France. Germany is the capital of pork: boiled knuckle and smoked loin; thick broiled chops served with mustard, plain roast leg served with cabbage. Pork's relatives, ham (*Schinken*) and bacon (*Speck*), also abound in Germany; the most famous ham is a smoked variety from Westphalia, traditionally served with slices of buttered bread and glasses of *Steinhäger* (juniper-flavored brandy). Bacon is served plain or added to stews such as *Blundhuhn*, a combination of fava beans, bacon, fresh vegetables, apples, and pears. The variety of German *Würste*, or sausages, is immense; among the better known are *Leberwurst* (liver sausage), Brunswick *Mettwurst* (smoked pork sausage), *Weisswurst* (a white veal and herb sausage from Munich), and the famous Frankfurter, traditionally served in a roll with mustard. Austria, Belgium, Holland, and Switzerland share a similar enthusiasm for sausages. France leans toward pâtés and *rillettes* (potted meats) that are rich, spreadable mixtures made from pork, though some are blended with goose.

Beef is eaten in all regions. *Tafelspitz* is an Austrian and German specialty in which beef is braised and served with freshly grated horseradish. *Vlaamse karbonaden* is a Flemish dish in which beef is simmered in a rich beer broth. Veal is most commonly associated with Austrian cuisine, thanks to the celebrated *Wiener Schnitzel* in which thin veal scallops are coated with bread crumbs and then pan-fried.

As well as fish from the North Sea and the Atlantic (cod, herring, mackerel), seafood is in plentiful supply off the coasts of Brittany and Normandy. A classic French dish is *moules marinière*, mussels steamed with shallots and wine; the Belgians serve their mussels with fried potatoes. In addition, the rivers of the area yield freshwater carp, pike, and trout.

Bread is the staple of mainland Northern Europe, traveling the full range of flavors and colors, from dark brown German rye bread (pumpernickel) to the crisply baked white sticks of French bread known as baguettes. Rice features in Dutch cooking in the form of the dish *rijsstafel*, which is imported from Holland's erstwhile colony of Indonesia; it is a feast of meat, fish, and egg dishes all served with rice.

Throughout the area, potatoes are the almost automatic accompaniment to all main dishes. Sliced and deep-fried, they appear as *pommes frites* in Belgium and France; simmered in herb-infused milk then baked

Scandinavian cured salmon

Waterzooi (Belgium)
Fish soup with white wine

Svenska Köttbullar
Swedish meatballs

Königsberger Klopse
(Germany)
Meatballs in caper sauce

Leberknodel (Germany)
*Liver, bacon, and potato
dumpling*

Sole Normande (France)
*Sole and mussels in creamy
cider sauce*

Kalakukko (Finland)
*Rye bread layered with fish
and pork, and baked*

Dillkött (Sweden)
Veal in dill sauce

Karjalanpaisti (Finland)
Beef, pork, and mutton stew

Rösti (Germany)
*Fried potato cake with onion
and butter*

Poulet à la Normande
(France)
*Chicken cooked in Calvados
sauce with sautéed
apples*

Frikadeller (Denmark)
Veal and pork meatballs

Rote Grutze (Germany)
*A mold of summer fruits
served with milk or custard
sauce*

Sachertorte (Austria)
*Chocolate cake covered
with apricot jam and
chocolate frosting*

Stekta Äpplen med Sirap
(Sweden)
*Baked apples with golden
syrup*

Oeufs à la Neige (France)
*Poached meringues served
with custard sauce*

Rødgrod med Fløde
(Denmark)
Summer fruits with cream

with cream they become the golden brown *gratins* of France; formed into a crisp pan-fried potato cake, they become *Rösti* in Germany and Switzerland.

Apples are used in sweet and savory dishes such as the German specialty *Himmel und Erde* (Heaven and Earth), which is a puree of apples and potatoes topped with broiled blood sausage. Normandy apples feature in many tarts and other desserts.

Fruits are also used to fill the many cakes and confections enjoyed in North European coffeehouses. In Germany, *Schwarzwälder Kirschtorte* (Black Forest Torte) is a rich mixture of chocolate cake, cherries, whipped cream, and grated chocolate. Austria is renowned for its rich tortes (cakes), such as *Sachertorte* (chocolate cake filled with apricot jam and covered with chocolate frosting) and *Strudel*, made of thin pastry wrapped around a spiced fruit filling. The chocolate of Belgium and Switzerland is legendary, as are the spiced cookies, cakes, and buns of Holland; the best known are *Speculaas*, cookies that are made into windmill shapes and flavored with a mixture of ground sweet spices and almonds.

Dairy produce plays a vital part in the cuisine. Milk and butter (from France and Holland) are widely used in both sweet and savory recipes. Cheeses come in many hundreds of regional varieties. France is noted for its soft, pungent cheeses; other countries are associated with harder cheeses: Gouda and Edam (Holland), Gruyère and Emmental (Switzerland). The most famous Swiss dish is fondue, which revolves around a large pot of bubbling, melted cheese, sometimes flavored with kirsch or white wine, into which squares of bread can be dipped.

By contrast, the foods of Scandinavia tend to be lighter and altogether more fish oriented. This is due to the long, icy winters that turn dairy pastures into snowfields.

Mackerel, plaice, cod, haddock, and halibut from the sea and carp, pike, and trout from the rivers, are eaten widely. Salmon is often sliced thinly and marinated raw in salt, dill, and spices for *gravlax*. Herring are a more workaday alternative: they are smoked, cured or marinated, and eaten on their own or mixed into salads. In Finland they are even combined with meat in the dish *forshmak* (salted herring and chopped lamb). Other Finnish dishes are just as hearty: *karjalanpaisti* is a stew of beef, pork, and mutton; while reindeer meat is dried, smoked, or roasted and served with cranberries.

Dairy products feature in Scandinavia as well. Sour cream, sprinkled with sugar, is a traditional Norwegian breakfast, and also an ingredient in other fish and vegetable dishes traditional to the region. Milk and sour milk are popular beverages. The best-known cheeses of the area are Havarti (Denmark), Fontina (Sweden), and Danish blue.

Potatoes are another indispensable ingredient, particularly in Denmark. Here, they are cooked and pureed, made into salads, sliced and fried, or boiled in their jackets and then peeled and rolled in sweet caramel to give a crunchy coating.

Berries of all sorts thrive in Scandinavia, including rowanberries and cloudberries; from these are made soups, fruit compotes, and desserts such as Swedish *jortrontårta* (cloudberry tarts). Denmark is famous for its fruit-filled pastries, its rich confections containing apples and raisins, filled with spiced custard and sprinkled with chopped nuts and cinnamon.

119

RUSSIA

Spanning a range of climates from arctic to subtropical, and a spread of cultures from European to Central Asian, Russia has naturally absorbed many styles of cooking. From the North, the Swedes brought smoked herring and sour cream (*smetana*). From the Middle East came eggplants and mutton. From Germany came salted cabbage and the tradition of combining meat with fruit.

Root vegetables are the workhorses of Russian soups. Cabbage, carrots, parsnips, and potatoes are all used in the making of *shchi*, the hearty cabbage soup; *rassolnik* soup contains sorrel, cucumber, onion, and celery; *borshch* is a thick purple broth of beets, potatoes, carrots, onions, and cabbage. Breads are the most common staple: white sourdough bread (*balabouchki*), nearly black rye bread (*krouchenik*), and others with onion, cheese, and sesame seed flavorings. Flaky buckwheat (*kasha*) is also served to soak up stews and sauces. Pastry-wrapped salmon (*koulibiak*) is a court dish that has emigrated to the West, unlike the large range of pastries and puddings that rarely appear outside Russia. These include *krendiel* (sweet brioches), *gozhnaki* (walnut and honey cakes), and *kulich*, a sweet bread made with cinnamon, nutmeg, cardamom, and candied fruit peel, often served with *pashka* (sweetened cottage cheese pudding).

The main meal of the day is lunch, which consists of *zakuski* (a selection of hors d'oeuvres), soup, main course, then fruit or pastries. Vodka, plain or flavored (pepper, lemon, caraway seed), may be drunk, but an alternative is *kvass*, a kind of beer often flavored with fruit.

EASTERN EUROPE

For centuries, the countries of Eastern Europe have been pawns in the hands of larger empires: Roman, Austro-Hungarian, Ottoman, and Russian. Armies of countless different rulers have rampaged back and forth across the plains of Hungary, Poland, and Czechoslovakia, and through the hills of Yugoslavia, Romania, and Bulgaria.

To be′ sure, the victorious forces left their mark on the cooking of those countries. To this day, Turkish pastries are eaten in those parts where the Ottomans held sway, while Viennese-style cakes and strudels are still served in regions that were once ruled by the Austrian Hapsburgs. But at the same time as adopting the cuisines of their conquerors, the cooks of Eastern Europe remained loyal to their traditional dishes and methods of cooking.

Skewered spicy sausages, for example, are to be found throughout Eastern Europe. In Yugoslavia they are called *cevapcici* and are made of beef, lamb, or pork. Bulgarian *kebabche* are a similar mixture of veal and pork, and in Romania *mititei* (known as *mici*) are made of beef.

The longevity of many Balkan mountain dwellers is traditionally ascribed to their yogurt-based diet. Certainly yogurt appears

Assorted breads

with a large number of dishes throughout the area, as does sour cream. The Hungarian speciality *hortobagyi palacsinta* consists of pancakes filled with ground meat, onions, and paprika, surrounded by sour cream. The Poles serve a thick sour cream sauce with salt herring (*sledzie w smietanie*), and the Czech dish *svickova* (baked spicy beef and vegetables) is not complete without a pool of sour cream beside it.

Salting and smoking are the most common means of flavoring and preserving. For example, shredded cabbage is stored in barrels of salted water throughout the winter, and the Polish *kabanos* sausage is slowly smoked over juniper wood.

The taste of garlic leaps out of many cold meats and salamis, as well as from the cold Bulgarian *tarator* soup, in which it is combined with yogurt, cucumber, and ground walnuts. Dill, sorrel, and fennel add their distinctive flavors to soups and stews. Paprika (crushed, dried sweet red pepper) has become synonymous with Hungarian cooking and is the central flavoring of goulash, the thick beef, onion, potato, and tomato stew that is the country's well-known national dish.

Hardship has for centuries stalked this part of the world, with the result that East European chefs have long since developed an expertise in making a little meat stretch a long way. Thus, there is a profusion of different soups and vegetable-dominated stews found in each country. *Kapismak* is the classic Polish soup, filled with cabbage, celery, and bacon. *Gyuvech* (*ghiveciu* in Romania) is the name of a hearty Polish vegetable stew that usually includes peppers, beans, eggplants, and whatever meat is on hand.

Pork, followed by beef, is the most popular meat, especially in Czechoslovakia, where the specialties are roast pork (*veprova pecene*), pairs of pork sausage (*parky*), and sumptuous Prague ham, often baked in a thick bread crust. Lamb and suckling pig are served whole, but only on special occasions; chicken is more readily available. Country dwellers often have an advantage over the urban population in their access to game: wild boar from the Polish plains and venison, hare, and quail from the mountains of Romanian Transylvania.

Apart from Baltic herring, East Europeans mainly have to content themselves with freshwater fish—trout, carp, and the celebrated *fogas* (pike-perch), from Hungary's huge Lake Balaton.

Of all the vegetables, cabbage is the most popular, being used both to bulk up soups and stews and also to provide the "wrapper" for a rice, meat, and sauerkraut stuffing. This combination appears under different names: *tölltött kaposzta* (Hungary), *sarmi* (Bulgaria), *sarma* (Yugoslavia), and *sarmale* (Romania). In other words, stuffed cabbage, which is well-known in many countries.

Thick, hearty breads further supplement the cuisine. These come in many different forms. Romanians have *mamaliga*, which is a firmer version of Italian polenta. Bulgaria has a range of breads made with butter, cheese, and yogurt, which are dipped before each mouthful in a spicy, tarragon-flavored powder called *kubritsa*. Dumplings—*knedliky* in Czechoslovakia, *csipetke* in Hungary—appear as a matter of course in many dishes.

Buckwheat, a flaky, somewhat soapy-tasting staple, is widely eaten and is very popular in Poland. Pasta also features in some cuisines: Hungarian chefs use *tarhonya*, small pasta grains that are boiled then cooked with chopped onions; Yugoslavian pasta is particularly common on the Dalmatian coast (as is risotto), and the Polish dish *lazanki* can claim direct descent from lasagne, having been introduced in the sixteenth century by the king of Poland's young Italian bride.

All countries in this region have a well-developed pastry repertoire, of which the most elevated is Poland's. The tastiest creations of the Polish pastry chef include light *paczki* doughnuts filled with rose petal jam, deep-fried *faworki* (made with flour, cream, and rum), and little rectangular *mazurki* (pastry bases with a marzipan and chocolate topping). There is also a range of fluffy *babka* cakes, of which the most famous is the raisin-dotted *babka wielkanocna*, which is traditionally made at Easter.

MEALS

Breakfast in mainland Europe often consists of a variety of cold meats, cheeses, and breads. In many parts of Belgium, Austria, Holland, Switzerland, and Germany, hot coffee or chocolate is served. The two main meals of the day are interchangeable according to taste, but the larger tends to be after the day's work, in the evening.

Breakfast is a light meal in Denmark, Finland, and Sweden, usually just fresh bread and coffee. In Norway, where, in summer, daylight comes very early, it can be an enormous affair: fish, cold meats, fresh bread, hot waffles, cheese, and eggs, washed down with hot chocolate, milk or coffee. Lunch may consist of a hot vegetable soup and open sandwiches, called *smörrebröd* in Denmark and *violeipä* in Finland. Supper is another soup and a main dish. All countries have their versions of Sweden's famous *smörgåsbord*, which is a buffet meal of hot and cold dishes such as herring, cold meats, pâtés, salads, cheeses, and hot meat-filled pastry. Smörgåsbord is served in restaurants and homes, at lunchtime or as a evening meal.

Breakfast in Spain and Portugal is a brisk downing of coffee or hot chocolate and a pastry, or simply some toast. In Spain, a post-siesta snack (*merienda*) is usually eaten between 5:30 and 7 P.M., with dinner eaten as late as 11 P.M. The Portuguese take their evening meal much earlier (between 7 and 8 P.M.); in both countries, dinners are variations on lunchtime.

In Italy and southern France, buttered bread and strong coffee start the day, with lunch or dinner the larger meal according to taste and circumstances. In both countries fruit frequently takes the place of dessert, and in France cheese precedes the sweet course. The Sunday afternoon meal is a tradition in France: families gather around a well-laden table, often spending the rest of the day there, lingering over multiple main courses followed often by salad, cheese, dessert, coffee, and possibly a cognac or Armagnac.

Eastern European tradition does not frown on the early morning downing of a vodka or fruit brandy before venturing out into the winter subzero surroundings. This may also be accompanied by a steaming hot bowl of soup (*chorba*), filled to the brim with cabbage, beans, and small pieces of meat. City dwellers favor less hearty dawn fare—a mixture of cheese, bread, hard-boiled eggs, and salami is more typical—but in the middle of the day, rural and urban populations alike pause to enjoy the main hot meal of the day. The evening meal is usually a cold version of lunch, with warmth added by one of the region's many strong alcoholic distillations.

MENU GUIDE

Tarator (Bulgaria)
Cold garlic- and walnut-flavored yogurt soup

Caviar (Russia and Poland)
Salted sturgeon eggs

Rassolnik (Russia)
Sorrel and cucumber soup

Crni Rizoto (Yugoslavia)
Squid ink risotto

Hortobagyi Palacsinta
(Hungary)
Ground meat, onion, and paprika pancake

Sledzie w Smietanie
(Poland)
Salt herring and sour cream

Szeged halaszle (Hungary)
Goulash-style fish soup

Pui Cimpulugean (Romania)
Chicken stuffed with bacon, sausage, vegetables, and garlic

Pirozhki (Russia)
Hot savory pastries

Blinis (Russia)
Small buckwheat pancakes, often served with caviar

Hideg Fogas (Hungary)
Pike-perch in mayonnaise

Koulibiak (Russia)
Salmon baked in pastry

Cholent
(Poland and Russia)
Beef baked with onions, buckwheat, and potatoes

Mamaliga (Romania)
Polenta bread

Lazanki (Poland)
Pasta squares baked with ham, mushrooms, and cabbage

Paczki (Poland)
Light doughnuts filled with rose petal jam

Sharlotka (Russia)
Charlotte Russe—sponge cake with custard and fruit puree

NORTH AFRICA

Almonds*
Cardamom*
Cassia*
Chermoula
Chick-peas
Chilies*
Cilantro*
Cinnamon*
Cloves*
Couscous
Cubeb pepper*
Cumin*
Dates
Eggplants
Fenugreek*
Garlic*
Gingerroot*
Grapes
Harissa*
Honey*
La kama
Mint*
Nutmeg*
Olives*
Onions*
Oranges*
Parsley*
Pickled lemons
Pine nuts
Raisins
Ras-el-hanout*
Rosebuds
Sesame seeds*
Turmeric*
Wheat

(*see Index)

Like their Middle Eastern neighbors, the North Africans enjoy a daily cuisine that originated many centuries ago and many hundreds of miles away. They inherited the Persian penchant for combining meat and fruit, and have fallen willing victims to the Turkish sultans' weakness for sweets. Even today, in the smartest Tangier or Tunis hotel, North Africans are still roasting lamb in the same way that Arabian desert nomads did a thousand years ago.

But as well as absorbing the foods and flavorings of other peoples, the North Africans have developed their own highly individual cuisine. This is a cuisine in which a chef might use twenty-five spices in a dish, or just one; a cuisine in which one national dish—*bstilla*, or pigeon pie—contains as many as fifty carefully constructed layers of delicately spiced stuffing and another—couscous—is the embodiment of peasant rough-and-readiness. It is a distinctive mixture of forceful, spice-driven main dishes and delicate little nut and date desserts. Like the land that has shaped it, the cuisine of North Africa is a juxtaposition of the wild and the lush, the barren and the fertile.

INFLUENCES

Two thousand years ago, the land mass that is modern-day Morocco, Algeria, Tunisia, and Libya was just one country, known as the Maghreb. It was home to the Berbers, a pale-skinned, blue-eyed race who for many centuries had pursued a nomadic life within its vast and arid interior.

Having a long coastline, the Maghreb was open to any seaborne invaders or colonizers, and the first to arrive in numbers were the Phoenician traders from northwest Syria, in the first millennium B.C.. The Phoenicians made many long sea journeys and required meat that was easy both to preserve and to store; their solution was a dried sausage. This became the direct ancestor of the spicy North African *merguez*. After the Phoenicians came the Carthaginians, who introduced durum wheat and its by-product, semolina, which the resourceful Berbers adapted for couscous, now the staple of the area as a whole.

In the seventh century A.D., the invading Arab armies brought many spices and the word of the prophet Muhammad. Seven centuries later, the sweet-toothed Turkish Ottomans established a pastry repertoire that the North Africans have since elevated to a high state of refinement.

In 1715, European merchants and colonizers took over, following the Ottoman demise in North Africa. The Italians left their mark with pasta, the French with their language, and the British with tea, which they successfully encouraged the local inhabitants to mix with the traditional mint brew, thereby creating *chai bi naa'naa,* the mint tea that is now universally popular throughout the Maghreb region.

FLAVORINGS

Tastes vary among the different peoples of the Maghreb. The Moroccans like rich, full flavors (particularly saffron), the Algerians favor less spicy dishes, and the Tunisians find food bland without some chili- or gingerroot-generated heat.

Chefs express their own preferences in the range of spices they choose to put in their *ras-el-hanout.* Meaning literally "top of the shop," ras-el-hanout is a mixture of up to twenty-five different spices and flavorings, which may include cardamom, cassia, mace, chilies, cloves, cumin, fenugreek, nutmeg, lavender, and dried roses.

Another distinctively North African flavor is *chermoula*, a powerful puree of onion, garlic, cilantro, chilies, chili powder, paprika, salt, pepper, and saffron. Gentler, more aromatic flavoring comes from the Moroccan spice mixture *la kama*, a blend of black pepper, turmeric, ground ginger, cumin, and nutmeg, often used to bring soups and stews to life. Tunisian *harissa* is a fiery paste (see page 71) often served with couscous, and *tabil* is another Tunisian chili-based paste made with garlic, cilantro, and caraway seeds.

Main-course dishes will often come with pickled lemons, which serve as part relish, part vegetable.

OTHER INGREDIENTS

As in most Muslim countries, lamb and mutton are the most common meats and feature in many regional dishes. Merguez sausages are made of coarsely-chopped mutton, garlic, and ras-el-hanout. *Meshwi* is

Ras-el-hanout

spit-roasted lamb, and *choua* is steamed lamb with cumin. Rabbit and goat are also eaten, and poultry is the basis for many dishes, including *tajines*, which are slow-cooking stews, usually featuring fruit (dates or prunes) and honey. These dishes get their name from the tajine pot in which they are cooked; this is a round earthenware dish, sometimes ornately painted, topped by a tall, conical lid that looks like a witch's hat.

Wheat, rather than rice, is the main staple throughout the Maghreb. Northern Arabs eat the flat, round disks of lightly leavened Arabic bread, of which *kesra* is a tasty

variant, spiced with sesame and aniseed. Couscous, also a wheat product, is made of tiny semolina pellets. In many parts of the area, couscous made in the traditional manner is subjected to a delicate ritual that alternates steaming and hand-fluffing.

Local bakers are particularly skilled in the making of thin, near-transparent pastry, known as *malsouga* in Tunisia. This pastry is used not only for bstilla but also for the colorful range of brown, red, and gold pastries that are to be found stacked up beneath the fluorescent lights of North Africa's countless cake shops.

In those parts of the Maghreb that are not desert, vegetables abound. The most common are zucchini, peppers, fava beans, carrots, turnips, eggplants, celery, leeks, onions, and chick-peas. These usually form the vegetable content of the chicken or lamb stew that is served in a flavorful broth alongside mounds of couscous.

As well as the soil, the sea is a rich source of food: mullet, hake, sea bass, and pilchards are the most common catch. Chermoula is often used with fish, either as a marinade or as a flavor enhancer in fish soups.

MEALS

Many North Africans begin the day with soup, often *harira* (lamb) and lentil broth, flavored with saffron and la kama.

Before eating, all diners ritually wash their hands in water that is passed around the table in a jug. For special occasions, the meal might start with pigeon pie, continue with a chicken dish, and feature couscous as its centerpiece. This is cooked in a special, two-tiered casserole called a *couscousière*. Meat and vegetables are simmered in the lower level, sending steam up into the upper compartment, which contains the couscous. Before serving, the couscous is mounded on a platter and a hollow is made in the center. The cooked meat and vegetables are placed inside, and harissa is served on the side. Couscous is eaten with the fingers, the grains being rolled into balls and occasionally anointed with the broth in which the meat and vegetables have been cooked. Dessert usually consists of pastries, fruit, or a sweet semolina confection washed down by mint tea.

MENU GUIDE

Harira (Morocco)
Lamb and lentil broth

Merguez
Spicy sausages

Brik à l'oeuf (Tunisia)
Seasoned tuna and egg wrapped in thin pastry sheets and lightly fried

Chakchouka (Tunisia)
North African ratatouille made with brown sugar, often topped with beaten egg

Couscous
Semolina with meat and a vegetable stew in broth

Djej M'Ahmar
Chicken stuffed with couscous

Salata Meshwiya (Tunisia)
Salad made with tuna, egg, and vegetables

Bstilla (Morocco)
Minced pigeon pie

Djej Tajine (Morocco)
Chicken stewed with prunes and honey

Arnhab Chermoula
(Morocco)
Roast marinated rabbit

Zaytun Meshwi (Tunisia)
Olive-dotted beef balls

Dolma Gara (Algeria)
Stuffed zucchini

Tajine Malsouka
Meat, bean, and egg stew flavored with saffron and cinnamon encased in phyllo pastry

Limon Makboos
Pickled lemons

Mahancha (Morocco)
Thin almond-stuffed pastries

Righaif (Morocco)
Honey and sesame pancakes

Ghoriba (Tunisia)
Light pastry balls

Chai bi naa'naa
Mint tea

AFRICA

L ike the continent itself, African cooking can be described in only one word: "big." Bulging across the center of the globe, this vast land contains a riotous array of nationalities, cultures, and religions. Its climate, too, touches all ends of the meteorological spectrum: while the Kalahari Desert in the south might not see rain for years, Mount Cameroon, looming large in the west, has the world's second highest rainfall.

But for all Africa's diversity, its chefs are united by hardship: much of the soil is lacking in vital nutrients and many areas are subject to savage droughts. And where food is available, the equipment with which to cook is frequently primitive. Accordingly, the disparate strands of African cuisine are brought together by a thread of inventiveness. From the Sahara to the Cape, meals are characterized by tastiness, heartiness, and a determination to nourish and sustain against often inhospitable conditions.

TRADITIONAL INGREDIENTS

Atokiko (ground mango stone)
Avocados
Bananas
Bitter-leaf
Black-eyed peas
Camel butter
Cardamom*
Cassava
Chilies*
Cilantro*
Cinnamon*
Cloves*
Coconut*
Curry powder*
Dates
Dried fish*
Egusi (melon seeds)
Fenugreek*
Garden-egg (eggplant)
Gari
Garlic*
Gingerroot*
Lemon*
Maize (corn)
Mangoes
Millet
Nutmeg*
Ochroe (okra)
Palm oil
Pawpaw (papaya)
Peanuts*
Plantains
Rice
Sorghum
Sweet potatoes
Tomatoes*
Yams

(*see index)

INFLUENCES

A thousand years before the birth of Christ, powerful African kingdoms were exchanging gold, slaves, and ivory for the produce of India, China, Greece, and the Middle East. But of all these trading partners, it was Arab merchants who left the strongest imprint. From the north, their camel trains plodded across the Sahara bearing salt, spices, and herbs. From the east, their *dhows* came laden with mint, saffron, cilantro, cloves, and cinnamon. Nor was it just foodstuffs that arrived. The Arabs also brought the Islamic religion, and today the annual fast-feast cycle of Ramadan and Lebaran is observed by large numbers of African Muslims.

It was not until the fifteenth century that Portuguese explorers brought sub-Saharan Africa into direct contact with Europe. From this nation of seafarers came imports such as citrus fruits, chili, corn, pineapple, and tomato. Today, in their former colonies of Angola and Mozambique, the stamp of Iberian cuisine lingers in the crusty rolls eaten for breakfast and in dishes such as kid cooked in Madeira wine.

The Portuguese were just the tip of a massive colonial iceberg that melted over Africa in succeeding centuries. And where each European nation deposited its settlers, it also deposited its cuisine. In West Africa, the French instilled an appreciation of snails. In Kenya, the British introduced the genteel delights of strawberries, raspberries, and asparagus. South Africa felt the sticky bite of the Dutch sweet tooth: coconut, sweet potato, and creamy cinnamon custard tarts abound, as do delights such as *koeksusters*, sweet braids of dough that are deep-fried and then dipped in a sugary syrup coating.

With the Europeans came their indentured laborers, who added their own exotic tang to African menus. Throughout East and South Africa, pilaf rice, curry, and samosas remain as an edible legacy of Britain's Indian Empire. Dutch trading vessels left behind Malaysian slaves to long-lasting culinary effect. *Sosatie*, for example, is the name of a South African specialty made of cubed spiked mutton served with spicy sauce, which derives directly from the Malay word *sesate*, meaning "meat on a skewer."

FLAVORINGS

There is no smoke without fire in the African kitchen. And as stoves are lit throughout the continent, so cooks reach for their chilies. Of the many varieties to hand, the most common are the plump, bombastic Scotch bonnet and a fierce imp called pilli-pilli. A volcanically hot, but compulsory sauce, called *periperi*, is used almost universally as a condiment. Chili combines again with ginger, black pepper, cardamom, ajowan, and other spices in the mouth-tingling Ethiopian spice mixture, *berber* (see page 97).

Not all African flavorings are such palatebusters. Palm oil, for example, plays a prominent part in West African cooking, lending a pungent flavor and striking red-gold hue to every dish it touches. One such

preparation is *joloff* rice, originally from Sierra Leone, but now a festive dish enjoyed throughout West Africa, which combines chicken marinated in lemon with rice, in a sauce of palm oil, chilies, and tomatoes. The palm oil turns the rice a deep orange, and the finished dish is garnished with onion rings and tomatoes.

Elsewhere, the most common cooking oil comes from peanuts, which also provide a rich and versatile source of protein. All over the continent they are roasted as snacks or used as a flavoring in the cooking pot. Many versions of peanut stew—chicken simmered in a sauce thick with peanuts—can be found in almost every country. Little balls of pounded peanut paste are a popular and nutritious snack.

In the tropical regions, coconuts are a prominent ingredient, and their flesh can be grated into stews as a flavorful thickener or deep-fried in strips for succulent snacks. The milk, meanwhile, makes a rich stock for cooking rice, beans, sweet potatoes, and other vegetables.

OTHER INGREDIENTS

Spices may give spirit, but it is starches that keep body and soul together. And nowhere is this truer than in Africa. Whether grain, pulse, or root, these basic foodstuffs provide nourishment, bulk, and a more neutral complement to the fiery seasonings that are used throughout the continent.

These staples vary with Africa's climate. Where there is plenty of rainfall, as in West and Central Africa, rice reigns supreme. Elsewhere, corn and drought-resistant millet and sorghum come into their own. In South Africa, for example, corn is pounded into a standard filler described aptly as "stiff porridge" or baked into loaves of a hearty bread known as *mielie*. In Ethiopia, millet flour is turned into a sour flatbread, known as *ingera*, which is as vital to everyday eating as the *baguette* is in France. Any of these grains can be made into dumplings that are wrapped in banana leaves and steamed.

Roots such as cassava, yam, and sweet potato appear on every menu. And although foreign in origin, they have been given a robust versatility to match the nature of African cooking. They can be boiled or mashed, cut into chunks and splashed into stews, or sweetened with sugar, sprinkled with cinnamon, and baked, or pounded with palm oil and made into a deep orange "bread." Plantains—which are large, green, cooking bananas—are another versatile food that can be roasted, boiled, mashed, fried, or fermented, for use in a wide range of sweet or savory dishes.

Africa also has its own unique taste sensations. Where else, for example, might one make an omelet for twelve out of a single egg—ostrich offerings weigh in at approximately 3 lb (1.5 kg) apiece—or battle one's way through a giant Achatina landsnail? In what other continent might one spoon through a bowl of crocodile or snake stew? And on what other menu might a diner waffle between fried locusts and white ants?

MEALS

A typical African meal consists of just one course, usually a thick stew—short on meat, long on oil, brimming with vegetables, and bursting with spicy flavors—plus one of the substantial, starchy puddings or dumplings used as a tasty utensil to scoop up the juicy morsels. Desserts, meanwhile, come as nature provides them, in the form of fresh fruits such as pineapple, granadilla (passion fruit), or mango.

In Senegal, Christmas is marked by the lemony aroma of *yassa*, a dish in which chicken is marinated in garlic, cloves, chili, and lemon juice before being fried in palm oil and simmered in a lemon sauce. It is accompanied by rice on a large platter. Diners sit in a circle around the platter and eat with their hands.

And in those few places where the European influence still prevails, mealtimes carve the day into the orderly European trinity of breakfast, lunch, and dinner. Even then, the tastes of Africa are evident. A typical South African breakfast might start with a fresh papaya before progressing to bacon and eggs; a lunchtime barbecue might include skewers of wild game or spicy *boerewors* sausages as well as regular hamburgers; and dinner might consist of *bobotie*, Africa's answer to traditional Shepherd's pie—curried ground beef and flaked almonds topped with a white sauce.

MENU GUIDE

Egusi (Nigeria)
Soup flavored with melon seed, spinach, dried shrimp, and palm oil

Tatale (Ghana)
Plantain cake

Nkui (Cameroon)
Okra and corn soup

Akkras (West Africa)
Black-eyed pea fritters

Dovi (Zimbabwe)
Chicken and peanut stew

Doro Wat (Ethiopia)
Chicken and hard-boiled eggs in a chili sauce

Matoke Ngege (Uganda)
Plantain and fish stew

Paleva (Sierra Leone)
Beef and melon seed stew

Joloff Rice (West Africa)
Spicy chicken and rice dish

Ndizi Na Nyama (Tanzania)
Meat stew with plantain and coconut

Yassa (Senegal)
Chicken simmered in a pungent lemon sauce

Bobotie (South Africa)
Curried ground beef and almond pie, covered with a white sauce

Pondu (Zaire)
Cassava leaf with palm oil, eggplants, and dried fish

Dioumbre (Ivory Coast)
Mutton stew flavored with okra and palm oil

Sosaties
(Zimbabwe and South Africa)
Spicy mutton kabobs

Foofoo (West Africa)
A stiff pudding of mashed yam or plantain

Ugali (East Africa)
A stiff pudding of corn flour

Bassi Salte (Senegal)
Couscouslike dish made from millet

CARIBBEAN

Stamp and Go, Run Down, Dip and Fall Back—the dishes themselves tell the story of Caribbean cooking. Spread across the Gulf of Mexico like a string of tropical beads, the islands of the Caribbean offer an adamantly exuberant cuisine. Onto Amer-Indian origins have been added European, African, and Asian influences. The whole has then been stirred, seasoned, and served up in a unique compote of creativity.

Caribbean chefs make the most of a rich natural bounty. The fertile soil sprouts a profusion of tropical produce, while creeks, lakes, and rivers combine with the sea to provide a superabundance of fish and shellfish. Each nation has its own specialty—saltfish and ackee in Jamaica, *colombo* in Martinique, *jug-jug* in Barbados, to mention just some—but thanks to culinary island-hopping, every dish appears in different guises throughout the region. The result is a cuisine that, like the islands themselves, is hot, colorful, and decidedly eclectic.

TRADITIONAL INGREDIENTS

Ackee
Allspice*
Annatto*
Arrowroot
Bananas
Beans
Breadfruit
Calabash (gourd)
Calabaza (pumpkin)
Callaloo
Cassareep
Cassava
Chayote
Chilies*
Cilantro*
Cinnamon*
Cloves*
Coconut*
Curry powder*
Gingerroot*
Limes*
Mangoes
Molasses*
Mushrooms*
Nutmeg*
Okra
Pigeon peas
Plantains
Saffron*
Sweet potatoes
Tamarind*
Thyme*
Vanilla*

(*see Index)

126

INFLUENCES

In 1492, Christopher Columbus stumbled across a remarkably beautiful archipelago stretching between North and South America. He was two oceans and two continents away from his ultimate goal of India, nevertheless he dubbed his discovery the West Indies, and claimed for Spain as many islands as he could find.

The lands Columbus discovered were inhabited by two peoples, the Arawak and Carib Indians, who subsisted mainly on farming and fishing. The mainstay of their diet, however, was provided by nourishing roots such as cassava and sweet potatoes—a legacy that lingers to this day.

It was not long before the West Indies were swamped by Spanish settlers, who brought with them such staples as bananas, mangoes and coconuts. But the most devastating import crop was sugar cane. It grew well, and before long, Britain, France, and Holland were vying with Spain for a slice of the sweet Caribbean pie.

Islands were seized, fought over, and exchanged according to the vagaries of European politics. Today the cooking of each island reflects the outcome of those distant power struggles. French technique and Caribbean flavors merge in the cooking of Martinique and Guadeloupe. The presence of Holland is unmistakable in Curaçao's *keshy yena coe cabaron*, a scooped-out Edam cheese stuffed with shrimp. And jug-jug, a traditional Christmas dish from Barbados, is comprised of ground beef, pork, pigeon peas, and millet—no more than a homesick haggis from Scotland.

But above all it is the flavors of Africa that dominate Caribbean cooking. Okra, yam, pigeon peas, plantain, *taro,* a tuber that is similar in appearance to yam, is also known as *dasheen*. It closely resembles rutabaga in texture, and its leaves, which are called *callaloo*, all are staples that owe their origins to Africa.

Through the centuries, this culinary melting pot was enriched by the arrival of other immigrants: Jews fleeing the Spanish Inquisition, Britons leaving the newly independent United States, merchants from Lebanon and Syria, and, after the abolition of slavery, indentured laborers brought from India and China to work the land.

FLAVORINGS

The chili, in all its diverse manifestations, is the undisputed queen of the Caribbean kitchen. Every island—and possibly every household—has its particular version of hot pepper sauce, colored red with tomatoes or golden with turmeric. It can be made with just onion and chili or with a number of additional spices and flavorings.

Other flavorings are gentler to the tongue. The native spice annatto (see page 60), for example, has long been prized for the delicate flavor and strong red color it imparts to food.

Pepper sauce

Allspice, from the small round berries of a tree indigenous to Jamaica, is another valued ingredient, as is coconut milk. A flavoring peculiar to the Caribbean is *cassareep*. It is made from the juice of the cassava root that is boiled with sugar, cinnamon, and cloves until thick.

Curry powders are common throughout the region, reaching an apogee of complexity in Trinidad. And marinating, known as "seasoning-up," is a much-used cooking method on English-speaking islands. A typical seasoning-up may include chopped chives, oregano, celery leaves, grated onion, crushed garlic, mashed chilies, ground cloves, and lime juice. The resulting mixture is liberally rubbed over meats, poultry, or fish before stewing or barbecuing.

OTHER INGREDIENTS

Being islanders, it is hardly surprising that West Indian chefs make extensive use of seafood. Every conceivable kind of marine creature graces the Caribbean table—parrot fish, flying fish, red snapper, land crab, scampi, and conch. The list is endless—as are the different methods of cooking. Seafood is marinated in lime juice and then skewered on kabobs; slowly baked with herbs and garlic; simmered in a tamarind

and coconut sauce; fried in a seasoning of crushed gingerroot, garlic, and thyme; and stewed with pumpkin, or curried with green mangoes and potatoes.

The Caribbean abounds with tropical fruit and vegetables, almost all of which are put to excellent and imaginative use. Stuffed dishes are particularly popular—breadfruit with saltfish, green papaya with spicy meat, and pumpkin with shrimp. The cooking banana is a prime example of tropical versatility. The large green plantain, for instance, can be used unripe, ripe, or overripe, in sweet or savory dishes. It can be boiled, mashed, roasted, fried, chopped, or simply served as it is. Banana leaves, meanwhile, impart a delicate flavor when wrapped around cornmeal and meat packages, otherwise known as conkies in Barbados and tie-a-leaf in Jamaica.

Starchy roots such as yam, cassava, and sweet potato provide filling bulk in an equally versatile manner. They also cater for the sweet-toothed diner when transformed into delicious cakes, puddings, or pies and flavored with rum, molasses, coconut, raisins, nutmeg, and cinnamon.

MEALS

A popular start to the Caribbean day is cassava bread fried in butter, but heartier dishes are also common. The traditional Jamaican breakfast is saltfish and ackee—a fruit that appears aptly like scrambled egg. On the English-speaking islands, a brunch might consist of pudding and souse— blood sausage and the lime-marinated meat of pig's head, tongue, and feet.

A typical family meal consists of a big one-pot dish packed with vegetables, legumes, meat, or fish, cooked in a spicy sauce and served with slightly flattened cornmeal dumplings bobbing on top. This will be accompanied by *foo-foo* (pounded plantains) or hot buttered corn bread. Alternatively, a drier main course will be eaten with some starch such as boiled cassava or yam, foo-foo, rice and peas, cornmeal and okra, or bakes (fried biscuits) and a vegetable such as spiced eggplant, mashed pumpkin, or stewed okra. Dessert is usually fruit based, making good use of local produce for puddings, custards, and ice cream.

MENU GUIDE

Acras de Morue
(Guadeloupe)
Salt cod fritters with chilies

Janga (Jamaica)
Crayfish cooked in court bouillon with chilies

Crabes Farcies (Martinique)
Stuffed crabs with chilies, coconut milk, and lime juice

Conkies (Barbados)
Banana leaves filled with mashed sweetened plantains

Callaloo (All islands)
Soup with callaloo leaves, vegetables, salt pork, coconut milk, and spices

Keshy Yena coe Carni
(Curaçao)
Whole Edam cheese with beef stuffing

Pepperpot (All islands)
Meat stew with cassareep and chilies

Daube de Lambis aux Haricots Rouges
(Guadeloupe)
Conch and kidney bean stew

Fowl Down-in-Rice
(Barbados)
Chicken with rice

Colombo de Poulet
(Martinique and Guadeloupe)
Chicken curry

Berehein na Forno
(St. Maarten)
Eggplants in coconut cream

Coo-Coo (Barbados)
Cornmeal pudding with okra

Bakes (Trinidad)
Fried savory biscuits

Bullas (Jamaica)
Brown sugar and ginger cookies

Boija (St. Croix)
Sweet coconut corn bread

Gâteau de Patate (Haiti)
Sweet potato cake

SOUTH AMERICA

Spain's conquistadores never found El Dorado, the fabled city of gold, when they stormed into South America during the sixteenth century. But they did discover something just as valuable—an array of exotic foods that literally doubled the contents of the world's pantries, and changed global eating patterns almost overnight.

The resulting cuisine is an amalgam of New World ingredients and Old World cooking that varies from country to country. Brazil, for example, boasts an exuberant mix of African, Portuguese, and Guarani Indian flavors. In the Andean states of Peru and Ecuador, indigenous ingredients such as chilies and potatoes prevail. The rolling grasslands of Argentina provide beef in abundance, and Chile's lengthy coastline is an unparalleled source of seafood.

TRADITIONAL INGREDIENTS

Almonds*
Annatto*
Bananas
Black-eyed peas
Black turtle beans
Brazil nuts*
Cashews*
Cassava
Chick-peas
Chilies*
Cilantro*
Cinnamon*
Cloves*
Coconut*
Corn
Cuy (guinea pigs)
Erizos (giant sea urchins)
Hearts of palm
Lima beans
Mangoes*
Mustard*
Nutmeg*
Okra
Olives*
Oranges*
Papayas
Parsley*
Peanuts*
Pineapple
Pine nuts
Plantains
Pumpkin
Rice
Salt cod
Seafood
Sugarcane
Sweet potatoes
Tomatoes*
Walnuts*

(*see Index)

INFLUENCES

Rome's viaducts were still just a gleam in the architect's eye when the Incas were channelling hillside torrents into massive irrigation channels, some up to 1.2 miles (2 kilometers) long, to link the disparate valleys of their empire. They were fine agriculturalists, and the fruits of their labor crammed the marketplaces of imposing stone cities perched atop Peru's mountains. But these were no common marketplaces. South American civilization had grown up in complete isolation, and its cuisine was different from any to be found elsewhere in the world. The farmers of the Andean hillsides, for example, were pioneers in potato cultivation. Millennia before the rest of the world learned the art of freeze-drying, they were pounding their potatoes into pulp that was alternately frozen by night and thawed by day until it formed a dehydrated, rock-hard lump that could be either stored for the future or ground into flour for immediate use.

The potato was just one of the culinary surprises that greeted the Portuguese and Spanish invaders when they colonized South America during the sixteenth century. Some of the others included corn, chilies, tomatoes, beans, and guinea pigs.

Foodwise, the newcomers gave almost as good as they got. The introduction of cattle brought beef, butter, cheese, and milk into the kitchen. Wheat, rice, and sugarcane were further welcome imports. The Iberians also passed on the secrets they had learned during 800 years of Arab occupation. Egg and sugar rice cakes, puddings, and Portuguese desserts became popular in Brazil, the vast, potbellied land that Portugal had claimed for its own.

Slave labor that was brought over from the African continent added another layer of foreign flavor: more chilies, along with okra, palm oil, ginger, and melon seeds.

When the floodgates of European colonialism burst open during the late nineteenth and early twentieth centuries, more settlers arrived, bringing with them their own culinary customs and preferences. The resulting blend is a cuisine that varies from region to region, but is uniquely South American in its rumbustious vigor.

FLAVORINGS

Despite the many different peoples that have settled in South America over the years, it is the old, indigenous flavors that still dominate. The exceptions are rice, to which all of South America took with enthusiasm, and parsley and cilantro, which were adopted as the favorite herbs.

Peruvian cooking is notable for its lavish use of chilies, not only in food preparation but also in freshly made sauces that appear on the table at every meal. A Peruvian market, even today, is filled with piles of red, orange, yellow, and green chilies that come in a multitude of shapes, sizes, and degrees of hotness.

Another typically Peruvian ingredient is the native corn, available in many colors including purple. When simmered in water, this releases a beautiful color and a flowery, lemonlike perfume, providing an ideal liquid base for desserts that are thickened with cornstarch, or jellied.

In the northern countries, chefs infuse annatto seeds in their cooking oil to impart a light, delicate flavor and warm orange color to meat and poultry dishes.

In Colombia, coconut milk figures prominently as a cooking liquid. Sauces are thickened with nuts, and it is common to find meat cooked with the many indigenous tropical fruits. Nuts, too, are commonplace in Brazil—not only Brazil nuts, named after the country itself, but also peanuts, a reminder that, until divided by the earth's shifting crust, South America and West Africa were joined together.

Food from Brazil is also marked by the bright orange color of palm oil—an African import—and by the imaginative use of cassava. A vital staple for the native Guarani Indians, cassava root is ground to a meal that is toasted and sprinkled over dishes in the manner of Parmesan cheese, and imparts a distinctive, nutty taste.

OTHER INGREDIENTS

Of the many other items in South American kitchens, perhaps the most common is the potato. By the time the Spaniards arrived in Peru, the Incas had already developed over a hundred different varieties of potato —white, yellow, black, or purple in color, and in numerous sizes and flavors. One of Peru's most notable potato creations is *causa a la chiclayana*. This hearty and attractive dish consists of potatoes served with a sauce of ground walnuts, cheese, chillies, onions, and garlic and garnished with sliced ears of corn, fried fish or shrimp, hard-boiled eggs, cassava root, and black olives.

But potatoes are not all South America has to offer. Along both seaboards—the Pacific especially—there is an abundance of magnificent shellfish: abalone, scallops, conch, lobsters, and clams. In Chile, for example, a local dish to look out for is *erizos al matico*—giant sea urchins cooked with chopped onions, lemon juice, and seasonings. This is usually served as a first course but is robust enough to provide the bulk of a light lunch.

Across the Andes, in Argentina, it is beef that rules the roost. *Matambre*, which literally means "kill hunger," is a dish that comprises thinly sliced and pounded steaks, rolled around a mixture of spinach, carrots, and hard-boiled egg, and braised in a rich beef stock. In Uruguay, the same dish is served filled only with spinach. A bit farther inland, ground beef figures in *so'o-yosopy*, a robust Paraguayan soup with sweet peppers and chilies.

MEALS

Breakfast in South America consists for the most part of fruit or fruit juice, bread rolls, and tea, coffee, or hot chocolate. Lunch begins with appetizers, proceeds to soup, then a main course of meat, poultry, or fish, with vegetables and either potatoes or rice, and ends with fruit and coffee. Dinner is much the same, but possibly adds a separate fish course.

What exactly is eaten depends, of course, on where exactly the eater is. Each country has its own preferences. While salads are a common starter in any part of the continent, Ecuadorans are more likely to enjoy a plate of cooked vegetables—the high altitude means that water will boil at a lower temperature than normal, making the cook's task that much easier.

The cuisine varies not only from country to country but also, within the Andes nations (Peru, Venezuela, Colombia, Ecuador and Chile), it alters between highlands and lowlands. In Colombia, for example, a popular lowland dish is *sábalo guisado con coco* (shad fillets in coconut milk), while highland specialities include *ajiaco de pollo bogotano*—a chicken stew that uses two different types of potato and fresh corn. In the mountains of Ecuador, a first course of potato cakes, *llapingachos*, is served with tomato, avocado slices, and lettuce. On the coast, the same cakes appear fried in oil seasoned with annatto, and arranged alongside fried plantains and a peanut sauce.

From the German settlers came the art of making fine beers, and the French gave the continent both vines and wine-making skills. Coffee can be found everywhere, usually served very strong in a demitasse cup, with a little hot milk.

Empanadas Salteñas (Bolivia)
Small meat pies

Aguacates Rellenos (Ecuador)
Avocados stuffed with chopped ham, hard-boiled eggs, and mayonnaise

Ajiaco de Pollo Bogotano (Colombia)
Chicken stew with two kinds of potato and fresh corn

Llapingachos (Ecuador)
Annatto-colored potato cakes served with fried plantain and peanut sauce

Aji de Gallina (Peru)
Chicken in chili sauce

Sopa Paraguaya (Paraguay)
Corn bread made with two kinds of cheese

Feijoada Completa (Brazil)
Meat with black beans served with orange salad, kale, toasted cassava, rice, and chili and lime sauce

Pabellón Caraqueño (Venezuela)
Thin beefsteaks with rice, black beans, and plantains

Carbonada Criolla (Argentina)
Meat and vegetable stew with peaches and pears

Pudim de Bacalhau com Ovos (Brazil)
Baked eggs topped with salt cod in tomato sauce

Pichones con Salsa de Camarones (Peru)
Pigeons in shrimp sauce

Porotos Granados (Chile)
Beans with corn and pumpkin

Budín de Yuca (Guatemala)
Cassava-root soufflé

Torta de Zapallo (Ecuador)
Sweet pumpkin cake with cheddar-style cheese

Manjar Blanco (Chile)
Milk pudding

MEXICO

The cuisine of Mexico was born at the point of a musket, blending the dishes of the native peoples with those of their Spanish conquerors, and its fiery flavors linger like smoke from the encounter. From the ancient Aztec and Mayan civilizations come the basic foodstuffs such as corn, chilies, and tomatoes. Onto these has been grafted the Spanish love of sweets, marinades, and sauces. It is a hearty peasant kitchen relying on the region's profusion of fresh vegetables and dominated by the *tortilla*, a round pancake of unleavened corn flour that is as much a plate as a food. But the flavors are not without subtlety or variety. There are, for example, some fifty species of bean and over 140 different types of chili pepper, each of which has its own distinctive taste and appearance.

TRADITIONAL INGREDIENTS

Acitrón (candied cactus)
Allspice*
Annatto*
Avocados
Banana leaves*
Beans
Cactus paddles (nopales)
Chayote (squash)
Chilies*
Chocolate*
Cilantro*
Cinnamon*
Coconut*
Corn husks*
Epazote (herb)
Guavas
Hominy (corn)
Jerusalem artichokes
Jicama (root vegetable)
Lemon*
Lime*
Masa harina
Mushrooms*
Onions*
Oregano*
Papayas
Pine nuts
Plantains
Prickly pear cactus
Pumpkin
Pumpkin seeds
Squash blossoms
Sunflower seeds
Sweet corn
Tamarind*
Tomatillos
Tomatoes*
Tortillas
Vanilla*

(*see Index)

INFLUENCES

Like their South American neighbors, the Mexicans had climbed a long way up the culinary ladder before the Spaniards came. It was here, around 7000 B.C., that corn was first cultivated, as was the avocado. And shortly after, local tables were graced by the indigenous turkey, Muscovy ducks, venison, quails, pigeons, and a host of fish and shellfish. It was here, too, that chocolate was born.

These foods, along with potatoes, chilies, squash, tomatoes, and beans, formed the staple diet of the area when the Spanish overran the Aztec and Mayan civilizations in the early sixteenth century.

These conquistadores brought with them all the produce of Europe and, thanks to their trade links, exotic foodstuffs such as rice from India. One popular import was citrus fruit, which allowed coastal dwellers to develop *seviche*, which is the technique of marinating fish in citrus juice until it is "cooked" by the acidity (see page 174). Equally liked was pork, not least because it introduced lard to what had previously been a virtually fat-free diet. Foods that might once have been simply steamed in banana leaves or corn husks could now be fried or roasted.

It was not until the nineteenth century that Mexico regained its independence, but by that time the cuisine had solidified into a decidedly colonial whole.

Mexico's proximity to North America brought it bad news and good. Its neighbors seized large tracts of land, but at the same time took to their new subjects' food with uninhibited relish. North America gave Mexican cooking no new ingredients, but it did give it an unmistakable enthusiasm. It was *Norte Americanos* who gave the name *burritos*, "little donkeys," to the dish of tortillas stuffed with almost every conceivable filling. It was they, too, who came up with the idea of turning tortillas into deep-fried *taco* shells, ready to be filled with whatever ingredients were on hand. And, curiously, chewing gum originated not in America but from Mexico's *chicle*, made from the sticky sap of the *zapote* (sapodilla) tree.

FLAVORINGS

Chilies, onions, and pumpkin seeds are among the flavorings most commonly used in Mexican cooking. Close on their heels comes the tart green *tomatillo* (husk tomato), which is used nowhere else in the world. Mexican dishes themselves are not necessarily spicy, and often the chilies are made into an on-the-table sauce that can be heaped on to taste. Nor is there a monotony of chili flavor, thanks to the many varieties of pepper available. One popular type is the *poblano*, a hot, dark green pepper that forms the main ingredient in *chiles rellenos*—poblano chilies stuffed with cheese or spiced meat and deep-fried in a golden batter.

Salsa cruda and *salsa verde*, two of the most popular saucelike relishes, combine chilies and tomatoes or tomatillos to telling effect. Salsa cruda is simply tomato, chili, and onions. Salsa verde follows the same recipe but substitutes tomatillos for the tomatoes. Another popular relish is guacamole, made of pounded avocados flavored according to taste with tomatoes, chilies, onions, garlic, and cilantro. This is served as an accompaniment to many dishes, to be spooned onto food or simply scooped up with tortilla chips.

Cilantro—always the leaves and only rarely the seeds (coriander)—is immensely popular, figuring in numerous dishes, as does the indigenous *epazote*, a pungent-smelling herb essential to the cooking of black turtle beans. Annatto is used a great deal in the southern region Yucatán, and the juice of lemons and limes is squeezed into many dishes as a finishing touch.

Chocolate is perhaps the area's most famous contribution to global cuisine, and it features distinctively in Mexico's national dish, *mole poblano*—turkey steeped in a rich sauce thickened with nuts and seeds and flavored with tomatoes, chilies, and bitter chocolate.

OTHER INGREDIENTS

Because this region was the birthplace of corn, it is little wonder that its cooks make extensive use of it. Whole kernels (hominy) are cooked into hearty soups called *pozole*. Kernels are ground into a coarse flour (*masa harina*) for the making of tamales, meat or vegetable filled packets that are steamed in corn husks or banana leaves. And in the tortilla, finely ground corn becomes not so much an ingredient as an integral part of everyday life.

However, it is fresh fruit and vegetables that distinguish this cuisine. Thanks to the region's diverse topography, almost any edible plant can be grown somewhere, at some time of the year. The selection is enormous, ranging from avocados to mangoes to prickly pear cactus paddles.

Poultry and beef abound. These are usually stewed or grilled, as in *carne asada a la Tampiqueña*, the ubiquitous restaurant dish found throughout the country. This combines thinly sliced steaks served with an assortment of accompaniments: beans, tortillas, salsa, guacamole, cheese, and fresh onion slices. Pork, however, is the most succulent of the meats used, and it finds its

way into many traditional preparations such as spicy chorizo sausages, ground stuffings for peppers, and stews.

Seafood is also an important item in the kitchens of Mexico. And little wonder, considering that the Mexican coastline is over 6,000 miles (9,000 km) long. It is said that the Aztec emperor Montezuma had fresh fish delivered to him daily by relays of messengers traveling barefoot from the gulf to his capital of Tenochtitlán. Today, the seas provide coastal markets with an abundance of produce—such as red snapper, grouper, and shellfish—while rivers and lakes supply tasty freshwater fish including catfish, trout, and bass. Giant prawns, shark, and ray are among the many exotic species to be tasted, usually broiled with pepper and garlic.

MEALS

The Mexican day starts with *desayuno*, first breakfast, and consists of coffee or, more rarely, hot chocolate, and the sweet breads and pastries inherited from Spain. A second breakfast, *almuerzo*, comes at around mid-day and usually comprises a more substantial dish such as *huevos rancheros*, (country-style eggs) with *frijoles refritos* (refried beans) and a fresh chili sauce.

The high point of the day is *comida*, a sturdy afternoon meal served anytime between 2:00 and 5:30 P.M. The first course is usually a light soup such as consommé, followed by *sopa seca*, a "dry soup" that is actually a rice or pasta dish. Then comes a main course of fish, poultry, or meat with a salad or vegetables. After this comes a course of beans—usually pinto—served in a small bowl in their own thick cooking liquid. The whole might be accompanied by tortillas or *bolillos*, the Mexican equivalent of *petit pain* or small rolls. To round off the meal there is fruit, either fresh or stewed, or perhaps *flan*, caramel custard.

The Mexican day ends on a relatively subdued note. *Merienda*, a light supper, is served later in the evening and consists of bread, jam, blind (unfilled) tamales, and possibly some sliced boiled ham.

On special occasions, such as birthdays and weddings, eating might extend into the night, with *ceña*, a late dinner held most commonly in a restaurant.

Sopa de Lima
Lime soup

Guacamole
Mashed avocado with chopped onion, chilies, cilantro, and chopped tomatoes

Pozole Verde
Hominy soup with chicken, pork, and ground pumpkin seeds

Esquites
Fresh corn kernels fried with hot green chilies and chopped epazote

Calabacitas
Zucchini cooked with onion, garlic, tomatoes, and chilies

Hongos Guisados
Mushrooms with garlic, chopped epazote, chilies, and lime juice

Ensalada de Jícama
Jicama salad with oranges in a lime, cilantro, and chili dressing

Quesadillas Fritas
Corn tortilla turnovers filled with cheese

Frijoles Charros
Beans simmered with bacon and roasted chilies

Mole Poblano de Guajolote
Turkey in sauce of tomatoes flavored with chilies, pepper, cinnamon, and bitter chocolate

Pescado Adobado en Hojas de Maiz
Chili-marinated fish cooked in corn husks

Pescado a la Veracruzana
Fish with tomatoes, capers, olives, and chilies

Tamales de Dulce
Sweet tamales filled with candied fruit

Flan
Vanilla custard with a caramel sauce

NORTH AMERICA

TRADITIONAL INGREDIENTS

Apples
Avocados
Beef
Black-eyed peas
Blueberries
Catfish
Cheddar cheese
Chilies*
Chocolate chips*
Cinnamon*
Clams
Codfish
Crab
Cranberries
Crayfish
Cumin*
Dill*
Filé powder*
Gingerroot*
Ketchup*
Lima beans
Lobster
Maple syrup*
Molasses*
Okra
Oysters
Peanuts
Pecans*
Pumpkin
Rock Cornish hens
Salmon
Salsa*
Sarsaparilla*
Sour cream*
Squash
Sweet corn
Sweet potatoes
Turkey
Wax beans
Wild rice

* see Index

North America is an enormous expanse blessed with a wealth of natural resources: its vast grain fields have been called the breadbasket of the world. The continent boasts the world's largest cattle industry, and its lakes, rivers, and thousands of miles of coastline offer an unrivaled bounty of fish and shellfish.

The North American climate encourages a diverse range of foodstuffs that encompass the luscious citrus fruits of Florida, the carefully cultivated salad greens of California, the corn and wheat of the prairies, and the salmon, oysters, and berries from the Pacific Northwest.

This diversity of ingredients is fully matched by a variety of cooking styles that have been carried, over the generations, to the New World. Since North America's "discovery," nearly every nation in the world has seen some of its members emigrate to it, adding another layer of culture and tradition to the expanding weave of the continent's fabric. All the recipes brought with the immigrants were adapted to the indigenous ingredients, producing a unique cuisine. And like its culture, this is a cuisine that is constantly changing and adapting, ever open to new influences and ingredients.

REGIONAL STYLES

New England and eastern Canada When the first settlers arrived here, they found a native population skilled in exploiting the wealth of indigenous food-producing animals and plants. Squirrels, deer, and bears filled the woods; wild turkeys, pigeons, and quail abounded; fish and shellfish stocked the lakes and ocean; and squash, corn, and berries were there for the picking.

These early settlers used cornmeal in place of wheat flour for breads and puddings and maple syrup from the heavily wooded areas of New Hampshire, Vermont, and eastern Canada as a sweetener. Maple syrup is still used on pancakes and waffles and to glaze baked ham. It was these hardy colonists who were responsible, too, for such traditional favorites as Boston baked beans and their Quebec counterpart, *fèves au lard.*

The first British settlers brought with them a fondness for pies. These could be both savory—filled with meat, fish, or poultry—or sweet, stuffed with berries and fruit. Because every woman was able to produce a version of apple pie, this dish became, and remains, one of the big icons of North American culture.

Maritimers and coastal New Englanders still enjoy a diet rich in fresh seafood. Their chowders and stews are usually simple but always sustaining.

In the mid-1700s, German immigrants arrived in the farmlands of Pennsylvania and later settled large areas of southern Ontario. Now known as the Pennsylvania Dutch, a corruption of *Deutsch*, they brought a liking for sausages and hams and a knowledge of preserving techniques. These cured goods and condiments are still part of their traditional cuisine, as well as being appreciated throughout the continent. Also of German origin are the many yeast-dough coffee cakes, or festive specialties such as stollen and lebkuchen.

By the nineteenth century, Jewish families from Eastern Europe joined the Irish, Italians, Hungarians, and Germans that were flocking to a new life in the United States. Great numbers of these new Americans settled in New York City. Today this city can offer the cuisine of every nationality of the world—delicatessen fare with an Eastern European flavor, oriental dishes served in the ambiance of its bustling Chinatown, and some of the finest Italian food on the East Coast.

The Midwest and the Prairies Many Scandinavians settled in the Midwest and brought with them the tradition of smorgasbord, as well as extensive use of dairy products. The cuisine of the middle section of the continent reflects the influence of a farming heritage—with hearty meals and baked goods still highly prized by the region's East European descendants. Prairie classics include Ukrainian foods such as *pyrohy* (often pronounced *perogies*), which are potato dumplings wrapped in dough; and *paska,* a traditional Easter sweet bread.

The South The Southern colonies were blessed with a gentle climate, and the inhabitants were able to enjoy a lavish lifestyle famed for its generous hospitality. An enduring specialty of the area is Smithfield ham. With its distinctive flavor of hickory smoke, this is still cured with the same recipe used by the colonists in the small town of that name.

The Spaniards introduced domesticated livestock, including pigs, to Florida and it was not long before pork featured prominently in the southern cuisine. Bacon, ham, and pork sausages still feature in the traditional southern breakfast, served with grits (corn that has been dried, ground, and cooked into a porridgelike dish) and hash brown or home-fried potatoes. Ham hocks with collard greens and ham with red-eye gravy are also favorites.

French, Spanish, and African culinary traditions came together in Louisiana to produce Creole cooking. The center is New Orleans, and the cooking has something of the sophistication of that city, being often imaginative and highly flavored. Popular Creole dishes include *calas*, a breakfast favorite of deep-fried sweet and spicy rice balls; and bisques, which are rich, thick seafood soups.

Cajun, too, has its origins in the cuisine of France. It was brought to the bayous of Louisiana by the Acadians, French settlers who were expelled from Nova Scotia in the middle of the eighteenth century. It has since mixed with the Spanish, African, and Native American cuisines of the South. Jambalaya (a dish of rice, pork, sausage, ham, shrimp, and crayfish, seasoned with chili or cayenne pepper), and gumbo (a spicy soup or stew thickened with okra or filé and using a variety of meats, seafood, and vegetables) are well-known traditional Cajun dishes.

The Southwest In the early days, many settlers pushed west, attracted by the promise of homesteading land, and the vast uninhabited plains were soon populated by farmers and cattle and sheep ranchers.

Texas and the neighboring desert states of Arizona and New Mexico have produced a style of cooking known as Tex-Mex, characterized by chili-spiced flavors with an unmistakable Mexican influence. This region is home to the popular dish of *chili con carne*, which has traveled all over America to be adapted to local tastes. Other dishes that are enthusiastically eaten from coast to coast include *tacos*, crisp corn *tor-*

tillas (flat bread) filled with seasoned ground meat and salads, and *burritos* (flour tortillas rolled around a bean, meat, poultry, or vegetable filling with cheese and sometimes salsa). Many Tex-Mex dishes are flavored liberally with cilantro. Salsa, a spicy uncooked tomato relish, is another specialty from Mexico, as is the avocado dip *guacamole*.

The West Coast In sunny southern California, weather has had the biggest influence on cooking styles. Almost constant sunshine and lavish irrigation produce a wealth of fresh fruit and vegetables. Artichokes, avocados, citrus fruit, dates, and melons thrive in the southern part of the state. Northern California offers the various delicacies of San Francisco's thriving Asian communities—Chinese, Japanese, Korean, Thai, Vietnamese, and others. The nearby Napa and Sonoma Valleys produce some of the world's finest wines.

In the Pacific Northwest, salmon, clams, crabs, and oysters are abundant and among the finest in the world. Oregon and Washington are apple, peach, and pear-growing country, and the area is justly famous for its fruit pies. British Columbia's Okanagan Valley, with its hot, dry climate, yields such treats as sweet and sour cherries, apricots, and plums.

Blueberry muffins

MENU GUIDE

BLT
Bacon, lettuce, and tomato sandwich

Clam Chowder
Hearty soup with clams and vegetables

Corn on the Cob
Boiled ears of corn served hot with salt and butter

Hash Browns
Fried grated potato cakes

Muffins
Individual cakelike sweet breads made without yeast

Barbecued Spareribs
Pork spareribs cooked over an open fire and coated with spicy barbecue sauce

Eggs Benedict
English muffins topped with Canadian bacon, poached eggs, and hollandaise

Reuben Sandwich
Corned beef and Swiss cheese sandwich with sauerkraut, on rye bread

Caesar Salad
Romaine lettuce with an anchovy dressing and Parmesan cheese

Pumpkin Soup
A rich creamed soup of pureed pumpkin flesh

Broiled Salmon Steak
Atlantic or Pacific salmon marinated in lemon juice

Baked Alaska
Meringue covered cake layered with ice cream

Fruit Cobbler
Deep-dish fruit pie with a thick, biscuitlike topping

Shoofly Pie
Spiced molasses and brown sugar pie

Devil's Food Cake
A two-layer chocolate cake with a chocolate fudge filling and icing

CORNUCOPIA OF CORN

Sweet corn has been a regular feature of North American meals since before the first settlers arrived. Native Americans used this indigenous crop as a staple, and many of their recipes are recognizable in modern-day dishes.

Cornmeal Available white or yellow, this was favored by colonial cooks over the more expensive wheat flour.

Cornbread Cakelike bread made with cornmeal, often used for turkey stuffing. When baked in cast-iron molds shaped like corn cobs, it becomes corn pone.

Corn Chowder Milk-based soup with salt pork, potatoes, and fresh corn kernels.

Corn Fritters Pan-fried patties of corn kernels in a light milk and egg batter.

Hush Puppies Deep-fried cornmeal dumplings, most popular in the South.

Indian Pudding Cornmeal dessert with milk and molasses; colonists called this "hasty pudding," a name that is still used in some areas.

Grits Ground dried sweet corn; it is popular in the South, with butter and sugar, as a breakfast item.

Spoon Bread Baked custardlike cornmeal.

Succotash A Native American dish combining sweet corn kernels and lima beans.

Tortillas Flat, thin unleavened bread made from *masa harina*; essential in Tex-Mex cooking.

Traditional Cast-Iron Corn Pan
This pan is used to bake corn pone, small cornbread rolls shaped like corn cobs that are popular in the South.

OTHER INGREDIENTS

The influence of the longhorn breed of cattle on North American eating habits cannot be overestimated. This hardy animal, able to withstand cattle drives over great distances, produced beef that no longer had to be corned (a type of pickling) or preserved in salt. In addition, the opening of the railways brought vast new markets and soon steak houses opened in many cities. Until the mid-1980s when health concerns about animal fats came to the fore, beef dominated the North American diet, and roast beef, pot roast, steak, and hamburger were standard fare.

To go with the beef, tomato ketchup and mustard became the two essential condiments found in most North American homes. The preferred mustard is somewhat milder than its European counterpart and is smooth rather than whole-grain.

Sourdough bread was a specialty of the early pioneers, especially the gold prospectors who set out from San Francisco for Alaska and the Yukon and, having no yeast, were forced to find a substitute. For the dough, a mixture of flour, water, and sugar is left to stand until it begins to ferment and smell sour; this is then used as the starter to make the bread rise. What was born out of necessity is now considered a local delicacy, and in Alaska and the Canadian North scores of different breads are made with sourdough as the starter.

Another traditional bread enjoyed by many North Americans is the bagel. This is a round roll with a hole in the middle that may have poppy seed, onion, or garlic topping. It is often eaten with smoked salmon and cream cheese for Sunday breakfast or used for sandwiches.

Crayfish, or crawfish, are small lobsterlike freshwater crustaceans, once part of the diet of Native Americans, that are cooked in pies, gumbos, and stews or simply boiled and eaten with the fingers, especially in Louisiana.

One of the native fruits noted by Captain James Cook in the late eighteenth century was the blueberry. Blueberries are now cultivated in most southern regions of Canada and the cool northerly regions of the United States, and are popular eaten raw with cream, cooked in waffles and pancakes, or baked in muffins and pies.

The heritage of North American food has been strongly influenced by the German immigrants. The ubiquitous ground beef patty served in a bun takes its name from the city of Hamburg, and hot dogs derive from Frankfurt sausages. The fruit and vegetable preserves that originated with the Pennsylvania Dutch traveled west, and north to Ontario, with the early pioneers, as did their fruit batters and chicken pot pies. Many Pennsylvania Dutch recipes remain an integral part of the North American cuisine. It is said that they can also be credited with putting the hole in the middle of the ever-popular doughnut.

Another dish that has been successfully adapted by North Americans of all regions and ethnic backgrounds is the pizza. This flat pie made from a yeast dough and topped with various combinations of cheeses, vegetables, meats, and seasonings is now one of the most popular of meals.

Bakers' brick ovens were used in the pizza parlors that the Italian immigrants opened in New York City in the early part of the twentieth century, and they are still essential to making a true pizza. Today most major cities have gourmet pizza restaurants where the traditional mozzarella and tomato toppings have been replaced with more innovative items such as goat cheese and sun-dried tomatoes.

North Americans are also well known for their outstanding range of desserts. Cheesecake—hot, cold, baked, no-bake, flavored fruit or cream-topped—is found throughout the continent. The most traditional is made in a deep pan and has a crust of crushed graham crackers.

Ice cream, the ubiquitous and crowd-pleasing treat, is eaten out of a bowl, in cones, between cookies, on waffles, pancakes, and cakes, in sodas and coffee, in and on pies, and baked under meringue. New flavors are constantly being developed, and its place as North America's favorite dessert is still unchallenged.

MEALS

Big meals and snacking throughout the day are two ways to sum up North Americans' eating habits. The only consistent feature about their meals is that portions are generous in both homes and restaurants, and there is a strong tradition of hospitality. Breakfast can be anything from freshly squeezed orange juice, cereal, and toast, to pancakes or waffles served with maple syrup to eggs with bacon or sausages.

Coffee is universally drunk at breakfast and throughout the day, in preference to tea.

Lunch is usually the lightest meal of the day, with salads and sandwiches being the most popular meal choice in delicatessens or sandwich bars or as items taken from home to school or work.

North American dinners tend to be early in the evening, anywhere between 6 and 8 P.M., and will usually consist of a main course and a simple dessert. Roast chicken, mashed potatoes, green beans, and a salad, followed by ice cream, might be a classic example. Individual dinner rolls or small leavened and shortened rolls called biscuits might be served with the meat course.

Milk, juice, soft drinks, and coffee are the most common beverages in homes; cola is sometimes drunk at breakfast. Wine was once reserved primarily for restaurant outings, but more and more North Americans are drinking wine with their meals at home.

Brunch is a North American invention that combines breakfast with lunch. Today it is a popular choice on many hotel and restaurant menus on weekends. Reading the Sunday paper over brunch has become a ritual for many North Americans, and the menu might include sliced meats, bagels and lox (smoked salmon), pancakes, or eggs Benedict, along with coffee, orange juice, or even cocktails.

North Americans enjoy eating outdoors when they entertain, and picnics, clambakes, barbecues, and tailgate parties (food served from the back of a station wagon) are favored when weather permits.

North Americans also eat out a great deal, and so-called fast food chains populate every main street. A wide variety of food is offered, including burgers, pizza, chicken, Mexican specialties, and spareribs, almost all served with french fried potatoes, milk shakes, or soft drinks. Some chains specialize in pancakes, doughnuts, ice cream, or frozen yogurt with dozens of delicious and imaginative toppings.

Another North American innovation is the "drive through" fast food restaurant. Without ever leaving the car, diners can order from one point, then drive around and pick up their meal at another.

Thanksgiving is one of the most important family holidays. Its traditional menu celebrates the first harvest festival of the earliest European settlers. The occasion is often commemorated in a meal consisting of roast turkey with corn bread or oyster stuffing, giblet gravy, cranberry sauce, candied sweet potatoes, and pumpkin or pecan pie.

DISTINCTLY CANADIAN

Canada's culinary heritage boasts one of the oldest and most distinguished regional cuisines in North America—traditional French-Canadian cooking. The first French settlers of Quebec came primarily from Normandy and Brittany and brought the custom of simmering stews, soups, and savory pies in a black cast-iron pot. Among the traditional pies are the pork *tourtiere,* served on Christmas eve; *cipate* or *cipaille*, layers of pastry interleaved with a filling of game, poultry, pork, and vegetables; and *cipate aux bleuts*, a three-crust blueberry pie. Other Quebecois specialties are *ragout de boulettes*, a stew of meatballs and pigs' feet; *cretons*, a coarse pâté of savory potted pork; and *caribou*, a drink of red wine and spirits. *Pâté chinois* is a form of shepherd's pie. Among the foods native to the country is wild rice, the grain of a tall aquatic grass, which is now cultivated extensively. It is usually boiled and served with butter, but sliced almonds, fresh herbs, or sautéed mushrooms or onions may be added. From the Baffin and Beaufort regions comes the Arctic char, a prized fish of the salmon family with an exquisitely delicate flavor.

The Saskatoon berry is another native, something like the blueberry. The tiny pincherry makes a wonderfully tart jelly to serve with the abundance of game. New Brunswick is famous for its delicately flavored fiddlehead ferns. Other acclaimed products include Peace River honey, considered by many to be the finest in the world; Oka cheese, soft, with a pronounced, distinctive flavor; and Winnipeg Goldeye, a superb freshwater fish with a sweet white flesh.

INDIA

F rom time immemorial India has been renowned as the source of exotic spices. Its cuisine is famed for its variety and infinitely subtle blends of aromatic spices and seasonings that flavor meat, legumes, and vegetables. The word *curry* does not do justice to the sheer range of Indian dishes, which reflects the diversity of geography, culture, and religion that this vast country has to offer. What does not vary is the care and sophistication with which food is prepared and cooked, and the value that is attached to its excellence and flavor. From the rich meat-based dishes of the North to the simple legume-based diet of the South, food is a way of life, with many religious and social rituals surrounding it, and throughout the whole country it is a source of great enjoyment and celebration.

TRADITIONAL INGREDIENTS

Almonds*
Amchoor (mango powder)
Asafoetida*
Basmati rice
Buttermilk*
Cardamom*
Chick-pea flour
Chilies*
Cilantro*
Cinnamon*
Coconut*
Cumin*
Curry leaves
Dried fish
Fennel seed*
Fenugreek*
Garam masala*
Ghee*
Gingerroot*
Lentils
Limes*
Mangoes
Mung beans
Mustard seeds*
Nigella*
Onions*
Panch phoran*
Pistachios*
Saffron*
Sesame seeds*
Split peas
Tamarind*
Tomatoes*
Turmeric*
Yogurt*

(*see Index)

REGIONAL STYLES

Northern India It is the food of Northern India that has become familiar to millions, for this is the common cuisine of Indian restaurants all over the world. It is a cuisine that was profoundly influenced by the Moguls, Muslim conquerors of India and its rulers. The Mogul Empire was founded in 1526 by Baber, and lasted until 1857. From Delhi, their seat of power, their cooking style radiated outward to be adopted and adapted through much of the region. Their food had its roots in the Middle East, a legacy that can be traced back through dishes such as the Persian *pullaos*, saffron-perfumed combinations of rice and meat; and kabobs, barbecued skewered meat, perhaps ground and mixed with spices or with lentils (*shami*). Another well-known Mogul dish is *biryani*, the great festive casserole of meat and rice imbued with the fragrance of saffron and other spices. Another is *murgh masala*, a stuffed chicken marinated in spices and yogurt and then roasted. Among sweets is *zafrani chawal*, sweetened rice with saffron and nuts, and *gajar halwa* (carrot halvah). One of the great Mogul centers was Lucknow, the royal city, which was renowned for the luxuriance of its courtly life. Vast banquets were often held, the chefs striving each time to surpass past triumphs and astound the guests with their inventiveness.

Food in the Muslim-influenced north of India is meat-based, although for the large population of Hindus the cow is sacred, making beef a meat that is never touched.

Goat is the most commonly used meat in all regions, although lamb and chicken are also consumed, and there is a whole variety of ways to prepare them.

Unique to the state of Punjab is the famous *tandoori* style of cooking. The most well-known dish is tandoori chicken: the meat is marinated in seasonings and yogurt and then cooked at very high temperature in the traditional clay oven, called a *tandoor*. This results in a succulent combination of moist, fragrant meat on the inside with a flavorful spicy coating on the outside. Other delicious northern dishes include *kormas*, meats cooked in rich creamy sauces with yogurt and fruit, or nuts and saffron, and *koftas*, which are spicy meatballs, served alone or with a sauce.

While oil is more commonly used in Southern India, *ghee* (clarified butter) is the preferred cooking fat in the cooler northern climes. Spices are put to milder use here; *garam masala* (see page 79) is a typical blend of spices designed to warm the body, unlike the fierce blends more commonly used in the South. The great wheat-growing plains of the Punjab produce the flour from which roti (bread)—the essential component of every meal in Northern India—is made. The most common, everyday bread is chapati, a flat, unleavened circular bread that is cooked on a griddle and then transferred to hot charcoal and charred. Its purpose is twofold: it is a starchy side dish and an edible utensil for scooping up the rich and delectable sauces. Other kinds of roti include nan—a luxurious leavened dough that is slapped on the inside of the tandoor and baked—and paratha, a crispy fried bread that is rolled out and folded into fine layers, often stuffed with vegetables or *kheema*, ground meat.

Southern India From Bengal in the west, Gujarat in the east and Tamil Nadu on the most southern tip of the peninsula, the southern half of India incorporates a vast culinary repertoire. At the heart of this predominantly vegetarian cuisine is the use of grains and legumes, as always combined with skillfully blended spices. However, there are deservedly celebrated exceptions.

Goa, once colonized by the Portuguese, has a cuisine that is strongly influenced by the Europeans, with many meat-based dishes that blend East and West to exotic effect. Although there are many dishes that use meat, a style of cuisine more typical of the North, the taste is unmistakably southern, with widespread use of flavorings such as coconut milk, tamarind, chilies, cinnamon, curry leaves, and peanuts.

Chilies, ginger, garlic, and coconut are the characteristic flavorings of much of the region, and their uses vary according to custom and geography. The style of cooking alters subtly farther south. Oil, not ghee, is a staple ingredient, and steaming is a common cooking method, producing such snacks as *dhoklas* (steamed lentil cakes, found in Gujarat) and *idlis* (fermented steamed rice cakes, popular in Kerala).

Rice, such as the fragrant basmati variety that grows on the foothills of the Himalayas in the North, accompanies every dish. It is a vital component of each meal, used to absorb the spicy, liquid vegetable and legume curries that are commonly eaten. Another ubiquitous dish is *dal*, a blend of legumes and spices that offers a valuable source of protein in this predominantly vegetarian

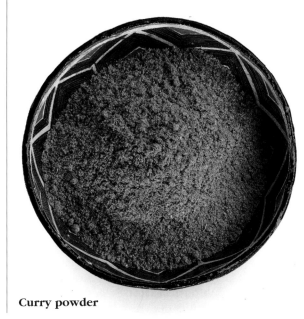

Curry powder

region. While *dal* is the word for split peas, the term is applied to all legume dishes of this type. Among the most common are those made from Egyptian lentils (*masoor*), black-eyed peas (*lobia*), and mung beans (*moong*). Lentils are also an important ingredient, with such dishes as *sambar* (lentils with vegetables) and *rasam* (lentils with garlic) that are prepared daily, being seasoned with different spices to give them variety. *Dhansak* is a dish that combines meat with lentils and is served with brown rice; *dosas* are lentil and rice pancakes. Another characteristic of the South is the use of small amounts of roasted or fried split peas to impart a nutty flavor to dishes.

Very spicy food helps the body perspire and thus lose heat, making it popular in this warm region. The fiery *vindaloo*—a Goan dish in which spices soaked in wine and vinegar are added to meat—is perhaps the most well-known example.

The magnificent exotic fruits that flourish in this hot climate add a rich dimension to the diet; red bananas are eaten as a nutritious snack, and mangoes may be pulped into juice and mixed with milk and nuts to provide a delicious and refreshing drink. Another use for the abundant supply of bananas involves banana leaves, which can be used as plates.

In the most southerly states, freshly roasted and ground coffee is the popular drink, while farther north the natively grown teas, such as Assam, are preferred.

Different areas use different ingredients. Buttermilk, for example, is a vital part of Gujarati cooking, as are gingerroot, chilies, and coconut. In Maharashtra, a primarily agricultural area with a long coastline, fish is a common ingredient and its flavor is enhanced by the coconuts from the palm groves that cover much of the state.

From here comes "Bombay duck," which is not of the quacking variety at all. It is actually the name given to dried fish that is a popular seasoning. It comes from a fish that is native to the waters around Bombay, whose local name is *bommaloe macchli*. After being caught, these fish are filleted and hung on frames to dry. In its dried form, Bombay duck can be added to curries, or pickled, or served as a snack with aperitifs.

In the fertile coastal strip that comprises the state of Kerala, coconut-scented fish dishes are prevalent, and the availability of coconuts, also grown here in great quantity, has given rise to the use of coconut oil in the local cuisine.

MENU GUIDE

Bhajia
Vegetables or fish deep-fried in a batter of rice and chick-pea flour

Samosas
Triangular crispy pastries with a spicy meat or vegetable filling

Pakoras
Vegetable fritters

Poppadums
Crispy fried wafers made from split peas

Poriyal
Cauliflower with chilies and mustard seeds

Koftas
Spicy meatballs

Mattar Paneer
Peas with fried cheese

Dosas
Rice pancakes with a spicy potato filling

Rhogan Josh
Lamb braised in a yogurt sauce with chilies and saffron

Murgh Tikka Masala
Chicken pieces marinated in yogurt and spices and baked in a clay oven

Tandoori Murgh
Chicken coated with spices and cooked in a clay oven

Tarka Dal
Spiced green lentils

Lassi
Yogurt drink, either sweet or savory

Kacchi Biryani
Rice pilaf with meat and spices

Nan
Leavened bread baked in a clay oven

Kulfi
Ice cream flavored with cardamom and nuts

Tamarind

CHUTNEYS

Few Indian meals are served without the tradi-·tional fruit or vegetable chutneys. Unlike Western chutneys, they often are not cooked but are more like relish salads and are notable for their fresh flavors. They can be mild or very hot.

Sesame Chutney *Often served at breakfast, this combines sesame seeds with cilantro leaves, mint, chilies, and tamarind.*

Tomato Chutney *A sweet-and-sour chutney made from tomatoes flavored with gingerroot, chilies, and often the spice mixture panch phoran (see page 90).*

Coconut Chutney *Eaten in the South, this combines chick-peas, flavored with freshly grated coconut, and ground spices.*

Raita *This is a mild yogurt mixture, usually made with cucumber, which is meant to offset the heat of curries.*

Ginger Relish *A commonly eaten spicy mixture of gingerroot, garlic, green chilies, and coconut that is said to aid digestion.*

Mango Chutney *A sweet fruit chutney to enhance the flavor of meat dishes.*

Cilantro Chutney *This is a very popular chutney, made daily in many homes, blending fresh cilantro with oil, mustard seeds, and asafoetida, eaten in small quantities with meals or served as a dip.*

Lime Pickle *A delicious, tangy, strong pickle in which the limes are mari-nated in spices and oil for several days until soft.*

Onion Relish *A simple side dish of raw onions, finely sliced and tossed with lemon juice and paprika.*

FLAVORINGS

Most dishes are seasoned by blending a combination of whole or freshly ground spices. The combinations are infinite, with each cook having a personal preference, though the basic principle is to make the masala so that no one flavor dominates the mixture.

There is a whole philosophy attached to the use of spices that has been handed down through the generations and that, subconsciously at least, every Indian cook applies. This goes beyond simply the flavor they impart, important though this is. Spices are considered to have medicinal properties: garlic, for instance, is good for the circulation of the blood; turmeric is an antiseptic and is often sprinkled on fish be-fore frying. Asafoetida is a pungent resin, derived from the rhizomes of a species of fennel, which helps the digestion; it is often combined with difficult-to-digest legumes. Gingerroot is another digestive that is often paired with lentils and other legumes.

Garam masala means "warm blend of spices," and these are usually highly aromatic, made with spices that are believed to warm the body. For this reason, they are traditional in the more temperate regions of the North.

Masalas can be wet or dry. The latter type, more typical of the North, usually includes bay leaf, cardamom, cinnamon, ginger, mace, and nutmeg, all of which are con-sidered warm spices. They are blended with ghee or sprinkled over a dish just before serving to add fresh aroma and flavor. The wet masalas of the South may contain freshly ground chilies, gingerroot, or onions, particularly in the hotter blends, which help the body to lose heat.

Another classic combination of spices is *panch phoran*, a Bengali blend of whole spices—cumin, fennel, nigella, fenugreek, and spicy *radhuni* seeds (black mustard seeds)—customarily used to flavor lentil and vegetarian preparations. *Tarka* is a combination of hot oil and spices, such as chilies and cumin seeds, which is often used to add interest to simple dal dishes.

Cumin, available in white or black var-ieties, is one of the most commonly used spices throughout India. Other popular spices and seasonings include coriander seeds, which are ground and used in meat and vegetable dishes; mango powder, made from dried mango fruit, which is used to impart a sour tang; tamarind, made from the pulp of pods soaked in hot water, also sour in flavor; and curry leaves, from the curry tree, which flourishes in many home gardens in the south.

Saffron and turmeric are favored throughout the country. Turmeric has a pungent flavor and imparts a characteristic yellow color to foods. Much more precious is saffron, the golden spice made from the dried stamens of a type of crocus found in Kashmir, most often used to imbue rice dishes with a subtle fragrance and color.

Fresh flavorings are used, too. Hot green chilies give a special spicy tang to many dishes, and fragrant fresh cilantro leaves are used both as a flavoring and a garnish. In southern Indian cuisine, fresh grated coconut and coconut milk are added to many dishes, lending a sweet, delicate flavor to fish and vegetable stews, and salads.

Apart from spices, other ingredients also influence the flavor, varying in their use from region to region. There are many kinds of oils that add another dimension of flavor to the ingredients. In Southern India, groundnut oil is widely used, giving a nutty flavor. In the coastal areas, where coconuts grow in abundance, coconut oil is used along with coconut milk to give the distinctive flavor of the South. In Bengal, a state that is crisscrossed by waterways, fish is widely available and much consumed. Mustard oil is used here too, imparting characteristic flavor to the regional cuisine. In Kashmir, it is sesame oil that gives a dis-tinctive flavor to the local cuisine. Ghee, which is butter clarified to the point where it contains no milk solids (see page 237), is used instead of the oil found in many Northern dishes and has a special nutty flavor of its own.

Thick, creamy buffalo-milk yogurt (*dahi*) is made daily in most kitchens. It is the basis of the classic yogurt, mint, and cucumber salad, *raita*, which is served with spicy main dishes. The yogurt adds richness to sauces and tones down the fire of spices, resulting in a creamy sauce such as the kind found in the meat or fish kormas. Dahi is also used for making *lassi*, a refreshing, cooling drink that can be either sweet or savory. Sometimes the seasonings are simply salt and black pepper (*lassi namkeen*); but rose water, sugar, and fruit can also be used.

Chenna is a kind of soft cheese made in the home for use in sweet and savory dishes—for example in the sweets *rasgulla* and *sandesh*, or the savory *mattar paneer* (cheese with peas). Chenna is made by adding vinegar and water to milk and bringing it to a boil before straining the milk through cheesecloth.

The cheese forms the basis of many other sweets, for which Bengal is a particularly famous center. Other ingredients commonly used in sweets are pistachio nuts, almonds, raisins, and coconut. Rice is combined with milk—in *zafrani chawal*, and in rice pudding made with rice and milk, like that familiar to many American children—and yogurt, which can be combined with saffron and sugar to make a creamy dessert. Flavorings, apart from sugar, of course, are cardamom pods and rose water, which give a delicate fragrance to the sweets.

Rather than being made in the home, sweets are generally bought from market stalls. Sweets have always been bought in the bazaars, and they hold a special importance on all occasions of celebration or religious festival. *Halwas* of every kind, based on milk and then sweetened and flavored with coconut, almond, or pistachio, are sold in numerous shops by the professional sweet makers, the *Halwais*.

MEALS

Traditionally, food in India is not eaten with a knife and fork: custom dictates that the right hand be used to pick up food, with the help of the rice or bread that is always served with it. Northern Indians use their fingertips, but the less formal manners that prevail in the South permit the use of the whole hand. It is taboo to use the left hand for eating, because it is considered unclean.

An ordinary meal consists of a rice dish (or bread in the North), a lentil dish, a vegetable, a meat, and a chutney. There are no separate courses, and even the dessert, if there is one, is served at the same time as the other dishes. Food is served in small dishes that are placed on a *thali*, a round metal tray given to each guest. Women serve the guests and the men of the household, and all sit on small mats on the floor.

In the South, the customary replacement for the thali is a banana leaf. These leaves are also used at formal events, such as wedding banquets, when a slice of lime will be salted and placed on a tender young banana leaf and served as a condiment.

Religious customs also dictate etiquette in the dining room. A purifying ritual that dates from 1500 B.C., the Vedic period of Hinduism in Southern India, is traditionally carried out on the rice that accompanies each meal. This involves a ceremony of combining rice with ghee. Rice is considered the most important ingredient in the meal and will be served with each course. In an Orthodox Hindu household, the guests will not be allowed in the kitchen since this is considered unclean. Orthodox families will not eat out in public for the same reason. Other religious restrictions include separate dining quarters for men and women, and the prohibition of alcoholic drinks.

SWEETS

Made by special sweet makers, the Halwais, Indian sweets are eaten as an afternoon or evening snack, often accompanied by a savory tidbit. They are also essential at all religious and festive occasions.

Barfi *A sugary, fudgelike sweet with a crumbly texture, sometimes called Indian fudge. Plain barfi is light brown; bright green pistachio-flavored barfi is called pista, and almond-flavored barfi, called badam, is a deep brown.*

Halwa *A distant relative of Middle Eastern halvah, this can be made with nuts or vegetables. Habshi halwa is made with pistachios, cashews, and almonds; gajar halwa, made from carrots, is orange.*

Jalebi *Crisp, orange squiggles of batter, these are deep-fried and then immersed in a syrup flavored with saffron.*

Laddu *These are bright yellow balls made from ground almonds, pistachios, and chick-pea flour.*

Sindhi Halwa *This is cut into squares or diamonds from a large two-colored slab; the green layer is flavored with pistachios and the yellow layer with almonds.*

Assortment of sweets

139

JAPAN

Clear, light, simple, and neat—such is the meaning of the word *sappari*, which defines the cooking of Japan, renowned for its attention to preparation and presentation. Appearance is as carefully considered as flavor, for it is believed that food is eaten with the eyes as well as the mouth. Harmony and balance are all-important, so alongside the emphasis on presentation goes a disdain of excess.

While a Japanese meal is meant to be beautiful, it should also include a measure of modesty. Central to this idea is the effort to respect true, unadorned flavors. Thus, a Japanese cook will always endeavor to bring out the natural qualities of an ingredient, in the belief that separate flavors should be shown in relief rather than blended to a whole. Today these culinary traditions coexist with an invasion of Western food. Steak bars and hamburger joints are popular for outings, though most meals prepared at home remain essentially Japanese.

TRADITIONAL INGREDIENTS

Bamboo shoots
Brown rice
Buckwheat noodles
Burdock
Chestnuts*
Chinese cabbage
Chrysanthemum leaves
Cloud ear mushrooms*
Dashi
Dried bonito flakes*
Dry mustard*
Eggplants
Fish paste
Garlic*
Gingerroot*
Ginkgo nuts
Lotus root
Matsutake mushrooms
Mirin
Miso*
Mooli*
Persimmons
Plums
Red beans
Rice wine vinegar*
Sake
Sanshō*
Seafood
Seaweed*
Sesame seeds*
Seven-spice seasoning*
Shiitake mushrooms*
Soy sauce*
Sweet potatoes
Taro
Tofu
Wasabi*
Watercress
Wheat noodles

(*see Index)

INFLUENCES

Invasions and colonialism are two primary factors that shape the way a nation eats, and Japan has had little of either. During the sixth century, however, Japan did absorb many ideas from neighboring China. The system of imperial rule and the religion of Buddhism were two of China's most important contributions, along with tea, which is arguably the national beverage.

All of Japan's ports were closed to foreigners between 1600 and 1868, consequently, Europeans had little opportunity for culinary exchange. The exception is tempura, the well-known dish of batter-coated, deep-fried foods, which was introduced by the Portuguese in the sixteenth century.

The tenets that shaped Japanese cuisine were laid down by Zen Buddhist monks. Every meal is designed to include a total of five dishes, each prepared in one of five ways: raw, simmered, steamed, barbecued, and fried. Each meal should include five flavors: bitter, salty, sweet, spicy, and sour. Red, green, yellow, black, and white are the requisite five colors.

A reverence for nature is inherent in both Zen Buddhism and the native Japanese religion, Shinto, and seasonality is therefore of utmost importance in the cuisine. Springtime delicacies include cherry-blossom rice in April and fragrant green *shincha*, or new tea, which appears in May. The moon is assigned to the month of September, when shimmering white dishes, such as abalone steamed over cucumbers or simmered bamboo shoots may be served. The mandarin oranges of winter, symbol of the sun, are the traditional offering of the new year.

The natural resources of this volcanic land are limited, and this has shaped the Japanese diet around crops such as rice and soybeans and the abundance of seaweed and fish from the surrounding oceans.

FLAVORINGS

Of all the Asian cuisines, Japan's is the most spice-free. Peppercorns are used today, though they are not traditional, leaving *wasabi* (see page 166), *sanshō* (see page 95) and dried chili peppers to do most of the seasoning. Even so, these are added quite sparingly. Sanshō berries have a similar taste to black peppercorns, and wasabi is best known as the fiery green paste that accompanies sushi. *Kinome* leaves come from the same tree that bears sanshō berries. They have a pleasing minty fragrance and are used mainly as a garnish.

There is one uniquely Japanese flavor and this belongs to *dashi*, an all-purpose stock that is made from *konbu*, or kelp, and dried bonito flakes. It is mandatory for all soups and simmered dishes, and it manages to find its way into many other dishes via marinades, dipping sauces, and dressings. *Dashi-no-moto* is the instant version, and it serves much the same purpose in Japan as bouillon cubes do in the West.

Along with tea, the Chinese left their legacy of soy sauce to the Japanese. Known as *shoyu*, Japanese soy sauce is less salty and somewhat sweeter than the Chinese version, because it contains more wheat. True *tamari* is a rich, high-quality, wheat-free Japanese soy sauce, which is very rare even in Japan. In the West, many shops sell a dark-colored liquid that is labeled tamari, regardless of its actual quality.

Sesame seeds, both white and black, are a staple, but as with most Japanese seasonings, they are used more as a condiment than as a flavoring that is cooked with the food. *Gomasio* is a mixture of salt and black sesame seeds, often placed on the table for sprinkling over rice and raw vegetables. Sesame oil lends its distinctive taste to the finest tempura oils.

For sweetness in marinades and dipping sauces, the Japanese prefer their sweetened rice wine, *mirin*, to sugar.

OTHER INGREDIENTS

With little land suitable for agriculture and livestock, the Japanese make good use of the products that they do have in abundance: soybeans, rice, seaweed, and fish.

Miso (see page 188) is fermented soy paste, available in colors ranging from chocolate brown to red to creamy white. When combined with dashi, it is made into a soup, *misoshiru*, which can be consumed at any time of the day, and sometimes several times a day. *Tofu* is soybean curd, which can be simmered, steamed, grilled, or fried.

Sushi

Sushi is the meeting place for some important ingredients. Here, rice flavored with Japanese vinegar that is sweetened with sugar is topped with raw fish, and sometimes rolled in thin sheets of *nori*, a kind of seaweed. Kelp and *wakame* (see page 220) are two other types of seaweed that figure prominently in Japanese cuisine, being used in salads and soups or as wrappers.

The Japanese are renowned for their *kobe* and *matsuzaka* beef. The cows are raised on a diet high in beer, and are massaged to ensure even distribution of the fat. This beef is not an item for everyday eating, and seafood is actually the mainstay of the diet. Dark-fleshed oily fish are highly prized, as is freshness. Tuna, mackerel, and salmon are popular, as are squid and octopus. Blowfish are considered a delicacy, though the liver is poisonous and consumption can be fatal. A restaurant must employ a licensed chef to serve it.

The Japanese are also devoted noodle eaters. Wheat noodles, *udon*, are the preferred type in the south, while buckwheat noodles, *soba*, are eaten from Tokyo to all points north.

MEALS

Rice, sprinkled with nori flakes, and miso soup are common breakfast fare; the miso is mixed using chopsticks, and the broth is then sipped from the bowl. Lunch is a light meal, often just a bowl of noodles, or a *bento* box. This is a multicompartment lunch box filled with a variety of cold dishes that is either bought on the way to work or delivered to the workplace.

The main meal of the day is in the evening. Traditionally, this meal consists of a simmered dish, a salad, and one fried, broiled, or steamed dish served with rice and a soup. All the courses are served simultaneously on a low table, and they are eaten in no particular order.

More formal meals usually begin with an appetizer course accompanied by small ceramic cups of *sake*, wine made from fermented rice. The main meal will include many dishes that combine colors, flavors, textures, and cooking methods. A bowl of rice, some pickles, and green tea will be served to conclude the meal.

MENU GUIDE

Nimono
Fish or vegetables simmered in soy sauce broth, served as an accompaniment

Umeboshi
Tangy, salty pickle of under-ripe apricots or plums

Dengaku
Skewered food coated with sweet miso paste

Kamaboko
Fish paste cakes

Misoshiru
Miso soup with tofu

Natto
Fermented soybeans, often served with raw quail eggs and soy sauce

Sushi
Vinegared rice with vegetables and raw fish sometimes wrapped in nori seaweed

Sashimi
Finely sliced raw fish

Oden
Stew with fish cakes, potatoes, carrots, and seaweed

Tempura
Seafood and vegetables dipped in a feather-light batter and deep-fried

Teppanyaki
Slivers of beef and fish cooked at the table on a hotplate

Tonkatsu
Breaded and deep-fried loin of pork served with sweet soy sauce

Kushi Yakitori
Skewers of chicken, vegetables or seafood basted with soy sauce

Sukiyaki
One-pot dish of thinly sliced beef and vegetables cooked at the table

O-cha
Green tea served at the end of the meal

KOREA

Bounded by the Sea of Japan on one side and the Yellow Sea on the other, the mountainous peninsula of Korea has been historically overshadowed by China and Japan. Centuries of invasion—both cultural and military—have ensured that its kitchens are rich with their influence. Chinese principles, for example, form the basis of Korean cooking, but a modern chef is also likely to be an expert at preparing Japanese specialties such as teriyaki and sushi.

Korea possesses an ancient cuisine with its own distinctive food. The national pickle dish, *kimchi*, is held in such reverence that Seoul boasts a museum devoted entirely to its 160 different varieties. From Seoul, too, comes a strong tradition of elaborate and highly decorative dishes developed over the years in the royal kitchens. But no amount of pomp can disguise the robust flavors and natural ingredients used in the dishes that typify a home-cooked Korean meal.

TRADITIONAL INGREDIENTS

Abalone
Adzuki beans
Agar-agar*
Barley
Bean curd
Bean sprouts
Chestnuts*
Chilies*
Chinese cabbage
Cilantro leaves*
Eggplants
Garlic*
Gingerroot*
Ginkgo nuts
Ginseng
Mung beans
Mushrooms*
Noodles
Pickled fish
Rice
Rice vinegar*
Rice wine
Scallions*
Seaweed*
Sesame oil*
Sesame seeds*
Soybean paste
Soy sauce*
Sweet potatoes
Watercress

(*see Index)

142

INFLUENCES

Almost every nation in the East seems to have invaded Korea, at some point or another. As early as 100 B.C., Chinese colonies were sprouting up along the peninsula and, shortly after, the ancient Korean kingdom of Silla was calling itself—with some pride— "Little China." In the thirteenth century A.D., Genghis Khan's Mongol hordes swept over the land. And right up until World War II, Japan's warlords were a constant menace.

With each invasion, Korean cooking gained a new and valuable input. From China and Japan came the principle of five flavors (sweet, sour, hot, salty, and bitter) as did the practice of emphasizing preparation time over cooking time. And it was from its southerly cousin, too, that Korea gained the *sot*, a version of the Chinese wok. Even the unruly Mongols left their mark on Korean cooking. The most eye-catching reminder of their presence remains the tabletop charcoal grill, shaped like the crown of a Mongolian horseman's hat, that is still used today.

Amid all the commotion, however, Korea retained its sense of identity. When Buddhism spread from China during the fifth century A.D., the Koreans steadfastly refused to embrace its vegetarian principles. Instead, they clung—as they still do—to their traditional diet of broiled or barbecued red meat. And the higher up the social ladder, the more jealously did they guard their culinary traditions. Even a century ago, the tabletop dish of *shinsollo*—combining seafood, chicken, meat, eggs, vegetables, and nuts, all cooked apart and then brought together for braising in a flavorful broth—was one that could be enjoyed only by royalty.

It is geography, however, that has probably had the greatest influence on Korean cooking. The surrounding seas offer almost limitless supplies of seafood and edible seaweed, the flat plains of the south are perfect for rice cultivation, and the mountains that cover most of the peninsula provide a variety of vegetables, herbs, and roots. In addition, the region's severe winters mean that, traditionally, food has had to be dried or pickled for storage, to be eaten during the harsh months.

FLAVORINGS

Korean cooking makes generous use of a few simple flavorings, most notably garlic, gingerroot, scallions, toasted sesame seeds, and sesame oil. Other important flavorings are soy sauce, bean paste, rice vinegar, and chilies—the last being a hallmark of the southern chef. Fermented soybeans and red chilies are combined in the popular flavoring *kochujang*, which is a hot, thick, dark paste. This is made in spring and then stored in large stone jars so that it can be used throughout the year.

Other long-lived flavoring is provided by *kimchi*. This is a spicy vegetable pickle that is served at every meal from breakfast to dinner. As well as being a ubiquitous condiment, kimchi plays a prominent role in soups, stir-fries, and stews. There are endless versions of kimchi, which can be made with Chinese leaf, radish, cucumber, Chinese turnip, onion, chili, garlic, and gingerroot. Kimchi is prepared in the autumn and almost every household has a large vat in which the ingredients are left to ferment, growing ever more potent by the week.

A widely appreciated item in Korea's daily fare is the native red ginseng, which is eaten as much for its flavor as for its reputed medicinal properties. Fresh ginseng root is eaten raw with honey or cooked in a vinegar sauce. Some restaurants specialize in *samgyae tang*, which is a steamed chicken stuffed with glutinous rice and ginseng. This dish is attributed with restorative properties.

A uniquely Korean flavor comes from the *ginkgo*. At 200 million years old, this is the world's most ancient genus of tree and its soft, yellow nuts are used to garnish a variety of festive dishes.

OTHER INGREDIENTS

As in most other parts of Asia, the basic Korean foodstuff is rice. It is usually the sticky, medium-grain variety, and in per-capita terms, annual rice consumption in Korea is among the world's highest.

A symbol of longevity, noodles are also popular fare. Noodle stands are a familiar sight on city streets, and a bowl of noodles will often be the lunchtime meal. Wheat flour and buckwheat vermicelli can be found, as well as the near-transparent noodles made from sweet potato or mung beans.

Other staples include barley, which, when roasted, makes up Korea's national drink, *poricha*—a barley tea that is drunk hot, lukewarm, or cold—and mung beans, which have a number of uses, most notably as an ingredient in *pindaettok*, a unique dish comprising a thick pancake of ground mung beans topped with vegetables and meat, which is often called Korean pizza.

From the many miles of coastline comes a plentiful supply of fish and seafood. The Koreans, however, are keen meat eaters, regarding a meatless meal as slightly second-rate; thus seafood is often used to flavor meat dishes rather than as an ingredient in its own right. Pork and chicken are widely

used in dishes such as *yukhoe*, but beef is the favorite, essential in the Korean version of steak tartar, and *pulgogi*, marinated strips of meat cooked at the table.

MEALS

Korean meals are eaten at a low table in the Chinese manner, with the dishes served all at once and eaten with chopsticks and spoons. Breakfast and lunch—both served with the inevitable kimchi—are usually light, with the substantial meal being reserved for the evening.

The trademark of a Korean meal is variety. A simple family dinner might include some 20 bowls containing an array of tempting tidbits. At least one (if not many more) will contain kimchi. Soup is another essential, as are *namul*, salad accompaniments of raw or steamed vegetables. And while pride of place may be given to a centerpiece such as pulgogi, the true essence of Korean cuisine is that no particular taste should predominate. Every flavor is balanced by another to produce a harmonic combination, evidence of the Japanese influence.

Given the emphasis on the whole, it is not surprising that Korean meals rarely include a separate dessert course; when a sweet course is served, it usually takes the form of fresh fruit. More often than not, the evening's intake concludes with poricha—maybe enhanced with a little ginseng—or a glass of sweet-potato liqueur called *soju*.

The Koreans are avid feasters, particularly on the occasion of a person's first or sixty-first birthday. Sixty is traditionally considered the average lifespan, so to have survived a year over is an achievement to be celebrated with a grand banquet.

Tabletop assembly and cooking are popular, as witnessed by one dish, *kujolpan*, or Nine Heavenly Varieties, where nine different fillings are arranged in the separate compartments of a black lacquered tray. The fillings—which may include shredded vegetables, strips of meat and omelet—surround a central stack of thin pancakes. Each diner fills a pancake, choosing any or all of the fillings, then rolls it up, and dips it in a sauce made of ground roasted sesame seeds, chopped scallions, rice vinegar, and soy sauce.

MENU GUIDE

Kongkuk
Soybean sprout soup

Twoenjang-Tchigae
Soybean paste soup

Kimchi
Korean pickled vegetables

Ttok
Rice cakes in chili sauce

Kimbap
Vinegared rice with vegetables and eggs rolled up in sheets of nori seaweed

Miyokguk
Seaweed soup

Minarinamul
Steamed watercress salad with soy sauce and sesame oil

Kajinamul
Steamed eggplant salad

Kulwigim
Deep-fried oysters

Pajon
Scallion pancake

Pindaettok
A thick pancake made of mung beans and topped with marinated meat, scallions, and chilies

Tubu-Tchigae
Bean curd stew with garlic, gingerroot, and vegetables

Chongol
Strips of beef, sliced vegetables, and bean curd cooked at the table in a large pot of simmering broth

Pibimbap
One-dish meal of rice with beef, vegetables, and a raw egg

Naengmyon
Buckwheat noodles in broth, served cold

Pulgogi
Barbecued marinated beef strips

Kalbi-Tchim
Spare ribs braised in soy sauce with spices

CHINA

A Chinese kitchen is the place where gastronomy, medicine, and religion meet. For many centuries, the people of China have seen food as promoting a physical and spiritual well-being that goes far beyond merely filling the stomach. Of primary importance is the quality of the ingredients—vegetables must be farm-fresh, meat newly slaughtered. Harmony of flavors and textures is also important, both within a dish and within a meal.

This preoccupation stems from Taoism, an ancient Chinese religion, which teaches that the world consists of two complementary principles: yin (negative) and yang (positive). Taoism also advocates living off the land, which is one reason a Chinese meal contains more vegetables than meat. A more practical reason is that only 7 percent of land in China is suitable for agriculture, barely enough to support humans, let alone animals. The Chinese farmer has always sought to get as many harvests as possible from the same soil in the same year and to grow plants that serve more than one purpose: the soybean, for example, produces oil, sauce, paste, and tofu. Meat, therefore, has always been a symbol of prosperity and security—the Chinese pictogram for a house represents a roof with a pig underneath it.

TRADITIONAL INGREDIENTS

Adzuki beans
Bamboo shoots
Bean curd (tofu)
Bean sauce (black and brown)
Bean sprouts
Beef
Chicken
Chilies*
Chinese cabbage
Cilantro*
Cinnamon*
Duck
Fagara*
Five-spice powder*
Garlic*
Gingerroot*
Hoisin*
Lamb
Lobster
Lotus root
Lychees
Miso*
Noodles
Oyster sauce*
Pork
Rice
Rice wine
Rock sugar*
Scallions*
Scallops
Sea bass
Seaweed*
Sesame seeds*
Shrimp
Soy sauce*
Star anise*
Water chestnuts
Winter melon

(*see Index)

REGIONAL STYLES

China's vastness and the diversity of its terrain and climate have made for several different and distinctive regional styles of cooking.

Cantonese is the type of Chinese cuisine that is most familiar to Westerners, due to the large numbers of people who have left Southeast China over the past century and opened restaurants abroad.

Peking or Northern cuisine is found in the largest area of China, and incorporates many Mongolian dishes. Szechwan (Sichuan) and Shanghai styles are generally spicier than those of other regions and are found in the eastern and western regions.

Cantonese This style of cooking has its historical origins in the southeastern city of Canton (modernday Guangzhou), but its most dramatic expression is to be found in prosperous Hong Kong. A sub-tropical climate prevails throughout the area, with heavy rainfall from May to September. The Pearl River (Zhu Jiang) delta thus abounds in green vegetables and tropical fruit—particularly lychees, peaches, oranges, and bananas. The coastal waters and the region's multitudinous rocky inlets are richly stocked with fish and many other kinds of seafood (crabs, scallops, clams, crayfish, and lobsters). Rice is harvested up to three times a year, and is grown alongside other staples such as wheat, sweet potatoes, and taro root. Nature's output is augmented with countless fish farms plus intensive pig and poultry units.

For natural ingredients, then, Cantonese chefs have a stock unsurpassed in any other part of China. This explains why of all the regional cuisines Cantonese is the least obtrusive and—if not properly executed—the most bland. The chef's priority is to bring out the full flavor of each ingredient, rather than to mask or adorn it with others.

As in all Chinese cooking, herbs and spices are few in number and modest in application. Most prominent are cilantro, gingerroot, garlic, chilies, cloves, tangerine peel, sesame seeds, and star anise, a pervasive, licoricelike spice. An alternative is five-spice powder (see page 86).

Chefs in this part of China make widespread use of dried ingredients, such as mushrooms (see page 161) and dried fish (see page 189), and of soybean sauces and pastes. Particularly popular is black bean sauce, a thin, salty liquid made of fermented black soybeans that have been pureed and mixed with garlic and star anise.

The classic Cantonese method of cooking is stir-frying. This involves heating a small amount of oil in a wok, which is designed to focus the heat in the center of the pan, allowing for a short cooking time. This method grew out of a shortage of fuel; a quick burst of cooking used up less wood or coal on the fire. Out of necessity, the Cantonese have developed an art.

With such a short cooking time, the secret of success lies in preparation. The ingredients must be chopped to uniform sizes so that they cook evenly; for this, Chinese chefs use large, heavy cleavers. These cleavers have an unwieldy look, but in the hands of an expert, they can slice scallions rapidly into tiny, silken threads.

Steaming is also a popular Cantonese method of cooking, particularly for fish. A typical Southeast Chinese dish is steamed whole sea bass, which has been placed in a bamboo steaming basket above a pan of boiling water and then anointed with oil containing lightly cooked slivers of scallions and fresh gingerroot. Here the more potent flavorings blend surprisingly well with the delicate fish, as in another Cantonese specialty, steamed scallops in black bean sauce. Chefs pride themselves on being able to mix contrasting flavors and still retain the distinctive taste of each one, without allowing any to dominate. Cantonese pickled vegetables, for example, are preserved in a mixture of salt, sugar, and vinegar, while in the sauce for sweet-and-sour pork, onions and green peppers go hand in hand with pineapple and cherries.

Finally, mention should be made of the delicious Cantonese roast duck. This is stuffed with scallions and bean paste, then glazed with a honey and vinegar marinade, and has a flavor deliciously suspended between sweet and sharp.

Cantonese wonton soup

Pekingese Centered on the Chinese capital Peking (now Beijing), this robust and hearty style of cooking is to be found throughout the north of the country. In contrast with the lush southeastern deltas of Canton, this is rugged territory, incorporating large tracts of sandy wilderness and the rocky Mongolian steppe that borders Russia. A harsh climate operates throughout the year, careening from intense heat in summer to extreme cold in winter, while in spring Beijing is peppered by violent dust storms that rise up from the surrounding desert.

Leafy vegetables do not grow here in huge quantities; cucumber, celery, and white Tientsin cabbage are most readily available. Rice, too, is not easy to cultivate in this climate. Instead, wheat, corn, millet, peanuts, and soybeans are the staple crops. Where southerners would eat rice, therefore, northern Chinese will eat steamed breads, buns, and noodles (made from wheat flour, egg, and water). Noodles are a symbol of longevity; noodle cakes are given as birthday presents, and the recipient will eat as many as possible to ensure a long life. In the shorter term, inhabitants of Beijing and other northern provinces keep out the cold by stocking up on boiled and sautéed dumplings (*chiao-tzu*), filled with shrimp and pork.

A sizable Muslim population exists in Northern China, which means that pork is much less commonly eaten than in other parts of the country. Beef has never been a universally popular dish; the Chinese farmer has been traditionally reluctant to eat his ox, considering it of more lasting use to him as a general beast of burden than as dinner.

Lamb is therefore the dominant meat, the most spectacular manifestation of this being Mongolian lamb firepot. For this dish, the meat is cut into thin, almost transparent ribbons: a skilled chef can get as many as ten servings from a 1-lb (500 g) joint of meat. The diners then use chopsticks to transfer the lamb pieces into the fire pot, which is a heated fonduelike container made of copper and filled with boiling water. After only a few seconds the meat is done, and it is eaten with thinly sliced raw leeks or scallions and cilantro leaves and accompanied by spicy red bean curd and sesame paste. When the boiling water has turned to lamb broth, noodles and cabbage are added and the soup is eaten.

MENU GUIDE

Steamed Scallops
Served in black bean sauce or with scallions and gingerroot

Pang Pang Chicken
Shredded poached chicken served cold with cucumber strips and spicy dressing

Peking Duck
Crispy roasted duck served with pancakes, scallions, and hoisin

Ma Po Bean Curd
Cooked with onion, garlic, gingerroot, and pork

Eight-Jewel Duck
Stuffed with nuts, dates, chestnuts, lotus seeds, raisins, shallots, and glutinous rice

Steamed Whole Sea Bass
Served with gingerroot and scallion, or in black bean sauce

Yangchow Lion Heads
Steamed meatballs and cabbage served in a broth

Mongolian Lamb Firepot
Quick-boiled lamb with vegetables and broth

Lotus-White Chicken
Stir-fried with egg whites

Drunken Chicken
Salt-rubbed, sherry-marinated chicken, served cold

Eight-Treasure Rice
Steamed glutinous rice pudding lined with nuts, lotus seeds, and candied fruit

Chicken Velvet
Finely minced chicken, lightly steamed or fried, served without sauce

Szechwan Cabbage with Pork
Pork boiled, deep-fried, and then steamed with spicy pickled cabbage

Ants Climbing a Tree
Ground pork served with cellophane noodles

DRIED INGREDIENTS

Dried ingredients play a crucial but often unseen part in Chinese cuisine. They are used to add flavor, texture, and color; often they impart a more intense taste than if they were used fresh.

Abalone

Sea Slug *Precooked and sliced, requiring several days' soaking before use.*

Agar-Agar *Vegetable gelatin made from seaweed, used in both sweet and savory dishes.*

Bird's Nest *Swallows' nests lined with hardened, re-gurgitated seaweed. Highly prized and highly expensive.*

Wind-Dried Sausages *Made of pork or duck.*

Dried Jellyfish

Dried Mushrooms *Mainly to add texture, although the delicate cloud ear mushroom is eaten on its own when reconstituted.*

Cloud ear mushrooms

Hair vegetable *A type of dried seaweed.*

Dried Oysters *For saltiness.*

Dried Red Dates *For sweetness.*

Dried Scallops

Dried Shrimp

Golden Needles *Bitter, dried buds of the tiger lily.*

Shark's Fin *Sun-dried fins from more than one type of shark. Chinese gourmets say it adds a matchless quality of flavor to a soup.*

Less rough-and-ready is Northern China's most famous dish, Peking duck. For this, only hand-reared, specially fattened ducks are used. First, boiling water is poured over the bird, followed by honey. Then the duck is hung in a windy place for 24 hours to dry the skin to a parchmentlike consistency, before the duck is roasted on a wire rack placed in the middle of an oven. The crisp, shiny red-brown meat is then shredded off the bones with two forks and served with small, paper-thin Mandarin pancakes. The correct procedure to follow when eating Peking duck is to smear the pancake with *hoisin* sauce (often known as plum or barbecue sauce), place one or two duck pieces on top, follow with a few shreds of scallion, and finally roll the pancake up and eat it with your hands.

Another typical Beijing dish is fish in wine sauce. Large pieces of fish are deep-fried in vegetable oil for a minute and then removed before being plunged into a sauce of wine, stock, scallions, and gingerroot and brought back to a boil. Pickled Tientsin cabbage, which is similar in shape to a romaine lettuce, is also typical. For dessert, crêpes filled with a sweet red paste made from adzuki beans are popular.

Szechwan The terrain of the Szechwan province (now Sichuan), and of neighboring Hunan, is characterized by steep mountains and deep river gorges, once home to many a giant panda. Summers here are humid and rainy, and winters are far milder than in Beijing, which lies some 1,000 miles (1,600 kilometers) to the northeast. Agriculture continues year-round; rice, wheat, rapeseed, corn, bamboo shoots, and citrus fruits are the most common crops. Chilies and Szechwan peppercorns, or *fagara* (see page 95), are also prominent in this cuisine, giving the food its characteristic hot taste.

Typical Szechwan-style flavorings are exemplified in the salty yellow bean sauce, made of pickled yellow soybeans, and in chili bean paste, which is a tingling hot mixture of garlic, dried chilies, fermented black beans, and mixed spices.

In the West, Szechwan cooking tends to be regarded as hot and spicy, but there is more to it than just heat. The best chefs aim to make each mouthful a mingling of many layers of flavor. They use chilies to stimulate the taste buds, then apply salty, sweet, and vinegary ingredients to provide a series of different tastes. Curing, pickling, and marinating thus play prominent parts. In most Szechwan homes, a bitter-tasting

pickle made from mustard greens in salt with chilies and garlic is used throughout the year to add a characteristic flavor to simmered, braised, and stir-fried dishes. One such dish is Szechwan cabbage with pork, which is made by first boiling pork, then deep-frying it, and finally steaming it with pickled cabbage, gingerroot, chilies, scallions, black beans, and rock sugar.

The most picturesque name for a Szechwan dish is Ants Climbing a Tree. This tasty dish combines rather characterless "cellophane" noodles (made from ground mung beans) with ground pork marinated in wine, flour, and soy sauce and then stir-fried in a sizzling garlic sauce. The Szechwanese imagine the little ground pork pieces as ants clinging to a noodle tree. Their sense of humor is also at work in a series of "fish-fragrant" meat or vegetable dishes that are so called because the flavorings—a pervasive mixture of chili paste, garlic, gingerroot and scallion—are the same as those traditionally used in cooking fish.

One of the most complex Szechwan dishes is smoked duck, which requires four different cooking processes. First, it is marinated in peppercorns, sage, gingerroot, and sugar. Then it is boiled in stock. Next, it is smoked over a mixture of tea leaves, sugar, bay leaves, and five-spice powder, and finally it is chopped and deep-fried.

Poultry features prominently in the cuisine of this landlocked area, and chicken provides a suitably blank canvas on which to paint the vivid taste pictures that are *Kung Pao* chicken (hot, sweet and sour, made with chilies, gingerroot, and peanuts) and *Pang Pang* chicken: plain poached chicken breasts, shredded and served cold with cucumbers, but covered at the last minute with a dressing made mainly from sesame paste, soy sauce, vinegar, and chili oil.

Shanghai A fourth, but less clearly defined style of cuisine operates on China's eastern extremities, centering on Shanghai and the Yangtze (Chang Jiang) delta, midway between Beijing and Guangzhou. Rivers and ponds dot the area, which is rich in wheat, rice, fish, and seafood. Shanghai crabs are famously tender, and the silver carp of nearby Hangzhou West Lake are considered to be the tastiest freshwater fish in China. The chefs of Shanghai are renowned for their red-braising method of cooking. This involves cooking meat, poultry, and fish, slowly and gently, in a mixture of thick, dark soy sauce and rice wine, then raising the heat to thicken the sauce.

MEALS

The classic composition of a Chinese family meal is one soup dish, one rice dish, and four meat, fish, or vegetable dishes. The soup comes first, then all the other dishes are put on the table at the same time.

Eating at home is very much a communal affair. The table is round, and the dishes are all placed in the center so that everyone is within equal stretching distance. The basic eating equipment is one small bowl (with a saucer underneath for bones), plus a pair of wooden or plastic chopsticks. Although hard for novices to master, in skilled hands these slender implements live up to their name of *faai jee*—"nimble little boys."

It is proper to first make a bed of rice in the bowl and then intermittently reach out with chopsticks to detach those parts of the main dishes that look most appealing. Good manners dictate that food from communal dishes should be placed at least momentarily on the rice before they are transferred to the mouth.

The correct way to eat rice in China is to bring the bowl up to the lower lip and carry little portions into the mouth with chopsticks. Spilling rice is thought to bring bad luck, and children who refuse to eat their last mouthful are told that for every grain they leave, a pockmark will grow on the face of the person they shall marry.

Every Chinese home is believed to have its own kitchen god, who in the last week of every year is called up to heaven to report on the behavior of each member of the household. While the god is away, the family tries to encourage a favorable report by smearing sticky candies onto his picture, which usually hangs above the stove. The kitchen god's return to Earth marks the beginning of the Chinese New Year (early February); he is welcomed back with firecrackers and small, doughy cakes filled with black bean paste (*jien duy*).

At family meals, dessert usually consists of fruit, served with a mug of tea from a large pot that will have been simmering throughout the day. The tea is kept hot in the mug by a lid: from a very early age Chinese children learn how, with just one hand, to lift the mug to their lips, pull back the lid, let the tea into their mouth, and then replace the lid. Tea is drunk without milk or sugar.

Particular favorites are jasmine tea, a green brew made fragrant with jasmine petals; oolong, a fruity, spicy tea grown in the Fujian province, and Lapsang Souchong, which has a strong smoky flavor (see page 268).

Many Chinese teas are thought to have intestine-clearing, medicinal properties. The same applies to *congee*, a thin, glutinous rice soup that is traditionally eaten for breakfast and into which is thrown whatever ingredients are on hand: perhaps soybeans, preserved eggs, pickles, dried fish, or water chestnuts.

At official banquets, the dishes are usually served one at a time, starting with tea, nuts, and fruit, then moving on to small, cold delicacies (pickled cabbage, marinated mushrooms), then the hot dishes (a stir-fry, a soup, Peking duck), and finally a whole fish. Toasts are drunk in Chinese beer and strong *mao tai* wine, made from wheat and sorghum, a milletlike cereal.

Stricter rules apply at domestic dinner parties. Of great concern to everyone is the ticklish business of who sits where. There is one fixed rule, and it dictates that the host and hostess should always sit with their backs to the door, and the guest or guests of honor should sit directly opposite them. Thereafter, it is up to the other guests to sort out among themselves the relative order of social importance, which is done with much polite gesturing as the guests invite each other to proceed ahead into the dining room. The desired result is that the least important guests end up sitting next to the host and hostess.

A selection of dim sum

DIM SUM

Dim sum means "touch the heart," and it is the phrase used to refer to the small snack dishes that the Chinese consume in great quantities in the middle of the day. Originally devised by teahouse owners in the Sung Dynasty (A.D. 960–1279), these little delicacies can often be difficult and time-consuming to make. Specialist dim sum chefs usually take over the whole restaurant kitchen, handing over to general chefs for the evening, when dim sum will not be on the menu.

Har Gow *Minced shrimp, covered with a thin, pastalike transparent skin, made of wheat starch.*

Paper-Wrapped Shrimp *A deep-fried mixture of minced shrimp, pork fat, ham, and bamboo shoots, wrapped in rice paper.*

Siu Mai *Little wheat starch skins filled in a variety of ways, for instance with a mixture of chopped pork, shrimps, mushrooms, scallions, bamboo shoots, carrot, and gingerroot.*

Char Siu *Cantonese red-roasted pork, marinated in soy sauce, rice wine, honey, sugar, and garlic.*

Char Siu Bao *A heavy, doughy dumpling, the size of a tennis ball, stuffed with red-roasted pork.*

VIETNAM

A land of swollen rivers and lush green paddy fields, Vietnam has a climate that ranges from monsoon tropical to cool and temperate. The result is a mixture of rampant vegetation and ordered, crop-rich farmlands. Green is the dominant color of Vietnamese cooking, in which the fragrance of indigenous herbs and vegetables neither gives way to the forcefulness of the Indian spices employed nor overpowers the more understated flavors that characterize its Chinese-style dishes. The outcome is a cuisine that gracefully blends the gentle and the vigorous.

TRADITIONAL INGREDIENTS

Aniseed*
Bamboo shoots
Banana leaves*
Basil*
Bean sprouts
Black bean sauce
Chilies*
Cilantro*
Coconut*
Curry leaves
Daikon*
Dill*
Duck
Eel
Five-spice powder*
Frog's legs
Galangal*
Garlic*
Jellyfish
Lemongrass*
Limes*
Mint*
Mushrooms*
Noodles
Nuoc mam (fish sauce)*
Palm sugar
Papayas
Peanuts
Rice
Rice paper
Rice vinegar*
Scallions*
Sesame oil*
Sesame seeds*
Shallots*
Shrimp
Star anise*
Tamarind*

(*see Index)

INFLUENCES

A thousand years of Chinese occupation, throughout the first millennium A.D., left a culinary mark on Vietnam that remains to this day. This is evident in its cooking methods (stir-frying and steaming), implements (bowl and chopsticks), and even its ingredients (soy sauce and noodles). On a deeper level, too, Vietnamese chefs have inherited the Chinese culinary principle of seeking to balance contrasting flavors and textures within a meal. This legacy is particularly noticeable in Northern Vietnam, which is still inhabited by a large Chinese population. Here, food tends to be milder than elsewhere in the country.

The French have also had a long relationship with Vietnam: first as traders, then as colonists. It was they who introduced the crusty *baguette*, European vegetables such as asparagus and green beans, pâté and even frog's legs. The Gallic influence is at its most evident in the cities of Southern Vietnam, where restaurants serve dishes such as French beans with crushed garlic and chili and frog's legs with chili and lemongrass.

FLAVORINGS

The generous use of herbs such as dill, lemongrass, cilantro, mint, and basil distinguishes Vietnamese cuisine from that of its Southeast Asian neighbors. Feathery dill is sprinkled over *canh chua ca*, a hot, sour fish soup comprised of white fish, fish sauce, chilies, and lemon juice. It also features prominently in the powerful-tasting *cha ca*. To make this dish, the chef first marinates fish in a tangy mixture of citrus juice, tamarind, turmeric, shrimp paste, and galangal. The fish is then charcoal-grilled, reheated at the table in fish sauce, and finally coated with a thick layer of dill and scallions before serving.

Lemongrass (*xa*) imparts its powerful lemony aroma and flavor to many salads, soups, and meat and fish dishes, such as *ga xao xa* (stir-fried chicken with lemongrass) and *thit bo xao xa ot* (grilled beef and lemongrass). The Vietnamese also love to mix their herbs. Mint, cilantro, and basil are piled onto cooked or marinated fish or meat and then topped with finely cut vegetables. These thick, aromatic clusters are placed on paper-thin rice pancakes or crisp lettuce leaves, rolled into neat little parcels, and then dipped into a variety of salty, sweet, and sour sauces.

The basis for many of these sauces is *nuoc mam,* or fish sauce. This is made by leaving layers of fish and salt in large wooden barrels to ferment for several months beneath fierce sunshine. The result is a clear, pungent, fish-flavored liquid, deep amber in color. The addition of lime or lemon juice, wine vinegar, hot chilies, garlic, and sugar features in another, still tangier sauce called *nuoc cham*. As well as serving as a dip, nuoc cham is used to provide an extra flavor dimension to soups, stir-fries, meat, and vegetable dishes.

Peanuts are frequently called on by the Vietnamese cook; roasted and crushed, they serve as a garnish, or they are combined with nuoc mam, garlic, chili, lime juice, and coconut milk to make a deliciously smooth satay sauce called *dau phong rang*. Traditionally, this accompanies eel fried with lemongrass, but it is also served alongside many meat and fish dishes. Sesame oil gives a nutty flavor to sauces, such as black bean sauce (black beans, garlic, fish sauce, sugar, vinegar, chili, stock, sesame oil, and seeds), while sesame seeds impart a nutty texture to finely sliced, charcoal-grilled beef. Scallions, an ingredient of many Vietnamese dishes, are used raw, or lightly cooked, to add last-minute bite to soups, spring rolls, or stir-fries. Shallots are either stewed in casseroles or deep-fried into crisp flakes and used as a palate-stimulating garnish.

INGREDIENTS

Rice appears at the Vietnamese table in many different manifestations. In its simplest form, it is plainly boiled to provide bulk accompaniment to soups, stews, and curries; alternatively rice is made into fine noodles and then deep-fried or steamed. Ground rice is made into thin pancakes that are steamed and then stuffed with any number of different fillings. A favorite is *banh cuoa*: pancakes filled with cooked pork and vegetables, topped with crispy fried shallots, and dipped into a spicy, sweet sauce. Finally, rice flour is the basis for the transparently thin wrappings of *cha gio* (spring rolls).

Widespread use is also made of glutinous rice, which is a starchier, stickier variety than its long-grained counterpart. It is particularly good in desserts; a Vietnamese specialty is glutinous rice soaked in coconut milk and then steamed inside banana leaves.

Pork is enjoyed throughout the country and is frequently incorporated with the bounty of seafood. It is combined with crab for pancake and spring roll fillings and with noodles and dried prawns for *mi quang*, a frequently served soup.

Chicken is a popular ingredient, either roasted with five-spice powder (*ngu vi huong*) or stir-fried with fragrant stalks of lemongrass. Beef is the central ingredient of *pho*, which is a well-known Vietnamese meat and noodle soup. It is made with fine shreds of raw beef that are combined with mint, scallions, and cilantro and then sprinkled over a bed of noodles. Steaming hot aromatic meat stock that is flavored with gingerroot and star anise is then poured over all the ingredients, partially cooking the raw

beef. Additional flavorings that are hot (red chili), salty (fish sauce), and sour (lime juice) are added in various quantities and combinations to suit individual palates.

As for vegetables, lettuce, white radishes, potatoes, asparagus, broccoli, carrots, artichokes, cucumber, cauliflower, zucchini, and eggplants are all used in varying degrees throughout the country. They are served raw or stir-fried for the shortest time possible to preserve color, flavor, and texture. Vegetables are often cooked with a minimal amount of pork and seafood, bestowing a gentle hint of flavor.

Fruit abounds in Vietnam, particularly in the humid South, and it is almost always eaten plain. Oranges, coconuts, lychees, star fruit (carambola), mangoes, bananas, custard apples, pomelos, watermelons, and guavas are the most popular and often combined to make sumptuous fruit salads.

MEALS

Traditionally, breakfast is a steaming bowl of pho, either homemade or bought from a favorite street vendor. Only a minority of Vietnamese prefer a Western-style breakfast of buttered bread with coffee or tea.

The Vietnamese lunch consists of rice, a clear soup, and a selection of light meat, fish, and vegetable dishes that are served with a full spectrum of dipping and flavoring sauces. The evening meal is usually similar to lunch but, being the largest meal of the day, consists of many more dishes.

On Sundays, the main meal is generally much more elaborate. Favorite dishes are scallops and crispy-fried, shredded seaweed, broiled pork balls with a sweet peanut sauce, or the traditional do-it-yourself dish *ta pli lu*. This involves diners being provided with a large platter of raw ingredients—chicken, beef, prawns, squid, and fresh vegetables—which are then cooked at the table in a pot of simmering, aromatic stock. Delicately scented jasmine tea provides a gentle and refreshing end to the meal.

Meals are eaten at a shin-high wooden table called a *divan*; diners generally sit on the floor to eat. Fresh fruits, rather than sweet baked desserts, are the usual way to finish a meal. If alcohol accompanies the meal it will almost invariably be rice wine.

MENU GUIDE

Pho
Rice noodles in broth with shredded beef or chicken

Canh Thit Nau Cua
Crab and pork soup

Cha Gio
Spring rolls

Bahn Tom
Shrimp pâté served on toast

Canh Chua Ca
Hot-and-sour fish soup

Ga Xao Xa Ot
Chicken with lemongrass

Ca Hap
Steamed sea bass

Ca Loc Hap
Fish steamed in coconut milk and gingerroot

Goi Dua Leo
Pork, squid, and peanut salad

Thit Ga Chien Gung
Chicken with gingerroot

Cha Ca
Monkfish and dill

Suon Chien
Barbecued spareribs

Kho
Fish or meat cooked in lemongrass and fish sauce

Ca Tim Nuong
Eggplants cooked with lime

Bau Xao
Zucchini with shrimp and pork

Banh Chuoi
Banana cake

Chuoi Va Thom Chien Gion
Deep-fried apple and banana slices

Chuoi Dua
Bananas in coconut milk

Hoa Qua Tuoi
Frozen fruit salad

Dau Xanh Vung
Mung bean cakes coated in sesame seeds

THAILAND

W ithin their culinary arsenal, Thai chefs have an array of flavors that range from the gentle to the explosive, from the shudderingly sour to the syrupy sweet, and colors ranging from the leafiest green to the spiciest red. Thailand is blessed with a climate that is neither too wet nor too dry; the result is a land that nurtures meat and vegetables in tropical abundance and seas and rivers that yield a shining harvest of fish and seafood. Confident in its own well-stocked pantry, Thailand has felt free to look outside its borders for inspiration. Thai cooking has embraced Indian spices, Chinese cooking methods, and that most unmistakably Pacific of flavors, the coconut. Yet it has borrowed piecemeal rather than wholesale, never subordinating itself to overseas influences, always making the newcomers play a Thai tune and retaining the indigenous cuisine. Thus, where the Chinese might steam fish plain, the Thais will add lemongrass; where an Indian curry might be flavored with only two spices, a Thai curry may contain many, along with herbs, fish sauce, and coconut milk. However, the real measure of Thai culinary skill lies not in the number of ingredients it employs but in the artistry with which they are used.

TRADITIONAL INGREDIENTS

Basil*
Bean curd
Beef
Chicken
Chilies*
Chili sauce*
Cilantro*
Coconut*
Corn
Cumin*
Curry paste*
Fish sauce*
Galangal*
Garlic*
Gingerroot*
Kaffir limes
Kapee (shrimp paste)
Krachai
Lemongrass*
Limes*
Mint*
Mushrooms*
Noodles
Oyster sauce*
Palm sugar
Peanuts
Pork
Rice
Scallions*
Sesame seeds*
Shallots*
Shrimp
Shrimp paste
Soy sauce*
Star anise*
Sugar*
Tamarind*
Taro
Turmeric*

(*see Index)

INFLUENCES

Geographically, Thailand stands closer to China than India, but its cuisine has adopted much from its more far-flung neighbors. From China, the Thais borrowed the wok, stir-frying, and steaming. What they chose not to take up was the Chinese practice of thickening sauces with cornstarch; consequently, Thai stir-fry dishes have always been lighter and more delicate than their Chinese counterparts. Similarly, Thailand adopted curries from India but invested them with three distinctly Thai characteristics. First, Thai curries are based on curry pastes, made from the pounding of wet herbs and spices, whereas Indian curries are generally flavored with curry powders, produced by the pounding of dry herbs and spices. Second, the Thais slice their main curry ingredients (meat, fish, or vegetables) into fine slivers rather than chunks. And third, instead of using dairy products such as ghee (clarified butter), Thai chefs employ coconut milk; this is produced by soaking grated coconut flesh in water and then draining off the thick liquid that results (see page 179).

Strangely enough, it was Europeans who introduced the ingredient that has come to epitomize Thai cooking: the chili pepper. Portuguese traders are credited with bringing this fiery addition to Eastern

cuisines; perhaps to compensate, they also brought with them the soothing egg custard, original ancestor of the coconut custard, *sung kha ya*, which is so popular throughout Thailand today.

FLAVORINGS

Ten varieties of the world's hottest chilies are grown in Thailand. The strongest of these is the miniscule bird chili; its innocuous size ($\frac{1}{2}$ in; 1 cm) conceals its prodigious capacity for searing the mouth. Chilies are put to a plethora of uses. When they are married with *nam pla* (a thin, salty fish sauce), *kapee* (shrimp paste), garlic, cilantro, and citrus juice, *nam prik* is born. This liquid acts as condiment, sauce, dip, and seasoning throughout Thai cooking. *Prik nam som* (chilies in rice vinegar) and *prik pon* (red chili powder) are other popular chili-based condiments.

Thai garlic, with smaller cloves and pinker skin than its Western relation, is used in vast numbers of Thai dishes; in addition, when crisply fried, it is used as a garnish, and when pickled in rice vinegar, salt, and sugar it becomes the condiment *kratiem dong* (pickled garlic).

The sour flavor of tamarind, the citrus flavor of lime juice, lemongrass, and Kaffir lime leaves, plus the heated flavor of

Thailand's three types of ginger—gingerroot, greater galangal, and *krachai (lesser galangal)*—add up to a perfume that pervades all Thai cooking. Chefs often combine this lively package of flavors with coconut milk to create the sparring between tingling piquancy and creamy sweetness that typifies the nation's cuisine. This phenomenon manifests itself most noticeably in the abundant red and green curry paste dishes such as *kiaw wan goong* (green prawn curry) and *kaeng pet kai* (red chicken curry). The color of the pastes depends on the color of the chilies used, and usual constituents of a curry paste (see page 81) include chilies (red or green), lemongrass, shallots, garlic, galangal, cilantro, cumin, white pepper, shrimp paste, and Kaffir lime skin or leaves.

Cilantro and mint leaves act as ornament and ingredient. Another prominent taste is basil, which imparts its fragrance throughout stir-fries, curries, and soups, as well as appearing shredded in salads.

OTHER INGREDIENTS

The invitation to a meal in Thailand is *kin khao*, which translates as "come and eat rice." There are two kinds that prevail: long-grain, or fragrant rice, which is the dietary mainstay of Southern Thailand, and the shorter-grained glutinous rice that is the main-course choice of Northern Thailand, as well as the basis for desserts throughout the country. Glutinous rice is more compact, and much more manageable, than the long-grained variety.

Rice noodles are also eaten throughout the country, arriving at the table in a number of different dishes. When stir-fried, they appear in the national favorite *pad thai*, along with dried shrimp, roasted peanuts, lemon juice, fish sauce, bean sprouts, scallions, chili, preserved turnips, cilantro, and sugar. When boiled, they luxuriate in soups such as *suki gai*, made with chicken, soy sauce, fish sauce, sugar, egg, red bean curd, pickled garlic, stock, chili powder, lemon juice, celery, and Chinese cabbage. When deep-fried to a crispy consistency, they are the centerpiece of the famous Thai dish *mee krop*, alongside garlic, shallots, chili, and pork.

Thailand's elongated coastline and its numerous rivers harbor a variety of fish and shellfish, which are prepared in many ways. They may be minced and shaped into balls, or stuffed, curried, or steamed with pickled plums and garlic. Broiled lobster with chili and garlic is a fine example of balancing delicate shellfish with hot chilies.

Pork plays a versatile role, often being combined with seafood in dishes such as *bu ja* (steamed crab with garlic, cilantro, and chili). Chicken and beef also appear in stir-fried vegetable dishes, as well as in curries such as *kaeng mussaman*. This combines beef, coconut milk, fish sauce, tamarind, potatoes, peanuts, and onions, in a rich Mussaman curry paste, which differs from other Thai curry pastes in containing cinnamon, cloves, star anise, and cardamom.

MEALS

Rice porridge is the traditional Thai way to begin the day, eaten with pickled radishes or other preserved vegetables and perhaps enlivened by some minced pork plus a few chilies. Lunch is generally bought from one of the multitude of street vendors who throng the pavements of every Thai town and who even make midday house calls in the more remote villages. The fare they peddle around lunchtime is usually noodle-based, perhaps a noodle soup, dotted with fragments of chicken, green beans, and bean sprouts. It might also be a fried noodle dish, sparingly strewn with a few meat and vegetable pieces but lavishly stimulated by a mixture of sauces that will include sugar, fish sauce, roasted fresh peanuts, and crushed dried chilies.

The evening meal is the most copious. There are many courses, which are all served simultaneously. Dessert, if served, usually comprises one liquid sweet dish, probably perfumed with coconut cream, and one dry sweet dish, perhaps based on sweetened bean paste. Fruit provides Thai meals with a refreshing climax.

Food is often garnished with exquisitely cut vegetables. Tomatoes are carved into the shape of roses, carrots into lotus petals, scallions into lilies and gingerroot into tiny crabs, which are usually accurate right down to their claws.

MENU GUIDE

Poh Piah Tod
Spring rolls

Kha Nom Jeen
Thai-style dumplings

Suki Kai
Chicken, vegetable, and bean curd soup

Yam Nua Saweo
Cucumber filled with beef

Tom Yum Kung
Hot-and-sour shrimp soup

Pad Thai
Stir-fried noodles with shredded meat and vegetables

Tod Mun Pla
Fish cakes

Hoy Op
Steamed mussels with basil and lemongrass

Laab Nua
Spicy minced beef salad

Kaeng Pet Dang Mhoo
Red pork curry

Kiaw Wan Goong
Green shrimp curry

Yam Talay
Hot-and-sour fish salad

Pla Kung
Shrimp and lemongrass

Satay
Barbecued skewered meat

Homok Talay
Seafood and coconut bouillabaisse

Mee Krop
Sweet crispy noodles

Khanom Maw Gaeng
Baked custard

Ta-Kho
Coconut milk with glutinous rice

Kruay Khaek
Fried banana

Met Kanoon
Sweet mung-bean dessert

SOUTH PACIFIC

A combination of rain, heat, and humidity makes the South Pacific a greenhouse when it comes to food growing. Bunches of tropical fruits swell and bulge from their trees, leafy vegetables sprout densely from the ground, and rice stalks wave in multitudes from the watery fields that dot the land.

Water is never far away, either in the form of a rice field, a river, or the sea. Fish and seafood abound, as do the number of ways to cook them: boiling in coconut milk, stewing in vinegar, frying in soy or fish sauce, or dousing with fiery dips and relishes. The chefs of the South Pacific adapt their cooking methods to express most eloquently the character of their main ingredients. With a treasury of herbs and spices, both indigenous and imported by many generations of seafarers, they have an almost unparalleled vocabulary of flavorings.

TRADITIONAL INGREDIENTS

Bananas
Banana leaves*
Basil*
Bay*
Buah keras/kemiri
Chilies*
Cilantro*
Cinnamon*
Coconut*
Cumin*
Dried fish*
Fennel*
Fish sauce (patis)*
Galangal*
Garlic*
Gingerroot*
Hoisin*
Jackfruit
Kalamansi
Ketjap
Lemongrass*
Limes*
Lychees
Mangoes
Noodles
Nutmeg*
Palm sugar
Papaya
Peanuts
Pineapples
Screwpine leaves
Shrimp paste (blachan/trasi)*
Soy sauce*
Soybean paste (miso)*
Sweet potatoes
Tamarind*
Turmeric*
Yams

(*see Index)

MALAYSIA

Most Malaysians live on a long tropical peninsula, which on its western shore borders the Strait of Malacca, a natural ocean corridor between the South China Sea and the Indian Ocean. The gentle coastline offers a natural landfall to seaborne traders, and in the fifteenth century A.D., merchants from China, India, and the Middle East came in great numbers to the thriving seaport of Malacca (today Melaka).

Of these early visitors, it was the Arabs and Indians who left the most lasting imprint on the society by carrying over the Muslim religion. In terms of cuisine, however, all have had a profound influence.

Indian spices, such as cumin and turmeric, proliferate in Malaysian curries; *satay*, the Malaysian skewered meat dish, can trace its origins back to the Arab kabob; and dishes of Chinese extraction such as spring rolls and *char siu* (honey-basted pork) have been part of Malaysia's cooking heritage for centuries.

The Chinese influence is particularly strong in Singapore, the island republic that sits just south of Malaysia. In the 1820s many thousands of Chinese laborers flocked here to work on the construction of Singapore City. They intermarried with the indigenous Malay women and produced a clearly identifiable culture, the *Nonya,* or Straits Chinese, who practice a style of cooking that combines a Chinese regard for texture and balance with a Malaysian fondness for chilies and curries.

Coconut milk, or *lemak*, lies at the heart of Nonya cuisine, as it does with nearly all Malaysian food. This is not the raw juice of the coconut (which can be extracted by drilling a hole in the shell), but the strained product of warm water mixed with shredded or dried coconut flesh. Lemak is the main source of liquid in Malaysian curries, but it is most prominent in the ubiquitous *laksa lemak* (coconut soup)—a delicious brothy hodgepodge of shrimp, lemongrass (*serai*), bean curd, garlic, onions, curry leaves, and candlenuts, called *buah keras*, which are similar to macadamia nuts. It also features prominently in puddings, such as *serikaya*, coconut custard.

Coconut flesh, shredded or dried, is a common ingredient in *sambals*, which are little platefuls of paste, sometimes moist, sometimes dry, which are used as a relish or an extra source of flavoring. Combinations include chili and shrimp, coconut and onion, or pineapple and cucumber.

Sambals frequently contain a fish paste called *blachan*, which is a pounded-down combination of fermented shrimp and salt. It has a powerful odor but, when cooked, blachan imparts depth of flavor rather than unrestrained fishiness, surprisingly enough. Another common fish flavoring is *ikan bilis*, which consists of tiny dried fish that are crumbled into soups and sauces to add an extra layer of taste. Soy sauce and hoisin (see page 242) are also used, though more often with dishes of Chinese than native Malaysian origin.

Powerful herbs and spices are used in abundance: lemongrass, cilantro, garlic, cumin, chili, turmeric, curry leaves, and gingerroot and its pine-scented relative galangal are among the best known.

Sweetness is supplied by brown palm sugar (*gula melaka*), and juice from the lime, lemon, and crushed tamarind pod (*asam*) add tartness. Malaysian cooks often employ the long, thin leaves of the screwpine tree, pandanus leaves, which lend foods a nutty flavor and a green coloring.

With a large Muslim population, and a significant Hindu one as well, the eating of beef and pork is limited. Only chicken is acceptable to the population as a whole. Chinese tradition, by contrast, imposes no such limits. Throughout Malaysia, fish and seafood are plentiful, particularly prawns, mackerel, pomfret, and snapper.

Peanuts give flavor and substance to the traditional satay sauce. Eggplants, bean sprouts, gourds, and Chinese cabbage are the other predominant vegetables, while the long list of fruits includes rambutans, lychees, bananas, pineapples, limes, and starfruit.

Noodles (*mee*) are a popular snack, but rice is the daily staple of Malaysian life. There are two main types: the long-grain rice that is familiar in the West, and glutinous rice. The last is starchier and stickier and comes in two colors: white and black. It is very often cooked inside a serving-sized container of braided palm or banana leaves, which gives it a delicate flavor.

Satay and peanut sauce

INDONESIA

Indonesia is an ocean jigsaw, a collection of some 13,600 islands, of which the three best known are Java, Sumatra, and Bali.

Between the seventh and twelfth centuries A.D., many islands owed allegiance to the Southeast Asian Hindu-Buddhist empire of Srivijaya. But when its power waned in the thirteenth century, islanders began to adopt the Islamic religion that arrived with the Muslim seafarers and this then spread to many points along their trading routes. Today, 90 percent of Indonesians are Muslim, though there is also a sizeable Hindu population on the island of Bali.

Indonesia shares many dishes and flavors with her Muslim neighbor Malaysia. Peanuts are the dominant taste. They feature in the conventional Indonesian dipping sauce for satay and in the sauce for the national dish *gado gado*, which is a cold salad of cooked vegetables served with prawn crackers (*krupuk udang*), and slightly bitter little chips called *emping*, which are made from the fried kernels of the nut from the giant melinjo tree.

Coconut milk, *santen*, is used in a large number of dishes, such as *ayam opur* (chicken cooked in coconut milk) and beef *rendang*, in which the meat is slowly cooked in spice-enhanced coconut milk. In some dishes, santen appears in the form of a thick sauce. While in others (rendang, for example), it is cooked until it is completely absorbed into the other ingredients.

As in Malaysia, sauces and pastes feature prominently. *Ketjap* (from which the word "ketchup" indirectly derives) is the Indonesian soy sauce. The two main types are *ketjap manis* (sweet, thick, and treacly) and *ketjap asin* (lighter and saltier). Both kinds are used in the making of sambals—spicy ground herb and spice mixtures that serve as both in-the-dish seasonings and on-the-table condiments. Examples are *sambal ketjap*, made with crushed chilies, garlic, ketjap manis, and juice from the Kaffir lime; and the all-purpose *sambal goreng*, which combines coconut milk, bay leaves, lime leaves, garlic, cumin, red chilies, galangal or *laos* (*lenkuas* in Malaysia), and *trasi*, the salted, fermented fish paste that is the Indonesian equivalent of Malaysia's blachan (see page 189).

MENU GUIDE

Acar/Achara
Pickled vegetable relish

Nasi Goreng (Indonesia)
Mixed fried rice

Char Kway Teo (Malaysia)
Stir-fried noodles with meat and shrimp

Martabak (Indonesia)
Minced meat pancakes

Char Siu
(Malaysia and Indonesia)
Chinese honey-basted roast pork

Dinuguan (Philippines)
Pork stewed in pig blood

Ikan Lemak (Malaysia)
Sweet-and-sour fish

Guinataan (Philippines)
Any dish cooked in coconut milk

Gado Gado (Indonesia)
Cold vegetable salad with peanut sauce and crackers

Pork Gulai (Malaysia)
Nonya dish of pork cooked in coconut milk

Chicken Relleno
(Philippines)
Stuffed chicken

Rendang (Indonesia)
Spicy beef and coconut milk curry

Kari-Kari (Philippines)
Beef or oxtail stew in peanut gravy

Nasi Kuning (Indonesia)
Festive dish of yellow rice

Lechon (Philippines)
Whole roast pig

Tahu Telur (Malaysia)
Bean curd omelet

Sinigang (Philippines)
Sour broth with tomatoes and acidic fruit

Lemper (Indonesia)
Chicken pieces encased in glutinous rice

MENU GUIDE

Lontong
(Malaysia and Indonesia)
Cold, compressed boiled rice, cooked in banana leaf containers

Singapore Laksa
Mixed seafood soup with rice vermicelli

Pancit (Philippines)
Noodles cooked in garlic and onions, with shrimp and pork

Ayam Opur (Indonesia)
Chicken cooked in coconut milk

Adobado (Philippines)
Pork and/or chicken stew cooked adobo style—in vinegar, garlic, and soy sauce

Laksa Lemak (Malaysia)
Coconut milk soup with prawns

Satay
(Malaysia and Indonesia)
Skewered beef, chicken, or turtle meat, served with peanut sauce

Paksiw Na Bangus
(Philippines)
Fish boiled in vinegar and salt

Gudeg (Indonesia)
Chicken with jackfruit

Chah Kangkung (Indonesia)
Stir-fried cabbage greens

Kilawin (Philippines)
Fish raw-cooked in vinegar and citrus juice

Gula Melaka (Malaysia)
Coconut, sago, and treacle pudding

Halo-Halo (Philippines)
Sundae of dried and preserved fruits mixed with ice shavings and ice cream

Serikaya
(Malaysia and Indonesia)
Coconut custard

Banana-Cue (Philippines)
Banana rolled in brown sugar and barbecued

Commonly used herbs and spices are lemongrass, cumin, cilantro, laos powder (dried and ground galangal), chilies, and turmeric; the latter gives the yellow coloring to the feast-day rice dish, *nasi kuning.*

Because of the country's island makeup, great emphasis is placed on fish. Most frequently pulled from the sea are red snapper, sea bass, pomfret, and the bony milkfish. Shrimp of all sizes abound, as do mussels and squid. Of the many freshwater species, one of the most prized for its thick, white meat is the *gurami.*

As in Malaysia, the large Muslim population eschews the eating of pork. Only on the predominantly Hindu island of Bali does the pig feature to any great extent in the chef's plans. Lamb is viewed as a special-occasion ingredient, while beef (or water buffalo) is a more everyday meat, although it is not eaten by Hindus.

Fruits grow abundantly in this tropical climate, among them papaya, pineapples, mangosteen, and several different types of banana, and in size they rise from little, crisp "rose-apples" (*jambu air)* the size of a golf ball to giant jackfruit (*nangka*). This is a boulder-sized fruit with fibrous yellow flesh inside its thick, rubbery-spiked skin. The jackfruit is a central ingredient in the traditional dish *gudeg.*

Indonesians eat largely the same vegetables as Malaysians: Chinese cabbage, cucumbers, bean sprouts, and *kacang panjang*, which are green beans that can grow up to 3 ft (1 meter) in length.

THE PHILIPPINES

The 350 years of Spanish rule, which lasted from the 1550s to the 1890s, have left the Philippines not just with a Spanish name (after King Philip II of Spain) but also a culinary legacy of a large number of dishes and flavors that have the distinctive stamp of Spanish style.

The small, savory snack dishes that make up the Philippine *merienda* buffet are the tapas of the South Pacific. *Arroz Valenciana* is a Philippine paella. The spicy chorizo sausage is a direct Spanish import, while other ingredients were imported from Spanish territories in the New World; corn, avocado, tomatoes, potatoes, and coffee all

came to the Philippines via Mexico, which for many years administrated this island region on Spain's behalf.

The other major influence on Philippine cuisine came from the Chinese merchants who were trading in this area, some as early as the tenth century. Dishes such as spring rolls and *lomi* (sticky noodles with meat and seafood) were firmly established in the Philippines long before the first Spanish galleon was sighted.

There is a sharpness and a tartness that runs through most Philippine food. Frequent use is made of the juice from the *kalamansi*, which is a sour citrus fruit halfway between a lime and a lemon. Vinegar also plays a central part in two of the most common styles of cooking—*paksiw*, meat or fish slowly boiled in vinegar and salt; and *kilawin*, the practice of "cooking" fish by marinating it in vinegar and kalamansi juice, as in the South American dish *seviche.* In addition, vinegar is combined with garlic and soy sauce to make *adobado*, a tangy pork or chicken stew.

A thick, salty fish paste called *bagoong*, and its thinner, lighter by-product *patis* (fish sauce), provide extra body for soups and stews and also for the large number of dips and relishes that are known collectively as *sawsawan*. Both bagoong and patis are mixed with ingredients such as garlic, pounded red chilies, vinegar, onions, and tangy tamarind or kalamansi juice, to provide a collection of dishes that range in flavor from the sharp to the fiery.

A gentler source of flavoring is coconut milk. This forms the basis for the style of dish known as *guinataan*, in which a mixture of chicken, pork, and vegetables is gently stewed until all the liquid has been absorbed. The term "guinataan" can also be applied to sweet dishes, such as a combination of yams, tapioca, banana, and jackfruit, again cooked in coconut milk.

The most frequently used spices are star anise, cloves, cinnamon, ginger, turmeric, and nutmeg. Herbs include rosemary, bay leaf, basil, and dill. Chili peppers—crushed, dried, sliced, or fried—also make numerous appearances in Philippine dishes.

In a country made up of over 7,000 different islands, fish naturally play a part in the diet. Anchovies, sea bass, swordfish, and milkfish are the most common, though stingray and abalone are also to be found.

Unlike their Southeast Asian neighbors, most Filipinos are not Muslim but Christian and therefore can countenance eating pork.

This is witnessed in the well-known dish *dinuguan*, a spicy stew of pork meat that has been cooked in pork blood. *Lechon*—whole roast pig—is reserved for feasts and special occasions: the guest of honor gets the meal under way by plucking off one of the cooked ears. Chicken and beef are also widely consumed, as are variety meats.

The Philippine staple is rice, both long-grain and glutinous. There is also a special purple rice, *pirurutung*, which is a decorative strain that is used only for puddings such as *puton bumbong*, a dish that is cooked in bamboo tubes and served with sugar and butter. Philippine cooking boasts a rich variety of dessert rice dishes, including the popular *pinipig*, which are individual cakes made of toasted glutinous rice, and *champorado*, chocolate-flavored sticky rice.

The favored vegetables are squashes, Chinese cabbage, onions, white turnips, palm hearts, and *kangkong*, a leafy swamp vegetable with a reputation for cheapness if not flavor. The fruits most commonly to be found on market stands are bananas, guavas, pineapples, mangoes, kalamansi, jackfruit, watermelons, and *durian*, a large, spiky-shelled fruit with an overpowering smell (some would say downright unpleasant) and a consistency much like soft cheese.

MEALS

Breakfast in Malaysia can be a filling affair, usually consisting of steamed buns or *nasi lemak*, a rich coconut milk porridge that can be sprinkled with *ikan bilis* (dried fish) and accompanied by anything from a hard-boiled egg and sambal to a full-size fish curry. Lunch is generally a lighter meal, perhaps a selection of little Chinese dim sum dumplings or else rice accompanied by a meat or vegetable dish, and washed down by scented Chinese tea.

The biggest meal of the day is dinner, which may consist of one rice dish and up to five fish, vegetable, or meat dishes, all accompanied by sambals. Usually the food is put in the middle of the table and all the diners are invited to help themselves. The style of cutlery depends on the origin of the food; Chinese dishes will normally be eaten with chopsticks and Malaysian dishes with either fingers (right hand only) or a

spoon and fork. Banana leaves usually play a part, either as rice containers, dinner plates, or heat-retaining wrappers.

On special occasions, Malaysians will get out the steamboat—a charcoal-heated pot much like a Swiss fondue set. First a bubbling stock is heated, then diners drop in pieces of meat, seafood, vegetables, and fish, removing them when done.

The meal pattern in Indonesia is much the same. The standard breakfast is rice porridge (*bubur ayam*), which is a bowl of rice mixed with omelet and crumbled dried fish (*goreng teri*). Another popular first-thing-in-the-morning dish is *nasi goreng*, meaning literally "fried rice," that is mixed with whatever leftovers are on hand.

Lunch will consist of rice or noodles and a meat or vegetable dish, perhaps a chicken or beef satay that has been cooked at a roadside stand. Dinner is eaten at any time after 6:30 P.M., and if it is a special occasion, the fare will most likely be *nasi gerar* (the Dutch *rijstaffel* or "rice table"): a vast collection of rice, soup, fish, meat, vegetable, and sambal dishes, selected so as to take the diners through the whole spectrum of tastes (spicy, bland, sweet, and sour) and textures (crisp, soft, crunchy, and chewy). Again, this is a serve-yourself meal eaten either with cutlery or with the fingers of the right hand; the left hand is considered unclean and should not be used, even to pass a dish to a neighbor. *Selamat makan* is the correct way to say *bon appétit* in Indonesia.

Filipinos also begin the day with rice, often fried with a hint of garlic and served with salted, dried fish. At lunchtime, they may have *pancit* (noodles with pork and shrimps) or *lumpia*, which are the local version of spring rolls. Late afternoon is the time for *merienda*, a selection of small savory dishes that can, in sufficient numbers, count as a full meal.

As in Malaysia and Indonesia, diners help themselves from communal plates, but in the Philippines it is much more common to eat with cutlery than with fingers.

Throughout all three countries, cooking implements are similar. The wok, either metal or earthenware, is the basic utensil. It is known as a *kwali* in Malaysia, a *wajan* in Indonesia, and in the Philippines it goes by the name of *carajay*.

Alcohol is never served to accompany meals in the two predominantly Muslim countries and only infrequently in the Christian Philippines. Alternatives are tea, coffee, fruit juice, and iced coconut milk.

AUSTRALIA AND NEW ZEALAND

British colonies for more than 200 years, both Australia and New Zealand combine heavy British-style dishes with a lighter, Asian-style cuisine. Examples of the heavier dishes are Lamington cake (sponge cake covered with a thick layer of chocolate) and the Adelaide Floater, a meat pie surrounded by pureed canned peas and topped with tomato sauce. Exponents of the lighter style borrow Southeast Asian flavorings such as lemongrass, cilantro, and ginger and marry them with home-grown ingredients such as beef and green prawns.

Roast meat plays an important part in the diet of both countries, particularly home-raised New Zealand lamb and Australian beef. A classic New Zealand dish is hogget, a whole roasted 1-year-old lamb. Australians also have a festive lamb dish, called colonial goose, which is a rolled, stuffed shoulder of lamb. Another popular form of cooking is barbecuing, a method originally perfected by the Aborigines.

Kangaroo, a gamy-tasting meat, is eaten in some parts of Australia, both roasted and braised. In New Zealand, venison is popular.

It is seafood, however, that is found in the greatest variety. Oysters, crayfish, prawns, red snapper, and John Dory are common to both countries. In Australia, the tropical northern region is home to tasty Queensland mud-crabs and the estuary-dwelling barramund fish.

Green vegetables grow in abundance in both countries, as do fruits both tropical and temperate, including apples, pears, peaches, kiwifruit, passion fruit, custard apples, and jackfruit. A selection of these make up the traditional filling for Pavlova, the famed meringue dessert that was invented in Australia.

VEGETABLE & FRUIT FLAVORINGS

MUSHROOMS

Wild, cultivated, or dried, the mushroom is a versatile and flavorful ingredient. It is classified as a fungus, which is a plant that contains no chlorophyll and does not flower. The flavor of mushrooms, which is due to glutamic acid, is intensely savory.

Mushrooms take well to most cooking methods: sautéing, braising, baking, and microwaving. They are even delicious uncooked. An all-purpose ingredient, mushrooms feature in cuisines around the world and can be used to enhance a wide variety of dishes.

CULTIVATED MUSHROOMS

Mushrooms that are grown commercially are called *cultivated mushrooms*. Cultivated varieties are the most readily available and the most versatile; they can be used as a flavoring, as an ingredient on their own, or as a container for stuffings.

Button Mushrooms The most immature variety, these milky white mushrooms are harvested at a very early stage of development. The flavor has not had much time to mature, but they are good in salads—alone or in combination—where their fresh, crunchy texture is best displayed.

Cup Mushrooms A little further along in development, these mushrooms are available with the cups either closed or open. The closed type are barely distinguishable from button mushrooms in appearance, although the taste is slightly stronger. Open-cup mushrooms have a speckled cap and exposed brownish gills on the underside. These are mature mushrooms with a fully developed flavor. They are delicious when filled with a savory, herb-specked stuffing and baked.

Cremini mushrooms

Fresh morel   **Dried shiitake**

Flat Mushrooms The most mature of all the common mushrooms, these also have the most intense flavor. Their fanned-out cap and exposed brown gills make them unattractive to many, but it would be a mistake to let their appearance interfere with their great flavoring potential.

Cremini Mushrooms A dark brown variety of the *agaricus bisporus*, this type has a pleasant flavor that can be appreciated in dishes both cooked and raw.

Cultivated Wild Mushrooms Some popular varieties are now grown commercially and are more widely available:

Oyster mushrooms have a pleasing chewy texture and neutral flavor, making them ideal for a mixed mushroom sauté. However, they have a high moisture content and should be cooked just to warm. High heat will draw out all the liquid, and with it all the texture and flavor.

Shiitake mushrooms are an Oriental variety now cultivated throughout North America and Europe. With a powerful and meaty flavor, these mushrooms lend themselves well to long cooking.

Common mushrooms *are always available and sold in a variety of sizes*

Cup mushrooms

Button mushrooms

Flat mushroom

WILD MUSHROOMS

In many countries, mushroom gathering is a popular pastime and an extremely rewarding one because wild mushrooms are one of the most delicious woodland offerings. Many mushrooms, however, are poisonous, and the inexperienced gatherer should be wary. Never eat any mushroom garnered in the wild if it cannot be positively identified as safe for consumption. There are a number of books available to aid identifying nonpoisonous edible mushrooms, although appearance varies from one area to another. For this reason, any suspicious type of mushroom should be authenticated by an expert. Therefore, when in doubt, do not eat.

There are many wild mushrooms; the most common are described below.

Boletus Known as *cèpes* in French and *porcini* in Italian, these have a rich flavor and pleasing texture. Their taste improves with cooking.

Chanterelles Beautiful orange-yellow mushrooms, these are extremely tasty. They can be gently sautéed and served on their own. Gray chanterelles are known as *girolles.*

Boletus *are stout, fleshy mushrooms with a powerful, meaty flavor to match*

Chanterelles *are horn-shaped mushrooms of varying size with an orange-yellow color*

Shiitake *can be eaten raw but their meaty flavor and unique texture are best appreciated when cooked*

Shiitake mushroom

Oyster mushrooms

Oyster mushrooms *lose their flavor when overcooked*

Horns of Plenty These are dark brown, almost black, mushrooms with a deep, rich flavor. They are less common, but easily recognizable in markets by their funnel-shaped stem. They offer a pleasing contrast when combined with other mushrooms.

Morels Considered to rival the truffle in flavor, these mushrooms are used in many European cuisines. The conical cap looks rather like a sponge with many small crevices. There are two types of morel: the lighter, or blond, morel is full of flavor, but the dark brown morel is considered by many to be superior.

Truffles The king of wild mushrooms, truffles have an incomparable flavor. Cost varies from year to year, and prices are prohibitively high. Wild truffles grow underground, around the roots of certain oak trees, and are gathered in the fall with the aid of dogs or pigs trained to sniff them out. Black truffles, which look much like small lumps of coal, are the most common, but there is also a white Italian variety that is considered by many to be the pinnacle of mushroom flavor.

159

MUSHROOMS IN THE KITCHEN

A delicious mushroom dish starts with the selection of good-quality ingredients. Loose mushrooms are always the best choice; plastic packaging suffocates the mushrooms, making them soggy. Only cultivated mushrooms will keep, and even then only for a short period. About three days in the vegetable compartment of the refrigerator is the maximum. Wild mushrooms are best used on the same day they are purchased.

CHOOSING AND STORING

Avoid buying mushrooms that are wrinkled or soft to the touch; the caps should be smooth and firm or springy to the touch with no traces of moisture.

Although mushrooms are best purchased in small quantities for use as needed, they can be stored, unwashed, for about three days. Cover them with a damp cloth or place in a paper bag punctured for ventilation and refrigerate until needed.

COOKING WITH MUSHROOMS

Mushrooms are quite porous, which makes cleaning them a delicate task. Cultivated mushrooms can be gently rinsed, but for salads it is best to trim the stems and wipe the caps with a paper towel to keep them crisp and dry. While it is common practice to peel mushrooms, this is not necessary unless the color or texture of the cap is uninviting; be sure to reserve the trimmings for the stockpot. Wild mushrooms should never be rinsed or peeled. Simply trim off the thick, rough part of the stems and gently brush off any dirt with a soft brush.

COOK'S CHOICE
DUXELLES

Makes about 1 lb (500 g)

*1 small onion or shallot,
finely chopped*

4 tbsp unsalted butter

*1 lb (500 g) mushrooms,
finely chopped*

2 garlic cloves, finely chopped

Salt

Freshly ground black pepper

2 tbsp chopped parsley

In a skillet, combine the onion and butter and cook gently until soft. Add the mushrooms and garlic, and season to taste. Cook over low heat, stirring occasionally, until all the liquid has evaporated, about 20 minutes. Stir in the parsley. Add to rice dishes or stuffings, or serve with roast meats.

While most mushrooms are best when cooked, cultivated mushrooms work well in salads. Sliced button mushrooms are delicious when tossed with an olive oil and lemon juice dressing, topped with slivers of Parmesan cheese, and sprinkled with fresh herbs, such as chervil or chives.

In some countries, it is an autumn tradition to serve a mixture of wild mushrooms sautéed in butter as an appetizer. All wild mushrooms take well to this treatment. Heat butter or oil in a large skillet and add the mushrooms. Cook over high heat until tender; cooking time depends on the variety. Chopped garlic or shallots can be added, but only in small quantities so as not to mask the delicate flavor of the mushrooms.

A small, supple brush is best for cleaning

PREPARING MUSHROOMS

Slicing
Hold the mushroom by the stem and cut the cap into thin horizontal slices. Reserve the end slices for the stockpot.

Julienne
Cut into thin slices. Stack the slices and cut lengthwise into thin strips.

Chopping
Slice into thin julienne strips. With a small, sharp knife, cut across the julienne to obtain finely chopped mushrooms.

Dicing
Cut thick, crosswise slices; do not let them separate. Cut the same thickness across the existing slices for a thick dice.

DRIED MUSHROOMS

While the flavor of fresh mushrooms is incomparable, many varieties take well to drying. The taste of certain mushrooms, such as morels and boletus, is even more intense when dried. It is always useful to have a small package of dried mushrooms on hand. Just a few dried mushrooms can greatly improve the flavor of almost any savory dish, or stretch a small amount of stewed, fresh mushrooms.

Morels *are very expensive but reconstitute beautifully; 1 oz (30 g) is sufficient to flavor a recipe meant for 5–6 people*

Cloud ears *need reconstituting in several changes of warm water before use*

Shiitake *can be a bit tough when rehydrated but are successfully added to sauces and stews*

Boletus *are usually Italian in origin and will have been graded before being sliced and dried for packaging*

RECONSTITUTING DRIED MUSHROOMS
Reconstituted dried mushrooms can be used in place of fresh in most recipes. Be sure to adjust the cooking time because they can be a bit tough and require additional simmering.

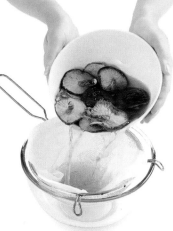

1 Soak the mushrooms for 15–30 minutes in warm water to cover. Strain through a lined sieve. The liquid can also be added to the dish.

2 Dry on paper towels and pat with another paper towel. They should be dry before use or they may dilute the flavor of the finished dish.

In some recipes, generally stews or other long-cooking dishes, dried mushrooms can be substituted for fresh. The general rule is to allow one part dried mushrooms for every eight parts fresh.

Morels These are the most expensive of the dried mushrooms, but only a few add quite a lot of flavor. When reconstituting (see right), be sure to stir occasionally to loosen any dirt or grit that may be lodged in the caps. Dried morels can be added to sauces or rice dishes, but they have a particular affinity with anything made with cream, eggs, or butter. A creamy morel sauce is the classic accompaniment to chicken, and a few reconstituted dried morels, sautéed in butter, greatly enhance scrambled eggs.

Boletus Because these often have a spongy texture, many cooks prefer to use them dried. They are an excellent addition to risotto or pasta sauce, and porcini dust, which is available in many specialty stores, can be added to almost any savory dish, with or without mushrooms.

Shiitake When dried, these have a smoky flavor, although they tend to be a bit tough when reconstituted. For best results, chop shiitake finely before adding to soups, stews, or sauces.

Cloud ears These are another Asian variety, sometimes known as tree ears. While they add little in flavor, they are valued for their gelatinous, seaweedlike texture. This type is a common ingredient in Chinese soups and stir-fries.

ONIONS

Finely chopped, sliced, or whole, the onion is one of the most useful vegetable flavorings available to the cook. Native to Asia, it has been a kitchen ingredient for thousands of years. The ancient Egyptians preferred them raw, while the Greeks valued onions for what they believed were their curative powers. Some varieties native to the United States were eaten by Indian tribes.

There are hundreds of onion types that vary in color, size, and flavor, and they are generally distinguished by their color and the time of year they are available. Flavor depends on the climate where they are grown; the milder the climate, the sweeter the onion. Pungent when raw and sweet when cooked, onions can enhance just about any dish.

TYPES OF ONIONS

Yellow Onions The most common onion, this type accounts for more than 75 percent of the world's production. It is a strong-flavored onion that keeps well and is best suited for long cooking in stews, soups, or sauces. When adding to the stockpot, include the outer brown skin for an attractive golden color.

Sweet Onions Popular types include Spanish, Bermuda, Maui, Vidalia, and Walla Walla. These are delicious when stuffed and baked, or coated and fried for onion rings. Sweet onions, thinly sliced and sautéed with sliced mushrooms and herbs, make a delicious accompaniment to broiled or pan-fried steaks. They can also be slowly simmered in wine and herbs and served with a pot roast.

Red Onions Also known as Italian red onion or purple onion, this type ranges in shape from round to oblong and has a pleasant sweetness. For maximum color, these are best used raw because cooking causes the color to bleed, although the flavor does not suffer. For a delicious addition to sandwiches, thinly slice a red onion and marinate in vinegar mixed with salt, pepper, and herbs.

Pearl Onions These tiny onions are harvested before they grow larger than 1 in (2.5 cm) in diameter. They have a papery skin that can be difficult to remove (see right). Ideal for pickling, these are delicious when served *glacés*, or glazed, as a vegetable, or added whole to soups or stews.

Dry onions have a papery outer skin and should not show any signs of sprouting

Yellow onion is strong in taste and keeps well; it is available year-round

Pearl onions are picked when the plant has just formed bulbs

Scallions should have firm bulbs and green, unblemished stems

Shallots

Red onions have a vibrant, fresh color and sweet flavor; they are very attractive sliced thinly into rings and used raw as a garnish

Shallots With a flavor more subtle than that of the onion and less pungent than that of garlic, these are the most refined members of the onion family. Shallots are indispensable for many classic French sauces such as *béarnaise* or *Bercy*. A fine wine vinegar infused with a shallot for several weeks makes a flavorful dressing for salads. Roasted whole, shallots can also be served with roast meats or poultry. Finely chopped (see right), they can be mixed with a fine wine vinegar and seasonings and served with raw shellfish, such as oysters or mussels.

Scallions Also called salad onions or green onions, these long slender onions are merely immature yellow onion bulbs. Mild and sweet, they are best sliced and added raw to salads, soups, or stir-fries. Larger scallions, with a slightly more developed bulb, can withstand light cooking. The Welsh onion, also called a Japanese bunching onion, is a small bulb with six stems that resembles the scallion. It can withstand slightly longer cooking and most resembles the leek in flavor.

CHOOSING AND STORING

Most onions are bought dry, with a papery outer skin. This skin, which protects them from moisture loss and light, is formed after harvesting, when they are left to dry. All that onions require for keeping, beyond this protective skin, is a cool, dark, properly ventilated place. For maximum storage time, choose onions that are firm and have a crisp, dry skin. Avoid those that are beginning to sprout or feel hollow because these will not keep; they may already be rotten on the inside. Once cut, the unused half can be wrapped in plastic wrap and refrigerated, but most of the pungency will be gone after one day. Fresh onions can be stored, unwashed, in plastic bags in the refrigerator, where they will keep for about five days, but they are best bought in small quantities for use as needed.

PREPARING ONIONS

Avoid peeling or cutting onions ahead of time because they lose flavor rapidly. It is best to reserve one chopping board for onions because the pungent flavor is easily picked up by more delicate foods.

To prepare an onion: Cut a slice off the top, leaving the root end intact. Peel off the skin and slice the onion in half lengthwise.

To chop an onion: Prepare as above. Place the onion, cut side down, on a chopping board. With a sharp knife, cut horizontal slices from the top just to the root end but not through it. Cut a series of even, lengthwise slices from the top. Finally, cut the onion crosswise into a dice.

To slice an onion: Prepare as above. Place the onion, cut side down, on a chopping board and cut thickly or thinly in vertical slices to obtain half-moons.

To cut onion rings: Peel the onion and slice just a bit off one round side to serve as a flat base. Place on a cutting board, cut side down. Hold the onion steady with one hand and cut downward into thick or thin slices; separate into rings as required.

CHOPPING SHALLOTS AND ONIONS

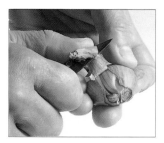

1 Remove the outer skin with a small knife and separate the bulb into sections.

2 Place on a work surface and slice horizontally towards the root, leaving the end uncut.

3 Repeat, slicing vertically, still leaving the root end intact and uncut.

4 Holding the root end, chop across to obtain a fine dice. Reserve the root end for stock.

PEELING PEARL ONIONS

Tiny pearl onions can be difficult to peel. This simple method shows how to remove the skin by plunging the onions into hot water, which softens the skin so it can be slipped off. Once peeled, the onions can be "glazed" for serving alone as a vegetable or adding to stews. Place peeled onions in a small saucepan, add butter and cook gently until golden brown. Add salt, a pinch of sugar, and water to cover. Cook over low heat in a covered saucepan until onions are tender.

Soaking
Place the onions in a bowl and add boiling water to cover. Soak for 2 minutes to soften without cooking.

Peeling
Drain the onions. When they are cool enough to handle, trim the root ends and peel away the skins.

GARLIC

One of the most controversial flavorings in the kitchen, garlic rarely leaves anyone indifferent. This distinctive ingredient is either loved or hated. A member of the lily family, garlic is thought to have originated in Central Asia. Each head, or bulb, of garlic is made up of several small cloves that are held together by an outer skin. There are many different varieties grown all over the world, varying in color, size, and flavor. The most common are the white skinned, pink skinned and purple skinned; the last is held to be the best. Elephant garlic is a giant variety and an ancestor of the modern-day leek. While the cloves are quite large, the flavor is very delicate. Garlic has many reputed medicinal properties, and it was once believed to repel evil spirits. But folklore aside, garlic remains a useful and flavorful ingredient for the contemporary cook.

BUYING AND CHOOSING GARLIC

Garlic is available throughout the year, but watch for the plump and succulent bulbs that appear in stores at the end of spring. The delight of garlic enthusiasts, these are particularly delicious when roasted whole. The most important thing to look for when buying garlic is freshness. The head should be compact and firm to the touch, and it should not be sprouting. For maximum flavor, the peeled cloves should be white; avoid using any that are gray, yellow, or stringy. Processed forms of dried garlic include flakes, powder, and garlic salt. Garlic puree is also available in tubes and in jars. This is superior to the dried forms, but it is best to use fresh garlic whenever possible. The flavor of fresh garlic is incomparable, and the health benefits are lost when it is dried.

Garlic powder

Garlic flakes

Pink garlic head

Pink garlic clove

Fresh garlic heads should be firm and compact

White garlic head

STORING GARLIC

Fresh garlic is at its best at the beginning of the season and should not be stored. Decorative, braided strings of garlic are available but these are not recommended for the restrained garlic user because the heads tend to dry out more quickly than they can be used. The most effective means of keeping garlic is in a cool, dry, well-ventilated place away from light. When stored properly, the bulbs should keep for several months.

COOKING WITH GARLIC

The odor of raw garlic tends to linger on kitchen work surfaces, although this can be circumvented by reserving one chopping board to use solely for members of the *Allium* genus (garlic, onions, shallots, etc.). With only one chopping board, the alternate solution is to wrap the garlic cloves in plastic wrap before crushing. However, this method is not practical when chopping. A garlic press is also useful for keeping odors contained, although it can impart a metallic taste to the garlic. The best way to crush garlic is with a mortar and pestle. With this method, the cloves are thoroughly crushed, thereby releasing a maximum of flavor, and work surfaces stay odor-free.

Garlic's strong flavor, characteristic of all members of the *Allium* genus, comes from an oil released when a clove is cut. Chopping releases even more, and crushed garlic is the most potent of all. Like its relative the onion, the powerful flavor of garlic is easily subdued by cooking. Garlic cloves can be used whole, crushed, or sliced. Quantity is really a matter of personal taste, although garlic should be used sparingly when

White garlic cloves

Garlic Press
To ensure that each batch of garlic contains only freshly pressed pieces, thoroughly wash and dry the press after each use. An old toothbrush, reserved especially for this purpose, is very handy.

Makes about 60–70 cloves

6–7 whole garlic heads
About 2 cups (500 ml) extra-virgin olive oil
Sprigs of fresh thyme
1 bay leaf

Preheat the oven to 375°F (190°C). Separate the garlic cloves but do not peel. Toss the garlic in oil just to coat. Wrap in foil and close securely. Roast until tender, 20–30 minutes. When cool enough to handle, place in a sterilized jar with a seal and add oil to cover generously. Add the thyme and bay leaf and seal. Store in a cool, dark place for at least 1 month before using.

combined with delicate flavors because of its dominance. When frying garlic, never let it burn or it will impart a bitter taste to the dish. However, it can be allowed to color slightly when used to enhance cooking oils, since the clove of garlic is discarded before the dish is served.

Whole heads of garlic can be rubbed with butter or oil and roasted along with meat or poultry. Serve the roasted garlic cloves in their skins with the main dish or discard the skins and mash or puree before adding to the sauce or gravy.

When using cooked or raw garlic as an ingredient in dishes that will be stored for several days, be sure to remove any small green shoots found in the center of the cloves. These shoots have a slightly bitter taste that develops over time and can be imparted to the finished dish. However, it is not necessary to remove these very small green shoots from the cloves if the dish is to be consumed immediately.

Warmer regions tend to produce the most flavorful garlic, so it is no surprise that the dishes of the Mediterranean and the Middle and Far East use large quantities. One classic French recipe calls for forty cloves of garlic. These are roasted with a chicken and then pureed and incorporated into the sauce. The chicken takes on a subtle and delicious garlic perfume, and the sauce is just slightly sweet from having so many slowly roasted cloves of garlic in it.

The Italians use garlic to add a delicate flavor to spinach leaves. First, a crushed and peeled garlic clove is speared on the end of a fork, then olive oil is heated in a skillet and the clove is rubbed around the pan for a few seconds. Finally, the spinach is added and stirred with the garlic fork. This gives a pleasant garlic taste without being too overpowering. This method is suitable for many other vegetables.

Garlic soup is a favorite in Spain. In this dish, garlic cloves are browned in olive oil until just golden, and then simmered in an earthenware pot with crushed pieces of fried bread, a pinch of paprika, and beef stock. When the cloves are tender, an egg is cracked into individual soup bowls and the hot broth is poured over.

In Tunisia, a condiment called *tabil* is made by pounding together garlic, sweet red peppers, fresh chili peppers, caraway seeds, and fresh cilantro; this paste is used to enhance the flavor of soups and stews.

Pickled garlic is a popular condiment in China and Thailand. Whole, peeled garlic cloves are preserved in sweet or tart vinegar. This pickle is delicious when added to Asian noodle dishes. It can also be served to accompany roast chicken or cold cuts.

The simplest way to enjoy the flavor of garlic is with bread. For a strong garlic taste, blend together crushed garlic, salt, and softened butter. Spread on French bread and brown under the broiler. A less pungent version can be made with roasted garlic.

PREPARING GARLIC

Place the garlic cloves on the work surface. Lay the flat edge of a knife on top and push down to crush. The garlic will crack out of its skin, making it easier to peel. Alternatively, plunge the cloves into boiling water for 30 seconds. Drain, then peel when cool. Crush with the flat edge of a knife, then slice or chop as required.

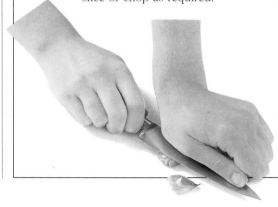

A TOUCH OF GARLIC
Rub a crushed clove around the base of a fondue pot to impart a hint of garlic flavor to the ingredients. This is also ideal for porcelain baking dishes or wooden salad bowls.

HORSERADISH, WASABI, AND DAIKON

Roots with a peppery bite are an essential flavoring element in the kitchen. Some, like radishes, need no other embellishment; others are more often pounded or grated for sauces or other condiments. Horseradish and radish are members of the same botanical family and are native to Eastern Europe. Wasabi is another root, often called Japanese horseradish, although the two are not related. Fresh wasabi is rare outside Japan, but powder or paste can be bought at specialty stores. These roots are useful for stimulating the palate, which makes them ideal for hors d'oeuvres.

Horseradish Although the young, tender leaves of this plant can be eaten in salads, it is the root that is most often used. When buying fresh, choose firm roots without any blemishes and avoid those that are sprouting or slightly green because they may be bitter. To prepare fresh horseradish, peel the skin down to the flesh; peel only the amount necessary. Grate or shred in a food processor; using a hand grater can produce very strong fumes, causing burning and watering eyes. Grated fresh horseradish loses its pungency quickly, so prepare in small quantities; it can also be frozen.

Dried horseradish flakes can be reconstituted and used as fresh, but horseradish is more commonly found in the form of a prepared sauce or relish.

Wasabi This root has a fierce aroma and a very biting taste. Sashimi, the Japanese dish of raw fish, is usually served with grated wasabi, or wasabi paste mixed with a soy dipping sauce. For sushi, wasabi paste is used for flavor and to help the fish adhere to the rice filling. Wasabi paste can be served with fish or meat dishes.

Grated horseradish *should be obtained just prior to use; combine it with cream, mayonnaise, or vinegar for a relish*

Horseradish sauce

Horseradish root *contains oils similar to mustard seed and has a powerful, painfully hot taste*

Wasabi powder

Wasabi paste

MIXING WASABI

Wasabi paste is available at Oriental markets, although it does not keep as well as the ground form. To prepare, mix equal quantities of powder and tepid water and stir to blend. Leave for at least 10 minutes to allow the flavor to develop. Serve with sushi or sashimi, or add in small quantities to barbecue sauces or mayonnaise-based salad dressings.

Daikon Also known as mooli or Japanese radish, this is simply a white, winter radish. It has a fresh, slightly peppery taste and a clean, crisp texture that make it an ideal salad ingredient, although it can also be steamed or stir-fried. Available throughout the year, it is at the peak of its flavor during the winter months. Choose roots that are

Peeled and sliced finely, the flesh is ideal combined with other vegetables

firm to the touch and slightly shiny, and be sure to use within one week because daikon does not keep well.

In Japan, where daikon is most common, it is shredded or grated and served with raw fish dishes. Mixed with lemon juice or vinegar, it is used to accompany broiled fish. It is also sliced or cut into decorative shapes or carved for elaborate garnishes. The Chinese incorporate it into a sweet-and-sour pickle. In its pickled form, daikon is called *takuan* in Japan and *kimchi* in Korea. Slivered daikon can be used to enliven clear soups and stews and can be sprinkled over vegetable dishes. Shredded daikon is also used to tenderize octopus.

Daikon shapes

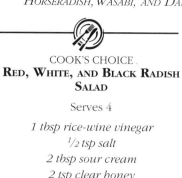

RED, WHITE, AND BLACK RADISH SALAD

Serves 4

1 tbsp rice-wine vinegar
¹/₂ tsp salt
2 tbsp sour cream
2 tsp clear honey
Freshly ground black pepper
6–8 large red radishes
1 small daikon, about 6 in (15 cm) long, peeled
1 small black radish
1 small red onion, finely chopped
2 scallions, thinly sliced
Lettuce and snipped chives for garnish

In a small bowl, combine the vinegar and salt and stir to dissolve. Add the sour cream, honey, and pepper to taste. Cover with plastic wrap and refrigerate for 2–3 hours to allow the flavors to blend. Slice the red radishes and daikon crosswise into paper-thin slices. Peel most of the skin from the black radish, leaving several thin stripes for color; slice thinly crosswise. Combine the radishes and onions and toss with the dressing. Serve on a bed of lettuce, garnished with chives. Use it as an unusual appetizer or salad accompaniment to an Oriental-style meal.

Pickled daikon

Whole fresh daikon *is milder than other radish types and is often found in Oriental markets*

RADISHES

Radishes range in color from white to red to black, and the varieties are numerous. The common red radish is delicious in salads, but it can also be cooked. When stir-fried, red radishes turn a stunning eggplant color and make an ideal accompaniment for roast meat. The black radish, with crisp, white flesh, is gaining popularity outside its native Eastern Europe. Its pungent flavor is best when eaten raw. The thick skin can be left on when thinly sliced, otherwise it is better peeled.

Black radishes

Red radishes

OLIVES

The domesticated olive tree, *Olea europaea,* has flourished throughout the Mediterranean region since pre historic times and produces one of the oldest known fruits. Olives, olive leaves, and olive oil are all mentioned in ancient Greek and Roman writings, as well as in the Bible, and many olive motifs can be discerned on ancient Egyptian artifacts. A beautiful tree with silvery green leaves, the olive can continue growing for hundreds of years. It does not need rich, fertile soil and grows happily on stony, mountainous ground that is unsuitable for other crops. An evergreen, it flowers in springtime and produces berries that, depending on the weather, can be harvested from October throughout the winter.

Mediterranean countries are the major olive producers, with Spain and Italy providing more than 50 percent of the crop, but the olive tree flourishes wherever a Mediterranean-type climate exists, and both California and Mexico have large olive-producing industries as well.

TYPES OF OLIVES

Most olives and olive oils come from either the *Sativa,* the most widely cultivated olive tree, or the *Oleaster,* the wild tree that is still confined primarily to its native Mediterranean region.

The difference between green and black olives is ripeness. Unripe olives are green, and fully ripe olives are black. Olives cannot be eaten straight from the branch; they must first be cured to remove their bitterness. There are two main curing methods: one for green olives, the other for black. Green olives must be soaked in a lye solution before brining, while black olives can be brined right away.

Olives are generally cured whole, but they are often cracked to speed up the curing process because the bitter juices are more easily extracted from bruised fruit. Varieties such as the Spanish *manzanilla*

Green olives
are picked while they are still immature

Black olives
are fully ripened fruit that can be brined right away

and the French *picholine* are better picked green, while others, such as the Greek *kalamata* and the tiny French *niçoise,* are best when harvested fully ripe.

Spain produces mostly green olives, which are often pitted and stuffed with various ingredients including almonds, pimientos, anchovies, capers, or onions.

Italy produces mainly black olives such as the acidic *liguaria,* the mild *ponentine,* the wrinkled *gaeta,* and the salty *lugano.*

California's most popular olive is the *sevillano,* which can be whole or cracked, and is usually salt-cured.

The Moroccans have a flavorful purple-mauve olive, which is picked when only half-ripe, and cracked before curing.

The most popular Greek olive is the deep purple *kalamata,* which is brine-cured. The plump, tasty black olives from Megara in Attiki are cured in salt.

French green olives

Spanish black olives

Greek green olives

Italian black olives

French black olives

Spanish green olives

Greek black olives

Italian green olives

FLAVORING OLIVES

Olives packed in brine can be enhanced simply by storing them in olive oil. First, drain and rinse the olives well to remove all traces of brine. Then, put them in a sterilized jar and add olive oil to cover.

For more flavor, add herbs and spices to the oil. The process is the same as above, simply add the flavorings before pouring in the oil. For example, combine olive oil with a little balsamic or red-wine vinegar. Put the olives in the jar, layer evenly with a few strips of lemon zest, a crushed garlic clove, some dried oregano, and some lightly crushed peppercorns, and pour over the oil and vinegar. Leave to mellow for one week before serving. Many herb-and-spice combinations are possible, but for an authentic taste, marry olives with flavors from their country of origin. Lemon peel and coriander seeds are good with Greek olives, while *herbes de Provence* (see page 51) enhance French olives, and garlic and black pepper with a few anchovies will set off any Spanish olives.

Olive bread
is made with both olive oil and chopped olives

COOK'S CHOICE
TAPENADE

Makes about 10 oz (300 g)

5 oz (150 g) pitted ripe olives, preferably niçoise
8 anchovy fillets
2 oz (60 g) capers, drained
2–3 garlic cloves, peeled
¹/₂ cup (125 ml) extra-virgin olive oil
Freshly ground black pepper

Put the olives, anchovies, capers, and garlic in a food processor and mix until just blended. With the machine running, slowly pour in the oil. (For a coarser mixture, whisk in the oil by hand.) Season with pepper to taste. Store in the refrigerator, tightly covered, for 2–3 days. Use this highly flavored puree with toast, hard-boiled eggs, raw vegetables, or pasta.

Tapenade on toast
makes a spicy snack and is a useful first course in an informal meal

COOKING WITH OLIVES

The quintessential cocktail snack, olives have many other uses in the kitchen. Olives can decorate canapés, pizzas, and buffet table presentations, and they feature in dishes such as *salade niçoise* and Greek-style salads. In Italy, France, and North Africa, olives are paired with poultry, cooked slowly in meat stews, or baked in breads.

Pureed olives, mixed with a little olive oil, are a useful condiment that adds an olive flavor without the inconvenience of the pit. The puree can be mixed into meat stews, vegetable casseroles, and tomato-based sauces, or rubbed on roasts before cooking. On its own, it is a light and flavorful sauce for pasta, hot or cold.

Tapenade, the *provençal* black olive spread (see right), is the classic pureed olive mixture. Serve it accompanied by toasted French bread and chilled rosé wine.

STUFFING OLIVES

Olives with a seasoned butter stuffing make an attractive and delicious appetizer. For example, blend ¹/₂ cup (125 g) butter, 2 tbsp finely chopped anchovy fillets, a squeeze of lemon juice, and freshly ground black pepper.

1 *Place an olive in the pitting tool with the stem end pointing up. Squeeze the handles together to extract the pit.*

2 *Place the anchovy butter in a piping bag and carefully fill the center of each olive with a rosette of flavored butter.*

Mediterranean-style pizza *is dependent upon black, sun-cured niçoise olives for its distinctive taste*

TOMATOES

Both a fruit and vegetable, the tomato is surely one of the most versatile flavoring ingredients. Brought from South America to Europe in the sixteenth century, the tomato was quickly integrated into the cuisines of Mediterranean countries. Tomatoes have been cultivated in the United States since the 1700s. The Northern Europeans, however, regarded the tomato with some caution, fearing it poisonous, and it was not until the nineteenth century that the tomato became an acceptable food in the northerly climes. Tomatoes are at their peak of flavor when picked ripe off the vine and can be grown successfully in gardens in a warm, sunny climate. Those less fortunate must content themselves with store-bought tomatoes, often picked before maturity to prevent spoilage during transport. When obtainable, the best way to enjoy the flavor of a fresh, ripe tomato is to serve it sliced as a salad, drizzled with olive oil and a scattering of fresh herbs. Ripe tomatoes are also delicious when baked with an herb-specked bread crumb topping. Long, slow cooking is the best way to appreciate less-than-ripe tomatoes. But whether cooked or raw, the tomato has earned its place in cuisines around the world.

In many countries, tomato growers are cultivating varieties with an emphasis on taste rather than looks. There are also quite a few interesting hybrids, which range from round to long, and from green to yellow. The following types are widely available and serve all manner of culinary purposes.

Beefsteak Tomatoes An extra-large variety of tomato with a firm texture, these are best for eating raw in salads and sandwiches. Their size also makes them an excellent choice for stuffing, both cooked and raw.

Plum Tomatoes Most popular in Italy, these elongated tomatoes are available fresh, or peeled in cans. Their dense flesh, which has few seeds, and excellent flavor, make them particularly well suited for long cooking in sauces and stews.

Common Red Tomatoes Available all year round, these are at their most flavorful during the summer. An all-purpose tomato, these are good for slicing for salads or sandwiches. After being peeled and seeded (see below), these can also be used for soups and sauces.

Cherry Tomatoes Small but packed with flavor, these can be added whole to salads or skewered for kabobs. Hollowed out and stuffed, they make a very attractive and delicious item for cocktail hors d'oeuvres or the buffet table. For a delicious accompaniment to broiled meats, sauté briefly in olive oil and sprinkle with fresh thyme.

Yellow Tomatoes Less acidic than red tomatoes, these also have a less pronounced flavor. Available in several shapes and sizes, they can be substituted for red tomatoes in any cold dish or combined with red tomatoes for an interesting contrast. Small pear-shaped yellow tomatoes make an attractive garnish when combined with other miniature vegetables.

Common red tomato
is an all-purpose food that is good for cooking and eating

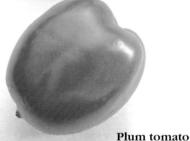

Plum tomato

PREPARING TOMATOES

1 Bring a pan of unsalted water to a boil. With a small knife, loosen a column of flesh around the core of the tomato and remove it.

2 Cut a small cross on the base. Immerse in a saucepan of boiling water. Lift out gently as soon as the skin starts to curl away.

3 As soon as the tomato is cool enough to handle, peel away the loosened skin with the tip of a small knife.

4 Cut the tomato in half and squeeze the halves to extract the seeds. Scrape away any remaining seeds with the tip of a knife.

Salad Tomatoes
Although tomatoes lend themselves admirably to any number of cooked dishes, their flavor is best appreciated in the raw state. Along with taste, they add color and texture to salads, and as the different types attest, a variety of shapes.

Beefsteak tomatoes *are large and substantial; sliced into rings or chunks they provide meaty pieces*

Cherry tomatoes *are the midgets of the family and are used whole*

Yellow tomatoes *are valuable for providing visual appeal and are available in round and pear shapes*

COOK'S CHOICE
TOMATO SAUCE WITH HERBS

Makes about 3³/₄ cups (1 liter)

2–3 tbsp extra-virgin olive oil
1 onion, chopped
Salt
Freshly ground black pepper
2 garlic cloves, chopped
5 lb (2.5 kg) tomatoes, peeled, seeded, and cored
8 oz (250 g) fresh mixed herbs such as basil, oregano, thyme, marjoram, savory, parsley, rosemary, sage, or bay leaf

In a saucepan, combine the oil and onions over low heat and cook until soft. Season to taste. Add the remaining ingredients and 1 cup (250 ml) water. Bring to a simmer, then cover and cook gently over low heat for about 1 hour. Puree in a food processor fitted with a metal blade. Return to a clean pan and cook, uncovered, to reduce, about 1 hour. Taste for seasoning. Serve the sauce immediately or freeze. Serve hot with pasta dishes or meat loaf; serve cold with fish or vegetable terrines.

TOMATO PRODUCTS

While tomatoes are available year-round, they are not always at the peak of flavor. Tomato products, however, are an adequate substitute in cooked dishes. Canned plum tomatoes come either whole or chopped, and can be enhanced with paste or puree. Strained tomato sauce can be used in hot or cold dishes. Sun-dried tomatoes have a strong, slightly smoky flavor. In small quantities they make an excellent addition to any cooked dish.

Sun-dried tomatoes

Tomato puree from a tube

Chopped canned tomatoes

Whole canned tomato

Canned tomato paste

Strained tomato sauce

CITRUS FRUIT

The cultivation of citrus fruits goes back at least 2,000 years. Originally from India and China, oranges and lemons gradually worked their way west. The ancient Greeks valued lemons both for their medicinal properties and their culinary contributions. Oranges were brought to Europe during the Crusades, and cultivation began in warm regions, where the trees then flourished. In the sixteenth century, the Spanish took oranges with them to the New World, and groves were planted in temperate areas such as Florida, California, and many parts of South America. Centuries of cultivation and crossbreeding have resulted in many varieties and hybrids. In the kitchen, this diversity translates into an ingredient that lends its skin, flesh, and juice to a variety of culinary preparations.

Valencia orange
is a sweet orange variety that is grown in many places around the world but not in Valencia, Spain

Satsuma *is a Japanese seedless mandarin with a green tinge to its skin*

Clementines *are Algerian in origin and a cross between the bitter orange and tangerine*

Grapefruit
a yellow rind covers a white-fleshed fruit

Limes

Mineola *are seed-free grapefruit/ tangerine crosses*

Lemons *have many uses in cooking; the juice, flesh, and skin are valuable flavorings*

Kumquats *are Eastern in origin but now grown mainly in Brazil; they are the smallest citrus fruits*

The citrus family
This group of fruits is constantly being enlarged by the many hybrids developed for taste, lack of seeds, and ease of peeling. Citrus fruits add color and flavor to many dishes both sweet and savory.

Ruby-red grapefruit
produces an attractive juice but fewer seeds being present rather than a pink color indicates sweetness.

TYPES OF CITRUS FRUIT

Oranges The first cultivated oranges to flourish in Italy and Spain were, like their early ancestors, quite bitter. Available only for a short period in winter, the modern Seville orange is probably the closest in flavor to those early oranges. Seville oranges are much sought after for marmalades and sauces, where their tang acts as a foil to rich meats, such as goose or duck. Blood oranges, with a delightful tart-sweet flavor and mottled crimson-orange color, are available only in season, which is generally in the winter months. Their red juice makes them invaluable for many preparations. Freshly squeezed, they produce an invigorating and beautiful breakfast drink, or a delicious addition to desserts and fruit salads. The skin of blood oranges may or may not be speckled with red—this depends on which side of the tree they grow. Nor does the skin color necessarily reflect the color of the flesh. Sweet oranges fall roughly into three categories: Jaffas are renowned for their juiciness, flavor and easy-to-remove peel; thin-skinned Valencia oranges are also full of juice, and navel oranges—easy to peel, juicy, and virtually seed-free—can be distinguished by their navellike growth at one end.

Mandarins This family of small, aromatic citrus fruits with easy-to-peel skins includes many varieties, such as satsumas and clementines. Satsumas are Japanese in origin. Less round than an orange, their light-colored skin peels away very easily, making them a simple and delicious snack. Clementines—hybrids of the bitter orange and the tangerine—look much like small

Orange cups
Hollowed-out oranges make an excellent container for orange ice cream or sorbet.

oranges. Peeled, segmented mandarins are often canned in a sugar syrup, and they take well to jams and preserves. Their small segments make them ideal for fruit salads. Mineolas are a hybrid of the tangerine and grapefruit. Similar to oranges in appearance, they combine good flavor with the advantage of no seeds. Tangelos are a flavorful juicy fruit and are a cross between tangerines and other citrus fruit.

Pomelos These are the largest members of the citrus group with thick yellow-green skins and thick inner membranes. Not as juicy as the grapefruit, their flesh is very refreshing.

Grapefruits A newcomer to the citrus family, the grapefruit was developed from the pomelo during the nineteenth century. Grapefruits are quite large, with an aromatic skin and a sharp but not sour flavor. Pink grapefruits are much sweeter. The large ugli (pronounced oo-gli) is a cross between a mandarin orange and grapefruit, but it most resembles the grapefruit in flavor. It is delicious sprinkled with sugar and baked. The ugli can be used interchangeably with grapefruit in most recipes.

Lemons This citrus fruit is almost unpalatable when raw, but its kitchen uses are many. The juice, flesh, and skin are valuable flavorings; the acidic juice can also be used as a cooking agent (see page 175). Segments and julienned peel can be used to garnish dishes, both sweet and savory. The juice can be added to salad dressings or used to deglaze skillets (see page 249).

Limes While this ingredient typifies the cuisines of tropical climates, it is not as valuable overall as the lemon. The juice can be used to flavor mousses, soufflés, and drinks, and the peel can be candied for a garnish. Limes are good when used in combination with other citrus fruits.

KUMQUATS

The small golden kumquat is unique among citrus fruits. While most have a bitter skin, kumquats are more sweet on the outside than within. This olive-shaped fruit can be eaten whole, either raw or cooked. The heat of cooking releases the full aroma of the skin, making them a welcome addition to braised duck or pork dishes. Dipped into a sugar syrup (see page 194), kumquats make a refreshing dessert to follow a rich meal. They are ideal for candying or preserving in syrup.

USING CITRUS PEEL

When a recipe calls for the zest of a citrus fruit, it is referring to the colorful, outer part of the skin and not the inner white part, known as the *pith*.

Cutting julienne
Peel strips of zest with a vegetable peeler. Slice strips lengthwise into thin, julienne strips.

Zesting
Working from one end, hold zesting tool firmly against the fruit and pull down toward the other end.

Drying skin
Cut the skin (peel) into strips and leave to dry. Use to flavor meat or fish stews, mulled drinks, or sugar.

CITRUS FRUIT IN THE KITCHEN

Aromatic zests, tart juices, and fresh bright color are the contributions of citrus fruits to the cook. Cuisines the world over make use of citrus fruits to season and enhance savory dishes. Along with salt, freshly ground black pepper, and olive oil, a squeeze of fresh lemon juice is often the only other seasoning required for broiled foods such as chicken or fish, or cooked vegetables such as broccoli or carrots. *Crêpes Suzette* and *tarte au citron* are much-loved citrus desserts from France. North America has its Key lime pie and candied citrus peel is an essential part of the traditional Italian Christmas cake, *panforte*. But whatever the recipe, an orange or a lemon in the fruit bowl will always offer the cook a world of flavoring and garnishing possibilities.

CHOOSING AND STORING

Citrus fruits are available year-round, but the fall and winter months provide the best quality and the biggest selection. When choosing, the same rules apply for all citrus fruits. Fresh, top-quality fruit should have a light sheen with no signs of bruising. The skin should be tight with an even grain. Avoid any fruit that is dry and shriveled. Fruit that feels heavy for its size is a good sign of juicy flesh on the inside. Citrus fruits generally keep from 3 days to 1 week at room temperature, and anywhere from 2 weeks to 1 month in the refrigerator. Because the peel is often called for in recipes, it is best to choose untreated or organically grown fruit. When in doubt, blanch the peel in boiling water for a minute or so to reduce the effects and bitter taste of pesticides or coloring agents. Chemical treatment affects only the skin and should not be able to penetrate through to the flesh.

SEVICHE
Raw fish marinated in citrus juice is called *seviche*. Fish should be very fresh, and many varieties can be used. Oily fish, such as mackerel and salmon, are delicious when paired with the tang of citrus juice.

COOKING WITH CITRUS FRUIT

Citrus fruits contain varying degrees of sugar and acid. However, while an acidic tang is characteristic, sugar predominates in most —oranges, tangerines, and grapefruits, for example. The flesh can be appreciated in its natural state, or use segments (see below) in a variety of preparations. The juice is both a seasoning and a cooking agent, and the zest offers a colorful and flavorful garnish.

Flesh A salad of grapefruit segments, avocados, and smoked salmon makes an unusual and mouth-watering appetizer, as does a savory salad of oranges, thinly sliced onions, and olives, dressed with salt and extra-virgin olive oil. In sweet dishes, the acidic nature of citrus fruits is best tamed by poaching in a light syrup (see page 196). Serve poached orange segments or slices alongside a bitter chocolate mousse and garnish with a sprinkling of

---

PREPARING CITRUS FRUIT

Peeling zest
With a vegetable peeler, slice away the zest, taking care not to include the pith. If skin is treated, blanch before use.

Removing inner skin
Cut a slice from both ends. Slice downward, taking care to remove all visible traces of skin and pith.

Cutting segments
Remove inner skin. Cut into a segment, separating flesh from membrane. Slice the other side and dislodge.

Slicing fruit
After removing inner skin, place the fruit on its side. With a sharp knife, cut downward into thin slices.

candied julienne peel. Even tangy lemon segments can be used when poached; arrange them on top of a lemon curd tart and glaze with strained apricot preserves (see page 258) for a refreshing conclusion to a meal or as an afternoon treat.

Juice For a maximum of juice, it is best to use fruit at room temperature. Before juicing, roll the fruit, pressing down with the palm of your hand; this breaks some of the inner membranes, helping to extract as much juice as possible. Once squeezed, the uses for citrus juice are many.

Orange and grapefruit juice are almost universal breakfast items, and lemonade is a classic summertime drink. Combine orange juice with garlic and freshly grated gingerroot and use as a marinade for broiled chicken. Or, prepare a stir-fry of pork tenderloin marinated in orange juice, soy sauce, crushed chilies, and fresh garlic. Lemon juice can be combined with grated lemon zest, rosemary, garlic, and olive oil for an all-purpose meat seasoning. A simple dressing of fresh lemon juice, olive oil, salt, and black pepper can be used to season salads, poached or broiled fish, or steamed vegetables. Most fruit salads also benefit from a squeeze of fresh lemon juice; the sweetness of the fruit combines with the subtle acidity of the citrus juice, making for a more complex and delicious flavor.

The acidic nature of citrus fruit juice can be exploited for marinades and "raw cooking," and lemon and lime juice are used as a cooking agent in many Latin and South American countries. Known most commonly as *seviche*, fish is combined with citrus juice, chilies, onions, and varying herbs and spices, and then left to "cook." After about 5 hours

of marinating, the fish turns opaque—as it does when cooked by conventional heating methods—and is ready to eat. Exact marinating time depends on the type and quantity of fish. Citric acid also has a bleaching effect, which is useful with ingredients that discolor rapidly when sliced, such as apples, artichokes, and celery root or when pristine whiteness is required of ingredients such as mushrooms.

Skin It is the zest that contains all the aromatic citrus oils. Like other vegetables and fruits, citrus fruits are often treated with chemical pesticides and dyes to enhance their natural coloring. While this rarely affects the fruit on the inside, it does affect the skin. Choose untreated citrus fruit when preparing recipes that call for the zest. If the fruit is treated, blanch zest before use. For easy removal, place the zest slices in a sieve or a cheesecloth bag and immerse in boiling water for 1–2 minutes.

Grated lemon, lime, or orange zest can be added to sauces or marinades for a hint of citrus tang. Thickly sliced zest can be dried and added to a bouquet garni or a jar of sugar. The flesh can also be scooped out, leaving a container for sorbet, ice cream, or fruit or vegetable salads.

The ideal garnish for ice creams, tarts and cakes, julienned citrus zest can be boiled in grenadine syrup for a splash of bright pink color. Freshly grated lemon zest is useful for marinades and is essential in the classic Italian seasoning mixture gremolada (see page 44), which is sprinkled over braised veal shanks just before serving. It is also delicious combined with freshly ground pepper, salt, olive oil, and Parmesan cheese for a simple pasta sauce.

COOK'S CHOICE
CITRUS SALAD

Serves 4–6

3 blood oranges
2 navel oranges
2 tangerines
1 ruby-red grapefruit
3 tbsp orange-flower water
Confectioners' sugar
Candied violets for garnish

Remove the inner skin and slice all the fruit (see page 172), being careful to save any juice. Arrange the fruit, alternating sizes and colors, on a large plate. Mix the juice and orange-flower water and sprinkle over the fruit. Dust with sugar to taste. Garnish with the candied violets and serve.

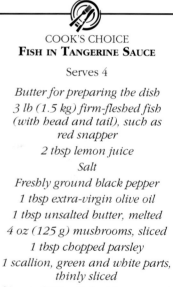

COOK'S CHOICE
FISH IN TANGERINE SAUCE

Serves 4

Butter for preparing the dish
3 lb (1.5 kg) firm-fleshed fish (with head and tail), such as red snapper
2 tbsp lemon juice
Salt
Freshly ground black pepper
1 tbsp extra-virgin olive oil
1 tbsp unsalted butter, melted
4 oz (125 g) mushrooms, sliced
1 tbsp chopped parsley
1 scallion, green and white parts, thinly sliced
2/3 cup (150 ml) freshly squeezed tangerine juice
1 1/4 cups (300 ml) dry white wine

Preheat the oven to 400°F (200°C); butter a baking dish large enough to hold the fish. Rinse the fish and pat dry. In a bowl, combine the lemon juice and salt and pepper to taste and stir to dissolve. Stir in the oil and butter. Place the fish in the dish and pour the lemon juice mixture over. Sprinkle on the mushrooms, parsley and scallions, and add the tangerine juice and wine. Bake until the fish flakes easily when tested with a fork, 20–30 minutes. Serve with the sauce.

CITRUS FRUIT GARNISHES

Sweet or savory dishes flavored with citrus fruit can be garnished with them as well. Place on top of food or on plates for an attractive presentation.

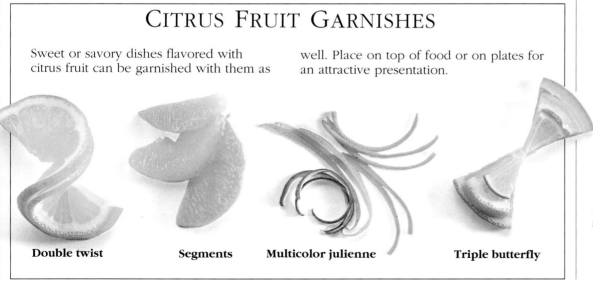

Double twist   **Segments**   **Multicolor julienne**   **Triple butterfly**

NUTS

In technical terms, a nut is a one-celled fruit encased in a dry shell. And while acorns, chestnuts, and hazelnuts are true nuts, the term is also loosely applied to seeds or edible fruit kernels that are enclosed in a hard shell—almonds and cashews, for example. Nuts have been used as a source of food and oil for centuries. As early as 200 B.C., the Romans distributed sugar-coated almonds on special occasions. When the Spanish carried their culinary traditions to the Americas, they found the Aztecs already using peanuts and pecans. A predominant ingredient in the cuisines of the Middle East, nuts such as almonds and pistachios feature in both savory sauces, such as Turkish *tarator* made with walnuts, and in many confections, such as *baklava*. Peanuts and cashews are used in stir-fries throughout Indonesia and the Far East. In African cuisines, nuts are a staple, and hazelnuts and almonds enter into recipes for many European desserts and candies. In many savory dishes, nuts have an affinity with spicy curries and chilies; in sweet dishes, they go well with cinnamon, honey, and chocolate.

TYPES OF NUTS

Almonds Related to the peach tree, the almond tree is a native of the eastern Mediterranean region and has been cultivated for thousands of years.

There are two types of almond—sweet and bitter—and the last is often confused with apricot kernels. Often called Chinese almonds, apricot kernels have a flavor remarkably similar to sweet almonds, and they are used to flavor many products such as almond extract and almond-flavored liqueurs. When raw, these can be toxic in large quantities and must be blanched or roasted beforehand. Sweet almonds are used whole or ground in cakes, pastries, butters, pralines, fillings, and nougat. Chopped, diced, slivered, and sliced, they are used for coating and garnishing. They also appear in many savory dishes, especially those with chicken, fish, and rice.

Brazil Nuts Not actually nuts, these seeds come from the tropical rain forests of Brazil. The edible part is one of two dozen seeds contained in a hard, brown

Slivered nuts

Cashews

Ground nuts

Walnuts *contain kernels that are hard to peel; the skin is usually left on for eating*

Hazelnuts

Pecans *feature in the cooking of the American South, and are found in cakes and pastries or stuffings for poultry*

Sliced nuts

Brazil nuts

Pistachios

Almonds

Chopped nuts

three-sided shell. Brazil nuts have a very high oil content, which gives a richness to their slightly sweet flavor but also limits storage time. Large Brazil nuts can be grated into cake batters, or dipped in chocolate to serve with coffee or as a dessert (see page 182).

Cashews The cashew tree is native to South America, but it now flourishes in many parts of Southeast Asia and India. Roasted, salted cashews are a popular cocktail nibble. In cooking, whole cashews feature prominently in Indian vegetarian dishes and Chinese stir-fries, and ground cashews are often used to thicken curries.

Hazelnuts Also known as filberts or cobnuts, these are small, round, brown nuts. Their sweet, rich flavor lends itself well to all kinds of pastries. Freshly ground hazelnuts are an excellent addition to cake or cookie doughs, and they can be folded into meringues before baking. Chocolate and hazelnuts marry very well. In savory dishes, chopped or sliced hazelnuts can be sprinkled over steamed or boiled vegetables. Hazelnut oil (see page 226) is very rich, and it makes an excellent addition to salad dressings or sauces, especially those served with veal or duck.

Pecans A type of hickory nut, these are native to the American South, though they are now cultivated in parts of Australia. The growing, harvesting, shelling, and sorting of these nuts is a lengthy and complicated process, which accounts for their high cost. Pecans have a subtle, refined flavor; this is surprising, considering that they have such a high fat content. Pecan pie is a Thanksgiving classic in the U.S., and these nuts can also be used in cakes, ice creams, and stuffings for roast poultry.

Pistachios Native to the Middle East, the green pistachio nut is sold in its shell or shelled and blanched. Irresistible as a cocktail accompaniment, pistachios are also a versatile ingredient. Their vibrant green color makes them an ideal garnish and a colorful addition to sausages, meat pâtés, and other charcuterie items. Chopped pistachios are essential in Middle Eastern rice dishes and in Greek, Turkish, and Arabic pastries. They are used in all kinds of baking and make a delicious ice cream.

Walnuts The walnut tree is native to Asia, but it now grows in many other countries. French walnuts are held to be the finest, especially those that come from the Dordogne region in the Southwest. The color of a walnut shell reflects its quality; the lighter the color, the higher the grade. Popular as a snack, walnuts also make an excellent addition to fruit and vegetable salads, stuffings, and a myriad of baked goods. Ground walnuts can be added to sweet pastry doughs, and they also enter into many sauces from cuisines around the world: the Turkish *tarator*, the Mexican *chiles en nogada*, and the Italian *sugo di noci*. Walnuts also produce a flavorful and highly prized oil (see page 227), which makes an excellent salad dressing.

MAKING PEANUT BUTTER

Peanuts are not a nut at all, but a legume. They grow on long tendrils, just below the ground, which is why they are sometimes called *groundnuts*. Native to Brazil, peanuts are now grown in many temperate areas of the world. Peanut butter is popular in American homes, where it is added to many baked goods or used as a sandwich spread with jam or jelly. It is also a valuable ingredient in the cuisines of Southeast Asia.

1 Place about ³/₄ cup (125 g) blanched, lightly roasted fresh peanuts in a food processor and mix. Add 1–2 tbsp oil.

2 Process until the peanuts reach the desired consistency, either smooth or slightly crunchy. This will make about 2 oz (60 g) of peanut butter.

CHESTNUT PRODUCTS

Chestnuts are available bottled and canned, either whole or pureed. Sweetened chestnut puree topped with a dollop of crème fraîche (see page 235) is a French dessert classic known as *Mont Blanc*. It can also be used as a crêpe or cake filling. Dried whole chestnuts can be reconstituted by soaking.

Canned chestnuts

Dried chestnuts

Chestnut puree

DECORATING WITH NUTS

Small in size and big in flavor, nuts lend themselves well to a number of decorative preparations. Marzipan, which is a paste made from ground almonds, egg whites, and sugar, is quite versatile. It can be colored and rolled flat to place over cakes instead of frosting, or it can be molded into shapes. Chopped or sliced nuts add flavor and texture to many foods such as soft candies, meat pâtés, and soft cheeses. Pistachios, on their own or with other nuts, add a touch of color; light colored nuts can be toasted for extra color. Almonds and hazelnuts have perfect bite-size shapes, and their flavors marry well with both sweet and savory dishes.

MARZIPAN SHAPES

The almond paste is colored, then kneaded to make it more pliable. Small amounts are molded by hand, and special tools are used to add the finishing decorative touches. Marzipan shapes can be eaten as a candy, or used as an edible garnish.

FRESH NUTS

Whole, chopped, or toasted nuts are ideal for a simple yet elegant decoration. Chocolate candies can be rolled in chopped nuts; walnut halves add texture to plain marzipan. Pâtés and cheeses can be decorated with nuts for additional flavor and texture.

MAKING NOUGATINE

Nougatine is made from a mixture of chopped almonds and sugar in equal quantities. It can be rolled out thinly and cut into shapes to decorate cakes and pastries. It can also be cut into larger circles or squares to line molds, or use as bases for elaborate gâteaux.

1 In a copper saucepan, heat 1 cup (200 g) sugar with 2 tbsp lemon juice until dissolved. Add 1 ¾ cups (200 g) blanched, chopped almonds and cook until caramelized. Turn out onto a lightly oiled work surface and knead with a metal spatula.

2 While still warm, roll out to a thin sheet. Work quickly because the nougatine becomes brittle as it cools. If necessary, transfer the nougatine to a lightly oiled, nonstick cookie sheet and place in a low oven to warm.

3 With a sharp knife, cut into strips and then into squares or triangles. Use the shapes for the sides of frosted cakes, or arrange triangles in a pinwheel pattern on the tops of cakes. Any leftover scraps can be reheated and reused.

COCONUT

The fruit of a palm tree native to Malaysia, coconuts are another "false" nut. The hard, brown fibrous shell, which is familiar to most, is the mature, ripe form of coconut. But in coconut-growing areas, both unripe and ripe coconuts are eaten. Immature coconuts are green on the outside, and the shell is still fairly soft.

They are often sliced open and served with a straw and a spoon; one is for drinking the sweet juice, the other for scraping out the soft, jellylike flesh. Throughout the Tropics, coconuts are a common ingredient in dishes both sweet and savory, although they are most often used in spicy, chili-flavored preparations.

When choosing coconuts, feel the weight; good-quality coconuts will be heavy with no visible moisture or mold around their "eyes." When shaken, there should be a distinct sound of liquid sloshing inside.

To crack the shell, hold the coconut steady and pierce the three "eyes" with a skewer or screwdriver. Drain off the liquid. To keep the coconut from slipping, place it on a dishcloth. With a hammer, hit all around the middle until it splits. Continue hammering to break into smaller pieces. With a small knife, separate the flesh from the shell and peel away the brown skin with a vegetable peeler.

For most recipes, freshly grated coconut is superior to the store-bought shredded kind, both in flavor and texture. Creamed coconut is an adequate substitute for fresh, and is much less time-consuming to use.

Slivers of fresh coconut can be sprinkled on fruit salads, rice puddings, or chocolate desserts. Similarly, the sweet, rich flavor of coconut seems to have a particular affinity for highly-spiced savory dishes, especially those with chicken and shrimp.

Fresh coconut

Creamed coconut

Flaked coconut

COOK'S CHOICE
SHRIMP IN COCONUT SAUCE

Serves 4

2 fresh hot green chilies, seeded and chopped

1 large onion, chopped

1 stalk lemongrass, chopped

4–5 fresh basil leaves, finely chopped

1 tsp ground turmeric

Small piece of fresh gingerroot, peeled and chopped.

1 cup (250 ml) coconut milk

1 lb (500 g) raw jumbo shrimp, shelled

Salt

About 3 tbsp toasted coconut flakes

Puree the chilies, onion, and lemongrass in a food processor or blender. Transfer to a heavy saucepan; stir in the basil, turmeric, gingerroot, and 1 cup (250 ml) water. Bring to a boil, reduce heat, and simmer until the water has almost evaporated, 6–8 minutes. Add the coconut milk, shrimp, and salt to taste. Cook gently, stirring frequently, until the shrimp are firm, 4–5 minutes. Sprinkle with the coconut and serve.

MAKING COCONUT MILK

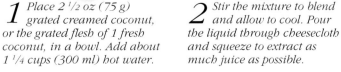

Not the same as the liquid inside fresh coconuts, coconut milk is made by infusing water or milk with fresh or creamed coconut.

1 Place 2 ½ oz (75 g) grated creamed coconut, or the grated flesh of 1 fresh coconut, in a bowl. Add about 1 ¼ cups (300 ml) hot water.

2 Stir the mixture to blend and allow to cool. Pour the liquid through cheesecloth and squeeze to extract as much juice as possible.

CHOCOLATE

The botanical name for the cacao tree, *Theobroma cacao,* translates as "food of the gods," and few would disagree. When Hernán Cortés conquered Mexico in 1519, the Aztecs were already making a drink, called *chocolatl,* from the bean of this tree. In the centuries since then, the versatile cocoa bean has continued to provide pleasure as a drink, snack, candy, savory flavoring, simple garnish, and elaborate decoration. Chocolate has a flavor that combines well with many others. Hazelnuts and almonds are a good match, as are spices such as cinnamon, nutmeg, and cloves. Mint is a classic partner, as are raspberries and oranges, and vanilla enhances its flavor. Even coffee seems more satisfying and full-flavored when accompanied by a chocolate. For added sophistication, chocolate desserts can be laced with brandy or other liqueurs.

PRODUCTION

The cocoa tree thrives in equatorial climates. Thus, the finest bean, *criollo,* comes from Central and South America and India. The largest crop comes from the *forastero* beans that are grown in Africa and Brazil. After harvesting, the beans are fermented to remove bitterness and develop the flavor content and then dried. Roasting follows, which exposes the inner section, called the nib. Various bean nibs are blended to obtain the desired flavor and then ground to a paste that is more commonly known as *cocoa mass*—the heart of chocolate's flavor. This paste is enhanced with sugar, cocoa butter, and flavorings, and passed through a series of rollers for blending. Thin, dry sheets of chocolate are obtained, but these must be "conched," a process developed by Rodolphe Lindt in 1879. Conching is a lengthy and costly procedure that enhances the texture and flavor. Inferior-quality chocolate is made by replacing the cocoa butter with a synthetic substitute, and replacing the conching process by the addition of soy lecithin for smoothness.

STORING AND CHOOSING

Chocolate and cocoa powder should be stored in a cool, dry place. Chocolate should not be refrigerated; the temperature is too low and the environment too moist. Refrigeration also encourages sugar bloom, those grayish-white streaks that appear on the surface. Fat bloom is similar, although it is caused by improper heating during either manufacture or storage. Bloom is the result of temperature fluctuations and reflects improper storage. It will not affect the taste, but it is unsightly. Although costly, plain chocolate that has been manufactured with care is always the best choice for eating and cooking.

TYPES OF CHOCOLATE

Chocolate can be unsweetened, bittersweet, bitter, or milk. With the exception of white chocolate, eating and cooking chocolate are made from cocoa mass that is blended with cocoa butter, sugar, and flavorings, and this is called cocoa solids.

The final taste of the chocolate does depend on the type, but the quality depends on several factors. Each type of bean has a particular taste, so individual bean types and the way in which they are blended have a direct impact on flavor. Equally important are the fermentation and roasting processes, as well as the method of manufacture.

Unsweetened Chocolate Also known as *baker's chocolate*, this type is cocoa solids without any additional sugar or flavorings. Used largely by manufacturers of chocolate products, it is bitter, grainy, and trouble-some to melt. It can be difficult for the home cook to obtain. In recipes that call for unsweetened chocolate, substitute 3 tablespoons unsweetened cocoa powder plus 1 tablespoon unsalted butter for each 1 oz (30 g) unsweetened chocolate.

Semisweet Chocolate Containing a minimum of 43 percent cocoa solids, this type also includes bittersweet and bitter chocolate; the last has the lowest sugar content. Recipes that call for semisweet chocolate will be most successful when made with a chocolate that contains a minimum of 50 percent cocoa solids, although some chocolates can contain as much as 70 percent.

Milk Chocolate As the name implies, this type contains milk along with the cocoa solids. It was developed in Switzerland in 1875. At that time, some of the cocoa solids were replaced with condensed milk, although nowadays it is made more frequently

Cocoa powder

Chocolate square

Chocolate chips

Chocolate shavings

Semisweet chocolate *made from quality beans, with a high percentage of cocoa solids, is the preferred type for cooking and eating*

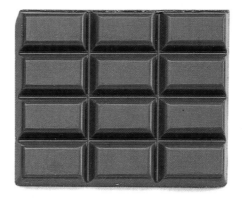

Milk chocolate *does not have enough cocoa solids to be used successfully in cooking and baking, except in specially adapted recipes*

Chocolate pieces *Manufacturers score their products in a variety of shapes and weights.*

with dried milk. For cooking, it should not be used in place of semisweet chocolate because it has a lower percentage of cocoa solids and the flavor of the finished dish will suffer. Milk chocolate is more sensitive to heat and is often harder to work with.

Couverture Chocolate The high proportion of cocoa butter in this type ensures a glossy appearance and smooth texture in finished dishes. It is used primarily by professional confectioners to coat and dip chocolates; hence the French name *couverture,* or "covering." Because of its high cocoa butter content, it should be "tempered" before use. Tempering involves heating and cooling the chocolate, which allows it to retain its gloss after hardening. Melted chocolate is warmed up to 115°F (46°C), then spread thin on a work surface and stirred until it is almost cool enough to set, about 80°F (27°C).

Then the chocolate is scraped back into a bowl and heated until it reaches 90°F (32°C). Only couverture will give satisfactory results when tempered.

Cocoa Powder With only 18 percent cocoa butter, this is less fatty than all other chocolates and is generally unsweetened. In 1882, C. J. Van Houten invented the cocoa press, which performs the task of extracting all the cocoa butter from the roasted beans. This produces dry cakes of cocoa, which are then ground into powder. "Dutching" is another Van Houten innovation, developed later, which neutralizes cocoa's acid, making cocoa powder easier to dissolve.

Hot Chocolate Mix This is a sweetened product for use as a hot drink preparation. It should not be substituted for cocoa powder because the added sugar and flavorings will interfere with the recipe.

WHITE CHOCOLATE

Technically this is not chocolate at all because it contains only cocoa butter, milk, and sugar; there is no cocoa mass. Inferior-quality white chocolate will contain a high percentage of vegetable fat, and some manufacturers omit the cocoa butter altogether in favor of this meager substitute. White chocolate is sensitive to heat and very difficult to handle. In the kitchen, it is best used melted or grated, for garnishing, where its white color offers an eye-catching contrast to dark chocolate.

Cocoa butter

HOT CHOCOLATE

For most, hot milk flavored with sweetened cocoa powder is a familiar and well-loved beverage. When made with whole milk and high-quality cocoa powder, this can be a satisfying treat; however, the flavor and texture of hot chocolate made from melted chocolate is incomparable. Choose semisweet chocolate with at least 50 percent cocoa solids. Finely chop 8 oz (250 g) chocolate and melt. Bring 3³/₄ cups (1 liter) milk to a boil. Whisk half of the milk into the chocolate until frothy. Add sugar to taste. Over low heat, slowly add the remaining milk, whisking constantly. Serve warm with whipped cream. For a richer beverage, replace half of the milk with cream.

Hot chocolate

White chocolate

Chocolate in the Kitchen

Although chocolate is used primarily as a flavoring for sweet dishes, the taste of bitter chocolate blends well with many savory dishes. In Spain and Italy, small amounts of chocolate are used with onion, garlic, tomatoes, and spices in a sauce for meat and fish dishes. Ground dried chilies are combined with chocolate for the traditional Mexican *mole* sauce. Try adding a small square of semi-sweet chocolate to a meat or game stew at the very last moment; it will reduce any bitterness, and the chocolate flavor will be only barely perceptible.

Melting Chocolate

Although a seemingly easy task, great care should be taken when melting chocolate. It burns very easily and this makes the flavor bitter, and if overheated, it becomes hard and granular. Be careful not to let any stray drops of water fall into the chocolate or it will "seize," or stiffen and solidify. Many recipes call for the addition of butter or oil when melting; this adds richness, without interfering with the melting process.

The most common method for melting is the *bain marie,* or water bath. A double boiler can be used, but a heatproof bowl that fits snugly over a saucepan will also work. Place a small amount of water in the saucepan—do not allow the bowl to touch the water. Bring the water to a boil and remove from the heat. Place the chocolate in the bowl and return the pan to the heat, if necessary, stirring to melt. Do not cover; this will cause steam to condense on the pan lid, forming water droplets that will fall into the chocolate and make it seize. The microwave is ideal for melting chocolate. Break chocolate into pieces and place in a microwave-safe bowl. To melt 2½ oz (75 g) chocolate, cook on full power, uncovered, for 2–3 minutes, according to microwave output. Stir to melt completely; the chocolate will retain its shape until stirred.

Bain marie
The gentle, even heat of simmering water facilitates even melting.

COOK'S CHOICE
Tomato and Chocolate Sauce for Game

Serves 6

3 thick bacon slices, chopped
2 large tomatoes, peeled, seeded, and chopped
2 large onions, sliced
2 carrots, chopped
2 garlic cloves, crushed
3¾ cups (1 liter) game stock
1 tbsp chopped fresh flat-leaf parsley
2 whole cloves
Pinch of freshly grated nutmeg
1 tbsp sherry vinegar, or red-wine vinegar
Salt
Freshly ground black pepper
2–3 tsp grated unsweetened chocolate
1 cup (250 ml) dry sherry

In a saucepan, cook the bacon over moderate heat until brown. Drain off the excess fat and add the tomatoes, onions, carrots, garlic, and stock. Stir in the parsley, cloves, nutmeg, and vinegar, and season to taste. Bring to a boil, cover, and simmer for 45 minutes. Strain and return to a clean saucepan. Add the chocolate to taste and stir in the sherry. Simmer the sauce, uncovered, for 5–10 minutes; adjust the seasoning if necessary. Serve with roast game birds such as quail and partridge, or with braised hare.

Coating and Fondue

Firm fruit, such as pear slices, melon cubes, banana slices, strawberries, or even starfruit, can be dipped in melted chocolate for a light and unusual dessert. Candied citrus peel works well, and chocolate-coated nuts, such as almonds or walnuts, are also delicious. Melt the chocolate (see left). Dip in the fruit or nuts, lift out quickly, and turn around several times for an even coating. Hold upwards to set. Dry on waxed paper at room temperature and serve within the hour; do not refrigerate. For fondue, serve a variety of fruit and nuts with a bowl of melted chocolate, or arrange on skewers. Add a little melted butter to the chocolate, for a smoother consistency and richer flavor.

Dried fruit

Nuts

Fresh fruit

Dipping fruit
For coating, use bite-sized ingredients, such as berries and nuts.

DESSERT BASICS

BASIC CHOCOLATE CAKE

Makes one 8 in (20 cm) cake

*Melted butter for the cake pan
4 large eggs
¹/₂ cup (125 g) sugar
³/₄ cup (100 g) all-purpose flour
4¹/₂ tbsp unsweetened cocoa
powder
1 tsp unsalted butter, melted and
cooled (optional)*

Preheat the oven to 375°F (190°C). Line the base of a round, 8 in (20 cm) cake pan with waxed paper and brush with the melted butter. Mix together the eggs and sugar in a heatproof bowl. Place over low heat, or a double boiler, and whisk until just warm to the touch. Do not overheat or the eggs will cook and form lumps. Remove from the heat and beat with an electric mixer until light and fluffy, about 15 minutes. Meanwhile, sift together the flour and cocoa powder. With a spatula, fold the dry ingredients into the egg mixture in three batches. Fold gently but thoroughly; there should be no visible pockets of flour. Fold in the butter with the last batch, if using. Pour into the pan and bake until the cake just comes away from the sides of the pan, 30–40 minutes. Turn out onto a wire rack. When cool, slice the cake horizontally into thirds with a long, serrated knife and fill.

From a simple homemade cake to an elaborate glazed, filled, and garnished dessert, chocolate cake is the perennial favorite of children and adults alike. The recipes given here are blueprints; they can be used together, as shown, or separately to add a bit of chocolate flavor to other desserts. For example, the cake can be split and filled with raspberries and cream. Or, blend the chocolate batter with a plain batter for a marbled effect. The ganache can be flavored with coffee, cinnamon, or mint and used to fill a plain cake or jelly roll; it can also be used to fill a baked tart shell for an instant chocolate tart. The chocolate frosting can be used to coat plain cakes, or those flavored with ground almonds or hazelnuts, or it can be served right away as a warm dessert sauce.

The garnish can be simple, like a dusting of cocoa powder, or more elaborate, like chocolate leaves or coated nuts

Put the filled cake on a wire rack set on a cookie sheet to catch drips when frosting; leftover frosting can be re-used

To obtain even layers, cut with a gentle sawing motion, turning the cake while slicing; a piece of cardboard will help to transfer the layers as they are divided

When filling, use a metal spatula to spread an even layer that extends all the way to the edge of the cake

CHOCOLATE FROSTING

For one 8 in (20 cm) cake

*12 oz (350 g) semisweet chocolate
¹/₂ cup (125 g) unsalted butter at
room temperature*

Finely chop the chocolate and place in a saucepan with ¹/₂ cup (125 ml) lukewarm water. Melt over low heat. Meanwhile, cut the butter into small pieces. Remove the chocolate from the heat and stir in the butter, a few bits at a time, until well blended. Pour over the cooled cake; use a metal spatula to help smooth the frosting if necessary. Chill for at least 1 hour before garnishing and serving.

CHOCOLATE GANACHE FILLING

Makes about 1 cup (250 ml)

*8 oz (250 g) semisweet chocolate
1 cup (250 ml) heavy cream*

Chop the chocolate finely with a sharp knife; the smaller the bits, the more quickly and evenly the chocolate will melt. Place the chopped chocolate in a heatproof bowl. In a saucepan, bring the cream to a boil. Pour the boiling cream onto the chocolate and whisk constantly until smooth and thoroughly combined. Refrigerate until just set and cooled, about 1 hour. Beat the ganache with an electric mixer until it doubles in volume, about 10 minutes. When cool, refrigerate until needed. (The ganache can be made up to 1 week in advance if kept covered in the refrigerator. Warm slightly before beating.)

CHOCOLATE GARNISHES

Chocolate decorations always give a professional look to finished desserts. It is best to make more than are needed because they are fragile and can break when handled. Any remaining decorations can be stored in an airtight container in a cool place for several weeks.

Some of these decorations are very delicate and even the weather can affect them. Professional confectioners and bakers tend to work in environmentally controlled areas. For best results at home, avoid working in excessively hot or humid conditions.

The simplest garnish is a dusting of cocoa powder: Hold a sieve over the surface to be coated, then add some cocoa powder and tap the sides gently. Move the sieve as necessary to obtain a thin, even layer. For a more sophisticated decoration, hold a paper doily just above the surface to be dusted and proceed as before. A stencil design made out of cardboard can be used more than once. For example, a series of 1 in (2.5 cm) lines will result in a lovely striped pattern that can be used again and again.

Another simple, attractive garnish can be obtained with a sprinkling of grated chocolate. A hand-held grater is ideal. When grating, hold a chilled block of chocolate with a piece of foil to prevent the heat of your hand from melting it. A food processor fitted with a metal blade can be used when very fine shavings are desired. With the machine running, drop the chocolate pieces through the feed tube; be sure the chocolate is at least coarsely chopped beforehand or the blades may jam.

CHOCOLATE SCROLLS

To obtain long thin scrolls, first melt the chocolate and then pour it onto a board or work surface. Using a metal spatula, spread to an even thickness of about 1/8 in (3 mm). Allow the chocolate to cool for about 30 minutes. Place the edge of a long-bladed knife or metal spatula on the surface, pointing away from you at a 45° angle. Scrape off a thin layer of chocolate in long scrolls. Use a teaspoon instead of a knife to obtain short, rounded curls.

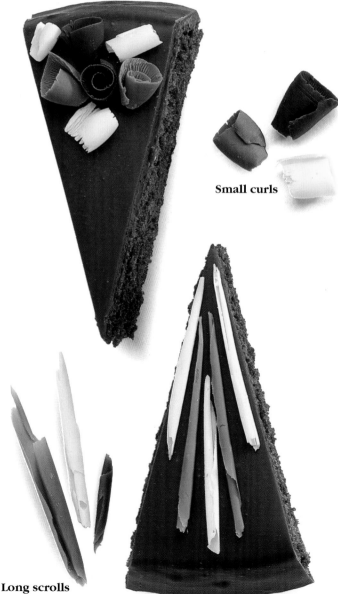

CHOCOLATE CURLS

Small curls can be made using chocolate at room temperature. (The chocolate will splinter if it is too cold; soften it between the palms of your hands first.) Using a vegetable peeler, "shave" the chocolate lengthwise over a plate. If the chocolate is an awkward shape, make an even block by melting it with a little vegetable oil, about 1 tsp per 1 oz (30 g) of chocolate. Pour the mixture into a small rectangular pan or mold and refrigerate until set. Allow the block to soften to room temperature, then shave it in the same way.

Small curls

Making scrolls
With a straight-edged knife or metal spatula, push the blade across the chocolate to form long, thin curls.

Long scrolls

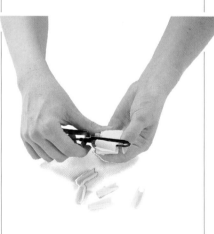

Making curls
Slowly and firmly draw the blade of the vegetable peeler across the widest side of a chocolate block at room temperature.

PIPING CHOCOLATE

Confident cooks can pipe melted chocolate garnishes directly onto the surface of a frosted cake. Novices may prefer to pipe onto waxed paper and then transfer the shapes to the cake when hardened. Two paper cones can be prepared from an 8 x 14 in (20 x 35 cm) piece of paper, cut in half diagonally. When the cones are made, melt the chocolate (see page 182). With a small spoon, fill one cone three-quarters full and pipe as shown right. Point cone upward between piping shapes to prevent leakage.

Making a paper cone
Fold the short side of a triangle over to the right-angled corner to form a cone. Wrap the long point around and tuck it inside the top.

Piping the chocolate
Place the design under waxed paper and then pipe chocolate over the outline. Do not force the chocolate; let it fall evenly from the tip.

Removing the shapes
When the shapes have set, lift off each with a metal spatula. Handle as little as possible because they are fragile.

CHOCOLATE LEAVES

Any fresh nonpoisonous leaf with distinct veins, such as rose, bay, or lemon, can be used. Wash the leaves and pat dry with paper towels. With a pastry brush, small painting brush, or small metal spatula, coat the underside of each leaf with melted chocolate. (This gives a more distinct pattern.) Leave a bit of the stem uncoated so that the leaf can be separated from the chocolate when set. Dry on wire racks and refrigerate until firm. Then, starting at the stem, with cool hands, carefully peel the chocolate away from the leaf.

Alternating dark, milk, and white chocolate triangles makes a lively garnish

Shapes

Tri-color leaves can turn a plain cake into something extremely decorative

Leaves

CHOCOLATE SHAPES

Pour melted chocolate onto a cookie sheet lined with baking parchment or waxed paper, or onto an oiled work surface. Spread to an even thickness of 1/8 in (3 mm) and allow to cool for about 30 minutes; it can be refrigerated. Invert the chocolate layer onto another sheet of parchment or waxed paper and trim the edges. Using a ruler, trace lines for squares or diamonds and cut out. Squares can be cut diagonally in half to make triangles. Alternatively, use small pastry cutters to make other shapes, such as circles. Refrigerate until firm.

Making leaves
Coat the underside of non-poisonous leaves with melted chocolate and peel away the leaf when dry.

Making shapes
Using a small decorative cutter, press into the chocolate, then chill shapes until firm. Alternatively, use a ruler and a thin-bladed knife.

Extracts, Essences, & Sweeteners

SAVORY EXTRACTS AND FLAVORINGS

Concentrated savory extracts have been an essential flavoring in cooking for hundreds of years. In the East, they are based mainly on soybeans and fish, and are used for both flavor and color. In the West, stocks are the best known and most widely used seasoning base. Intensely savory reductions of liquid simmered with vegetables, meat or fish bones, and herbs, stocks can be prepared at home or purchased in the form of bouillon cubes or in cans. Other concentrates include yeast extract, which is made from salt and the yeast by-product of beer and spirit distillation, and dried fish. But whether Eastern or Western, animal or mineral, what all of these products have in common is the ability to reinforce the flavor of foods.

Miso This flavoring of Japanese origin has been around for thousands of years. It is made by salting and fermenting soybeans together with a grain such as rice, barley, or wheat, and a special mold, then aging the resulting paste for several years.

Each region has its own traditional type of miso, ranging in color from a light cream, to tawny brown, to deep chocolate. The flavor varies according to the type of grain, but it always has a winelike pungency. Some versions are thick and smooth, others are chunkier.

Miso was originally intended as a preservative, and it is still used for many Japanese pickles, but along the way it has evolved into a very important seasoning, primarily in Japan and Korea. It is most often paired with Japanese soup stock, *dashi*, for miso soup. In Japan, this is traditional at breakfast, though it can be drunk at any time of day. It is also used to flavor sauces for salads, vegetables, and bean curd, and in dips for tempura. When using miso in hot dishes, add just before serving; it should not be allowed to boil.

Skewered meat, fish, and vegetables can be spread with plain miso and then grilled. *Denagaku*, a popular Japanese dish, is grilled bean curd coated in a sauce of miso blended with sake, dashi, sesame seeds, mirin, sugar, a few teaspoons of lemon juice, grated lemon rind, and thickened with beaten egg yolks.

Yellow miso, *shinshu*, is an all-purpose miso; red miso, *aka*, is a very salty version. White miso, *shiro*, made with two-thirds rice, is very smooth and sweet. It is used in pickles and as a topping for broiled meat. The strongly flavored *hatcho miso* is most often eaten on its own, and barley miso, *mugi*, is dark with an earthy flavor.

Red miso *is very salty and should be used sparingly in stocks, soups, and casseroles*

Trasi *is a firm paste made from fermented shrimp; it is extremely pungent*

Yellow miso *is the all-purpose bean paste version, popular throughout Asia for enhancing the taste of many dishes*

Savory extracts
From East to West, savory extracts and flavorings enhance the taste of many dishes.

Malt extract *provides the keynote for several well-known milk drinks*

Meat extract *adds a salty, concentrated taste to many foods, from soups to drinks*

Yeast extract *is a blend of salt and brewer's yeast*

Beef bouillon cubes

Chicken bouillon cube

Bouillon granules

Fish Paste Made from salted and fermented prawns or shrimp, fish pastes are popular throughout Southeast Asia. Known as *trasi* in Indonesia, *blachan* in Malaysia, and *kapee* in Thailand, these vary in appearance from a gray watery paste to crumbly brown blocks. Regardless of the form, they all have a very strong fishy taste and smell, and need to be used with care. Fish pastes are an acquired taste, so it is best to add them sparingly. When using in uncooked dishes, the block forms of fish paste must be cooked first. Cut off a piece and toast over a low gas flame, or place under the broiler until roasted, then proceed with the recipe. European anchovy paste is a similar product,

but it is no substitute for the pungent pastes of Southeast Asia. In Western kitchens, anchovy paste is used as a seasoning for ground meat mixtures, stews, and sauces, or on its own as a spread for toast or crackers.

Meat Extract In the West, meat juices are concentrated into thick, commercially made pastes. Some, like Bovril, are mixed with vegetable extracts, flavorings, and spices. Most often, these extracts are diluted with hot water for drinking, although they can also be used to impart a meaty flavor to soups, casseroles, and gravies. They can also be enjoyed straight from the jar, as a spread for sandwiches and toast.

Stock Extract For convenience, meat and vegetable stock extracts are also available dried in cubes or freeze-dried into granules. Flavors include beef, pork, ham, lamb, fish, and chicken, as well as pure vegetable. Both cubes and granules should be dissolved in hot water before use; they can be added directly to dishes that are high in liquid.

Yeast Extract First produced in the 1800s, this type of extract was developed by the French scientist Pasteur and the German chemist Liebig. Even before the role of vitamins in daily nutrition was discovered in 1912, yeast extracts, such as Marmite, were well-established health products. Yeast extracts are popular in Great Britain, Australia, and parts of Canada as a spread for bread and toast.

Malt Extract Made from fermented barley, this extract has a distinctive sweetish flavor. It is used in Western kitchens for baking and in malted milk.

COOK'S CHOICE
MISO SOUP

Serves 4–6

6 in (15 cm) square of konbu seaweed
3 tbsp bonito flakes
4 oz (125 g) red miso
4 oz (125 g) soft tofu
2–3 scallions, sliced

Wipe the seaweed with a damp paper towel and make several incisions with a knife. Bring 4 cups (1,200 ml) water to the boil and add the seaweed. Cover and leave for 10 minutes. Remove the seaweed and add 1 cup (250 ml) water. Return to a boil. Add the bonito shavings and stir. Strain the soup base and return to the pan. (Alternatively, replace the seaweed and bonito flakes with concentrated *dashi*, available in Japanese groceries, and mix with the same total quantity of boiling water.) Stir in the miso. Slice the tofu into small cubes and divide among warmed soup bowls. Add the scallions to the soup, stir, and pour over the tofu in the bowls. Serve immediately.

DRIED SEAFOOD

Dried seafood has long been a staple ingredient in Chinese cuisine. Some seafood, such as dried oysters, scallops *(conpoy)*, and squid, must be soaked before use; the soaking liquid is also added to the dish, like dried mushrooms. Bonito flakes, or *katsuo-bushi*, are essential for *dashi*, Japanese soup stock.

Dried powdered shrimp

Dried scallops

Bonito flakes

Bonito flakes are dried, woodlike shavings that are obtained with a special tool, called katsuo-kezuri-ki

SWEET ESSENCES AND FLAVORINGS

Essences are produced by extracting the essential flavors of a very wide range of plants, through either maceration or distillation. The best liquid essences are made wholly from natural ingredients; however, good essences are expensive to produce. Some manufacturers may add cheap substitutes and synthetic flavors to their products. In the kitchen, essences are used to flavor desserts and baked goods, as well as sauces and dressings. Flavorings are usually the dried form of an aromatic plant that has been ground to a fine powder. Sweet flavoring powders are used mainly in the manufacture of candy and soft drinks.

Fruit and nut essences *such as lemon, strawberry, almond, and hazelnut are used primarily in baking and confectionery*

Strawberry essence

Hazelnut essence

Kola nuts *are dried and used in a variety of popular soft drinks; they contain a small amount of caffeine and so provide a mild stimulant*

Cola drink

Kola powder

Sarsaparilla *is made from the cordlike roots of the South American plant smilax; the roots are dried and used to flavor a carbonated drink, once popular in the U.S.*

Sarsaparilla powder

Sarsaparilla drink

Licorice roots *are dried and ground to a powder, or the bittersweet juices are extracted to make delicious black candy*

Licorice root

Licorice candies

190

Herb extract
A few drops of an herb extract will reproduce an herb's flavor when it is not available fresh.

are best to added to uncooked dishes, or at the end of cooking, because heat will diminish their flavoring potential.

Nut Essences These are a simple and flavorful way to add interest to plain cakes, cookies, and tarts.

Vanilla Extract Widely available, this can be used in almost all kinds of baked goods to enhance the main flavor.

Herb Extracts Available in some specialty stores, only a few drops of these intensely concentrated extracts are needed to add extra layers of herbal flavoring to soups, stews, and casseroles.

Licorice This distinctive bittersweet flavor is a classic the world over. It is used mainly in confectionery items, such as licorice whips and pipes, black jelly beans, and liquorice allsorts. Pieces of licorice root can also be infused in hot water for a flavorful and soothing tisane, and licorice powder can be used to enliven fruit juices and dried fruit salads. Licorice is also used in the production of some liqueurs, most notably Italian Sambuca.

Cola and Sarsaparilla Once prescribed as medicines, these flavorings were held to have revitalizing properties. Some soft drink manufacturers capitalized on the ostensible efficacy of these ingredients and included them in their products. Cola is now the basis for the most successful soft drinks.

Fruit Essences Strawberries, raspberries, and pomegranates are ideal for distilling into essences (or macerating into syrups) that keep well through the long winter months. Use these essences to flavor all kinds of food, from ice creams and sorbets to tarts and cake fillings. They make an interesting addition to fresh fruit salads, and can also be used to enhance savory dressings and sweet dessert sauces. These fruit flavorings are also used to give sweetness and flavor to many kinds of drinks, and they are a vital constituent of many classic cocktails.

Fruit Oils Extracted from the essential oils in the skins of citrus fruits, only a few drops of these are needed to infuse a dish. They

FLAVORING PASTRY CREAM
Blend together 10 tbsp sugar, 7 tbsp cornstarch, and 2 eggs. Pour on 2 cups (500 ml) scalded milk. Continue stirring over heat until the mixture thickens. Transfer to a bowl, stir in a few drops of a fruit or nut essence and leave to cool.

COOK'S CHOICE
GRAPEFRUIT AND GRENADINE SORBET
Serves 6

4 ½ cups (1 liter) pink grapefruit juice
1 cup (200 g) superfine sugar
2 tbsp grenadine
Cookie cups (see page 203)
Fresh mint for garnish

Combine the grapefruit juice, sugar, and grenadine in a bowl; stir to dissolve the sugar. Freeze the mixture in a metal bowl. When the mixture has solidified, break into chunks and place in a food processor; meanwhile, return the empty bowl to the freezer. Process the frozen chunks until the mixture is smooth. Return to the chilled bowl and freeze until set, 30–45 minutes. Serve scoops of the sorbet in cookie cups and garnish with the mint.

GRENADINE

Grenadine is a syrup made from pomegranate juice. It is bright red in color and has a sweet, fresh flavor. It is completely nonalcoholic, but plays an essential part in any good barman's repertoire.

No classic Daiquiri, for example, would be complete without it. Other cocktails flavored with grenadine include Tequila Sunrise and Planter's Punch.

Grenadine is a natural coloring and is valued for its ability to tint cocktails as well as desserts and candied citrus peel. It looks particularly effective when added to sorbets, ice cream, and fruit salads. Try it with grapefruit halves, or use in a salad dressing for avocado. Do not confuse grenadine with pomegranate syrup, which is

the unsweetened, boiled-down juice of sour pomegranate seeds. This syrup is used primarily in Middle Eastern cuisine, where its intensely concentrated flavor is used to enhance many dishes, most notably Iranian *faisinjan*. This dish combines duck or chicken, cut in pieces, with a sauce that is thickened with walnuts and perfumed with pomegranate syrup.

Pomegranate seeds make an attractive garnish that can be sprinkled over ice cream, mousse, or fruit salad

LIQUEURS, SPIRITS, AND WINES

Almost any part of a plant—seeds, leaves, roots, fruit, and kernels—can be macerated with or infused in alcohol to provide a spirited flavoring. Alcohol-based drinks, although normally imbibed straight from the glass, do have a useful range of culinary applications.

Wine adds richness to long-cooking dishes, while fruit and nut liqueurs can be added at the last minute or flambéed for a burst of flavor. Spirits and brandies work well in marinades and dessert coffees; they can also be poured over fruit or ice cream for a simple dessert.

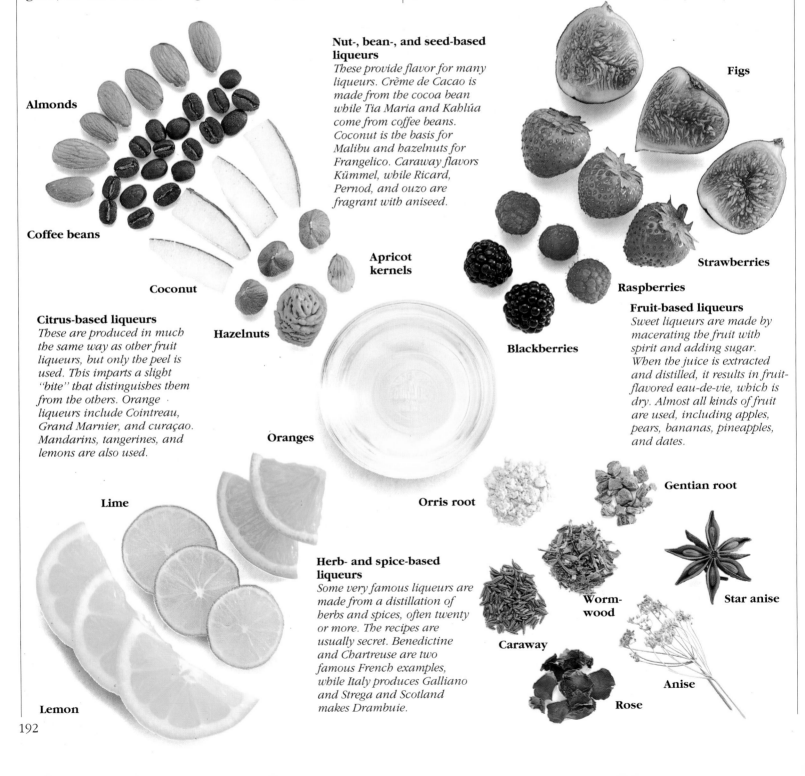

Almonds

Coffee beans

Nut-, bean-, and seed-based liqueurs
These provide flavor for many liqueurs. Crème de Cacao is made from the cocoa bean while Tia Maria and Kahlúa come from coffee beans. Coconut is the basis for Malibu and hazelnuts for Frangelico. Caraway flavors Kümmel, while Ricard, Pernod, and ouzo are fragrant with aniseed.

Figs

Coconut

Apricot kernels

Hazelnuts

Strawberries

Raspberries

Blackberries

Citrus-based liqueurs
These are produced in much the same way as other fruit liqueurs, but only the peel is used. This imparts a slight "bite" that distinguishes them from the others. Orange liqueurs include Cointreau, Grand Marnier, and curaçao. Mandarins, tangerines, and lemons are also used.

Fruit-based liqueurs
Sweet liqueurs are made by macerating the fruit with spirit and adding sugar. When the juice is extracted and distilled, it results in fruit-flavored eau-de-vie, which is dry. Almost all kinds of fruit are used, including apples, pears, bananas, pineapples, and dates.

Oranges

Orris root

Gentian root

Lime

Herb- and spice-based liqueurs
Some very famous liqueurs are made from a distillation of herbs and spices, often twenty or more. The recipes are usually secret. Benedictine and Chartreuse are two famous French examples, while Italy produces Galliano and Strega and Scotland makes Drambuie.

Worm-wood

Star anise

Caraway

Anise

Rose

Lemon

192

FORTIFIED WINES

Some wines, mainly port, sherry, and Madeira, are fortified with an added dose of brandy. With the exception of fino sherries, these wines are sweet and have a remarkably full flavor that can be used to add richness to winter casseroles, game sauces, and even some fish dishes. Port is often added to duck dishes and pâtés. Madeira goes well with ham and other pork dishes, and sherry enhances soups and sauces, especially those that are poultry based. Fortified wines are also used in sweet dishes such as custards, sabayons, trifles, savarins, and sugar syrups for poached fruit.

Port

Sherry

Many pâtés are flavored with port

COOK'S CHOICE
SHRIMP MARSEILLAISE

Serves 4

2 shallots, finely chopped
2 tbsp unsalted butter
1 lb (500 g) large peeled shrimp
1 tbsp anise-flavored liqueur
¹⁄₂ cup (125 ml) dry white wine
¹⁄₂ cup (125 ml) fish stock
²⁄₃ cup (150 ml) heavy cream
Salt
Freshly ground black pepper

In a saucepan, combine the shallots and butter over low heat and cook until soft, about 1 minute. Add the shrimp and continue to cook for 1 minute longer. Add the anise-flavored liqueur and the white wine, cover and bring to a boil. Simmer for 30 seconds. Remove the shrimp and keep warm. Add the fish stock and return to a boil. Cook rapidly until reduced by at least half. Add the cream and cook until thickened, about 5 minutes. Season to taste. Arrange the shrimp on serving plates and pour the sauce over them. Serve immediately.

All alcohol-based drinks can be used to flavor foods. The easiest way is to add the alcohol directly to the pan, either by deglazing (see page 249) or by pouring it into liquid preparations such as soups and stews. To impart a deep, mellow flavor rather than an overpowering dose of alcohol, be sure to boil the mixture for at least 1 minute to allow the alcohol to evaporate.

Recipes that do not include an alcoholic flavoring can be easily enhanced by one. When choosing an alcohol to partner a particular food, consider the drink's ingredients. Cherry-flavored Kirsch is the obvious ally for any dish made with cherries. The strong juniper flavor of gin goes well in dishes made with game, and Calvados, French apple brandy, can be used in apple dishes. Origins are another clue to successful flavor pairing. For example, add a splash of Italian red wine to pasta sauces or an anise-flavored liqueur from southern France to season fish or shellfish dishes.

Flambéing is the culinary technique most often associated with wines, spirits, liqueurs, and brandies. When these are heated, their alcohol burns off, leaving behind only flavor. Table-side flambéing makes for a spectacular presentation, and in the kitchen it adds an attractive golden brown appearance as well as helping to caramelize dishes that contain sugar. This technique is simple but precautions should be taken when flambéing in a home kitchen. Keep hair tied back and your face well away from the pan. Also, be sure there are no obstructing shelves or cabinets directly above the cooking area.

These alcohols can also be used as the base for quick and delicious desserts. Pineapple slices and kirsch are traditional; orange curaçao goes well with peaches, or splash some ginger wine on fresh melon. On a lighter note, fresh strawberries and raspberries are even more delicious in a crystal coupe of pink champagne.

Whipped cream is the ideal base for an alcoholic flavoring. Add a nut-flavored liqueur to whipped cream for chocolate desserts or use black-currant-flavored cassis and serve with fruit salads.

Many ice creams also take well to a dash of liqueur or brandy. Flavorful matches include green apple sorbet with Calvados, rum-raisin ice cream with rum, and French vanilla with something rich—hazelnut Frangelico, almond-scented Amaretto, or coffee-flavored Kahlúa.

To a cup of after-dinner coffee, add a splash of brandy or *crème de vanille*, or whisky and cream for Irish coffee.

Angostura bitters
Made in Trinidad, Angostura bitters rely on the bitter but aromatic bark of the Cusparia tree plus a combination of dried fruit and spices. A few drops can be used to flavor spirits for cocktails and to enhance fruit salads, ice creams, savory sauces, and soups.

SUGAR

Sugar is one of the oldest flavorings and condiments, and its use in Asia goes far back in recorded history. Its earliest form was as a liquid sugar extracted from sugarcane. Early Europeans relied on honey and fruit to sweeten their food. When they finally "discovered" sugarcane, they described it as a reed that produced honey without the aid of bees. Christopher Columbus introduced sugarcane to the West Indies, where it was, and continues to be, widely and successfully cultivated.

In the seventeenth century, the increasing popularity of beverages such as coffee, tea, and cocoa had a direct impact on the European demand for sugar, making sugarcane a precious commodity. But it was not until the 1800s that the sugar beet was considered as an alternative source; its sugar is identical in strength and quality. Today, sugar is obtained from both sugar beets and sugarcane, and is available in a variety of forms: raw, refined, brown, cubes, and even flavored sugars.

Sugarcane is a tropical plant grown mainly in plantations in the West Indies and South America. It is a perennial plant that grows to a height of 20 ft (6 meters). The cane is usually 1–2 in (2.5–5 cm) in diameter and closely resembles bamboo.

Sugar beet is grown as a field crop in temperate regions across Europe and the great plains of North America. Sugar is extracted from the swollen root, which looks rather like a fat parsnip.

PRODUCTION

After harvest, sugarcane is taken to factories for processing. The canes are crushed and then fed through powerful rollers that extract the sugar juice. This juice is then mixed with a substance that draws out the

Made from a blend of refined and unrefined sugars and honey, this gives a distinctive flavor to braised pork and duck dishes

Turbinado (or Demerara) sugar

Raw (or golden granulated) sugar

Light brown (or muscovado) sugar

Dark brown (or muscovado) sugar

Chinese rock sugar

Granulated sugar *has a medium-fine texture that makes it the best all-purpose sugar*

Superfine sugar *is much finer than granulated sugar; it dissolves quickly and is good for baking*

Confectioners' sugar *is the most finely textured of all sugars; use for sweetening foods and garnishing*

impurities. Next, the juice is thickened by evaporation, boiled in vacuum pans, then seeded with tiny sugar crystals that encourage crystallization.

When the appropriate crystal size has been obtained, the mixture is spun in high-speed centrifuge machines, resembling clothes dryers, which separate the raw sugar crystals from the syrup base. For white sugar, the crystals are separated from the molasses syrup, then they are refined further for color and texture. Brown sugars are made from refined white crystals that are coated with a thin layer of molasses.

In sugar beet production, the root is sliced and then infused in hot water. Otherwise, processing is identical to that of sugarcane: the resultant liquid is purified, concentrated, and seeded with sugar crystals. When the appropriate crystal size is reached, the sugar is spun, washed, and dried. Unlike cane sugar, the molasses by-product is used only in cattle feed.

TYPES OF SUGAR

Unrefined Sugar True unrefined sugars are not white in color, they are brown. This is due to the molasses syrup that is allowed to stay on the crystals, instead of being refined out and added later. In the U.S., unrefined sugar is found in health food stores and other specialty markets.

HERB AND SPICE SUGARS

Sugar can be flavored with flower petals, such as rose, lavender, or rose geranium, and spices such as cloves, aniseed, ginger, cinnamon, vanilla, or cardamom pods. Use these sugars to add extra flavor to custard sauces, cakes, and other baked goods. Make sure petals and spices are quite dry or the sugar will have lumps.

Molasses Sugar A dark unrefined sugar, this contains a high percentage of molasses, which is responsible for its strong flavor and sticky texture. *Barbados sugar* is one of the most widely available types of molasses sugar and is delicious in chutneys, fruitcakes, gingerbread, and toffee.

Brown (or Muscovado) Sugar Light and dark brown sugars are not as strong-tasting as molasses sugar but their color and flavor will depend on the amount of molasses added. Well suited for baking, they can also be used to add color and a rich flavor to steamed puddings, spice cakes, cookies, autumn fruit crisps, and baked apples. These sugars also add color and sweetness to savory dishes such as glazed ham, barbecue sauce, and chutneys.

Turbinado (or Demerara) Sugar This sugar came originally from Guyana. The distinctive large crystals are obtained by regulating the conditions under which the sugar syrup is spun. High-quality turbinado should be slightly sticky with an aromatic flavor. It is particularly good in baked goods, such as cookies, cakes, and crisps, and with hot beverages such as coffee and mulled wines.

Raw (or Golden Granulated) Sugar This is a dry, free-flowing sugar with a buttery taste. Its light golden crystals are made by a unique process that produces a very clear and brilliant juice for crystallization. This type is unsuitable for cakes and delicate pastries because the coarse texture makes it difficult to blend into batters.

Granulated Sugar This is the sugar for everyday use in the kitchen and at the table. In savory cooking, it is the best type to caramelize for added color and depth of flavor, as is often done in Caribbean cuisine. This is also the best type to use for making flavored sugars (see left).

Superfine (or Caster) Sugar Granulated sugar is milled further to produce this fine sugar, which is ideal for use in cakes, angel food cakes, meringues, and any recipe where the coarser texture of granulated sugar might affect the consistency of the finished dish.

Confectioners' (or Icing) Sugar This is powdered granulated sugar. As its name implies, it is used mainly for icing and decoration, although it is also useful for delicate pastry preparations, such as tart crusts, which benefit from the absence of more coarsely textured sugars. Store in a cool, dry place, and always sift before use because this sugar is prone to lumps.

SPECIALTY SUGARS

Flavored or colored sugars can be used in place of ordinary sugar for drinks, or decorating cakes and pastries. Chocolate sugar can be stirred into *café au lait* and rainbow crystals make an attractive addition to the coffee tray. Swizzle sticks are also pretty alternatives to sugar cubes, but they are best used with coffee, tea, and other hot drinks to ensure that the sugar dissolves.

Chocolate-flavored sugar

Rainbow crystals

Colored decorating sugar

Sugar swizzle stick

SUGAR IN THE KITCHEN

Although sugar is used mainly as a sweetener, it does have many other applications. It inhibits the growth of microorganisms, making it useful for sweet preserves and chutneys; it is a yeast activator for breads, and a texture enhancer and flavoring for home baking. Sugar undergoes changes upon heating, which facilitate candymaking, and it is essential for pastries and baked goods, not only as flavoring but as decoration. Sugar is used for most decorative frostings—from glaze to buttercream—and it can be heated to the caramel stage and spun or molded into a whole variety of patterns, shapes, and sculptures. At its first stage of cooking, the syrup is ideal for poached fruits, sorbets, and frozen soufflés, and for preserving fruits in alcohol. For extra flavor, the sugar syrup may be infused with spices, such as vanilla and cardamom, or flavorings such as lemon peel.

Sugar syrups are simple mixtures of sugar and water and they have a variety of different uses in the kitchen. Differing strengths of syrup can be achieved by increasing or decreasing the quantity of sugar in a given amount of water.

Light syrups are used for poaching fruit, bottling apple slices, or freezing delicate fruit such as melon and pineapple. Allow ²/₃ cup (125 g) sugar to 2¹/₃ cups (600 ml) water.

Medium syrups, for fruit sorbets and frozen soufflés, are made with equal quantities of sugar and water. An even heavier syrup is needed for fondant icing or for bottling peaches. Allow about 3 cups (600 g) sugar to 2 cups (500 ml) water.

COOKING WITH SUGAR

Sugar syrup for candies, pastries, and poached fruit is made by boiling a mixture of sugar and water. Simple sugar syrups can be prepared in an ordinary saucepan, but for those that must be brought to high heats—as when making caramel—unlined copper pans should be used.
To prevent any sugar that splatters from burning, use a pastry brush dipped in water to brush down the sides of the pan.

Sugar syrup will keep unrefrigerated for several days, or for several weeks if kept cold. For extra flavor, it can be infused with vanilla pods, star anise, or citrus peel. Or, boil a handful of lime flowers in the water, strain and proceed with the syrup-making, using the flavored water. The result will be subtle yet delicious.

A sugar syrup changes its composition as it is boiled. The stages through which the sugar passes are known as thread, soft-ball, hard-ball, soft-crack, and hard-crack. Each of these stages corresponds to a specific temperature and is used in the preparation of different kinds of pastries, sweets, and even savory dishes. Professionals often test

Fudge

Marshmallows

Taffy

Hard candies

Peppermint fondants

Nougat

Humbugs

Toffees

Soft-ball 239°F (115°C)
Use for fondants, fudge, and buttercream. Test by dropping into cold water. It should be able to hold a small ball shape.

Hard-ball 248°F (120°C)
Use for almond paste and Italian meringue. Test in cold water; it should roll into a harder ball than at the soft-ball stage.

Soft-crack 257°F (125°C)
Use for caramels, toffee, and taffy. Test in cold water; it should be brittle, but still sticky on the fingers.

Hard-crack 295°F (146°C)
Use for almond brittle and glazed fruits. Test in cold water; it should be very brittle with no stickiness.

DECORATING WITH FROSTING

A sugar syrup heated to the soft-ball stage can be used to prepare buttercream frosting, which is ideal for cake decorating. To fill and coat a 9 in (23 cm) cake, combine 6 tbsp water and ¹/₂ cup (100 g) sugar in a saucepan. Heat until the sugar dissolves, then boil until it reaches 239°F (115°C) on a sugar thermometer.

In a large bowl, whisk together 4 egg yolks. With an electric mixer, slowly beat in the sugar syrup and continue beating until cool, 5–10 minutes. Cream 1 cup (250 g) unsalted butter and add to the syrup mixture in batches, beating constantly. Place in a pastry bag and decorate.

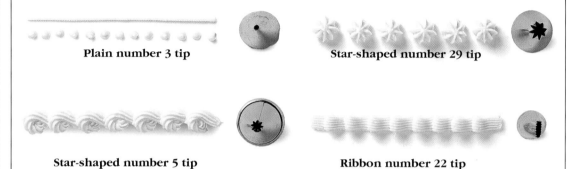

Plain number 3 tip

Star-shaped number 29 tip

Star-shaped number 5 tip

Ribbon number 22 tip

the temperature with their fingers, keeping a bowl of ice water nearby, but the home cook will obtain the best results with a sugar thermometer. Always be sure to put the thermometer in the mixture when beginning to heat, or it will break.

When the mixture reaches 350°F (177°C), the syrup starts to change color. This is the beginning of the caramel stage and it is possible to judge it by eye without the thermometer. When the syrup is a tawny brown color and just beginning to smoke, remove it from the heat and immediately place the pan in a shallow basin of cold water to stop the cooking. The unlined copper pans, which are essential for caramel making, are great conductors of heat, so it is important to cool the pan down right away or the caramel may burn, even off the heat.

Pulled sugar candies and blown sugar decorations are made by highly skilled confectioners who have been trained to sculpt and mold scaldingly hot sugar syrups. They must work on heatproof surfaces, often under special lamps that maintain the heat necessary to retain the pliability of the sugar. This sugar is white, but color can be added with food coloring. For blown sugar decorations, a tube is inserted in the sugar mass. The confectioner then blows air into the sugar through the tube, much like blowing up a balloon.

For the home cook, confectioners' sugar offers the most accessible form of sugar decoration. A very simple cake decoration

is achieved by placing a stencil over the top of the cake and sprinkling with confectioners' sugar. Paper doilies are handy for ready-made stencils, but patterns can also be cut out of ordinary cardboard. Decorate just before serving and do not place the stencil directly on the surface of frosted cakes.

Sugar-based icings (see above) can be used plain, or flavored with chocolate, liqueurs, or fruit purees. Intricate decorations can be made with an assortment of metal or plastic pastry bag tips, or a simple cone made from waxed paper (see page 185) can be used for lettering or a lattice pattern.

COOK'S CHOICE
ENGLISH TOFFEE

Makes about 1¹/₂ lb (750 g)

Butter for the pan
1³/₄ cups (350 g) sugar
1 cup (250 ml) heavy cream
¹/₈ tsp cream of tartar
¹/₂ cup (120 g) unsalted butter
1 tsp vanilla extract

Butter a square pan. In a pan, combine the sugar, cream, and cream of tartar over high heat. When boiling, cook for 3 minutes, stirring constantly. Add the butter and cook to 257°F (125°C) on a sugar thermometer. Add the vanilla and pour into the prepared pan. Cool, then score into squares. Wrap in waxed paper and store in an airtight container.

COOK'S CHOICE
CARAMEL APPLES

Makes 12 apples

12 eating apples
12 wooden skewers
2¹/₂ cups (500 g) sugar
8 tbsp unsalted butter

Wash and dry the apples and push a large skewer into the center of each. In a saucepan, combine the sugar, butter, and 2 tbsp water. Cook gently until the sugar dissolves. Bring to a boil and heat to 257°F (125°C). Dip the apples into the hot caramel. Leave to set on waxed paper.

Sugar sieve
For confectioners' sugar decorations, always use a sieve to sift out any lumps.

SYRUP

There are many different types of commercial syrups—golden syrup, molasses, maple syrup, corn syrup, and treacle—and while their flavors and colors vary, they are all essentially liquid forms of sugar. Most syrups are by-products of cane and beet sugar refinement. They are made from the liquid that is left over after the sugar crystals have been removed, which is then reduced to obtain a thick syrup. Corn syrup is derived from sweet corn kernels and is relatively mild in flavor. It is sometimes mixed with molasses for added color and flavor, and then it is known as dark corn syrup. Along with golden syrup, it is used in baking to flavor cakes and cookies, and for candy.

Molasses and maple syrup are popular sweeteners in North America, where they lend their distinctive flavors to many baked goods and some savory sauces. Cane syrup tastes like molasses and is the result of simmering sugar cane juice until thick and golden brown. Another molasses syrup, although a golden and tart one, is sorghum. This is extracted from the stalks of the sorghum plant and is widely used in the southern U.S. Barley malt syrup, also known as malt extract, has a delicate flavor and is high in vitamins and iron. Nowadays, treacle is probably the least-used sweetening syrup; many desserts, such as treacle pudding and treacle tart are, in fact, made with golden syrup.

Liquid sweeteners
Syrups are liquid forms of sugar and most are popular as toppings. Darker syrups tend to have stronger, more distinctive flavors, while lighter syrups are more delicate. Mild varieties such as golden syrup and corn syrup can be used interchangeably.

Syrups vary in consistency and strength of flavor, and this may affect the ways in which they are used in the kitchen. The following is a selection of some of the different types.

Molasses This is a very dark syrup that is produced during the manufacture of sugar cane. Americans nicknamed the heavy molasses from the West Indies "blackstrap syrup," and this name is now applied to any type of dark syrup. Molasses is an unrefined syrup with a very thick texture and a strong taste that leans towards the bitter side of sweet. Once a common household item, today its use is confined to specialty cakes and cookies, and some toffee.

Treacle A smoother syrup, this is made by blending molasses and refinery syrup. Although less bitter than molasses, the flavor is still distinctive. Treacle ranges in color from light gold to black and is slightly thinner than molasses. It is most common in traditional English baked goods, and it is essential for black-treacle toffee.

Golden Syrup This is a very smooth, clear syrup with a bright golden color. The flavor is sweet and mild, and in Britain it is often used in batters for flapjacks and other baked goods. Pour into cored apples with raisins for baking, or drizzle over a steamed pudding. It is especially nice as a sweetener for oatmeal, and in Britain, it is traditionally served with pancakes on Shrove Tuesday.

Corn Syrup A rather runny, mild-flavored syrup, this is popular in all kinds of baking. It can also be used in barbecue sauces, candies, and sweet-and-sour dishes.

Maple Syrup Made from the sap of the black maple and sugar maple trees, both of which flourish in America and Canada, this is a thin, runny syrup that has a very distinctive flavor. Maple syrup is graded for quality; the lowest grades are often made from corn syrup that has simply been flavored with maple syrup. Maple syrup is delicious poured over vanilla ice cream or British-style hot crumpets and scones. In baking, it can be used to enhance the flavor of robust sweet breads and in any cake, cookie, or pie made with nuts. It can also be used in savory dishes, such as glazed ham or as a sweetener for relishes such as cranberry sauce. Maple syrup also has a particular affinity with boiled vegetables, especially brussels sprouts, where the sweetness acts as a foil for their bitter edge.

Corn syrup

Molasses

Maple syrup

Black treacle

Golden syrup

HONEY

This sweet substance, made from the nectar of flowers, has been used in cooking since very ancient times. Neolithic man probably robbed beehives for his honey, but by the Bronze Age, domesticated beekeeping was widespread. Ever since then, honey has been used as a sweetener and a preservative as well as a flavor enhancer. Many Europeans used it to sweeten their wine or brewed it into an alcoholic drink. In the Middle East, it has long been used in sticky-sweet phyllo pastries. Honey's popularity has endured to the present day and its culinary uses range from sweet to savory. The flavor and appearance are determined by the flower. Lavender honey is a deep gold with a perfumed flavor, while acacia honey is clear and pale with a delicate flavor.

Honey imparts its own distinctive flavor to the food with which it is cooked, so it is important to choose the right honey for the job. Ordinary commercial blends are fine when an unobtrusive honey flavor is desired; however, single-flower honeys have more personality and often more taste. Herb flowers, such as thyme and rosemary, produce aromatic and flavorful honeys that stand out in any dish. Orange blossom and clover honeys are both delicately perfumed and mild in taste.

Not only does honey add flavor; it also improves the keeping qualities of baked goods; it even gives a better texture to bread crusts. For baking, the thinner honeys mix more easily into batters; warming the honey also facilitates blending. Straight from the jar, honey adds pleasant sweetness to cereals, toasted bread or biscuits, ice creams, yogurt, and soft cheeses such as cottage cheese. Fruit, such as apricots, peaches, pears, and plums, are delicious when poached in a honey syrup consisting of one-third honey to two-thirds water.

In Europe, honey is traditionally used in baking—for example, in Dutch honey cake and German Christmas cookies. Many of the phyllo pastries from Greece and Turkey are soaked in a sweet honey syrup.

Honey is also used in savory cooking. Oven-roasted hams with a honey glaze are popular in America and many parts of Europe, and in America. Honey lends itself well to spicy barbecue sauces, and honey-flavored vinegar makes a remarkable vinaigrette.

The Chinese use honey to baste roast pork and duck, and in Turkey, chicken is often cooked with honey and almonds.

To store, keep honey in a cool, dry place; refrigeration is not absolutely necessary since it will last for a very long time without deteriorating. In fact, many honeys will crystallize at low temperatures.

Nutritionally, honey is made up of fructose and glucose sugars, which are considered to be easier to digest than the sucrose of sugar beet or sugarcane. Fructose is the sweetest of all sugars, so use less honey than sugar when substituting one for the other.

Honeycomb

English clover honey

French lavender honey

Greek Hymettus honey

COOK'S CHOICE
HONEY MADELEINES

Makes about 24

Butter for preparing the pans
7 oz (200 g) unsalted butter
1 tbsp single-flower honey
2 3/4 oz (80 g) flour, sifted
7 oz (200 g) superfine sugar
2 3/4 oz (80 g) ground almonds
1 vanilla pod, split
6 egg whites

Thoroughly coat madeleine pans with butter. In a saucepan, melt the unsalted butter over medium heat. Stir in the honey and allow mixture to cool without solidifying. In a bowl, combine the flour, sugar, and almonds and stir to blend. Scrape out the vanilla seeds with a small spoon and add to the flour mixture. In another large bowl, beat the egg whites until frothy. Fold in the flour mixture, then the melted butter; blend thoroughly. Spoon the batter into the pans and place in the refrigerator for 1 hour. Preheat the oven to 375°F (190°C). Place the pans in the oven and bake until just golden around the edges, 12–15 minutes. Ease the madeleines out with the tip of a knife and cool on wire racks. Serve warm, or store in an airtight container for 2–3 days.

Honeys range in appearance from light and clear to thick and opaque; the flavor depends on the flower from which it came

FRUIT PUREES, ESSENCES, AND SYRUPS

The seasonal appearance of fruit, often in copious quantities, has encouraged cooks to develop ways of capturing these flavors for future use. Preserving, bottling, and concentrating fruit flavors into syrups are the traditional methods; freezing is a more recent development, but no less useful. The many and varied flavors of fruit are used in cake and pastry recipes, jams and jellies, candies, and a wide range of alcoholic and soft drinks. They also turn up in savory dishes, mostly in chilled soups or in sauces, where their tartness acts as a foil for fatty meats such as duck or pork. Very often, the fruit is lightly processed to make better use of its flavor and texture. The fruit flesh may be pulped with the juice to make versatile purees or the two may be separated and the juice used alone.

Black currant syrup

The most familiar type of fruit puree is made from apples. Apple puree turns up in traditional desserts from around the world: Normandy apple tart, Swedish apple cake, English apple charlotte, Austrian apple strudel and American apple pie. Sometimes the puree is plain, sometimes it is flavored. Popular additions include lemon zest or juice, and spices such as cardamom, nutmeg, and cinnamon. Apple and blackberry is a favorite combination in Britain.

Indeed, mixing fruit flavors allows for more complex and interesting tastes. In some European countries, gooseberry is traditionally cooked with elderflowers as the two coincide in season. Gooseberries are also very good mixed with strawberries, raspberries, and oranges. Other tart berries, such as huckleberries, need to be subdued with the addition of a sweeter fruit, or with cream. Apricot puree, thinned with fresh orange or lemon juice, makes a flavorful sauce for ice creams, sweet soufflés, and mousses. Herbs and spices can also be added. Rhubarb has an affinity with gingerroot, and a squeeze of lemon juice subdues rhubarb's bite. Plum with cardamom, or pears and raspberries with mint, are just some of the possible flavor combinations.

Soft fruits are easily pureed for sauces, and while they are delicious on their own, they can also be combined. Try papaya with lime, blueberry with peach, strawberry with red currant, blueberries with blackberries, or raspberries with orange juice served with a dark chocolate cake. Enhance the flavor of the puree by adding a splash of kirsch, cassis, or almond-flavored liqueur. The same mixtures are delicious used as a base for ice creams and sorbets.

Fruit sauces are traditional with some savory foods, too. Applesauce is served with roast pork and potato pancakes, red currant sauce can be served with lamb, cranberry sauce is a classic with turkey, and in England, gooseberry sauce is the traditional accompaniment to baked mackerel.

Other savory sauces are made by adding both sugar and vinegar to the pureed fruit for a sweet-and-sour flavor. An apricot glaze for barbecued spare ribs can be made in this way.

Fruit soups are very popular in Central and Northern Europe. These are sometimes based on apples, as in apple and celery soup or carrot and apple soup; sometimes on cherries, as in the German chilled cherry soup with dumplings or the Hungarian yogurt and sour cherry soup.

In Scandinavia, fruit purees are cooked with cereals for a dish that is a cross between porridge and soup. When seasoned with salt, it becomes a savory supper dish; when sweetened with sugar or honey, it is served as a dessert.

Apricot puree

Fruit essence *is extracted from the skins of citrus fruit, which contain the flavorful essential oils; this dissipates in the heat of cooking, so use as a last-minute flavoring for sauces or custards*

200

Pear, *like other hard fruit, must be cooked before straining*

Apricots *are delicious paired with banana*

Apple *is found in pureed form in many world-famous dishes*

Strawberries *are among the soft fruits that need no prior cooking*

Raspberries *must have their seeds filtered out before being pureed*

Cherries *are cooked as purees for warm and cold soups*

Kiwi fruit *may need straining after pureeing to remove all the seeds*

Blackberries *produce more juice when cooked first*

Blueberries *need gentle cooking to soften their skins*

Rhubarb *lends itself to purees but benefits from a squeeze of lemon*

Mango *puree is easily obtained from ripe fruit*

FRUIT PUREES

Thick fruit purees have always been used as fillings for pies and crêpes and as a base for mousses and fools. Thinner purees can be used for both hot and cold sauces. The latter are often known as *coulis*, which is quite simply a French word that is applied to all sieved sauces, although the term was once reserved for savory meat and fish sauces. Most fruit can be used for purees; soft fruit can be used uncooked, while firmer fruits usually need to be stewed first. As a rule, fresh fruit is always best, but both frozen and dried fruits can also be used. Modern electric appliances, such as food processors and blenders, are quite handy for making coarse and medium purees, but a really smooth and delicate puree can be obtained only by hand-sieving through a fine nylon mesh.

Soft fruits—strawberries, raspberries, loganberries, ripe peaches, mangoes, kiwi fruit, bananas, pineapple, and melon—are prepared simply by hulling, peeling, or removing the stones. The flesh is then forced through a nylon sieve or pureed in a food processor or blender and sweetened to taste. Sugar is standard, but honey has an affinity for many fruit flavors, especially peaches and apricots. It may be necessary to heat the honey slightly for easier blending.

Firmer soft fruits, such as red currants, blueberries, and blackberries, may require gentle cooking to release all the juices or to soften the skins. Place the fruit in a non-reactive saucepan with very little water and place over gentle heat. When warmed through, proceed as for other soft fruit. Hard fruit, such as apples, pears, and rhubarb, must be cooked. Allow 2–3 tablespoons water to every 1 lb (500 g) fruit; slightly more water may be needed to cook pears. The advantage of precooking is that it affords the opportunity to add an extra layer of flavor. For example, add a slice of fresh ginger, a star anise, or a sprig of fresh thyme to the fruit. Remove before pureeing.

Some fruits have a tendency to discolor. Bananas and apples are prime examples; add lemon juice before cooking to preserve their color. The ascorbic acid (vitamin C) in the juice inhibits the oxidation process and it also imparts a pleasant tang to the mixture. Speed will keep discoloration to a minimum, so peel mangoes, apples, and pears as quickly as possible and do not prepare them until the last minute. Alternatively, squeeze the juice of a lemon into a bowl of water and add the peeled fruit. This will keep it from discoloring, but it will also dilute the flavor.

FEATHERING
For a spiderweb pattern, pipe a spiral of cream onto a fruit puree base. Draw a skewer across from the center to the edge, then from the edge to the center. Repeat around the plate. Hold the plate steady when serving or the design will be marred.

A trio of textures
The many different textures of fruit result in a variety of different textured purees.

PUREEING FRUIT

Purees can be fine or coarse; fine purees lend themselves to sauces or coulis, while more substantial purees can be eaten as desserts, or relish accompaniments to cooked meats. Purees can be processed using electrical machines, hand-cranked food mills, or by forcing through a sieve; they can be made with fresh, frozen, or cooked fruits. Be sure to adjust the processing method to match the desired consistency. For example, a fine-mesh nylon sieve will result in a very fine puree. Also, some fruits, such as kiwi fruit, which can be processed in a mill or blender, may need further sieving to remove all the seeds.

1 Fruits with a lot of seeds, such as raspberries, gooseberries, and passion fruit, need to be forced through a sieve to remove the seeds. If desired, add lemon juice to thin.

2 A food processor can be used for soft fruit, such as pineapple, to make a coarse puree, or for cooked fruit, such as apples, to make finer puree.

COOK'S CHOICE
FRUIT FOOL IN COOKIE CUPS
Serves 4–6

1 lb (500 g) fruit puree, such as gooseberry, rhubarb, or apple
Sugar to taste
1 cup (250 ml) heavy cream
4 tbsp unsalted butter, softened
1/3 cup (60 g) sugar
Vanilla extract
2 egg whites
1/2 cup (60 g) all-purpose flour, sifted
Raspberry puree
Light cream for feathering

To prepare the fool, force the puree through a fine-mesh nylon sieve. Add sugar to taste and set aside. In a bowl, whip the heavy cream until it just begins to stiffen. Fold the puree into the cream until well blended. Chill until serving. For the cookie cups, preheat the oven to 375°F (190°C). In a bowl, cream together the butter and sugar until light and fluffy. Add the vanilla, continue mixing and gradually add the egg whites. Gently mix in the flour. Line cookie sheets with baking parchment. Take a teaspoon of the mixture, and with circular movements, smooth it out with the back of the spoon. Place in the oven and bake until just golden around the edges, 5–7 minutes. With a spatula, lift off and transfer the soft cookies to upturned glasses or bowls for a cupped shape. Work in small batches as the cookies cool and harden very quickly. To serve, coat the bottoms of dessert plates with raspberry puree and feather with the cream (see page 202). Fill the cookie cups with the fool, place in the center of the puree and serve immediately.

Use fruit purees for flavor and color

Once prepared, fruit purees have many uses. They can serve as the base for ice creams or sorbets, or they can be folded into yogurt for a simple but flavorful dessert. Purees also make excellent dessert sauces. Rich chocolate desserts go well with a raspberry puree base. For an attractive presentation, simply place a spoonful on a dessert plate and tilt the plate, swirling the puree to coat. Place the cake or pastry in the center of the puree. Use a single puree or combine them for more flavor and color. Vanilla ice cream can be served on a plate that has been coated with strawberry puree to one side and kiwi puree to the other—garnish with a sprinkling of fresh blueberries. Passion fruit puree has a wonderful flavor and a bright red-pink color; pair it with apricot puree and serve with pound cake.

Freezing is the best way to preserve the flavor of fruit purees for future use. To freeze, pack the puree in plastic containers, allowing some room for expansion, and cover with airtight lids.

Figs

Prunes

Apricots

DRIED FRUIT

Dried fruits can be used for purees. Use them alone, in combination, or with fresh fruit; for example, pair dried apricots with cranberries or dried figs with pears. Spices, such as cinnamon and cloves, go well with the musky flavors of dried fruit. Puree as for fresh fruit, but soak overnight or simmer gently to soften before use.

FRUIT SYRUPS

Syrups are clear, sweetened juices, the strongest of which used to be known as cordials. Most familiar as a flavoring for drinks, fruit syrups are a versatile ingredient that can also be used as a sauce for desserts, cakes, and puddings. They are essential to fruit sundaes and ice cream sodas, and make a pleasant sugar syrup alternative for fruit salads. They can also be used to enhance mousses, ice creams, and candy. Use fruit syrups undiluted, or add water, soda, milk, or thinned yogurt to make drinks such as shakes or sodas. Provided they are stored properly in a cool, dark place, syrups can be kept for up to a year; they can also be frozen. Fruit syrups can be store-bought, but they are also easy to make at home, where the sugar content and flavor can be personalized.

Fruit juice can react with certain substances, so it is important to ensure that the pans and utensils used are not made of zinc, copper, or iron. Once the juice has been extracted, work quickly to keep discoloration to a minimum. Fruit syrups must be made with fruit that is at its peak; underripe fruit has an unsatisfactory flavor and is not juicy enough. However, overripe fruit will give the juice a musty flavor, and moldy fruit can adversely affect the keeping qualities of the finished syrup.

The best fruits to choose are flavorful, juicy berries, such as black currants, blackberries, raspberries and loganberries. Other choices include strawberries, gooseberries, elderberries, apples, and rosehips. Citrus fruits such as lemons, limes, and kumquats also make good syrups. For these, both the zest and the pulp can be used in combination for extra flavor.

FRUIT WATERS

Fruit waters are made by infusing fresh fruit with water and sugar for a refreshing drink. Pureed berry fruits work the best, although any strong-flavored fruit can be used. For 1 lb (500 g) fruit, add 2 1/2 cups (600 ml) water and 10 tbsp sugar. Strain before serving. For firmer fruit, dice, place in a saucepan with the water, and bring to a boil. Stir in the sugar, cool, and strain. Citrus waters are made by adding the zest to boiling water. Cool, stir in the juice, and sweeten to taste. Serve chilled, in tall glasses without ice, which would dilute the flavor. Garnish with fruit or fresh mint sprigs.

Homemade syrups can be flavored in many ways. Combine fruit, such as apple and blackberry, add herbs such as mint, sweet cicely, and lemon thyme, or infuse with spices such as cardamom, whole vanilla beans, and cinnamon sticks.

The pulp that remains after all the juice has been extracted can often be put to good use. Strawberry, gooseberry, apricot, and apple pulp can be pureed and sieved to make a fruit fool or mousse. The pulp from berries, especially raspberries and blackberries, is usually too full of seeds to yield much puree, but it can be used for making fruit wine. The pulp from rosehips, however, cannot be reused.

Some fruit syrups tend to lose their color faster than others, although a little vegetable coloring may be added to give a more attractive appearance. The addition of lemon juice also helps preserve color. Apple

MAKING SYRUP

Any fruit can be used to make syrups, although berries are the easiest. Use alone, combine with other fruit, or flavor with citrus peel, herbs, or spices.

1 Prepare a puree (see page 202), then strain through a sieve lined with cheesecloth. Gather the corners of the cloth together and twist tightly to force out the juice.

2 Add 1 lb (500 g) of sugar to every 1 1/4 cups (300 ml) of juice. Place over low heat and stir to dissolve the sugar, then boil. Less sugar may be used, but it will reduce keeping time.

3 Lower the heat. With a spoon, skim off any scum. Dip a pastry brush in water and clean the sides of the pan to prevent burning. Cool before using.

Fruit syrups

Colorful and deliciously sweet syrups can be used to enhance a wide range of recipes. They make attractive toppings poured over scoops of ice cream; mixed into shakes and sodas they add color and an extra taste dimension; stirred into fruit salads they increase the range of flavors.

Fruit salad with syrup

Strawberry milk shake

Black currant soda

COOK'S CHOICE
RASPBERRY SUNDAE

Serves 4

4 scoops vanilla ice cream

2 cups (250 g) fresh raspberries

2–3 tbsp raspberry syrup

4 scoops raspberry ripple ice cream

1/3 cup (80 ml) heavy cream, whipped

4 tbsp silvered almonds, toasted

Place one scoop of vanilla ice cream in the base of four sundae dishes. Add some raspberries and a little raspberry syrup. Next, add the raspberry ripple ice cream and the remaining fruit. Pour on the remaining syrup and top with whipped cream. Decorate with toasted almonds.

FLAVORING TIPS
Use syrups for flavorful sundae, soda, and shake combinations:

Strawberry ice cream with orange syrup and a dash of Grand Marnier

Fresh peaches, vanilla ice cream, and raspberry syrup

Toffee ice cream, fresh banana slices, pineapple syrup, and whipped cream

---

juice, on the other hand, tends to darken with processing, and this can be a problem for the home cook. Freezing fruit syrup helps to counteract the problem of fading colors. Instead of using bottles, pour the syrup into small plastic containers, leaving room at the top for expansion, then freeze. Ice-cube trays are also effective. Each cube will be sufficient to make one 1-cup (250 ml) drink. Freezing also solves the problems of sterilization for bottling, which is a lengthy and complicated process; unless the bottles are specially made, they tend to break in the preserving pans.

Despite the processing, most fruit syrups are a good source of vitamin C. This is particularly true of rosehip and black currant syrups, which are delicious when mixed with orange or grapefruit juice for extra nutrition at the start of the day.

Fruit syrups are concentrated, so a little goes a long way. A couple of spoonfuls will flavor a sauce, and the same amount will make a refreshing drink diluted with water, white wine, thinned yogurt, or soda. Fruit syrups are the ideal edible gift because they can be made in large quantities. Use colored bottles for attractive presentation and tie with pretty ribbons to decorate.

FRUIT JELLIES

Fruit jellies are a traditional British confection, not unlike American gumdrops. To prepare, heat together 1³/4 cups (450 ml) fruit juice, 7 tbsp sugar, and 4 tbsp liquid glucose, stirring until the sugar dissolves. Add 1 oz (30 g) powdered gelatin and stir to dissolve. Pour into a moistened pan, about 1/4 in (6 mm) deep. Leave to set in a cool place. To cut, use a sharp knife; dip the blade in hot water to make slicing easier.

Alternatively, use cutters for festive shapes. Use single juices or combine a light- and a dark-colored juice for layered jellies. Let the bottom layer set slightly before adding the top layer. Serve plain, or roll in superfine sugar for a crunchy coating.

EDIBLE
LEAVES
& FLOWERS

FLOWERS

One of the most visually appealing ingredients available to the cook is undoubtedly a sprinkling of fresh edible flowers. The culinary use of flowers dates back thousands of years; the first recorded mention was 140 years before the Christian era. In the Far and Middle East, rose and orange blossoms have always been used; in the Mediterranean region, stuffed zucchini flowers have been deep-fried or braised as an appetizer for years. Some flowers, such as lavender, rose, nasturtium, jasmine, and orange blossom, can lend their delicate flavor to sorbets, custards, jams and jellies, liqueurs, wines, and teas. Other blossoms—cornflowers, geraniums, chrysanthemums, and marigolds, for example—are rather dull in flavor but add a splash of color, which has the effect of stimulating the palate.

When choosing flowers to use with or on foods, there are several important guidelines that should be followed. Firstly, be sure to use only edible blossoms, such as the flowers shown here. Ensure that the flowers selected have been grown without the help of pesticides or other chemical sprays. Flowers from the florist are quite often treated, so those from a reliable source, such as an untreated home garden, are best. Even if the flowers are being used as a decoration and not as an ingredient, any flower that comes into contact with food should be suitable for human consumption. If in doubt, check with a local horticultural society or poison control center. All of the flowers shown are nontoxic and safe for culinary use.

If gathering flowers from the garden, they should be picked early in the day and in dry weather. Rinse quickly under gently running cool water. Do not gather more than one day in advance as the blossoms wilt quickly. Before using in any preparation, remove the pistils, stamens, and the white part at the base of the petals. This is called the "heel" and, where visible, it should be cut off because it will impart a bitter flavor to the finished dish.

Many flowers, such as lavender, hibiscus, heather, and rosebuds, can be dried for use out of season. One of the best uses for dried flowers is for flavoring sugars. Grind the dry petals, then mix 1 part petals to 4 parts sugar. Let the mixture sit for at least 1 month to allow the flavor to mellow before using.

Fresh flowers are preferable for flavoring butter. Wrap unsalted butter in cheesecloth, place in a bowl of flower petals, and leave overnight in a cool place to infuse the butter. To best enjoy the delicate flavor, spread on thin slices of bread and serve with flower jellies and jams.

Carnation

Pansies *lend a touch of vibrant color to salad leaves*

Violet

Borage *can be used to garnish drinks and soups*

Chrysanthemum

Variegated geranium

Cornflowers

Geranium

Baby's breath

Lavender

Marigolds *can be used in
savory dishes; chop finely,
and with one or two leaves,
add to omelets, cream
cheese, soufflés, and
vegetable terrines*

Nasturtiums
*can be shredded
and added to
risotto or mixed
with olive oil to
top hot pasta*

**Daylily
(Hemerocallis)** *can
be floated in a soup
tureen or punch bowl;
some lilies are poisonous
so check with
a reference
source before
using*

Honeysuckle *is
one of the more
fragrant flowers
that can be used
to good effect to
flavor cakes,
sorbets, and soft
drinks*

Gladiola *can be used
to top cakes and
gâteaux and may be
served with ice creams*

Rose *has many
uses with food
both as a
garnish in fresh
and crystallized
form and as an
ingredient*

Wild roses

Freesia *is highly
scented and makes a
wonderful flavoring
for sorbets if infused
in a sugar syrup*

Sweet pea *makes a
very attractive garnish
for vegetable dishes*

FLOWERS IN THE KITCHEN

Edible blossoms are an unusual and colorful garnish that can be used to great effect in dishes both sweet and savory. They impart a delicate flavor to sorbets, jams, and salads, for example. Zucchini flowers are even robust enough to be lightly fried, while dried flowers are a common ingredient in many spice mixtures.

A scattering of colorful petals and flowers is most striking when set against a background of lightly dressed salad greens. Be sure to use lettuces that match the flowers in texture and complement them in flavor. Delicate lettuces and salad herbs, such as lamb's lettuce and chervil, are best. Use a dressing that is light in vinegar or lemon juice. A highly acidic dressing will both discolor the petals and overwhelm their subtle flavor. Toss the leaves beforehand and arrange on individual plates; add the flowers just before serving for the most appealing and colorful appearance. Herb flowers, such as borage and chive, are ideal for salads, as are peppery nasturtium blossoms. Cornflowers, violets, and marigolds are also useful for their color. In sweet dishes, roses are the obvious choice, and they marry well with many fruits, especially cherries.

A selection of brightly colored edible flowers can turn an ordinary salad into something eye-catching

Flowers in salads
Never add flowers to a salad before tossing, because the dressing will spoil the color and fresh appearance of the delicate flower petals.

Ras-el-hanout

COOK'S CHOICE
STUFFED ZUCCHINI FLOWERS

Serves 4

12–14 zucchini flowers
1 cup (250 g) ricotta cheese
4 tbsp freshly grated Parmesan cheese
1 small bunch fresh basil, chopped
Freshly grated nutmeg
1 egg, beaten
Salt
3/4 cup (90 g) all-purpose flour, sifted
Vegetable oil for frying

Rinse the flowers and pat dry. In a bowl, combine the cheeses, basil, nutmeg, and egg, and season to taste. Fill each flower with the mixture and close, twisting the tip to seal. In a bowl, whisk the flour with 1 cup (250 ml) water added gradually; it should resemble heavy cream. Heat the oil in a skillet. Dip each flower into the batter and fry until golden, about 2–3 minutes on each side. Drain on paper towels, sprinkle with salt, and serve hot.

RAS-EL-HANOUT
Ras-el-hanout is a North African spice mixture that translates literally as "top of the shop." It is used to flavor rice, couscous, and tajines, the slowly cooked stews common to Morocco and Tunisia. There is no one specific recipe; North African grocers often mix their own, so the combinations can vary. A typical blend could include peppercorns, cardamom, mace, galangal, nutmeg, allspice, cinnamon, ash berries, cloves, ginger, turmeric, nigella, lavender, rosebuds, orrisroot, cassia, and fennel seeds.

Rose petal ice cream is traditional in concept but very contemporary in terms of today's cuisine

COOK'S CHOICE
ROSE PETAL ICE CREAM

Serves 6

2 cups (500 ml) milk

Petals from 1 large rose, or to taste, rinsed

8 egg yolks

10 tbsp sugar

1 cup (250 ml) heavy cream, whipped

Red food coloring (optional)

Fresh or crystallized rose petals for garnish

Place the milk in a saucepan and bring to a boil. Add the rose petals, cover, and leave to infuse for 15 minutes. In a large heatproof bowl, beat together the egg yolks and the sugar until thick. Strain the rose petals out of the milk and then return the milk to boiling point. Pour a little of the hot milk onto the yolk mixture and whisk to blend, then pour it all into the saucepan of milk, lower the heat, and stir constantly with a wooden spoon until thick. Draw your finger across the back of the wooden spoon; if it leaves a clear mark, the mixture is cooked. Cool, then fold in the cream and food coloring, if using. Churn in an ice cream machine according to manufacturer's instructions. Garnish with rose petals and serve immediately.

Candied violets *can be made at home or bought readymade; they are the perfect decoration for many desserts*

Fresh rose petals are the ideal garnish for this refreshing dessert, but crystallized petals can be used to delicious effect, too

CRYSTALLIZING ROSE PETALS

The ideal dessert decoration, crystallized rose petals can be bought or made at home. Separate the petals and trim away any white parts. Be sure to work in a dry environment, because they are very sensitive to humidity. Many other edible flowers can be crystallized, including violets and borage.

1 Dissolve 2 oz (60 g) gum arabic (or edible gum) in 1¼ cups (300 ml) warmed rosewater. Allow to cool. (Gum arabic is found in specialty stores.)

2 With tweezers, dip each petal into the rosewater mixture and coat lightly and evenly. Shake the petal gently to remove excess liquid.

3 Dip the coated petals into sugar and place on waxed paper to dry. Store in an airtight container lined with waxed paper.

FLORAL WATERS AND CORDIALS

The use of floral waters in cooking dates from the Middle Ages. Orange blossom and rose were the most commonly used extracts, which, along with elderflower, gained popularity in seventeenth-century England. Nowadays floral waters are used primarily in the cuisines of India, the Middle East, and Eastern Europe, where they flavor everything from meat stews, to pastries, to after-dinner coffees. Floral waters are available in specialty stores, but be sure to use only floral waters for cooking, since some are destined for cosmetic use only.

ROSE WATER

In Turkey, rose water flavored candies, such as Turkish delight, are traditionally served with coffee

A diluted form of attar of roses (pure rose oil), rose water is an ancient flavoring. Indeed, before the birth of Christ, Persia was exporting rose water as far afield as China. Once a favorite flavoring in Elizabethan England, rose water still reigns supreme in the highly perfumed sweet dishes of India and the Middle East. In India, a festive creamed rice dish, known as *kheer,* is flavored with cardamom and rose water and decorated with silver leaf. In Turkey, rose water scents the sweetmeats served with the strong coffee: A heavy sugar syrup, fragrant with rose water, is thickened with cornstarch and mastic to make *loukoum,* better known as *Turkish delight.* It may be used to soak the rich, sweet pastry known as *baklava.* Delicate rose-scented sorbets, ice creams, mousses, and candies make an unusual conclusion to a meal.

Try rose water sprinkled over fresh strawberries or used to perfume sweetened whipped cream

Rose water

Orange-flower water

ORANGE-FLOWER WATER

A highly scented blancmange can be made with orange-flower water

Distilled from orange blossoms, orange-flower water is used to greatest effect to enhance oranges or to add a delicate perfume of flowers to citrus fruit salads, sorbets, and candies. Like rose water, it is a powerful flavoring and should be used with restraint. As a culinary ingredient, it was most popular in Medieval times; orange-scented blancmange, still appreciated today, dates from this period. Today, it enjoys great popularity in the Middle East, where a mixture of orange-flower water and sugar is often given to children before bedtime. When this drink is prepared with boiling water, the infusion is called white coffee, and it makes a relaxing and digestive drink for all ages. To prepare, allow 1 teaspoon orange-flower water per small cup and add boiling water to fill. Sweeten with sugar or, better still, with orange-blossom honey. Although it is most commonly used to perfume puddings and pastries, a spoonful will also enhance salad dressings and stews.

To prepare simple cordials, sweeten store-bought floral waters and blend with water, or use fresh or dried flowers to make a syrup (see below) and create more original beverages. Choose highly scented edible blossoms, because these will make for the most flavorful syrups. Elderflowers, roses, violets, clove-scented pinks, primroses, lilacs, and orange blossoms are all intensely perfumed and make delicious syrups.

In hot weather, cordials are more refreshing when diluted with chilled soda water or sparkling fruit juice, or they can be combined with sparkling or still wine for an unusual aperitif. In cold weather, teas or tisanes (see page 274) can be mixed with floral syrups for a warm and soothing drink, or combine syrups with hot mulled cider or wine, and wintery spices such as cloves and cinnamon sticks.

Floral syrups can also be used to flavor candies, custards, cakes, fresh fruit salads, ice creams, and sorbets. A tablespoon or two of a floral syrup can also add a subtle difference to a salad dressing, barbecue sauce, marinade, or dipping sauce.

COOK'S CHOICE
RATAFIA OF CARNATIONS

Makes 4^1/$_2$ cups (1 liter)

8 oz (250 g) scented carnation petals
5 tbsp superfine sugar
1 clove
1 very small cinnamon stick
4^1/$_2$ cups (1 liter) vodka or white eau-de-vie

Remove all flower heels, if any. Combine all the ingredients in a large bottle or glass jar. Seal and leave to infuse in a cool, dark place for at least 1 month, stirring occasionally. When the petals lose their color, strain and rebottle the ratafia.

COOK'S CHOICE
CHERRY AND ROSE PETAL BRANDY

Makes 4^1/$_2$ cups (1 liter)

1^1/$_2$ lb (750 g) sour cherries
8 oz (250 g) cherry leaves
2^1/$_2$ cups (500 g) superfine sugar
6 scented roses, petals only
2 oz (60 g) dried jasmine flowers
4^1/$_2$ cups (1 liter) brandy

Pit the cherries and crack the pits. In a jar, combine the cherries, pits, leaves, and sugar. Add the rose petals, jasmine flowers, and brandy and stir. Seal. Infuse in a cool, dark place for at least 1 month. Strain into bottles and store in a dark place.

Any edible blossom can be infused in a sugar syrup for use in unusual and refreshing drinks

Floral cordials

COOK'S CHOICE
SUMMER PUNCH

Makes about 4^1/$_2$ cups (1 liter)

1 orange, sliced
1 apple, sliced
1 tbsp orange-flower water
1 tsp vanilla extract
4^1/$_2$ cups (1 liter) sparkling water or tonic water
^{1}/$_2$ cup (125 ml) floral syrup, such as elderflower
Lemon and orange slices for garnish

In a large pitcher, combine the orange, apple, orange-flower water, and vanilla. Pour over the sparkling water or tonic water, cover, and leave to infuse for at least 2 hours. Alternatively, refrigerate for slightly longer. Stir in the elderflower syrup. Serve over ice cubes, and garnish with the lemon and orange slices.

MAKING FLORAL SYRUP
For a basic syrup, place about 1 lb (500 g) flower petals (white heels removed) in a saucepan and add 2^1/$_2$ cups (600 ml) of water, or more if necessary to cover. Bring to a boil, cover, and infuse for 30 minutes. Strain and return to the pan with 1^3/$_4$ cups (350 g) sugar, or to taste. Simmer for 10 minutes. Infuse the petals alone or create floral, fruit, herb, and spice combinations: violets sweetened with honey, hawthorn or may blossoms with borage flowers, elderflowers and orange blossoms with dried apple.

WRAPPINGS

An often under-exploited technique, wrapping with leaves offers a means of presenting food in an attractive, flavorful and easy-to-manage manner. *Dolmades*, the Greek dish of grape leaves stuffed with rice, is the classic example. Fragile ingredients, such as fish, which are easily broken during cooking or serving, can be wrapped in lettuce, spinach, or grape leaves for reinforcement. This not only enhances the flavor, but it makes them easier to get from kitchen to table and offers a stunning presentation. Large, tough leaves, such as corn husks or lotus, are ideal wrappers, but they are inedible and must be discarded. Some edible leaves should be blanched to remove bitterness or to render them supple enough for wrapping. Do not limit the use of leaves to ingredients that must be held together: Experiment with any filling that could benefit from a delicate infusion of leafy flavor.

Lettuce Leaves The long, outer leaves of romaine lettuce make an excellent wrapping for steamed fish, served whole or in fillets. The more tender, pliable tips are well suited to the traditional Thai manner of serving egg rolls: A raw lettuce leaf is lined with fresh mint, the egg roll is placed on top, and the package is rolled up and dipped into a sweet-and-sour sauce.

Spinach Leaves With their assertive flavor and deep green color, these are ideal leaves for wrapping. For an attractive presentation, line small buttered ramekins with blanched spinach leaves and fill with a vegetable mousse. Bake in a water bath and turn out before serving.

Cabbage Leaves Particularly suitable for slow cooking, stuffed cabbage leaves is a classic dish in many countries. The leaves can be filled with meat or rice, or both, and served with a tomato-based sauce. For easier rolling, it is best to remove the tough central core before stuffing.

Grape Leaves A familiar and popular wrapping, these have a pleasant lemony tang and are suitable for many ingredients, such as fish or quail, and many cooking methods. Blanching before stuffing is imperative: Fresh leaves need their slight bitterness subdued, and leaves packed in brine are very salty. Always adjust the seasoning accordingly when using preserved grape leaves.

Lettuce leaves

Grape leaves

White cabbage leaves

Spinach leaves

PAAN LEAVES
Throughout India, it is customary to offer a paan leaf bundle at the end of the meal as a breath freshner and an aid to digestion. The paan leaf is filled with a mixture of bitter, sweet, and sour flavors, such as: betel nut, coconut, cardamom, aniseed, sugar balls, and melon seeds. The leaf is secured with a clove.

MAKING STUFFED GRAPE LEAVES

Grape leaves stuffed with a savory mixture—such as the cooked rice, sultana, onion, pine nut, and parsley mixture shown here—are a classic. They can be served cold with thick Greek yogurt as an appetizer, or warm with tomato sauce as a main course. The leaves should always be blanched before filling. Rice is essential, but try other ingredients: crushed tomatoes, chopped spring onions, mint, cumin, and minced lamb.

1 Place a grape leaf, vein side up, on the work surface. Place a spoonful of filling at the base of the leaf, just above the stem.

2 Bring the leaf tips up alongside the filling, making the shape slightly more rectangular. Roll securely to make a tiny bundle.

3 Serve cold as an appetizer or warm as a main dish. If filled with raw stuffing, simmer in a covered pan until tender, about 2 hours.

Lotus Leaves These are usually available dried and are most familiar as a wrapping for steamed Chinese dumplings, or dim-sum. Only fresh young leaves can be eaten raw.
Corn Husks Frequently used in Central and South America, these are employed for the sweet, nutty flavor they impart to food, but they are not edible.
Banana Leaves These enormous leaves can be up to 10 ft (3 meters) long and 2 ft (60 cm) wide. They have a very delicate flavor, which is quickly absorbed by the ingredients they enclose. Banana leaves are a common feature of Asian and West Indian cuisines.

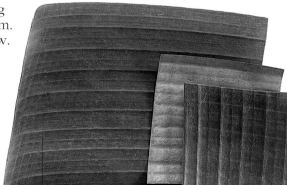

Large enough to wrap most foods, banana leaves impart a delicate flavor to ingredients but are inedible

Banana leaves *are used most commonly in dishes of Asian or West Indian origin, where they protect barbecued, baked, or steamed fish and poultry*

WRAPPING WITH CORN HUSKS

Parboil two corn husks. Lay one husk on top of the other to form a cross. Place stuffing in the center and, starting with the bottom husk, fold over to form a square. Secure with long, thin strips of corn husk. Remove husks before serving.

Dried corn husks

Dried lotus leaves

LETTUCES AND CHICORIES

In the past, spring heralded the arrival of leafy vegetables; nowadays, many varieties are available all year-round. Edible leaves come in many forms and flavors: there are a great number of commercially grown types, including lettuces and chicories (also known as endives), and some wild varieties such as nettle and dandelion. Rich in vitamins A and C, leaves are best used immediately after gathering because both the flavor and nutritional value are quickly lost. When choosing, look for leaves that are glossy and firm, and avoid those that are limp, discolored, or blemished. For storage, clean and dry thoroughly and keep in a cool, well-ventilated place. Before storing, remove all plastic wrapping because this tends to foster humidity and encourage rot. Whether destined for the salad or soup bowl, having a year-round supply of lettuces and chicories is a great advantage for any cook.

Lettuces and chicories provide a wide range of flavors, colors, and textures. Their traditional place is in the salad bowl, but many types can also be cooked successfully. The more robust chicories are delicious when braised and served alongside roast meats or poultry. Or, try a leafy, lettuce chiffonade garnish (see page 47), which offers a more substantial alternative to the traditional chopped parsley or chives.

Loose-leaf Lettuce Also known as salad-bowl lettuce, this type is so named because the leaves are easily separated. This makes them a practical plant for the vegetable patch. You need only pick the required number of leaves while the lettuce remains firmly planted, and this guarantees a lasting supply of garden-fresh lettuce leaves for the salad bowl.

These lettuces tend to have a more delicate flavor and texture, so for salads that are well balanced, combine loose lettuces with more robust leaves. Among the increasing number of varieties are *lollo biondo*, a very bright green lettuce with a distinctive frilly edge, and *lollo rosso*, which is tinged with red. *Red oak leaf lettuce*, also called *feuille de chêne*, has rich red leaves, a fine flavor, and a pleasing texture, and mixes well with other salad leaves.

Round Lettuce *Butterhead, Bibb,* and *Batavia* are good examples of this type, which is characterized by a compact head, a solid core, and soft, tender leaves. The darker outer leaves provide a strong flavor; the paler inner leaves are more delicate. Round lettuces are a universal favorite for the salad bowl.

Long Lettuce *Romaine*, also called *Cos*, is the classic long lettuce. It is robust, with a mild, almost nutty flavor. In salads, these dark green, flavorful leaves stand up well to powerful ingredients such as anchovies or Parmesan, making Cos the best lettuce to

Romaine *combines a crisp texture with a mild taste*

Lollo rosso

Red oak leaf lettuce

Crisphead lettuce, *also called iceberg and Webb's Wonder, has a tightly packed firm head and a crunchy texture, if little taste*

216

Chicories *are a group of lettuces that provide a pleasant bitterness when mixed with milder leaves; they are also excellent when cooked in vegetable dishes*

Chicory *may be regarded as the prettiest member of its family with its lacy head of white, yellow, and green leaves*

Lollo biondo *is one of the newer varieties of lettuce and it has dense, ruffled leaves that form a compact bunch without a heart*

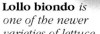

Radicchio

Batavia

Belgian endive *is one of the most versatile of all the chicories as it is well suited to both salads and braising*

use in Caesar salad. Slightly smaller varieties, such as *Little Gem*, have the added advantage of a storage period which is longer than most lettuces.

Chicories Many vegetables known as endives are members of the chicory family; consequently, much confusion arises. With their slighty bitter taste and sturdy texture, most of the chicories lend themselves well to both cooking and salads. The compact, spear-shaped shoots of *Belgian endive*, called *chicory* in the U.K., owe their pallor to cultivation: They are actually grown in sandy soil in the dark, much like mushrooms. Make sure that leaf tips are tinged with yellow; if turning green they are likely to be old. The leaves can be separated and chopped coarsely for use in salads, or left whole for baking or braising. To reduce bitterness when cooking, it is best to remove the central core. *Chicory,* also known as *curly endive,* or *frisée,* fans out to display its sprawling, lacy leaves and it is a treat when combined with hot bacon, croutons, and a poached egg. *Escarole* is a chicory that looks like a cross between lettuce and chicory. The flavor is quite bitter; for salads it should be torn into small pieces. It is delicious when braised in meat stock. *Radicchio,* a red-leaf variety of chicory, is favored by the Italians. It has a glorious color, which makes it a valuable contribution to any monotone green salad. The cup-shaped leaves offer a decorative container for hot or cold salads, and the heads can be sliced in halves or quarters and barbecued.

LEAVES AND SALAD HERBS

Many of the leafy plants that grow wild in the Mediterranean region, such as mâche and arugula, have been used in cooking since Roman times. These are now enjoying renewed popularity and are cultivated for year-round availability. Nasturtium leaves, with their distinctive peppery flavor, are also gaining favor and they make a delicious addition to any green salad. Nettles and dandelion are among the most flavorful and easily obtained, provided that an untended field is accessible. Always make sure that leaves gathered in the wild have not been chemically treated with products unfit for human consumption. Also, avoid gathering plants growing close to the roadside, where they are exposed to dirt and gas fumes. All of these leaves should be picked in the spring, while they are at their most tender and before the flowering varieties have begun to bloom.

Arugula (Rocket) Gathered by the ancient Romans, this was appreciated for its sharp peppery flavor. It is related to mustard and has fiddle-shaped leaves that look similar to radish tops. Arugula is one of the ingredients of mesclun, the traditional Niçoise mixture of tiny salad leaves. Quickly sautéed in olive oil, arugula can also be tossed with pasta and served hot.

Mâche (Corn Salad) There are several varieties of this small leaf that traditionally grew wild. The most common variety has long, narrow leaves, while the marshland type has small, compact, rounded leaves. Ideal for salads, mâche is delicious when tossed with a walnut oil dressing and served with diced beets and a sprinkling of shelled walnuts. It also marries well with corn; canned will do, but fresh baby corn, lightly blanched, is best.

Dandelions A nuisance to the gardener, dandelion leaves are the cook's delight. The most tender leaves appear in the spring, and the jagged, slightly bitter leaves make a

Leaves are long and spear shaped with a spicy bitterness

The pointed, spinachlike leaves contain oxalic acid, which gives sorrel its sour bite

Mâche

Watercress

Arugula *is used to great effect in Italian cuisine, where it is added to salads, tossed with pasta, or stirred into risotto*

Sorrel

delicious salad when young. Older leaves should be blanched or wilted with a hot dressing to tenderize them before serving (see right). If gathered from a garden or field, be sure that the dandelions have not been treated with pesticides or other chemicals unfit for human consumption.

Nettle Only the young, tender tips are suitable for cooking; the stalks and lower leaves are not edible. Puree for soup or a vegetable accompaniment. Finely chopped nettles can also be added to a soft cheese, such as goat cheese or ricotta, and used as a filling for ravioli.

Sorrel The most acidic of all the edible leaves, this is very high in vitamin C, which accounts for its tart flavor. One or two torn leaves, tossed into a mixed salad, is all that is required to add a refreshing note. Likewise, only a small amount is required to impart sorrel's characteristic piquant flavor to a cooked dish. As with spinach, its volume diminishes significantly when cooked, so raw quantities should be carefully calculated. Allow about 2 lb (1 kg) raw sorrel for each 1 lb (500 g) cooked.

Purslane Often considered to be no more than a weed, this plant has crisp, succulent leaves that are actually quite delicious. It can be cooked like spinach and served with cream or butter or added raw to salads.

Nasturtium The leaves of this plant can be used in a number of ways. With their slightly peppery flavor, whole leaves are a welcome addition to green salads. Chopped or shredded, the leaves can be blended into soft cheese for a sandwich filling, or added to scrambled eggs and omelets.

Watercress To thrive, the shoots of this plant must grow in the cleanest of water; hence, most of the watercress available in stores is now cultivated. Delicious in a cream-based soup, watercress can also be chopped and added to butter and used to flavor meat or fish. Watercress is fragile and does not keep well; use within one day of purchase for maximum flavor.

Garden Cress Familiar as a garnish, this can also be combined with egg salad as a sandwich filling. Cress is easily grown at home (see page 62) or it can be bought growing in small containers.

COOK'S CHOICE
NETTLE SOUP

Serves 4

1 lb (500 g) young nettle shoots, washed
4 shallots, finely chopped
2 tbsp unsalted butter
1 large potato, peeled and diced
Salt
Freshly ground black pepper
Heavy cream and croutons for garnish

Separate one-third of the nettle leaves and chop finely. In a stockpot, combine the shallots and butter and cook over low heat until soft, about 5 minutes. Stir in the whole nettle leaves and cook for 1 minute. Add the potato and 4½ cups (1 liter) of cold water and season to taste. Cover and simmer until the potato is cooked, about 20 minutes. Transfer to a food processor or blender and puree, in two batches if necessary, until smooth. Taste for seasoning. Stir in the chopped nettles and the cream, sprinkle on the croutons, and serve immediately.

WILTING LEAVES
The robust leaves of dandelions can be tenderized by wilting with a hot dressing. Wash the leaves and place in a bowl. In a skillet, cook diced slab bacon in olive oil until brown, then sprinkle over the leaves. Deglaze the pan with wine vinegar (see page 249), pour over the leaves, season, and toss.

Nasturtium

Purslane

Garden cress

Nettle

Dandelion

SEAWEED

In the West, plants that grow in or around the sea have been acclaimed for their medicinal properties, to the detriment of their culinary possibilities. Ignored by the Ancient Greeks and Romans, Westerners have subsequently had little enthusiasm for the number of edible sea vegetables that are native to their shores. But seaweed—rich in minerals, vitamins, and protein—has long been a staple in the diets of most Asian populations. Seaweed has been harvested off the shores of Japan since the 1600s, and it is here that its many uses are best appreciated. Most seaweed is available dried. It is easily reconstituted by soaking first in water, then boiling until softened. With a pleasantly subtle flavor and great visual appeal, seaweed can be adapted to myriad culinary preparations: from a seasoning for soups and poaching broths, to an ingredient in salads and stir-fries, to a gelling agent in desserts.

Konbu Known also as *giant sea kelp*, this can be used raw, freshly cooked, or dried. More than any other sea vegetable, it takes pride of place in the cuisine of Japan, although it features in many Korean dishes as well. It is the foundation for the numerous broths and stocks (*dashi*) that flavor so many Japanese dishes. When added to the cooking water of tough or hard ingredients, such as legumes, konbu strips impart not only flavor: they help to soften the ingredient, making it more digestible. Strips can also be braided and deep-fried to make attractive basket-shaped containers. *Tororo konbu* is bleached, finely shaved strands, which become sticky when cooked. It can be used either in soups or as wrappers for bundles of rice. Konbu rolls are a traditional Japanese dish in which dried fish, usually herring, is rolled in sheets of konbu and then simmered in a flavorful broth.

Nori Along with kelp, this is the most widely consumed of all the seaweeds. In English, this is called laver. Most often sold in sheets, its principal use is as a wrapper for sushi (see page 221). To lightly crisp nori, releasing its delicate sweet flavor, pass the sheets over a flame, or place in a hot oven for a few minutes before crumbling over a salad or into a soup.

Wakame The seaweed that most resembles land vegetables, this has a mild flavor and lovely green color; it is the ideal type for the first-time seaweed taster to try. The texture after reconstituting is very tender, making it popular in salads, sprinkled over rice dishes, or added to pickles.

Hijiki This type requires little preparation as it is usually precooked before drying. Looking very similar to tea leaves, this seaweed's bulk is increased immensely when soaked, so only very little is needed. Hijiki is very good sautéed or dipped in batter and deep-fried for tempura.

Agar-Agar Known also as *kanten* in Japan, this is most widely used as a gelling agent. Both varieties can be enjoyed on their own, although the white type makes a delicious salad: soak the seaweed for a few minutes until it softens, then toss with cucumber strips, toasted almonds, and a dressing of sesame oil and soy sauce.

Nidashi konbu

Konbu

Tororo konbu

Konbu rolls

FRESH SEAWEEDS

Many of the seaweeds found around the coasts of Europe can be used fresh, either cooked or raw. Laver is a seaweed that has been a traditional food in the British Isles. It is reduced to a spinachlike puree, then mixed with oatmeal and called laver bread. It makes a delicious accompaniment to thick slices of pan-fried bacon or poached fish. Dulse and sea lettuce can be shredded for garnishes or salads. Not strictly a seaweed, samphire is a vegetable that grows near ocean shores. To best savor it, steam, toss with melted butter or vinaigrette, and serve as an accompaniment to seafood.

Laver bread

Samphire

Tissue thin, this Japanese seaweed is popular as an ingredient, flavoring, and wrapping

Wakame

Nori

Hijiki

Red agar-agar

White agar-agar

COOK'S CHOICE
WELSH LAVER BREAD AND POACHED SKATE

Serves 4

Juice of ¹/₂ lemon or to taste
³/₄ cup (60 g) rolled oats
1 lb (500 g) laver, fresh or frozen
2 tbsp cider vinegar
4 small skate wings
4 tbsp oil
Lemon slices and parsley sprigs for garnish

In a bowl, mix together the lemon juice, oats, and laver. Mold into small patties, about 1¹/₄ in (3 cm) in diameter, and spinkle lightly with a little more oatmeal. Place enough water to cover the skate wings in a shallow pan and bring to the boil. Add the vinegar and the skate, and poach for 8–10 minutes. Meanwhile, gently heat the oil in a frying pan and add the laver bread patties. Fry 2 minutes on each side. Serve with the skate and garnish with lemon and parsley.

An Asian staple
Seaweed is widely used in the cuisines of Japan, Korea, and parts of China.

PREPARING SUSHI

Nori sheets and rice in sweetened vinegar are mandatory for sushi; beyond that, the choice of fillings is up to the cook: mushrooms, spinach, pickled gingerroot, and dried squash shavings are just some examples.

1 *Place a lightly toasted nori sheet on a bamboo mat. Spread with vinegared rice, leaving one edge of the nori exposed. Place the filling on top of the rice.*

2 *Use the mat to help roll the nori around the rice. Squeeze the mat gently to make it firmer. Leave the roll to rest for 5 minutes.*

3 *Unroll and remove the bamboo mat. Using a sharp knife, slice the sushi rolls into 1 in (2.5 cm) rounds. Serve with soy sauce and wasabi paste (see page 166).*

OILS, VINEGARS, & DAIRY PRODUCTS

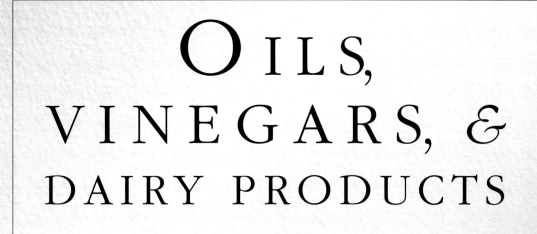

OLIVE OIL

Olive oil is one of the oldest culinary oils. In ancient Athens, the olive was a symbol of the city's prosperity, and its oil was used both in cooking and as fuel for oil-burning lamps. The Romans also spread olive cultivation throughout their empire, from Africa to the Iberian peninsula. There was even an ancient Roman philosophy of longevity that linked two vital products of their daily life: wine and olive oil. Nowadays, olive oils are classified by category—from pure to extra-virgin—and these categories are determined by levels of acidity. This is important information because a high level of acidity detracts from the flavor of oil. It is this flavor that makes olive oil such a valuable ingredient, but with so many different categories and classifications, it can be difficult to ascertain the quality within from the label without. All olive oil labels should indicate the percentage of acidity, grade of oil, volume, and country of origin. If the label also shows the name of the producer and the farm or village where it was made, this is a sign that it has been produced with care, on a small scale, and the quality should be high.

PRODUCTION

The traditional method for making olive oil is to crush the olives between two opposing stone wheels until the fruit is reduced to a pulp. This pulp is then spread on mats that are stacked one upon the other and pressed down with weights. There are other more modern production methods, but this is the method used for oils labeled "cold pressed." Because the pressure from the weights is relatively low, heat does not build up in the pulp; hence, the "cold" pressing. Heat allows more oil to be extracted but also results in an inferior flavor, so cold-pressed oils are superior in quality.

Olive oil is graded on a scale that rates its level of acidity. Other factors, such as color, flavor, and aroma, are also considered, but the quality is closely linked to the percentage of acidity. The higher the level, the less aromatic and refined the oil will be. Extra-virgin olive oil, with only 1 percent maximum acidity, is the finest. It is followed by fine virgin olive oil, with a maximum acidity of 1.5 percent, and virgin olive oil, which can have as much as 3 percent. Pure olive oil also has a maximum acidity level of 3 percent, but it is made from a blend of different grades of oil.

In the end, for olive oils, quality is synonymous with flavor, and the best way to wade through the many available oils is to let your own palate be the judge.

TYPES OF OLIVE OIL

Olive oil is produced in most of the countries near the Mediterranean; only the most prominent producers are listed here.
Italian Olive Oil The oils from Tuscany and Umbria are held to be the finest. Their renown is the fruit of an extensive marketing

Cloudy oil
Air, heat, and light will cause olive oil to turn rancid, so it should be stored in a cool place in an airtight container. When chilled, or in cold weather, the oil may turn cloudy and even solidify. Such oil will clear again as it warms, so cloudiness should not be taken as an indication that the oil is past its prime.

The taste of the finest oils is light and fruity

The color of olive oil ranges from pale golden yellow to a dark, dense green

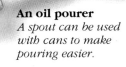

An oil pourer
A spout can be used with cans to make pouring easier.

operation, which may partially account for their reputation. There is, however, a local consortium and rigorous quality controls to maintain good production methods.

Spanish Olive Oil After Italy, Spain is the world's largest olive oil producer, although there are years when climatic conditions are more favorable to Spain and production there will surpass that in Italy. The Spanish olive oil industry is governed by an internal body that has established a quality control called "label of origin." Borjas Blancas, in the northeastern region of Lérida, is considered to produce some of the finest of the Spanish label of origin oils.

Greek Olive Oil In Greece, annual olive oil consumption is estimated to be around 24 quarts (23 liters) per person, which puts them at the head of worldwide per capita consumption. However, Greece is only the third largest producer. The quality tends to vary because controls are less strict than in other oil-producing countries.

French Olive Oil Unlike Greece, French olive oil production is low but quality is generally high. Most of the oil-producing groves are in the South, and oils from the areas surrounding Nyons and the Vallée des Baux are of superior quality.

COOKING WITH OLIVE OIL

Olive oil can be used in the same way that other cooking oils and fats are used, but some palates find its flavor too strong. For a less pronounced flavor, blend olive oil with a more neutral oil, such as sunflower or corn oil. (An overpoweringly unpleasant taste may simply indicate a low-quality oil.)

In the countries that surround the Mediterranean, olive oil is vital to the cuisine. It is as much a seasoning as a cooking medium. It can be drizzled over a platter of sliced ripe red tomatoes, or added to a hot vegetable soup just before serving, as is often done in Italy and France. Likewise, true Spanish gazpacho recipes call for the addition of a Spanish olive oil just before serving. All three countries have their own version

of grilled bread with olive oil. For Italian *bruscheta*, thick slices of country bread are charcoal-grilled then rubbed with garlic and topped with olive oil and sea salt. When crushed tomatoes are added, the Spanish call it *pan con tomate*. In France, croutons fried in olive oil can be served with a puree of potatoes and salt cod (*brandade*) or bowls of saffron-scented bouillabaisse.

Olive oil is essential to all Italian pasta sauces; when combined with garlic and chilies, it is a sauce in itself, delicious with spaghetti. Mayonnaise made with olive oil and flavored with crushed garlic is commonplace in southern Spain and France, and many uncooked, herb-based sauces, such as pesto, rely on olive oil.

While Europeans often use olive oil for cooking meats and sautéeing vegetables, in the Middle East, it is generally reserved for seasoning cold appetizers and salads, such as eggplant puree or hummus (garbanzo bean puree), or for frying fish.

Infused olive oils
Some Italian extra-virgin olive oils are already infused with truffles, porcini mushrooms, or lemon; some French oils are available with herbs and spices. These lend themselves well to seasoning any dish that calls for ordinary olive oil.

Storing oil
Light is the enemy of olive oil; it should be stored in a cool, dark place, preferably in a can or a dark-colored bottle. Oil purchased in bulk should always be poured into smaller containers.

NUT AND SEED OILS

For the cook, oils are a necessary ingredient. They add fat for browning and for consistency, and many oils add flavor. Oils derived from nuts and seeds also contribute to a well-balanced diet. Much attention has been focused on monounsaturated, polyunsaturated, and saturated fats—all of which can be present in nut and seed oils. These technical terms refer to the molecular structure of the oil, more specifically, to the number of hydrogen atoms present. Saturated fats, the least healthy, contain the maximum possible number of hydrogen atoms. The healthier polyunsaturated and monounsaturated fats have less than their maximum of hydrogen atoms, so they combine more easily with other substances within the body, such as oxygen. Olive oil is high in monounsaturated fats, while palm and coconut oils have the highest levels of saturated fats. Although there are general-purpose oils these can generally be divided into cooking oils—those that are fairly neutral in flavor and withstand heat well—and seasoning oils, which are best used to flavor uncooked dishes such as salads. Cooking oils include soy and corn oils; walnut and hazelnut oils can be heated, but are most successful as seasoning oils.

Almond Oil A pale oil made from sweet almonds, this is used in baking and confectionery. Use to coat cake pans or cookie sheets when preparing delicate baked goods, or heat gently with slivered almonds and serve with fish or cooked green vegetables.

Avocado Oil Extracted from the pits of avocados, and sometimes from blemished fruit, this oil is colorless with a faint aniseed flavor. It is used mainly in North America.

Coconut Oil Extracted from the dried kernel of the coconut, this is often used in commercial food preparations and in certain Indian dishes. It is high in saturated fats.

Corn Oil One of the most economical and widely used all-purpose oils, this is deep yellow in color and heavy in texture. Corn oil is high in polyunsaturated fats and has a high smoke point, so it is both healthy and ideal for most culinary preparations.

Cottonseed Oil Derived from the cotton plant, this is used in the production of margarine and blended cooking oils. It is also used in Egyptian cuisine, where it lends a distinctive flavor.

Grapeseed Oil A pale, delicate oil extracted from grape seeds, this can withstand a wide range of temperatures. When refrigerated, it will not cloud, making it ideal for mayonnaise, and it has a very high smoke point so it is excellent for frying and general cooking. It is high in polyunsaturated fats.

Hazelnut Oil This is a delicious, richly flavored oil that is extracted from the nut. Produced mainly in France, it is expensive and should be used with the finest vinegars for salad dressings, or as a marinade for fish or poultry. Its delicate flavor is lost when heated, but it can be whisked into a sauce at the last minute or used for baked goods in combination with hazelnuts.

OILS FOR FLAVOR

Nut and seed oils are generally used as a flavoring for cold food, or added to hot dishes at the last minute. Pumpkin seed, walnut and hazelnut oils, Asian sesame oil, cold-pressed peanut and pine seed oils all make superb salad dressings, vegetable seasonings, and marinades. Because they are quite flavorful—often to the point of being overpowering—they should always be used sparingly and in combination with a neutral oil, such as sunflower. They can also be used much the same as a pat of butter, to flavor cooked foods; toss steamed or boiled green beans with walnut oil just before serving.

Palm Oil Also known as palm nut oil or *dende* oil, this is extracted from the pulp of the fruit of oil palms. Orange-gold in color, it has a pleasant nutty flavor. Although it is a general-purpose oil, being light in color and taste and good for frying and making salad dressings, it does, however, turn rancid very rapidly.

Peanut Oil This is a very fine, almost tasteless oil for general use in salads, cooking, and frying. The cold-pressed variety has a mild peanut flavor that is good with fruit-flavored vinegars for salad dressings. Peanut oil is moderately high in monounsaturates and low in saturates.

Pine Seed Oil With a distinctive pine seed flavor, this oil is produced on a small scale primarily in France. It is quite costly but the flavor will never disappoint. Use it for salads; it is especially delicious when added to a dipping sauce for artichokes.

Pumpkin Seed Oil This is a dark brown oil with a pleasant flavor of toasted pumpkin seeds. It is popular in Austria, where most of it is produced. Use as a last-minute seasoning for steamed vegetables or fish.

Rapeseed Oil Also known as canola oil, this neutral-flavored oil is suitable for frying, cooking, or baking. It has a high smoke point and is low in saturated fats.

Safflower Oil With a bright yellow color, this oil is ideal for all culinary use, although the flavor is rather strong. Of all the cooking oils, this is one of the highest in polyunsaturated fats, lowest in saturated fats, and a good source of vitamin E.

Sesame Oil There are many types of this oil. European, or cold-pressed sesame oil, is light in color and nutty in flavor with a high smoke point, making it a good cooking oil. Asian sesame oil is made from toasted sesame seeds, giving it a darker color and more pronounced taste. Middle Eastern sesame oils are lighter in flavor than Asian ones, with a deep golden color. All are aromatic and capable of being heated to a high temperature.

Soy Oil A major component of blended oils, this is a high-quality, neutral-flavored oil that is low in saturated fats.

Sunflower Oil This is one of the best all-purpose oils. It is high in polyunsaturates, tasteless, pale, light in texture, and inexpensive. It can be used for frying, cooking, salad dressings, and mixing with other more strongly flavored oils.

Vegetable Oil This is an oil obtained from blending a number of oils in various proportions, and types and quantities are not necessarily given on the label. It may contain coconut or palm oils, which are high in saturated fats. Vegetable oil has little aroma or flavor, making it popular as a all-purpose culinary oil.

Walnut Oil A delicious topaz-colored oil with a rich, nutty flavor. Walnuts from the Perigord and Dordogne in France are said to produce the best oil. In these regions, walnuts are strictly graded for quality; it is even possible for one tree to have two separate grades of walnut. Production is small, therefore this oil is expensive. Walnut oil does not keep long, either opened or unopened, so buy in small quantities and keep in a cool place, but not in the refrigerator. It makes a delicious salad dressing, and in baking it adds flavor to cakes, especially those that contain walnuts. It is also good with fish, poultry, and vegetables, or use wherever a walnut taste will marry well with the ingredients.

Flavoring oils
Oils with a distinct taste should be chosen in order to enhance particular dishes; they are too overpowering to be used simply for general-purpose cooking. Such oils, particularly if they are not blended, tend also to be expensive so are best used where only a small amount is needed.

Grapeseed oil

Virgin sesame oil

Virgin pumpkin seed oil

Hazelnut oil

Walnut oil

COOK'S CHOICE
MÂCHE AND BEET SALAD WITH WALNUT OIL DRESSING
Serves 4

1 tbsp white-wine vinegar
Salt
1 tsp Dijon mustard
3 tbsp walnut oil
2 tbsp sunflower oil
Freshly ground black pepper
4 bunches mâche, washed
4 cooked beets, diced
2 oz (60 g) Roquefort cheese, crumbled
2 oz (60 g) coarsely chopped walnuts
Fresh chervil sprigs for garnish

In a small bowl, whisk together the vinegar and salt to taste. Add the mustard and blend. Slowly whisk in the oils until well blended. Add pepper to taste. Place the mâche in another bowl and toss with 2 tbsp of the dressing. Arrange the mâche on 4 salad plates. Divide the beets into 4 equal portions and mound in the center of each plate, then drizzle 1 tbsp of the remaining dressing over each mound of beets. Sprinkle over the Roquefort and walnuts. Garnish with the chervil and serve immediately.

BURNING POINT
If an oil is heated for too long to too high a temperature it may catch fire. Never use water to extinguish burning oil; instead, smother it with a lid, a flameproof or fire blanket, or a sheet of aluminum foil.

FLAVORED OILS

Oils infused with herbs and spices can add greatly to any recipe that calls for ordinary oil. There are a number of flavored oils available in supermarkets and specialty stores, but these are also quite easy to prepare at home. Extra-virgin olive oil lends itself most naturally to flavoring. For something truly extraordinary, infuse a high-quality olive oil with a truffle; a small quantity of oil can even be flavored with truffle shavings. Use the truffle oil to season pasta, risotto, or salad. Herbs and spices can be added alone, or in combination. There are no rules, although the ingredients should always be complementary. While these oils are destined mainly for seasoning, not cooking, robust herbs, such as thyme, rosemary, and bay, make good additions to oil for *fondue bourguignonne*.

SPICES

Spice-infused oils can be made year-round using any spices on hand. To enhance the flavor, some spices, such as caraway and fennel seeds, can be dry-roasted before infusing. Spices can be left whole, or they can be crushed slightly to allow more flavor to escape. Appropriate choices include: cardamom, star anise, juniper, coriander seeds, nutmeg, cinnamon, cumin, and cloves.

Cardamom

Juniper

Nutmeg

Saffron

Cinnamon oil

Basil oil

HERBS

Making herb-flavored oils is a good way of using summer herbs when they are inexpensive and plentiful. Use basil, bay, cilantro leaves, oregano, marjoram, chervil, chives, dill, mint, parsley, rosemary, sage, tarragon, and thyme. To best distinguish the tastes, use herbs separately, or combine with ingredients such as garlic and lemon peel for a good depth of flavor.

Sage

Rosemary

Basil

As an ingredient for frying and browning, oil is more versatile than butter, and the range of possible flavors is more varied. To the already long list of different oils with their different perfumes, add the number of herbs, spices, and other ingredients that can be infused, and discover an endless supply of seasoning alternatives. An excellent vehicle for flavor, oils need be infused only with a small amount of herbs or spices. Add a pinch of curry powder to oil and it will take on a delicious curry flavor, perfect for tossing with pasta or vegetables. Add a slice of gingerroot and it will become ginger oil, which can be brushed on beef marinated in soy sauce just before cooking. With a few star anise, oil becomes an excellent seasoning for chicken or shellfish dishes. Any home pantry will benefit from a constant and plentiful supply of flavored oils.

If using fresh herbs, wash and dry thoroughly, and bruise lightly to help release their flavor. Place the herbs in a clean bottle or jar with a clamp top and add oil to cover. Seal tightly and leave to stand in a cool, dark place for at least 2 weeks. Taste the oil; when it has a pronounced flavor it is ready to use. For a stronger flavor, add more herbs and leave to stand for a week longer. The oil can be left as it is, or the herbs can be strained. Bear in mind that the oil's flavor will strengthen on standing if it is not strained. However, the addition of a sprig of the appropriate herb is not only a most attractive finishing touch, it also makes the flavor of the oil readily identifiable. For spice-flavored oils, both whole and ground spices can be used although whole always have more flavor. Quantities are according to taste; the method is the same as for herb-flavored oil.

COOKING WITH FLAVORED OILS

Flavored oil can be used as an alternative to ordinary oil, although the results will not taste the same. A salad dressing made with olive oil is adequate, but can be delicious when made with an herb-infused olive oil. Chives, parsley, and chervil—all excellent salad herbs—are ideal used alone or in combination, to perfume a salad oil. A bottle of this oil is handy during seasons when these delicate herbs are hard to obtain. Herbs with a robust flavor (bay, rosemary, thyme, and sage) impart an earthy flavor to oils. Use them to enhance marinades for meat and game or as a marinade for small, firm goat cheeses. An excellent appetizer can be prepared from the marinated goat cheese: slice the cheese, place on rounds of French bread, and broil until bubbly; serve on a bed of salad greens tossed with a dressing made from the marinade oil.

A peanut oil spiced with cinnamon sticks makes a beautiful edible gift as well as a delicious oil for frying fruit fritters, cooking pancakes or waffles, or brushed on chicken for grilling. Peanut oil can also be infused with fruit—strawberries, lemons, pears, apples, oranges, and peaches—alone or in combination. Use the fruit-flavored oil when making mayonnaise or dressings to accompany cold meats.

COOK'S CHOICE
PENNE WITH VEGETABLES AND CURRY OIL

Serves 4–6

8 tbsp extra-virgin olive oil
2 tsp curry powder
Salt
6 medium carrots, diced
1 lb (500 g) peas, fresh or frozen
1 large onion, diced
2 yellow peppers
1 lb (500 g) penne

One day before serving, infuse the oil with the curry. The day of serving, bring a saucepan of water to a boil. Add salt, place the carrots in a sieve, and submerge in the water. Cook until just tender, 3–5 minutes. Remove the carrots and return the water to a boil. Cook the peas in the same water, about 3 minutes. Drain and set aside. In a skillet, combine 2 tbsp of the curry oil, the onion, and salt to taste. Cook over medium heat for 3 minutes. Add the peppers and cook until just soft, 1–2 minutes more. Taste for seasoning. Cook the penne in boiling, salted water until just tender. Add the carrots and peas to the penne just to warm, then drain. Transfer to a bowl, add the onion mixture and remaining curry oil. Toss to coat and serve.

MAKING CHILI OIL

While most oils can be flavored cold, chili oil is best heated. Keep the heat very low and supervise cooking; if the chilies are overheated, they will give off throat-burning fumes. Any oil can be used, and milder or hotter chilies can be substituted. Oils, such as Asian sesame oil, are best added after the original mixture is cooked in order for their distinctive flavors to have the greatest effect. A Mediterranean-style version, made with extra-virgin olive oil, is delicious when drizzled over pasta, pizza, or brushed over grilled meats just before serving.

1 *In a skillet, mix 1 cup (250 ml) peanut oil and 6 tbsp chopped dried red chilies. Cook 10 minutes over very low heat; allow to cool.*

2 *When cool, add 2–3 tsp ground cayenne pepper and 1–2 tbsp Asian sesame oil. Cover and let stand for at least 12 hours.*

3 *Strain through a lined funnel into a sterilized bottle. Add 2–3 whole chilies for a decorative effect. Keep in a cool, dark place.*

VINEGAR

The term "vinegar" comes from the French *vin aigre,* or sour wine, and it is also used to describe other soured, alcohol-based liquids, such as those made from cider, malt, or rice wine. Souring is a natural process that occurs when a liquid containing less than 18 percent alcohol is exposed to the air. Bacteria present in the air react with the alcohol to produce a thick, moldy-looking skin over the surface of the liquid, which is called the "mother." In simple scientific terms, the mother is a layer of yeast cells and bacteria that converts the alcohol into a natural acetic acid, and it is this acid that gives vinegar its characteristic sharpness. Although this reaction does occur naturally, it is not always consistent. To produce quality vinegars, the speed and temperature of this process must be controlled. This explains why it is not enough to leave an open bottle of wine or ale on the kitchen counter for a few days and expect it to turn into vinegar. If unmonitored, the souring process can result in loss of flavor, or in further bacterial action and the production of unpleasant bitter flavors. In the kitchen, wine vinegars are indispensable for salad dressings, marinades, and deglazing (see page 249). Rice-wine vinegar is vital for flavoring the rice in sushi, and malt vinegar is used in many pickles and, of course, on authentic, British-style fish and chips.

TYPES OF VINEGAR

In general, wine vinegars are required to have at least 6 percent acetic acid, and other vinegars range between 4–6 percent acetic acid. Slight variations in acidity levels will be only barely perceptible on the palate; they need be of concern only when preparing pickles or other preserves.

Wine, malt, and cider vinegar are strong, but distilled and spirit vinegars are even stronger. While any vinegar can be distilled, malt vinegar is most often used for this process. The distillation concentrates the acetic acid, increasing the level above 6 percent.

The vinegar made in any given country tends to reflect the produce. Wine-making countries, such as France, Italy, and Spain, produce wine vinegars. Where apples are a main crop, as in parts of North America, cider vinegar represents the bulk of production. Beer-brewing countries, such as Britain, produce malt vinegar. In the Far East, where wine is made from rice, a mild variety of rice wine vinegar containing 2–4 percent acetic acid is most widely used.

Wine Vinegar This is produced from both red and white wines, and the quality of the vinegar depends on the quality of the wine. The finest wine vinegars are made by the *Orléans* method, which allows wine to ferment slowly and naturally (at about 70°F; 21°C) in oak barrels until the mother forms on the surface. However, this method is lengthy and costly, and many manufacturers speed up the process by raising the temperature. This results in a less costly vinegar, but one that is also inferior in quality.

There are almost as many types of wine vinegar as there are wines. Champagne vinegar has a pale color and delicate flavor, while Rioja vinegar has a deep red color and a full rich taste. Sherry vinegar, with its deep caramel color and well-rounded mellow flavor, is matured in wooden casks similar to those in which the sherry is made and can be expensive. As wine making develops in North America and Australia, new kinds of vinegars, such as those made from the California zinfandel grape variety, are emerging.

A wine vinegar that is gaining recognition in cuisines around the world is *aceto balsamico,* or balsamic vinegar. Made in Modena in northern Italy, it is named for the Italian word for "balm" referring to the smooth, mellow character of this unique vinegar. Balsamic vinegar is made from unfermented grape juice that is aged in

Distilled vinegar

Malt vinegar

Cider vinegar

Rice vinegar

Red-wine vinegar   **White-wine vinegar**

Balsamic vinegar   **Champagne vinegar**

Fine wine vinegars
Champagne vinegar is an elegant substitute in recipes that call for ordinary white-wine vinegar. Balsamic vinegar can be very expensive, but a little goes a long way. Mixed with an extra-virgin olive oil, it makes a superb dressing for delicate salad leaves or a sauce for fish such as poached sea bass.

wooden casks. The quality of the finished product depends a great deal on the type of wood used and the skill of the vinegar maker. The finest vinegars are aged for a minimum of ten years; the maximum aging time can extend for many decades. Balsamic vinegar production demands an artistry equal to the production of a great wine. In Modena, fine aged balsamic vinegar may be served as an after-dinner drink. Traditionally made balsamic vinegar can be costly, although an industrially made version does exist and is an acceptable substitute for the traditional kind in most recipes.

Cider Vinegar Apple pulp or cider can be made into cider vinegar following the same method used to produce wine vinegar. There are recipes that call specifically for cider vinegar, but it has a strong, sharp flavor and so should only be used where it complements the other ingredients. Commercial cider vinegars, which are filtered, are a pale brown color. Home-produced versions can become cloudy, but this does not affect their taste or indicate an inferior quality. The flavor is not smooth and refined enough for most salad dressings, but it can be used successfully in fruit pickles.

Malt Vinegar Made from malted barley, this type is most often used as a pickling vinegar for onions and other vegetables. Malt vinegar has too strong a flavor for use in salad dressings, but is the perfect condiment for fish and chips. Powerful distilled malt vinegar, which is colorless, is for pickling watery vegetables, such as cucumber, which are likely to dilute the vinegar. It is also used in the manufacture of sauces and chutneys and is sometimes colored with caramel to produce brown malt vinegar.

Spirit Vinegar The strongest of all vinegars, this is used almost exclusively for pickling. It differs from distilled vinegar in that it contains a small quantity of alcohol.

Rice Vinegar Most common in the cuisines of Asia, this type is made from soured and fermented rice wines. Japanese rice vinegars are mellow and mild, while vinegar from China is sharp and sometimes slightly sour. Depending on the rice used, Chinese vinegars are red or white in color. Like vinegars in the West, rice vinegar is often flavored. Soy sauce and mirin, or sweet rice wine, can be added, along with spices and flavorings such as gingerroot, dried bonito flakes, chilies, sesame seeds, onions, horseradish, and mustard. There is also a black Chinese vinegar, which is obtained from wheat, sorghum, and millet instead of rice.

COOKING WITH VINEGAR

Vinegar is an essential ingredient in the kitchen and a highly versatile flavoring. Also used as a means of preserving foods, generally fruit, vinegar is also an excellent seasoning. High-quality vinegars can be costly, so it is important that they are stored properly to ensure maximum shelf life. Keep vinegars in a cool place away from light; they do not need to be refrigerated. Most vinegars can be kept almost indefinitely if stored correctly.

Vinegar is commonly used in sauces and salad dressings—particularly where a sweet-and-sour flavor is desired—and it can be used as a preservative for vegetables and fruits. It is also one of the principal ingredients in pickles and chutneys.

The importance of vinegar to the flavor of the finished dish is often overlooked. The best vinegars are made from the finest raw ingredients, and this is especially true for wine vinegars. A high-quality sherry vinegar, for example, can transform a simple green salad; an ordinary vinegar will result in an ordinary salad.

Certain kinds of vinegar are used to deglaze pan juices for piquant sauces or gravies. The addition of a little vinegar can enliven many sauces, especially tomato-based ones, but remember to use a light touch. Vinegar goes surprisingly well with soft fruits, such as raspberries and strawberries, and a dash of a mellow vinegar adds distinction to fresh fruit salad.

A classic dish from Modena pairs sliced strawberries and balsamic vinegar. Drizzle fresh strawberries with a high-quality balsamic vinegar and leave to mellow for 30 minutes before serving. A few drops of balsamic vinegar, used to deglaze panfried liver or duck, can transform an ordinary dish into something special.

When deciding which vinegar to use in a dish, always choose the most appropriate flavor. Malt vinegar is made from grain and is strongly flavored, so it is best with straightforward food such as fish and chips, cold meats, or when preparing relishes and chutneys. Cider vinegar is the best choice for deglazing pork chops accompanied by sautéed apples.

Wine vinegars are ideal for mayonnaise and all kinds of salad dressings. They are also used in many classic butter sauces, such as *béarnaise*, often made with white-wine vinegar and served with fish. A dash of fine wine vinegar adds distinction to rich meat or game stews.

FLAVORED VINEGARS

Flavored vinegars have long been used in cooking, and they are enjoying renewed popularity. Fine wine vinegars are the most appropriate choice for flavoring, and they can be enhanced by a wide variety of herbs, spices, and flavorings. Flavored vinegar can take the place of ordinary vinegar in most recipes, provided that the marriage of flavors is judicious. White-wine vinegar infused with herbs, such as tarragon, or with shallots, makes an ideal ingredient in dressings for robust salad greens, such as romaine or chicory. Or, blend it with oil, cream, and seasonings and toss in a chicken or seafood salad. Flavored red-wine vinegars will give added depth to marinades, stews, or meat dishes. They can also be used to perk up a salad made with ordinary lettuce, while garlic-infused red-wine vinegar is a good choice for red cabbage salad. Wine vinegar can also be lightly perfumed with rose petals or imbued with the more distinctive flavor of flowers such as lavender, nasturtium, and violet.

Stronger sherry vinegar, flavored with sliced horseradish, rosemary, garlic cloves, or chili, makes an excellent last-minute seasoning for meat and poultry.

Appropriate partnerships

Be sure to pair flavored vinegars with appropriate partners. For example, a dash of tarragon vinegar at the end of cooking adds a pleasant touch to simple sautéed chicken breasts, and spiced vinegar is excellent with game.

MAKING HERB VINEGAR

Place 2 oz (60 g) fresh, clean herbs in a clean jar with a clamp-top lid. Bring 2 cups (500 ml) vinegar to a boil and pour over the herbs. Seal and leave to infuse for at least 2 weeks, shaking the jar occasionally. To store, strain the vinegar into a clean jar or bottle and seal with a cork (see page 233).

Rosemary vinegar   **Nutmeg vinegar**

COOK'S CHOICE
SPICED VINEGAR

Makes 4¹/₂ quarts (4.5 liters)

4¹/₂ quarts (4.5 liters) wine vinegar
1 nutmeg
1 small piece gingerroot, peeled
¹/₂ tsp whole cloves
2 tsp mustard seeds
4 tbsp salt
1 tsp black peppercorns
Peel of ¹/₂ orange
6 shallots, quartered

In a large earthenware crock or glass container with a lid, combine all the ingredients and stir to mix. Cover tightly and leave to steep in a warm place, or in the sun, for 3–4 weeks. Strain into a bowl, pressing to extract the flavor. Pour through a funnel into clean bottles and cork. Store in a cool, dark place. Use as a last-minute seasoning for grilled meats.

MAKING FLAVORED VINEGAR

Any soft fruit, particularly summer fruit, can be used to enhance the flavor of vinegar. It is best to use white-wine vinegar, which allows the color of the fruit to come through. Herbs and spices, such as peppercorns, cinnamon, or bay leaf, are a flavorful addition.

1 Combine 1 lb (500 g) fresh fruit, such as raspberries, blueberries, apricots, or figs, and 5 cups (1.25 liters) vinegar in a sterilized glass jar with an airtight seal. Leave in a warm place to steep. Shake the jar occasionally.

2 Strain the raspberries and vinegar into a saucepan, pressing to extract flavor from the berries. Add 1 tbsp sugar and stir to blend. Place the mixture over low heat and simmer for 10 minutes. Transfer to sterilized jars. For a more attractive presentation, add a few fresh berries or pieces of fruit.

The possibilities for making herb-flavored vinegars at home are endless. Use red- or white-wine vinegar and fresh ripe fruit or very fresh, unblemished herbs to produce distinctively flavored vinegars. For maximum flavor, heat the vinegar gently before steeping. Use the seasonings alone or in combination with one another to add a personal touch to dishes. Some suitable combinations include lemon and thyme, rosemary and bay, or cranberries, cloves, and honey. For fruit vinegar, frozen fruit can be used, but do not use canned fruit in syrup. For a more attractive presentation, add a few fresh berries or pieces of fruit to the bottle after straining. Fruit vinegars also benefit from the addition of honey.

Cherry vinegar

Rose-petal vinegar

CORKING VINEGAR
For homemade vinegars, old bottles may be used over and over again provided that they are sterilized. Corks cannot be reused, and they should be replaced with each new batch of vinegar. New corks need to be trimmed to fit the bottles. They must then be sterilized in a pan of boiling water for a few minutes; this also helps to soften them slightly. To seal the bottles, push the corks into the bottles. With a wooden mallet or hammer, pound the cork into the neck of the bottle, leaving no more than $\frac{1}{4}$ in (5 mm) exposed cork.

STORING FLAVORED VINEGAR
A dark cabinet in a cool place, or a cellar, is the ideal place for keeping homemade flavored vinegar. A low storage temperature is important, and not only for preserving the vinegar's flavor; if the vinegar is kept in a warm environment, it may ferment and pop its cork. This fermentation is generally a sign that the vinegar is no longer fit for human consumption. As a rule, any home-bottled vinegar that develops a questionable appearance or odor should be discarded immediately.

BUTTERMILK, SOUR CREAM, AND YOGURT

Milk or cream thickened by heat, or sharpened by bacterial cultures, or both, becomes buttermilk, sour cream, or yogurt. These dairy products have a unique role in the kitchen. All three can be used as the basis for dips and dressings, in cake batters or bread doughs, and can greatly enhance many soups. Cuisines the world over use cultured dairy products in a number of ways. Sour cream is used extensively in the cuisines of Central and Eastern Europe. Yogurt is used in both sweet and savory dishes throughout India and the Middle East, and in North America, buttermilk flavors many baked goods or serves as the foundation for fruit-flavored drinks.

Cultured dairy products are difficult to use in cooking because they curdle when over-heated, and for this reason, they must never be boiled. For best results, always add them at the end of cooking time, and stir in by spoonfuls. Alternatively, a teaspoon or so of cornstarch can be stirred in before heating. This will help to stabilize these delicate ingredients and reduce the risk of curdling.

Yogurt Thought to be Turkish in origin, yogurt has been used for centuries through-out India, the Middle East, Turkey, and the Balkan regions of Eastern Europe. There are many different types of this popular cul-tured dairy product: Much depends on the milk from which it is produced: either whole, low-fat, or skimmed cow's milk, or water buffalo's, camel's, goat's, or sheep's milk. Yogurt is produced by adding bacteria (that are beneficial to the digestive tract), to the milk, which is usually pasteurized and homogenized. These bacteria break down the milk sugar, or lactose, to produce lactic acid, which gives yogurt its charac-teristic sharpness. Yogurt can be enjoyed on its own, but it can also be used as a marinade to tenderize tough meats, or as a thickener for sauces. There are many different types of yogurt. *Plain yogurt* is the most basic; it is simply milk with the two yogurt cultures: *Lactobacillus bulgaricus* and *Streptococcus thermophilus.* Plain yogurt that has been incubated in its carton will be soft textured. A firmer set results when the yogurt is incubated in large tanks. Low-fat yogurt is made from skim milk and contains between 0.5–2 percent fat. Very low-fat yogurt has less than 0.5 percent fat. Commer-cially sweetened fruit yogurts are generally made using low-fat yogurt. Unflavored, plain yogurt is ideal to use as a starter for homemade yogurt (see above).
Greek-style yogurt is made from either sheep's milk or cow's milk. It is characterized by a thick, creamy texture and an especially rich flavor. Sheep's milk yogurt is relatively low in fat (about 6 percent) and is naturally thick. Cow's milk yogurt is much higher in fat (about 10 percent) and it must be strained to remove the excess moisture and to obtain the characteristic thickness. The acidity of cow's milk yogurt is balanced by the high fat con-tent, giving it a sweeter, milder flavor.
French-style yogurt is generally set, and is made from low-fat homogenized milk. As a rule, set yogurts can be used for cooking, although they are best appreciated when eaten in their natural state, with vanilla sugar (see page 195) or enhanced with honey or fruit compotes. To avoid the crunchy tex-ture of superfine sugar, use confectioners' sugar because it dissolves more easily.

MAKING YOGURT
Bring 2 cups (500 ml) pasteurized milk to a boil, then lower the heat and simmer for 2 minutes. Transfer to a glass bowl, cover, and cool to 110°F (43°C). In another glass bowl, beat 2 tbsp plain yogurt until thin. Slowly whisk in the milk. Cover and incubate for 8–10 hours in a warm place (about 75–85°F; 24–29°C). In warm weather, wrapping in a towel will often suffice. Alternatively, leave overnight in a gas oven with only the pilot light lit. Refrigerate and consume within 4 days.

Sour cream *is a versatile ingredient that can be used as a garnish for soups, a topping for potatoes, or for dips*

Yogurt

Buttermilk *is particularly effective in certain baked goods, where its acid helps the dough to rise*

Yogurt and mint

Sour cream and watercress

Cream cheese, buttermilk, and dried apricots

Dairy products in dips
The slightly tangy flavor of sour milk products offers the perfect base for dips served with vegetable crudités, crackers, breadsticks, or toast.

Buttermilk A by-product of butter making, this is the liquid that is drained from the churned milk after the fat has coagulated to form butter. Old-fashioned buttermilk was simply pasteurized before packaging, and it had a rich, full flavor. Nowadays, a culture is added and it is left to ferment for about 12–14 hours at a very low temperature, giving modern-day buttermilk a more acidic tang. Buttermilk marries well with the sweetness of fruits such as pears and cherries, and they can be processed together in a blender for a pleasant refreshing drink. In some recipes, where sharpness is welcome, buttermilk can be substituted for ordinary milk; try making fruit custards or flans with buttermilk. In baking, it is best to use recipes that are specially adapted for buttermilk because the quantities of yeast or baking powder are calculated to accommodate the acidity of buttermilk.

Sour Cream While sour cream is, in effect, sour, it is not ordinary cream that becomes sharp over time. Commercial sour cream is made from a homogenized cream that has about the same fat content as light cream, plus a bacterial culture. As with

buttermilk, it is the culture that imparts the tang. Especially popular in the cuisines of Central and Eastern Europe, sour cream is essential in the classic Russian dish Beef Stroganoff and beet soup, or *borscht*, which is common to many cuisines of the area. Sour cream can be used like ordinary heavy cream to enrich meat or game casseroles, sauces, and soups; sour cream with chopped fresh chives is the classic baked potato topping. Sour cream also provides the ideal base for crudité dipping sauces and salad dressings. A popular addition to chocolate cakes, cheese cakes, and coffee cakes, sour cream adds a pleasant tang and unctuous texture.

BUTTERMILK PANCAKES

Serves 2–4

2 cups (250 g) all-purpose flour
1 tsp sugar
1 tsp salt
2 tsp baking soda
1 ½ tsp baking powder
2 eggs
4 tbsp unsalted butter, melted (or vegetable oil)
2 cups (500 ml) buttermilk
Melted butter or oil for frying
Maple syrup

In a large mixing bowl, sift together the flour, sugar, salt, baking soda, and baking powder. In another bowl, lightly beat the eggs and stir in the melted butter and buttermilk. Make a well in the center of the flour mixture and slowly whisk in the egg mixture until thick. Allow to rest 20–30 minutes to thicken. If the batter is too thick, thin with a little more buttermilk. Heat a large, heavy-bottomed skillet or a griddle and add enough butter or oil to coat. Ladle the batter into the pan to form pancakes. Cook over medium heat until golden brown on the edges and bubbles on top burst open, 3–4 minutes. Turn and cook the other side until golden, 1–2 minutes. Transfer to plates and serve immediately with maple syrup.

CRÈME FRAÎCHE

An essential ingredient in all French kitchens, this is a much more distinctive version of sour cream. In some areas, crème fraîche is difficult to obtain, but it can easily be made at home. Place 2 cups (500 ml) heavy cream in a saucepan with 1 cup (250 ml) buttermilk. Cook over gentle heat until the mixture feels warm, but not hot, about 85°F (30°C). Transfer to a bowl, cover partially and leave at room temperature for 4–8 hours (hot weather will speed up the culturing process). Stir, cover securely, and refrigerate.

BUTTER

Made simply by beating cream until it thickens and separates, butter has been used through the ages for a variety of culinary preparations. According to one theory, the technique of butter churning was discovered unintentionally by early travelers in cold climates; milk carried on horseback for long journeys was churned into butter by the constant motion. Butter made from cow's milk is the norm in most countries, although goat and sheep's milk are used in Greece, water buffalo's milk is sometimes used in Italy, camel's milk in Africa, and yak's milk in Tibet. In the kitchen, heat alters the form and flavor of butter. It can be clarified (see page 237) for high-heat cooking methods, used alone as a spread, or seasoned with a variety of flavorings (see page 238).

Salted butter

Unsalted butter

PRODUCTION

While there are many different types of butter, production methods are essentially the same. Pasteurized cream is placed in great vats and churned vigorously. This beating causes the fat globules to pull together and solidify, leaving a liquid that is known as buttermilk. The buttermilk is drawn off, leaving small lumps of solid butter that are washed and drained. If necessary, any additional flavoring, such as salt, or coloring is added at this stage. The butter is then churned until it forms a solid mass that is ready for packaging.

The flavor of butter varies according to the cow and its diet. Springtime butter is held to be the best because the cows have more opportunity to graze and feed on fresh grass. In the winter, when their diets are higher in grain, they tend to produce a less flavorful and less supple butter.

These factors also affect the color. Some cows produce a deep yellow butter, others a paler one. For a consistent product year-round, natural dyes such as annatto (see page 60) or carotene can be added.

TYPES OF BUTTER

By definition, pure dairy butter must be at least 80 percent fat, but will also contain 10–18 percent water and 2–4 percent milk solids, or whey. There are two basic types of butter: sweet cream butter and lactic butter. Both of these may be salted or unsalted. Butter that is labeled "salted" contains at least 3 percent salt; "slightly salted" butter contains only 1–2.5 percent salt.

Sweet cream butter is made from pasteurized cream that is placed in a "cream-aging" tank at a low temperature for about 12 hours before churning. This butter has a sweet creamy taste and a golden yellow color, and is ideal for baked goods.

Pasteurized cream combined with a lactic acid culture produces lactic butter. During manufacture, the cream and lactic acid are blended and left at a higher temperature (65–68°F; 18–20°C), for a longer time than sweet cream butter. The resulting butter has a much lower moisture content, only about 10 percent, while sweet cream butter can contain as much as 18 percent moisture. For baked goods and pastries, especially puff pastry, low-moisture butter is preferable because humidity will interfere with the consistency of the finished dish.

COOKING WITH BUTTER

Butter adds substance, an unctuous texture, and, above all, an inimitable flavor to many culinary preparations.

The choice of butter for cooking is generally a matter of taste, although unsalted lactic butter is the preferred type for most culinary preparations for several reasons. The absence of salt is an advantage, allowing the cook more control over the flavor of the finished dish. This type of butter also has a higher percentage of pure butterfat and a lower percentage of water and milk solids, allowing it to better withstand heat without

STORING BUTTER

Butter is best kept in the refrigerator, but it easily absorbs other flavors, so it should be well wrapped and kept away from strong-smelling foods—especially melon and cauliflower.

Before refrigeration, ceramic containers were often used to keep butter fresh. Butter in the lid was chilled by cold salt water in the base. Today, these offer an attractive presentation; ice water can be used in place of salt water.

Ice water helps to keep molded butter fresh

Ceramic containers are attractive butter holders

CLARIFYING BUTTER

Clarified butter is butter that has been melted to remove the water and milk solids, leaving pure butterfat, which has a much higher burning point: 350°F (180°C). Clarified butter can be made in large batches and stored, wrapped well, in the refrigerator, where it will keep for several weeks.

1 Melt the butter over low heat without stirring. When completely melted, remove from the heat and skim the foam from the surface with a spoon.

2 Slowly pour the melted butter into a bowl, leaving the milky solids behind. Alternatively, after skimming, pour through a cheesecloth-lined sieve.

adding any unwanted moisture to delicate preparations, such as pastries and icings. Because butter contains water and milk solids, it burns at a lower temperature than other cooking fats. Adding oil to butter raises its smoke point and reduces the risk of burning. An indication of the water and milk solid content of butter can be seen when it is heated. When the temperature reaches the boiling point of water, the butter sizzles. This is the sound of the water boiling and evaporating. If the temperature continues to rise, the milk solids will separate, appearing as a white sediment. Further heating causes the milk solids to brown, which can add a pleasant nutty flavor, followed by black, or burnt, butter, which has a bitter flavor and is reputed to be unhealthy. With small quantities of butter,

such as the amount added to a skillet for sautéing, black can follow quite rapidly from brown, so care should be taken when using high heat. For frying or other high-heat cooking methods, clarified butter (see above) is best, but bear in mind that butter with fewer milk solids has less flavor.

Butter is an essential ingredient in many classic sauce recipes. The simplest is *à la meunière*, which is melted butter enhanced by a squeeze of fresh lemon juice. Roux—a mixture of butter and flour—is the basis for *béchamel*, and it is also used to thicken gravies, soups, and stews. Butter-mounted sauces are many, and they can be identified by their rich flavor and glossy appearance. *Beurre blanc* (see above) is a classic example, and any stock-based sauce can be mounted with butter by simply whisking in small cubes of cold butter just before serving.

A pat of butter has many uses: stirred into creamy scrambled eggs, it stops the cooking process and adds flavor; it prevents chocolate sauces from turning dull; and dotted over a fruit pie, it stops the filling from boiling over.

Butter stamps *are carved wooden implements that can be used to imprint butter with decorative patterns*

COOK'S CHOICE
BEURRE BLANC

Makes about 1 cup (250 ml)

1 large shallot, finely chopped
3 tbsp white-wine vinegar
1 tbsp dry white wine
6 tbsp heavy cream or crème fraîche
1 cup (250 g) unsalted butter, chilled and cut into small cubes
Salt
Freshly ground white pepper

In a saucepan, combine the shallot, vinegar, and wine over high heat. Cook until the liquid has almost evaporated, 1–2 minutes. Lower the heat, add the cream, and cook until reduced and thickened, 1–2 minutes more; whisk occasionally. Off the heat, whisk in the butter, a few cubes at a time, whisking constantly. Move the pan on and off the heat while adding the butter, and never let the mixture boil. Season to taste and serve immediately. (Although difficult to keep hot for a long time, the sauce can be kept warm over a bowl of hot water for up to 30 minutes; stir often to prevent the sauce from separating.) Serve with poached fish.

COOK'S CHOICE
BEURRE NOIR

Makes about 6 tbsp

4 tbsp unsalted butter
1 tsp white-wine vinegar
2 tbsp lemon juice
1 tbsp capers, drained
Salt
Freshly ground white pepper
1 tbsp chopped fresh parsley

In a saucepan, melt the butter over medium heat until it browns; do not allow to burn. Pour immediately into a small bowl and leave to cool slightly. In the same pan used for the butter, combine the vinegar and lemon juice and cook over high heat until reduced by half. Stir in the capers and season to taste. Stir in the butter and parsley and serve with broiled or poached fish.

FLAVORED BUTTER

On its own, butter is an excellent flavoring, but when combined with herbs, spices, and other ingredients, its taste potential is even greater. Garlic butter is perhaps the most well known, but the flavoring possibilities are endless. Anchovies, horseradish, tarragon, chives, basil, and chilies are just some of the choices for making savory butters to spread on canapés or sandwiches, or serve alongside broiled meat or fish. Sweet butters can be made with many ingredients: honey, cinnamon, fresh or dried fruit, nuts, vanilla, and chocolate, for example. Prepare with softened butter, then chill until firm or use to make garnishes. Flavored butter can also be frozen.

HERB BUTTER SHAPES

1 *Spread softened butter between two sheets of waxed paper. Roll out evenly, about ¹/₄ in (5 mm) thick. Transfer to a cookie sheet and refrigerate until firm.*

2 *With cutters, or a small glass, stamp out shapes or circles. Or, use a sharp knife and a ruler to cut out geometric shapes. Chill until ready to use.*

BUTTER ROSES

1 *Fill a pastry bag fitted with a wide ribbon tip with softened, flavored butter. The butter can be colored with food coloring if desired. Chill until firm enough to pipe.*

2 *Attach a square of waxed paper to a small jar. Pipe a central strip, turning the jar to form a tight spiral. To finish, twist the end of the tip toward you in a single steady movement.*

3 *Hold the tip at a 45° angle to the piped-out rose center. Starting just before the seam, pipe out one petal; twist bottom toward you to finish. Continue piping petals, overlapping them slightly and making them larger as you work away from the center. Turn the jar while piping for even petals. Chill until ready to use.*

BUTTER BALLS

One of the simplest butter garnishes can be made with a melon ball tool. Use one size and group different-flavored butters, or make an assortment of balls using different-size tools. Assemble into the grape cluster shown here or serve individually. For example, serve chive balls with baked potatoes or honey butter balls with warm muffins. Or, shape softened butter into balls and roll in herbs or spices to coat.

1 *Dip a melon baller into cold water, then press into a block of chilled butter. Plain butter balls can be rolled in spices or chopped herbs for flavor. Alternatively, prepare a flavored butter, reshape into a block, and chill until firm.*

2 *For textured butter balls, roll between two wooden butter shapers. Arrange an assortment of flavored or plain butter balls atop fresh grape leaves in a cluster formation. The butter grape cluster makes a stunning buffet centerpiece.*

Nonpoisonous leaves make a pretty and colorful background on which to display your butter "fruits"

Butter can be flavored from within or without and molded into many different shapes

CHOCOLATE-HAZELNUT BUTTER

Makes about 6 oz (175 g)

3/4 oz (20 g) plain chocolate, chopped

1 tsp superfine sugar

1 tbsp hazelnut-flavored liqueur

1/2 cup (125 g) unsalted butter, softened

1 tsp vanilla extract

2 tbsp ground hazelnuts

In a bowl, combine the chocolate, sugar, and liqueur and melt. Leave to cool. Blend the butter, chocolate mixture, vanilla, and hazelnuts. Let stand, covered, in a cool place for 1 hour to allow the flavors to develop. Chill to firm before serving with warm croissants, muffins, or toast.

MEDITERRANEAN BUTTER

Makes about 1/2 cup (125 g)

1/2 cup (125 g) unsalted butter, softened

2 tsp capers, chopped

2–3 anchovy fillets, chopped

1 garlic clove, chopped

1 tsp lemon juice

2 sun-dried tomatoes, chopped

Salt

Freshly ground black pepper

Blend together the butter, capers, anchovies, garlic, lemon juice, tomatoes, and salt and pepper to taste. Let stand, covered, in a cool place for 1 hour to allow the flavors to develop. Chill to firm before serving with veal, chicken, or seafood.

Paprika butter

Nutmeg butter

Sesame butter

Chive butter

Thyme butter

239

SAUCES, PRESERVES, & CONDIMENTS

SOY SAUCE

Salted and fermented soybeans were among the very first Chinese condiments. A thin liquid known as *jiang* was in use 2,000 years ago, and this is thought to be the ancestor of Chinese soy sauce. The sauce familiar today was devised in the sixth century. It is made from fermented soybeans and wheat, which are aged, sometimes for two years, before being strained and bottled.

Soy sauce was first used to preserve food for the winter months, though it is now a common seasoning and flavoring in kitchens from East to West. There are light and dark versions, each with their own uses—much like red and white wines—though traditional Northern Chinese cooks use only dark soy sauce, while the Japanese, who developed their own style of soy sauce, use light sauce.

Soybeans

Light soy sauce

Dark soy sauce

The procedure for making soy sauce combines roasted soybeans and a lightly ground grain, usually wheat, with a special mold starter. After the culture has been growing for several days, yeast and brine are added, along with a bacterial starter, much like the ones used to make yogurt. The resulting mash is left to age, which can take as long as two years. The sauce is then strained and bottled.

Chinese Soy Sauce Soy sauce is used in China much the way salt is used in the West. It seasons all kinds of Chinese dishes, from soups and dipping sauces to stir-fries and stews. The Chinese produce both a light and dark soy sauce. The latter is aged much longer, and it is also mixed with molasses. The resulting sauce therefore has a much stronger flavor and a deeper, caramel color.

Each type of soy sauce has its own place in Chinese cooking. Dark soy is used to flavor and color heartier dishes such as red-braised chicken, as well as many beef and pork dishes. Light soy sauce is used with seafood, vegetables, and in soups and dipping sauces.

Mushroom soy is made from dark soy sauce that has been infused with Chinese straw mushrooms; this is rich and full-flavored and can be used whenever dark soy is called for

Mushroom soy sauce

Japanese soy sauce

SOYBEAN SAUCES

Yellow bean sauce, popular in Northern and Western China, is used to flavor Peking noodles and was the traditional condiment for Peking duck. In Szechwan and Hunan cooking, it is often seasoned with chilies. Hoisin sauce, which is much sweeter and spicier, is used in Southern Chinese stir-fry dishes and is delicious as a marinade for meat and poultry, or as a basting sauce. Do not confuse hoisin sauce with Chinese barbecue sauce (see page 244), which is similar in appearance but not in flavor.

Yellow bean sauce

Hoisin sauce

A particularly dark version is made by infusing the soy sauce with straw mushrooms. Known as mushroom soy, this is rich and full-flavored, and can be used whenever a recipe calls for dark soy sauce.

Japanese Soy Sauce The Chinese introduced soy sauce to Japan, and the Japanese then developed their own varieties to suit local cooking methods and styles of cuisine. The fermenting and aging processes are similar, but Japanese soy sauce contains more wheat and is usually matured for no longer than six months. As a result, it is less salty and slightly sweeter.

The Japanese prefer much lighter versions of soy sauce; even their dark sauce would fall at the lighter end of the Chinese scale. In Southern Japan, an especially light sauce is used because the style of cuisine discourages the use of ingredients that obviously alter and "discolor" food.

The Japanese use soy sauce as both table condiment and flavoring. Like the Chinese, the Japanese will use the darker versions in red meat dishes and the lighter versions in clear soups and one-pot meals.

Other Soy Sauces True Japanese tamari sauce is a rich, dark sauce brewed without wheat. It is most commonly served in sushi restaurants and is rarely used in the home. In the West, the term *tamari* has been applied to a variety of Japanese-style soy sauces, available mainly in health-food stores.

Southeast Asia also has many soy sauces that vary from region to region. *Ketjap manis* is a very thick and sweet type of soy sauce

Decorative soy servers *such as these attractive porcelain pouring containers are made for use at the table*

used in Indonesia. *Toyo mansi* is a light-style soy sauce from the Philippines, flavored with a native fruit similar to the lemon.

Soy-Based Condiments These rich, flavorful pastes, made from fermented soybeans, are popular throughout China and Southeast Asia. The best are made with whole beans; ground bean sauces tend to be slightly more salty.

In Szechwan cooking, bean sauces, either plain or fired up with a few chilies, are an integral part of most dishes. Hoisin is a soybean sauce flavored with five-spice mixture (see page 95) and dried chilies. When mixed with sugar and sesame oil it becomes the sauce served with Peking duck.

(see page 95)

COOK'S CHOICE
MASTER SAUCE CHICKEN
Serves 4–6

*1 chicken, weighing about
4 lb (2 kg)
Salt
1¼ cups (300 ml) soy sauce
1¼ cups (300 ml) dry sherry
¾ cup (150 g) sugar
2–3 tbsp honey
1 star anise
1 small piece tangerine peel*

Wash the chicken thoroughly and pat dry. Season the inside lightly with salt. In a large saucepan, combine the soy sauce, sherry, sugar, honey, star anise, and tangerine peel. Bring to a boil, stirring to dissolve the sugar. Add the chicken. When boiling, reduce the heat and poach for 30 minutes, basting often. Turn the chicken and poach 20 minutes more. Remove from the heat; leave the chicken in the pan and allow to stand for 20 minutes; baste occasionally. Serve warm or cold. The sauce can be reused. Simply strain and refrigerate. Bring to a boil before using and adjust seasoning if necessary. The refrigerated sauce will keep for about 10 days.

USING TERIYAKI

Teriyaki glaze is a flavorful topping for barbecued, pan-fried, or baked food. Here, chicken breasts are dipped into teriyaki and broiled. Slice and top with the thickened glaze before serving.

1 For the teriyaki, bring 1¼ cups (300 ml) each of mirin, Japanese soy sauce, and chicken stock to a boil. Cool and pour into a shallow dish. Dip chicken breasts in the teriyaki, coating both sides.

2 In a saucepan, mix 3 tbsp of the teriyaki with 2½ tsp sugar and bring almost to a boil. Stir in 1½ tsp cornstarch dissolved in 2½ tbsp water and the remaining teriyaki. Stir until thick.

3 Cook the chicken. A broiler is best with teriyaki, but the chicken can be baked or panfried. To serve, slice the breasts across the grain and fan out. Spoon the teriyaki glaze over chicken and serve.

FISH SAUCES

The fish sauces that are popular seasonings in South-east Asian cuisine are distant relatives of the salted anchovy sauce of ancient Roman times and the anchovy essence used by many cooks today. Often these sauces are a by-product of fish that are fermented, layered with salt, and then placed in sealed crocks. The liquid that is drawn out of the fish by the salt is separated and strained for fish sauces; sometimes the remaining fish are pounded into a paste that is then used as a seasoning.

Western chefs using fish sauces to flavor stir-fries often add a pinch of sugar; the sweetness is a pleasant foil to the salty pungency of the fish sauce.

The main purpose of fermenting fish in Asian cuisines is to extract the juices for flavorful seasoning sauces. In Vietnam and Thailand, however, the fermented fish are pounded into a pungent seasoning paste that can be used in place of fish sauce in some dishes. A particularly flavorful version is made from ground anchovies mixed with fish sauce. Known as *mam nem xay*, the taste of this sauce has been likened to creamed anchovies.

Oyster Sauce This is a Cantonese specialty, originally made from oysters, salt, and water, although nowadays cornstarch and caramel are added as well. Used as an all-purpose seasoning for meat, fish, vegetables, and noodles, it has a pleasant savory flavor that is not overly fishy.

Fish Sauce Made from fish, usually anchovies or mackerel, fermented in salt, this sauce can be used as a kitchen seasoning or table condiment, much like soy sauce. Thai *nam pla*, Vietnamese *nuoc mam*, and Philippine *patis* are some of the better-known versions sold in the West.

Fine Shrimp Sauce Known as *kapee* in Thailand, this is also made by combining shrimp and salt, but it is left to ferment and dry in the sun, not in crocks. A similar sun-dried sauce is made from squid.

Barbecue Sauce This is made of dried fish and shrimp, chilies, garlic, peanuts, and spices. Use like a curry paste in stir-fries, or spread on meat for barbecuing.

Table condiments
A common ingredient in Asian sauces, stir-fries, and dips, some of the milder fish sauces can be used much as soy sauce is with Chinese food, though the taste will be more pungent.

Fish by-products
include sauces that have a strongly concentrated and pungent flavor; these are widely used in Chinese and Southeast Asian cooking

Fine fish paste   **Oyster sauce**   **Fine shrimp sauce**   **Nam pla**   **Fish sauce**

CHILI SAUCES

South American Indians were making chili pepper sauces well before Columbus arrived, and chilies have remained a very important flavoring in the cuisines of Mexico and the Caribbean. Today there are probably as many recipes as there are cooks, and chili sauces are used to enhance a variety of dishes: from omelets, broiled steaks, and chops to salads, marinades, and casseroles. Once discovered, chili peppers were taken to Europe and the Far East, where pepper sauces became extremely popular. Chinese, Korean, Vietnamese, and Thai cuisines all use hot sauces. Some are served on the side; others are used as an ingredient, resulting in a truly fiery dish.

Hot chili sauces
In the Caribbean, each island has its own style of pepper sauce. Most are made by steeping chilies in vinegar. Some are red from tomatoes, others are yellow from turmeric, but the common denominator is lots of chili-fired heat. Pepper sauces are used in preparations ranging from sautés to marinades, and as a table sauce. Tabasco sauce is a North American condiment made from extremely hot Tabasco peppers and matured for several years in oak barrels. A few drops will be enough to give soups, casseroles, and sauces a strongly piquant flavor.

Small, high-necked bottles are the standard containers for the fiery red chili sauces

These sauces can be green, yellow, or red in color, and many contain minced pepper and onion

Chili-flavored sauces
Salsa is the Mexican word for sauce, but outside Mexico it has come to mean an uncooked tomato-based relish, flavored in varying degrees by onions, cilantro, and chilies; some salsas use the very hot and slightly smoky jalapeño pepper. Salsas can be used as a topping for Mexican-style dishes, such as tacos and tostadas, and are delicious with most bean, rice, egg, and meat dishes. Tex-Mex-inspired barbecue sauces show a Mexican influence in their often high chili content. They are best brushed over charcoal-grilled steaks, ribs, or chicken, before and after cooking.

Saltier and thicker than their Caribbean counterparts, the chili seeds are clearly visible

Asian chili sauces
The Chinese treat chili peppers in much the same way as soybeans (see page 242). They are salted and fermented to produce pungent sauces, which are used in stews, stir-fries, and soups. In China, chili sauces are essential to the flavors of Szechwan and Hunan cuisine. They are also used in Korean cooking. In other parts of Southeast Asia, chilies are bottled fresh, retaining their red color, and are used as a table sauce or mixed with other ingredients such as peanuts, dried fish, and soy sauce to make sambals (see page 69) or satay sauce (see page 249).

TABLE SAUCES AND DRESSINGS

Many familiar table sauces in the West had their origins in the East. Recipes for ketchup and Worcestershire sauce, for example, were brought back to England by officers in the Eastern colonial service. The recipes for these sweet-and-spicy sauces were adapted to the English palate. They became popular in Britain, before spreading to tables in North America and, eventually, continental Europe. Native Western seasoning sauces, on the other hand, are largely French or Italian in origin. Oil and vinegar dressings have long been used to flavor salads, vegetables, and grilled or broiled meats. Emulsified sauces, such as mayonnaise, are comparatively new, developed in French court kitchens in the seventeenth century. Today, there is a wide variety of dressings and sauces, all based on traditional recipes, but with myriad innovative flavorings designed to suit the modern palate.

SWEET FOR SAVORY

Roast meats are often served with sweet sauces, placed on the table for diners to help themselves. The most popular combinations are applesauce with roast pork or duck, cranberry sauce with turkey, and lamb with mint jelly or a more piquant mint and vinegar sauce.

Applesauce

Mint sauce

Cranberry sauce

Worcestershire sauce
Originally an Indian recipe, this is now made from vinegar, molasses, anchovies, shallots, sugar, tamarind, and spices. This unique condiment—the nature and exact proportions of the ingredients remain the manufacturer's secret—can be used to add piquancy to sauces and savory dishes. Central to the effect of some cocktails, it makes a welcome addition to gravies, dressings, dips, and soups.

HP Sauce
This is a brown, spicy sauce based on vinegar, molasses, fruit, and spices. Served with red meats, its sharp taste makes an excellent contrasting accompaniment. Added to ground meats before cooking or poured on after broiling it helps to counteract blandness. Both hot and cold dishes, like soups, stews, and other sauces, will benefit from a teaspoonful or two.

Ketchup
Usually made of tomatoes or mushrooms, old English recipes refer to elderberry, oyster, anchovy, and walnut ketchup. Its name is thought to derive from the Malay word, ketjap, which is a soy-based condiment. Most often used as accompaniment to a variety of foods, including broiled meats and fried potatoes, it is often called for as an ingredient in relishes, sauces, dressings, soups, and stews.

A.1. Sauce
Another brown, sweet-spicy sauce, this is flavored with oranges, garlic, onions, and other herbs and spices. It is generally served with steaks, broiled chops, and hamburgers. It can also be added to hamburgers, meat loaves and meatballs for extra spiciness before cooking. In a pinch, it can be used as a marinade for chicken and beef.

Vinaigrette *is a versatile sauce that can be used as a dip, dressing, or marinade*

Blue cheese dressing *can be served with salads, baked potatoes, or hamburgers topped with bacon*

Thousand Island dressing *is flavored with ketchup, chili sauce, green pepper, pimiento, and chives*

Mayonnaise *can be used to accompany many dishes, both hot and cold*

Tartar sauce *is made from mayonnaise with chopped gherkins, shallots, capers, parsley, and tarragon*

FLAVORING MAYONNAISE

Mayonnaise has a pleasant, smooth texture and rich, neutral taste that lends itself well to many seasoning ingredients. Serve flavored mayonnaise in place of plain or use to create an assortment of simple and delicious canapés. Flavorings include pesto, horseradish, chutney, anchovy paste, pureed raspberries, *harissa*, curry paste, whole-grain mustard, chopped sun-dried tomatoes, *tapenade*, spices, fresh herbs, and citrus zest.

Tomato mayonnaise

Dill mayonnaise

Watercress mayonnaise

Curry mayonnaise

Salads can be simple or elaborate, side dish or meal, but whatever their role, they all need some form of seasoning. The simplest dressing is a vinaigrette. This need only contain wine vinegar, salt, and oil, although Dijon mustard is often added for flavor and a thicker consistency. Chopped shallots, garlic, fresh herbs, and soy sauce are other possible additions. Aside from heightening the flavor of salads, vinaigrette is a ready-made marinade that is ideal for chicken. Another oil-based dressing is mayonnaise, which gets its thickness from egg yolks combined with skillful whisking in of oil. The simplest way to alter the taste of these dressings is to use different oils. Olive oil is distinctive, although it is often too overpowering for some palates and it needs to be used with a neutral oil, such as sunflower. Walnut, hazelnut, and sesame oils are also delicious additions, but these too must be paired with milder oils. Flavored vinegars (see page 232) can also be used to great effect.

Once prepared, these dressings will enliven and enrich many dishes. Vegetable, meat, and seafood salads, crudité platters, and even poached fish, are delicious with a vinaigrette. The addition of crumbled Roquefort cheese makes a robust dressing for robust leaves, such as romaine or chicory. Mayonnaise with garlic is *aïoli*, also delicious with crudités or cold, poached salt cod.

247

HERB AND SPICE SAUCES

Sauces have partnered all manner of foods since Roman times. The word *sauce* is derived from the Latin *salsus*, meaning salty, and indeed, the most distinctive feature of Roman sauces was their extreme saltiness. The empire crumbled, but palates evolved, and much of the Medieval period was marked by a taste for highly spiced sauces. This was as much necessity as fashion, for the role of a sauce was often to mask the unpleasant taste of ingredients past their prime. The seventeenth and eighteenth centuries were the golden age of sauces in France. Refined and aromatic sauces, such as white sauce and hollandaise, were created for the French court and they remain present-day favorites. But the use of herbs and spices to enhance sauces is not unique to France. Italy has innumerable pasta sauces, India has many exotically-spiced chutneys, Britain has tangy mint sauce, and from the Americas comes a wide range of fiery-hot salsas. Today's cook will find the repertoire of classic sauces enriched by tantalizing flavor combinations from around the world.

COOK'S CHOICE
BÉARNAISE SAUCE

Makes about 1¹/₂ cups (300 ml)

1 cup (250 ml) white-wine vinegar
4 shallots, finely chopped
2 tbsp chopped fresh tarragon
1 tbsp chopped fresh flat-leaf parsley
4 egg yolks
1 cup (250 g) unsalted butter, chilled and cut into small pieces

In a saucepan, combine the vinegar, shallots, tarragon, and parsley. Cook over medium heat until reduced to about 3 tbsp. Strain and return the liquid to the pan. Whisk in the egg yolks and place the pan in a larger pan of warm water set over gentle heat. Stirring the mixture with a wooden spoon, add the butter, a few pieces at a time, stirring constantly in the same direction. When blended, remove the sauce from the heat, pour into a sauceboat, and serve with hearty foods such as broiled steak, lamb, and salmon.

Béarnaise sauce *is ideal with broiled meats*

COOK'S CHOICE
RAVIGOTE SAUCE

Makes about 1 cup (250 ml)

¹/₄ cup (60 ml) wine vinegar or lemon juice
Salt
1 tbsp Dijon mustard
³/₄ cup (175 ml) extra-virgin olive oil
Freshly ground black pepper
1 tbsp capers, chopped
1 small shallot, chopped
3 tbsp chopped mixed herbs: tarragon, parsley, chervil, and chives

In a bowl, whisk together the vinegar or lemon juice and salt to taste until dissolved. Whisk in the mustard. Continue whisking and slowly pour in the oil. Add pepper to taste. Stir in the capers, shallot, and herbs until well blended. Serve with boiled artichokes or cold meat.

Cilantro *is a versatile sauce ingredient*

Ravigote sauce *is traditionally served with cold meat*

Basil *pounded with garlic, pine nuts, Parmesan cheese, and olive oil produces the classic pesto sauce*

There are classic combinations of sauce with the finished dish: juniper is the traditional spice with game, tarragon flavors *béarnaise* sauce for broiled steaks, and saffron imparts both vivid color and fine flavor to sauces for seafood. However, there is no need to adhere rigidly to established marriages of flavor. A cream sauce infused with ginger-root, cardamom, and cilantro can be a delicious partner for poached white fish. Likewise, a tomato sauce infused with bay, thyme, and oregano is typically Mediterranean—until pepper, cloves, cinnamon, and a dash of chocolate are added, as is often done in the *mole* sauces of Mexico.

To maximize flavor and appearance, freshly chopped herbs are best added toward the end of cooking; to infuse long-cooking sauces, use aromatic herb bundles (see page 55). Spices add exotic pungency to sauces; always buy whole and grind as needed. Thoughtful use of herbs and spices will often lift a sauce above the average. A grating of nutmeg is the finishing touch for an onion sauce *par excellence*, while milk that has been infused with parsley, bay leaf, and thyme yields a superior *béchamel* sauce. Experiment with unknown seasonings and unconventional blends. For the imaginative cook, the possibilities are limitless.

COOK'S CHOICE
SPICED YOGURT SAUCE

Makes about ²/₃ cup (150 ml)

1 tbsp peanut oil
1 tsp ground cumin
3 cardamom pods, seeds only
¹/₂ tsp paprika
Pinch of ground turmeric
²/₃ cup (150 ml) yogurt
1 tsp lemon juice
2 tbsp chopped fresh cilantro leaves
1 tsp fresh grated gingerroot
Salt
Freshly ground white pepper

In a heavy skillet, combine the oil, cumin, cardamom, paprika, and turmeric and cook for 1 minute. Remove from the heat and stir in the yogurt, lemon juice, cilantro, and gingerroot. Season to taste with salt and pepper. The sauce can be served hot with steamed vegetables or cold with hard-boiled eggs. It is ideal for neutral foods, such as white-fleshed fish.

Cardamom *lends its exotic taste to many Indian and Middle Eastern sauces such as the recipe above*

Spiced yogurt sauce *can be served hot or cold*

Satay sauce *can be used for dipping or with broiled meats*

DEGLAZING
The term *deglaze* comes from the French *déglacer,* to dissolve into liquid. It refers to the action of scraping cooked-on bits from the bottom of pans as they are dissolved by the added liquid. Water is often used, though wine, stock, and vinegar offer more depth of flavor. Deglazing works best with panfried meats. When the meat is cooked, remove it from the pan and keep it warm. Immediately add the liquid, raise the heat, and scrape the bottom of the pan until it is clean. Boil just long enough to reduce slightly (or to cook off some of the alcohol from wine or acidity from vinegar). If any burning occurred, do not deglaze the pan or the sauce will be bitter. For more flavor, add sautéed shallots or fresh herbs just before serving.

COOK'S CHOICE
SATAY SAUCE

Makes about 1³/₄ cups (450 ml)

³/₄ cup (100 g) roasted, unsalted peanuts
2 tbsp peanut oil
1 onion, finely chopped
1 garlic clove, finely chopped
1¹/₂ tbsp ground coriander or fennel seed
¹/₃ tsp ground turmeric
1 tsp ground cumin
1³/₄ cups (350 ml) coconut milk
2 tbsp chili sauce
2 tsp brown sugar
2 tbsp lemon juice
Salt

Roughly grind the peanuts with a mortar and pestle. Heat the oil in a pan, add the onion, and cook for 1–2 minutes. Stir in the garlic and spices and cook until aromatic. Add the peanuts, coconut milk, chili sauce, and sugar. Stir and simmer for 2–3 minutes. Stir in the lemon juice and salt to taste. Serve with broiled beef or chicken kabobs.

FRUIT AND VEGETABLE SAUCES

When one thinks of a sauce, it is usually a stock- or cream-based sauce. However, many delicious sauces can also be based on fruit and vegetables. The addition of a few spoonfuls of vegetable puree will give a sauce extra color, texture, and flavor. Likewise, many fruit sauces are based on fruit purees (see page 202) or flavored with juice. For savory dishes their sweetness is balanced with acidity, usually by adding a dash of vinegar or a squeeze of lemon. Vegetable purees need only be diluted with cream, wine, or stock, and perhaps enriched with a pat of butter, for a deliciously simple and fresh-tasting sauce.

COOK'S CHOICE
SAVORY APPLE SAUCE

Makes about 1½ cups (300 ml)

3 apples, peeled, cored, and sliced
2 tbsp ground almonds
1 onion, chopped
Grated zest of 1 orange
1 slice white bread, toasted and crumbled
½ tsp ground quatre-épices (see page 75)
3 tbsp white wine
3 tbsp white-wine vinegar

In a saucepan combine the apples, almonds, onion, orange zest, and bread. Add the *quatre-épices*, and moisten with the wine and vinegar. Bring to a boil and cook until the apples are soft, about 15 minutes. Pass through a sieve and serve hot. This is a traditional accompaniment to roast pork and potato pancakes and is also good with poultry.

Apple sauce *is delicious served with roast pork or potato pancakes*

Plum sauce *makes a good partner for roast duck*

Cranberries and oranges *are delicious in fruit sauces to be served with poultry*

Maltaise sauce *can enliven poached fish or asparagus*

COOK'S CHOICE
CHINESE-STYLE PLUM SAUCE

Makes about 2½ cups (600 ml)

1 large cooking apple
½ lb (250 g) red plums, halved
½ lb (250 g) apricots
½ cup (125 ml) white-wine vinegar
¾ cup (150 g) superfine sugar or more to taste
1 dried red chili, chopped
1–2 star anise
Soy sauce

Peel, core, and dice the apple. Place in a pan, add 4 tbsp water, cover, and cook until the apple is soft. Add the plums, apricots, vinegar, sugar, chili, and star anise. Cover and simmer for 45–50 minutes. Sieve to remove the pits and star anise. If the sauce is very thick, add a little water. If it is too tart, add more sugar. Add soy sauce to taste. Serve hot or cold or use as a basting sauce.

Tomatoes and mush-rooms *lend themselves well to slow-simmered sauces*

250

When preparing a sauce, consider its color as well as its flavor. For instance, pair a rich red tomato sauce with spinach gnocchi or a pale green avocado and sour cream sauce with delicate pink salmon. A sorrel puree can be stirred into a *béchamel* sauce served with veal, whisked into a hollandaise to accompany salmon, or thinned with cream and poured over poached eggs.

The sweet-sour flavor of fruit sauces makes them excellent partners for both game and rich meats such as duck, goose, and pork. Cherries make superb savory fruit sauces, as do apricots, rhubarb, and quinces.

Citrus fruits are most useful in sauces. Just a squeeze of blood orange juice added to hollandaise transforms it into maltaise sauce, delicious with asparagus. It can also be added to fresh tomato sauce, served with fish, for extra tang. Berries can also be used to great effect in cookery sauces. Cranberries with turkey is an American classic, and in Britain gooseberry sauce is often paired with baked mackerel.

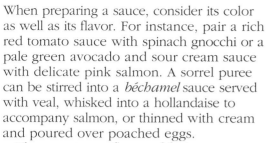

Sweet corn sauce *is an unusual partner for roast meats*

COOK'S CHOICE
SWEET CORN SAUCE

Makes about 2¹/₂ cups (600 ml)

12 oz (350 g) sweet corn kernels
1¹/₄ cups (350 ml) milk
²/₃ cup (150 ml) sour cream
1 tsp paprika
Salt
Freshly ground white pepper

In a food processor, combine the corn, milk, sour cream, paprika, and salt and pepper to taste and puree. Transfer to a saucepan and cook, stirring constantly, over low heat for 5 minutes. Taste for seasoning. Serve with roasted meat.

COOK'S CHOICE
MALTAISE SAUCE

Makes about 2¹/₂ cups (600 ml)

6 egg yolks
1 tbsp lemon juice
Salt
Freshly ground black pepper
2 cups (500 g) unsalted butter, chilled and cut into small pieces
Juice of 1 blood orange, strained

In a heatproof bowl set over a pan of simmering water, whisk together the egg yolks, lemon juice, and a pinch each of salt and pepper. When blended, whisk in the butter, a few pieces at a time, until thick and glossy. Whisk in the orange juice and serve immediately, with poached fish or asparagus.

Broccoli and anchovy sauce *goes well with pasta*

Roasted red pepper sauce *can be used as a dip*

COOK'S CHOICE
BROCCOLI AND ANCHOVY SAUCE

Makes about 1¹/₄ cups (300 ml)

Salt
12 oz (350 g) broccoli florets
5 tbsp extra-virgin olive oil
6 anchovy fillets, chopped
1 garlic clove, finely chopped
1 tbsp unsalted butter
Freshly ground black pepper

Bring 9 cups (2 liters) of water to a boil. Add salt and the broccoli, cover, and cook until tender, 7–8 minutes. Drain. In a skillet, combine the oil, anchovies, and garlic over medium heat, crushing with a wooden spoon until the anchovies are thoroughly mashed. Add the broccoli florets, butter, and pepper to taste. Cook to warm through, about 5 minutes. Taste for seasoning. Serve immediately with hot pasta and freshly grated Parmesan cheese and black pepper.

COOK'S CHOICE
ROASTED RED PEPPER SAUCE

Makes about ²/₃ cup (150 ml)

2 red peppers, roasted (see page 69)
3–4 garlic cloves, peeled
2 oz (60 g) white bread, crusts removed
4–6 tbsp extra-virgin olive oil
1 tbsp lemon juice
1 tsp crushed chilies, optional
Salt
Freshly ground black pepper

In a food processor, combine the red peppers and garlic and process until smooth. Place the bread in a shallow bowl. Add just enough warm water to moisten, then squeeze out the excess. Add to the pepper mixture and process again. Transfer to a bowl and stir in the oil and lemon juice, and chilies if using. Season to taste. Serve with fish, or as a dip for crudités.

PICKLES

The preservative qualities of vinegar and salt are essential to pickles. In the past, all kinds of food were pickled to extend them beyond their seasons. Corned beef is one example of a nonvegetable pickle that is still popular, though today pickled foods are eaten more for pleasure than out of necessity. Pickles can be condiment, sauce, or salad and they have been popular throughout the ages and in many countries.

Piccalilli was introduced to England in 1664 under the title "To pickle lila, an Indian pickle," and it is served with cold cuts. Peppers and artichokes pickled in vinegar are both an integral part of the Italian antipasto platter, and tart *cornichons* are traditionally served with French pâtés. In Korea, pickled cabbage, or *kimchi*, is served as a snack, appetizer, and table condiment, and vinegared salads are a popular Japanese first course.

SALTING

Some vegetables are "watery" and must be brined or salted to draw out the water before pickling. This not only ensures better flavor, but prevents the vinegar from being diluted, which inhibits its preservative qualities. For brining vegetables such as cabbage or onions, allow $^1/_3$ cup (60 g) coarse salt for every $2^1/_2$ cups (600 ml) water. For salting vegetables such as cucumbers and tomatoes, allow $^1/_2$ cup (100 g) coarse salt for every $1^1/_2$ lb (750 g) of vegetables. For both methods, leave for 24 hours and rinse thoroughly before proceeding.

Pickled spiced pears

COOK'S CHOICE
PICKLED ONIONS

Makes about 2 lb (1 kg)

2 lb (1 kg) pickling onions
10–12 tbsp coarse salt
4$^1/_2$ cups (1 liter) spiced vinegar (see page 232)

Peel the onions and place in a bowl. Dissolve the salt in $4^1/_2$–$6^3/_4$ cups (1–$1^1/_2$ liters) water and pour over the onions. Leave overnight, then drain and rinse. Pat dry and pack into sterilized jars, using a wooden spoon to ensure that there are no large spaces. Fill with cold vinegar; seal with vinegar-proof lids. Keep for 3–4 weeks before using.

Pickled onion

COOK'S CHOICE
PICCALILLI

Makes about 3 lb (1.5 kg)

3 lb (1.5 kg) diced mixed vegetables: cauliflower, pearl onions, carrots, beans, red and green peppers, and celery
1$^1/_4$ cups (250 g) coarse salt
2 tbsp dry mustard
1 tbsp ground turmeric
1 tbsp ground ginger
4$^1/_2$ cups (1 liter) distilled vinegar
2$^1/_3$ cups (275 g) sugar
2 tbsp cornstarch

In a bowl, toss all the vegetables with the salt and let stand overnight. Drain, rinse thoroughly under cold water, and drain again. In a saucepan, combine the mustard, turmeric, and ginger with a little of the vinegar and blend to a paste. Stir in the remaining vinegar and the sugar. Bring to a boil, stirring until the sugar dissolves. Add the vegetables, cover, and simmer until just tender, 15–20 minutes. Using a slotted spoon, transfer the vegetables to warm sterilized jars, filling them to within $^1/_2$ in (1 cm) of the rim. Dissolve the cornstarch in a little more vinegar and add to the sauce in the pan. Cook over low heat, stirring continuously until thick, then pour over the vegetables. Seal with a vinegar-proof lid and store in a cool place for at least 1 month before serving.

Piccalilli

Almost any kind of fruit or vegetable can be pickled, but they must be as fresh as possible and in good condition. Never use overripe fruit or tired vegetables, although pickling is often a good way to use up ill-formed or less attractive fruit and vegetables.

The most popular pickles are made with onions, beets, red cabbage, walnuts, and cucumber, but carrots, button mushrooms, artichoke hearts, cauliflower, and peppers, and fruits such as melons, peaches, and pears are also well-suited to pickling. Beets are the only problematic vegetable because their color bleeds.

Malt vinegar is the most commonly used type of vinegar, but cider and wine vinegars are recommended for delicately flavored pickles, with little or no added spice. White or colorless vinegar shows off the pickles to better advantage than brown malt vinegar. Whatever the vinegar, it should have an acetic acid level of at least 5 percent to ensure the preservative properties. Spiced vinegars impart the best flavor to pickles. These are available commercially, although they are easy to make at home (see page 232). Alternatively, vinegar court bouillon is even easier. To a saucepan of vinegar, add any or all of the following ingredients: ginger, cinnamon, cloves, allspice, black peppercorns, garlic, mace, and bay leaf. Bring just to a boil, then remove from the heat and

infuse for at least 30 minutes. Use hot or cold; cold vinegar is good for keeping brined vegetable pickles crisp and crunchy.

Sweet pickles are made with a spiced sugar and vinegar syrup: allow 2½ cups (500 g) sugar to 2 cups (500 ml) vinegar then steep the spices in this mixture. Sometimes spirits, such as brandy or rum, are substituted for the vinegar.

Most recipes call for salt, and it is important to use coarse or kosher salt rather than table salt. The latter is treated with anticaking additives to keep it flowing freely, but these can affect the pickling vinegar adversely, reducing its preservative qualities.

Before adding the pickle, sterilize jars by filling with hot water. The jars must also have lids with plastic-coated linings, which prevent corrosion that can lead to rust and contamination. The fittings for clamp-top jars should be sterilized in boiling water before filling. Be sure that the lids are airtight, or the vinegar will evaporate and expose the ingredients to the air and all its harmful bacteria.

Vegetable pickles are ready to eat in about 2–3 months; fruit pickles require a bit more time. Pickles can be kept for as long as 1 year, but after that time raw vegetable pickles loose their crispness. Pickled red cabbage is the exception; it should be eaten within one month.

FRUIT IN ALCOHOL
Like vinegar, alcohol prohibits the growth of microorganisms. It is best suited to fresh or dried fruit, such as cherries, prunes, berries, or plums. In general, combine 1 cup (250 g) sugar with 1 lb (500 g) fruit. Place in clean jars and add alcohol to cover: rum, brandy, kirsch, vodka, or any flavor liqueur. Spices such as vanilla, cloves, cinnamon, star anise, or ginger are all welcome additions. Use after 3–4 weeks.

COOK'S CHOICE
PICKLED SPICED PEARS
Makes about 4 lb (2 kg)

4 lb (2 kg) firm pears
½ lemon
1 in (2.5 cm) piece fresh gingerroot, peeled
3–4 cloves
1 cinnamon stick
2½ cups (600 ml) white-wine vinegar
3 cups (600 g) sugar

Peel, halve, and core pears. Place in a pan of water, add the juice of the lemon, and simmer gently until tender, about 1 hour. Place the gingerroot, cloves, cinnamon, vinegar, and sugar in a preserving pan large enough to hold all the pears. Cook over low heat, stirring constantly, until the sugar dissolves. Bring to a boil and simmer for 5 minutes. Add the pears and simmer until tender, 15–20 minutes longer. Pack the pears carefully into preheated jars. Boil the syrup for about 5 minutes to thicken and pour over the pears, making sure they are well covered. Seal the jars. Use after 1 month.

LAYERING VEGETABLES

Decorative pickles can be obtained by layering very lightly cooked vegetables in a clear pickling liquid. These jars are attractive on open kitchen shelves or counters but they will not last quite as long as those that are kept in a cool, cabinet, away from light.

1 Prepare an assortment of different-colored vegetables: cauliflower, green beans, carrots, broccoli, red peppers, pickling onions, and mushrooms are all suitable. Blanch each vegetable separately in salted water. Then drain and slice as desired.

2 Layer the vegetables in sterilized clamp-top jars. In a saucepan, combine equal amounts of white-wine vinegar and extra-virgin olive oil and bring to a boil. When cool, pour over the vegetables. Tuck in a bay leaf for extra flavor.

CHUTNEYS AND RELISHES

Popular sweet-and-sour condiments, chutneys are highly spiced preserves, often with the consistency of jam, while relishes are slightly crisper. Chutneys are made by stewing fruit and vegetables in a vinegar, sugar, and spice sauce. The long cooking concentrates the flavors and softens the textures, resulting in a condiment that is much darker and often more richly flavored than crisp, fresh-tasting relishes. Chutneys originated in India, where their Hindu name, *chatni*, means "strongly spiced." They

have been a familiar item in the West since the nineteenth century, when they were introduced by returning British colonials. The palate-reviving sweetish flavor of chutneys and relishes makes them the perfect partner for fiery foods, such as curries, and more neutral foods, such as cold meats. Modern chefs have revived interest in these condiments, creating innovative recipes and serving them with a variety of foods: rich duck, delicate fish, and even robust deep-fried camembert or brie.

Limes, mangoes, and apples are the traditional fruits for chutneys, although cherries, gooseberries, cranberries, plums, and all the citrus fruits can be turned into delicious chutneys as well.

Dried fruit and nuts are welcome additions because they add an extra layer of both flavor and texture. Golden and dark raisins are classic, and they offer a pleasant contrast to light-colored fruits such as peaches and oranges. Less run-of-the-mill options include dried figs, dried bananas, and dried cherries. Dates add sweetness to tart fruits such as gooseberries and pineapples or to chutney mixtures that combine such improbable partners as pumpkins and onions. Dried apricots can even be used on their own for an intensely flavored chutney.

Crisp, crunchy vegetables are the ideal candidates for relishes. Corn is also good; the texture is pleasing and the taste falls

USING SWEET CORN
If corn kernels are scraped, the milky liquid will cloud the relish. For a clear preserve, carefully separate the kernels from the core of the cob, row by row, with the tip of a small sharp knife.

somewhere between sweet and savory depending on how the mixture is blended. And while fresh corn has a limited season, it is an abundant crop, and relishes provide a flavorful medium for preserving it for year-round enjoyment.

Warm aromatic spices—cinnamon, ginger, cardamom, cloves, and allspice—are best for flavoring chutneys. Brown and white mustard seeds are good for relishes, and dry mustard can be used when conspicuous specks are unwanted. Pickling spice (see page 75) is also appropriate.

Stainless steel or unchipped enamel saucepans are recommended. It is best to avoid iron, brass, and copper as they react negatively to the acidity of vinegar mixtures and can impart a bitter taste to the food. Likewise, stir with a wooden spoon. For storage, use sterilized jars and choose plastic-lined, vinegar-proof lids.

SEALING WITH WAX

All homemade preserves will have better keeping properties if they are sealed with a layer of paraffin wax. This method is especially good for chutneys and relishes, which tend to shrink over time.

1 Choose unscented, colorless candles or a block of paraffin wax. Break into small pieces and place in a can. Bring a pan of water to a boil, place the can in the water, and lower the heat.

2 When the wax is melted, pour it carefully into jars that have been filled to within 1/4 in (5 mm) of the rim and fitted with a circle of waxed paper. Hold the hot can with a towel or pair of tongs.

3 When cool, cover with a square of plastic wrap or cloth to protect from dust. To remove the wax, insert the tip of a knife just under the wax to break the seal. The waxed paper will come away too.

COOK'S CHOICE
CORN RELISH

Makes about 3 lb (1.5 kg)

9 corn cobs
1 green pepper, finely chopped
1 red pepper, finely chopped
2 large onions, finely chopped
1¹/₂ cups (300 g) light brown sugar
2 tbsp coarse salt
1¹/₂ tbsp dry mustard
4¹/₂ cups (1 liter) cider vinegar

Scrape the kernels from the corn cobs (see page 254). In a large, stainless steel saucepan, combine all the ingredients and bring to a boil. Reduce the heat and simmer gently until soft, 15–20 minutes. Transfer to sterilized jars with vinegar-proof seals. Keep in a cool, dark place.

COOK'S CHOICE
DATE AND ORANGE CHUTNEY

Makes about 4 lb (2 kg)

1 lb (500 g) untreated oranges
3¹/₂ cups (750 g) sugar
7 tbsp golden syrup
2 tbsp coarse salt
¹/₄ tsp crushed dried chilies
6 ³/₄ cups (1¹/₂ liters) malt vinegar
1 lb (500 g) onions, chopped
1 lb (500 g) dates, stoned and chopped
1 lb (500 g) raisins

Grate the orange zest and set aside. Remove the pith from the oranges (see page 175) and discard the seeds. Finely chop the orange flesh. In a large, stainless steel saucepan, combine the sugar, syrup, salt, chilies, and vinegar. Bring to a boil over high heat, stirring to dissolve the sugar. Add the oranges, onions, dates, raisins, and half the grated zest. Reduce the heat and simmer until thick, about 1 hour. Stir in the remaining orange zest. Spoon into warm, sterilized jars. Leave to cool, then seal. Store in a cool, dark place.

Corn relish

Date and orange chutney

Crisp vegetable relish

Green tomato and apple chutney

COOK'S CHOICE
CRISP VEGETABLE RELISH

Makes about 10 lb (5 kg)

1 white cabbage, shredded
4 carrots, grated
6 onions, thinly sliced
1 red pepper, thinly sliced
1 green pepper, thinly sliced
1 tbsp coarse salt
4¹/₂ cups (1 liter) malt vinegar
1 tbsp mustard seeds
3¹/₄ cups (750 g) sugar

Place the cabbage, carrots, onions, and peppers in a plastic colander. Add the salt and toss to blend. Leave overnight to drain. In a bowl, combine the vinegar, mustard seeds, and sugar and stir to dissolve. Put the vegetables into sterilized jars or a bowl and add the vinegar mixture to cover. Leave 1 week before using. Seal, or cover with plastic wrap. In the bowl, this will keep for 2–3 months, refrigerated, if the vegetables are always covered with the vinegar.

COOK'S CHOICE
GREEN TOMATO AND APPLE CHUTNEY

Makes about 8 lb (4 kg)

2 lb (1 kg) green tomatoes, chopped
2 lb (1 kg) tart apples, peeled and chopped
¹/₂ lb (250 g) onions, chopped
1 lb (500 g) raisin
3³/₄ cups (750 g) light brown sugar
2 tsp ground ginger
2 tsp black peppercorns, crushed
2 tsp quatre-épices (page 75)
2 tbsp coarse salt
2 garlic cloves
3 cups (700 ml) wine vinegar

Combine all the ingredients, except the vinegar, in a stainless-steel saucepan. Add 6 tbsp of the vinegar and cook over low heat, adding the remaining vinegar gradually as the mixture boils. Stir as the mixture thickens about 45 minutes. When thick, transfer to sterilized jars. Seal when cool. Store in a cool, dark place.

SWEET PRESERVES

The perennial favorite for spreading on breakfast toast, sweet preserves have lost some of their original purpose. What was once a necessity—preserving the bounty of spring and summer fruit for enjoyment all winter long—is now purely a pleasure, and neatly stacked rows of colorful jams and jellies are as much a feature of modern-day supermarkets as they were of old-fashioned pantries. Although commercial preserves are widely available, and of good quality, there is nothing quite so satisfying as making them at home, not to mention the superior flavor. Most fruits are suitable for preserving. They can be used alone for traditional jams, such as strawberry or apricot, or they can be combined for something more unusual: grape and pear, rhubarb and fig, or apple, cranberry, and quince. Elderflowers add a touch of muscatlike flavor, nuts such as walnuts or almonds can be included for flavor and texture, and sophistication can be added with a dash of brandy or even an orange-flavored liqueur. Herbs and spices are also a welcome addition. Try vanilla with pears, mint and sage with gooseberries, or plums with basil; sweet preserves made with herbs sometimes border on the relish side and are best served with savory dishes. If made and sealed properly, most home-made preserves keep for well over 1 year in a cool, dark, dry place; but it is best not to keep them too long—the flavor fades and the quality deteriorates. Whether made at home or store bought, sweet preserves fulfill a useful and delicious purpose in the kitchen.

Strawberry jam
One of the most popular preserves, this is a classic for spreading on breakfast toast or hot muffins.

Tropical fruit conserve
Made with pineapple and coconut, this tropical flavor combination is ideal for a festive breakfast or brunch.

Orange cheese
Fragrant with oranges, this thick preserve can be spread on toast; it can also be molded and served on its own.

Lemon curd
The tart flavor of lemon is tamed for this preserve, which can be piped into prebaked tart shells, or spread between layers of sponge cake.

Mint jelly
The classic accompaniment to roast lamb, this can also be used with other savory dishes such as broiled meats or kabobs.

Tomato jam
The flesh and flavor of tomatoes lend themselves well to preserve making, resulting in an unusual condiment for cold meats.

Apple

Apricots

Fruits for Preserves

There is no such thing as a fruit that cannot be preserved. However, whether or not the preserve gels depends on the levels of pectin, acid, and sugar present. Some fruits—tart cooking apples, red and black currants, gooseberries, quince, cranberries, and citrus fruit—are high in both pectin and acid and, with sugar added, produce firmly set jellies. Pectin levels are highest when fruit is barely ripe; overly ripe fruit may result in a more loosely gelled preserve. Jams and preserves can be made quite successfully with fruits that have a moderately high pectin level: apricots and raspberries, for example. Low-pectin fruits—strawberries, cherries, peaches, pears, pineapples, grapes, figs, rhubarb, and melon—require additional pectin in the form of powder or liquid.

Cranberries

Lime

Types of Preserves

All sweet preserves—jams, jellies, conserves, marmalades, fruit butters, cheeses, and curds —have two things in common: fruit and sugar. It is the texture, and sometimes the fruit used, that determine their different names.

Preserves A general term used to describe all the products that follow, this also refers specifically to a product in which whole fruits, such as strawberries or peaches, are briefly cooked in a sugar syrup. The fruit is removed and the syrup is cooked down to concentrate the flavor. When reduced, the fruit is returned to the syrup. This allows for a maximum amount of flavor without over-cooking the fruit. Use as a dessert topping or, if spicy, serve with roast meat or game.

Jam Made from whole berries or larger fruit that has been chopped, jam is usually gelled, but not hard, and has a spreadable consist-ency. Fruit for jam is cooked until tender, sugar is added, and the jam is boiled until it reaches the gelling point. Raspberries, gooseberries, plums, and rhubarb are some of the fruits that are ideal for jam making.

Conserves A type of jam, a conserve is a fruit, usually whole or sliced, preserved in syrup. In Victorian and Edwardian England, they were very fashionable, and were eaten with a spoon as a dessert. Nowadays, con-serves sometimes contain dried fruit, nuts, or citrus peel along with the fruit. They are generally richer and sweeter than conven-tional jams, and much more syrupy.

Jelly Made from strained, sparklingly clear fruit juice, jelly should be firmly gelled. Jellies require a bit more preparation than other preserves. The pureed fruit must be placed in

---

HERBS FOR FLAVOR
Many preserves are greatly enhanced by the addition of herbs. Mint and lemon balm marry well with most sweet preserves. Basil, sage, thyme, and rosemary can also be used. Apple jelly, with a smooth texture and mild flavor, can be transformed by a bay leaf or even some rose geranium leaves.

Mint

Basil

Rosemary

---

a tightly woven cloth sack, called a jelly bag, and left overnight to allow the fruit juice to drip through. Jellies can be used for spreading or for glazing fruit-topped pastries. They can be flavored with herbs and spices for more unusual condiments, excellent with roast poultry, pork, or game. For example, infuse a puree of apples or quince for jelly with cloves, sage, ginger, or cardamom.

Marmalade The name *marmalade* is derived from a Portuguese quince preserve called *marmelado,* from the word *marmelo,* or quince. The term was originally used in Britain to describe a preserve made with bitter oranges that was popular in the 1700s, and the name stuck. Marmalade is made from citrus fruit that is sliced and simmered in water until tender, then boiled rapidly to the gelling point. Presliced oranges in cans are available to speed up the process.

Fruit Butters and Fruit Cheeses These are the traditional preserves that graced the tea tables of Victorian and Edwardian Britain. Made from single or combined fruit purees that are cooked with butter and sugar, these are very thick spreads, much like soft cheese or butter, hence the names. Creamy fruit butters can be spread over bread or toast, while firm-textured fruit cheeses can be molded and sliced to serve alongside cold meats or poultry.

Fruit Curds In addition to fruit, these contain eggs and butter, making them very rich preserves. However, the presence of dairy products also reduces the storage time; about 3 months in the refrigerator is the maximum. Traditionally made with citrus fruit, they can also be made of passion fruit.

SWEET PRESERVES IN THE KITCHEN

With their large percentage of sugar, jams and jellies can be used as a sweetening agent in some dishes. For example, a spoonful of raspberry or red currant jam stirred into a beef or lamb gravy adds a hint of fruit flavor without the cloying sweetness of pure sugar. Any firmly gelled preserve can be used as a filling for layer cakes or jelly rolls or as a protective layer between an uncooked filling and a precooked tart shell.

Although they are sweet, some fruit and vegetable preserves can be combined with savory preparations. When firmly gelled and mixed with vegetable oil, jellies can be used as a simple, last-minute glaze for broiled meat. Tomato or carrot jam can be served alongside roast meat with stuffing as an unusual condiment. For a pleasant sweet-and-sour flavor and caramelized texture, melted marmalade can be brushed over a ham during roasting.

For jam or fruit curd tartlets, sprinkle the bottom of precooked shells with a small amount of ground almonds, then fill with jam or pipe out rosettes of fruit curd.

Sweet preserves can also be used as a decoration. Fill a paper piping cone (see page 185) with a dark-colored jelly, such as red currant, and pipe lettering, lines, or a feathered pattern (see page 202) on the tops of cakes or pastries that are covered with lightly colored frostings.

GLAZING MEATS
To glaze barbecued meats, mix a small amount of a smooth jelly—red currant, cranberry, or mint—with some vegetable oil. Brush over the meat about 2 minutes before the end of cooking time.

GLAZING TARTS AND FLANS
For a glossy glaze on fruit-topped pastries, brush with jelly that has been warmed slightly to thin it. Other preserves can be used but they should be sieved first for a smooth coating.

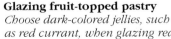

Glazing fruit-topped pastry
Choose dark-colored jellies, such as red currant, when glazing red or purple fruit and light-colored ones, such as apricot, for paler fruit.

MAKING PRESERVES

Fruit, sugar, and pectin, in varying quantities, are the fundamental ingredients of a sweet preserve. The fruit provides the sweetness, balanced by tartness, and the color. Pectin is the gelling agent, and it is found in the skin, pits, and flesh of fruit. For loosely gelled jams, the existing amount of pectin in the fruit will usually suffice. When a firm gel is required, or when pectin levels are low, extra pectin can be added. Pectin works best in the company of an acid, and while most fruits contain enough acid on their own, fresh lemon juice can be added to ensure a firm gel. Sugar is a sweetening and preserving agent; in large quantities, it draws the moisture out of food, thereby inhibiting the growth of microorganisms. The average proportion is $3/4$–1 lb (375–500 g) sugar to every 1 lb (500 g) fruit. This is the advised minimum, but the sugar can be increased to taste. Bear in mind that while some fruit can be very tart, an excess of sugar will result in crystallization. Alternative sweeteners include honey, molasses, treacle, and maple syrup. Obtaining the correct balance of acid, sugar, and pectin will result in successful preserves.

COOK'S CHOICE
ORANGE MARMALADE

Makes about 12 cups (3 kg)

12 small oranges, preferably untreated, organically grown
4 lb (2 kg) sugar
Juice of 1 lemon, strained

Place the oranges in a large heavy-bottomed pan, preferably a preserving pan. Add cold water, allowing about $2^1/2$ cups (600 ml) for every 1 lb (500 g) fruit. Cover and simmer gently until the fruit can be easily pierced with a skewer, about 1 hour. Remove the oranges and reserve the cooking liquid. When cool enough to handle, slice or chop the fruit as desired; remove the seeds and place in a square of cheesecloth. Tie the edges of the square together with kitchen string to form a bag. Add the sugar to the reserved liquid in the pan and cook over low heat, stirring constantly until the sugar is dissolved. Increase the heat and boil for 5 minutes. Add the bag of seeds (for pectin), the oranges, and the lemon juice to the liquid and bring to a boil. Cook until the mixture reaches 221°F (105°C) on a sugar thermometer, or test with a wooden spoon (see right). Remove the bag of seeds and skim the surface to remove any scum. When cool, pour into sterilized jars and seal. Store for up to 1 year in a cool, dark place.

MAKING MARMALADE
The flavor and quality of homemade marmalades ensure that making them is well worth the effort. Experiment with citrus fruit combinations and a wide variety of flavorings: herbs, spices, nuts, honeys, syrups, and liqueurs.

1 Place the fruit and water in a preserving pan and boil until tender enough to pierce with a skewer, about 1 hour. Strain into a colander placed over a large bowl.

2 Slice the fruit and chop coarsely or finely, as desired. Separate the seeds and tie in a square of cheesecloth.

3 To test for a proper gel, begin after 15 minutes of boiling. Dip a wooden spoon into the fruit mixture and remove. When done, drops will form on the edge of the spoon then fall from the spoon in a sheet of drips.

COOK'S CHOICE
LEMON CURD

Makes about 2 cups (500 g)

4 lemons, preferably untreated, organically grown
$1/2$ cup (125 g) unsalted butter, cut into cubes
$1^1/4$ cups (250 g) superfine sugar
4 eggs

Grate the zest of each lemon and squeeze the juice into a heatproof bowl. Add the butter and set the bowl over a pan of simmering water. Stir in the sugar gradually, stirring until the butter melts and the sugar dissolves. Place the eggs in a large sauce-pan and beat. Strain the sugar mixture into the pan with the eggs. Cook over low heat, stirring constantly; do not boil. Remove from the heat when the mixture is thick enough to coat the back of a spoon. When cool, pour into sterilized jars and seal.

Lemon slices

COFFEE,
TEA, &
SPICED DRINKS

COFFEE

Coffee originated around the Red Sea, most probably in Ethiopia, and there are records of coffee cultivation in the Yemen as early as the sixth century. By the thirteenth century, the growing, roasting, and grinding of coffee to make a strong-flavored infusion were widespread throughout the Arab world. News of the drink was brought to Europe by traders, but Christians were wary of this "invention of the devil." However, when Pope Clement the Eighth gave the drink his seal of approval after trying a cup for himself, the trend quickly caught on. The seventeenth century saw the spread of coffee drinking throughout Europe. Coffeehouses opened in Vienna, Paris, and London, and they soon became the favorite meeting places of politicians, artists, and intellectuals. By the eighteenth century, coffee production was well established in Java and the Caribbean. The coffee-drinking habit spread; one of the repercussions of the Boston Tea Party of 1776 was that Americans adopted coffee as their national beverage. Today, coffee is drunk around the world, and each nation has its own ways of preparing and serving it.

PRODUCTION

Coffee is now grown in more than fifty countries, although production is not at all straightforward. Because it is vulnerable to frost, coffee can be successfully grown only between the Tropics of Cancer and Capricorn. In addition, crop maintenance is labor intensive. The plants require careful tending, pruning, hoeing, and weeding, and in most areas picking is done by hand.

Just after harvesting, the ripe berrylike fruits are called "cherries." These ripen over a period of 6–8 months and turn a deep red when ripe; hence their name. Inside, there are two beans that have to be separated from the pulp and skin, and dried. This process is known as *curing*, and it can be done by one of two methods.

For the traditional "dry method" of curing, the cherries are laid out in the sun until completely dry, then the dried skins and pulp are removed by a hulling machine.

The wet method is a more recent development and it is employed for high-quality, hand-picked beans. The outer, fleshy layer is removed, then the cherries are soaked and fermented, followed by washing and drying. Finally, the skins are removed by a hulling machine.

In both cases, the hulled or "polished" green beans are sorted, graded, and packed for export. Roasting is usually done in the country of import. It is possible to buy green beans, but most coffee is sold after it has been roasted. The roasting process is necessary to reduce the acidity of the beans and to develop the aromatic oils that give the coffee its aroma and flavor.

Finally, grinding exposes a larger surface area to the water, ensuring optimum contact between grounds and water, resulting in a satisfying cup of coffee.

Fresh unroasted beans

Roasted beans

Ground beans

TYPES OF COFFEE

The flavor, character, and quality of coffee vary tremendously—not only among countries, but also among estates within the same country. The soil, altitude, and climate are all factors that contribute to the character of the bean, thereby affecting the final taste. There are four varieties of coffee plant, but only two are sold on any commercial scale.

The most important of these is *Coffea arabica*, which grows on steep mountain slopes at high altitudes. This bean produces coffee that is rich, aromatic, and full of flavor, and it accounts for 70 percent of world coffee production. Coffee experts agree that the arabica bean is far superior in flavor to other types.

The other main variety, *Coffea canephora*, produces the coffee known as *robusta*. Grown on the lower slopes, where cultivation is easier, robusta beans have a higher caffeine content than arabica beans and a rougher, almost earthy flavor that lacks delicacy and subtlety. It costs about half the price of arabica and is used in the cheaper blends of both fresh and instant coffee.

The following are some of the most common types of coffee available.

Brazilian Santos Brazil is the world's largest coffee grower, producing every grade of bean, but the majority is used in the manufacture of instant coffee. This type gets its name from the port through which it is shipped, and it is held to be the best of the Brazilian coffees. Usually medium roasted, this has a flavor that is soft and mellow but full-bodied.

Colombian A fine coffee, with roundness, body, and a good balance of flavor and acidity, this can be enjoyed either medium or dark roasted. *Medellin excelso*, with its slightly nutty flavor, is probably the most

Coffee extract *can be used as a flavoring for cakes, pastries, ice creams, and drinks*

Instant coffee granules *made with arabica beans are the best*

Instant coffee powder *is a good flavoring for recipes where liquid is unwanted*

DECAFFEINATED COFFEE
Caffeine is a stimulant that is present in coffee. It has the effect of making the nervous system more active, which is usually the desired effect, although some people react badly to it and prefer to buy coffee without caffeine. Decaffeinated coffee is available in all the regular coffee forms: whole beans, ground, and instant. Caffeine is removed by soaking the beans in water or by using solvents or carbon dioxide. The last is thought to be the best method as it does not affect the flavor and there is no residue. To qualify as decaffeinated, coffee must contain less than 0.9 percent dry weight of caffeine. A 5 fl oz (150 ml) cup of decaffeinated coffee contains about 3 mg caffeine. This compares to 115 mg for filter coffee, 80 mg for percolated, and 65 mg for instant coffee.

well-known Colombian coffee, but *Libana supreme* is reputed to have more flavor than other varieties of bean from this country.

Costa Rican Prized for the elegant richness of its flavor, as well as its delicate acidity, this is popular as a breakfast coffee. *Tarrazu* is one of the best from this area.

Guatemalan All the beans from this country have a characteristic rich spiciness and a smoky character. Medium roasting is recommended to bring out the full body and pleasant, flavorful acidity.

Indonesian The most well known are *Java* and *Sumatra*, and both have a heavy-bodied, smooth flavor with little acidity. Java beans have a unique, slightly smoky taste, whereas Sumatra beans have a flavor that is vaguely reminiscent of chocolate.

Jamaican Blue Mountain With a smooth, subtle delicacy and gentle acidity, plus a rather distinctive nutty flavor, this coffee is in great demand. Not surprisingly, this is one of the more expensive coffees.

Kenyan Aromatic with a clean, sharp, bright taste and good acidity, this is one of the classic coffees.

Kenyan Peaberry An especially prized type of coffee, this should be medium roasted and preferably drunk black.

Kona Kai Grown in Hawaii, this is another of the world's fine, rare coffees. Rich, earthy and full-flavored, with a pleasant acidity, this is best when medium roasted.

Mexican Maragogipe Originally from Brazil, this Mexican strain produces a fine coffee. *Mexican coatapec* is another good quality coffee, exported mainly to America.

Mocha Strictly speaking, this is the name given to coffee from Arabia, but in practice, the trade applies the name to coffee from Ethiopia. *Ethiopian mocha* has a rich, complex flavor that is often described as "gamy" or "winy." With an excellent aroma and good balance, it is the choice of many connoisseurs; the best example is *Harrar longberry*. This is also the type used for traditional Turkish coffee.

Mysore The best-known Indian coffee, this has a delicate aroma and smooth, soft flavor with no acidity. It is often blended with Mocha to give *Mysore mocha*.

Nicaraguan A mild nonacidic coffee, these beans make a coffee that is well suited to breakfast-time drinking.

Tanzanian Kilimanjaro Stronger than Central American coffees, but less acidic than East African coffees, this has a distinctive well-balanced flavor. It can be satisfactorily medium or dark roasted.

ROASTING AND BREWING

A good cup of coffee depends upon the correct choice of bean and grind for the occasion. Roasting is the first step to the final flavor because the application of heat develops the aromas of the bean. However, single types of beans, or blends, that are suitable for the breakfast table may not be appropriate after dinner. The grind will also affect the final flavor, as will the choice of equipment. For example, a very finely ground coffee is unsuitable in a percolator, but essential for espresso coffee.

Always make sure the equipment is clean and free from coffee residue. Use freshly drawn water and heat to just off a boil. Allow 1–2 teaspoons of coffee per $^2/_3$ cup (150 ml) water. Timing is vital—brewed for too short a time, the flavor will be weak and sour; too long, and the flavor will be destroyed, leaving only bitterness. For a stronger brew, add more coffee per cup. Freshness is essential; buy beans in small quantities and grind as needed. Also, be sure to match the grind with the preparation being used.

TYPES OF ROASTS

The degree of roasting determines the delicacy or richness of a coffee; strength is determined by the amount of coffee used.

Light This roast is used for beans with subtle flavors that would be marred by stronger roasting and it gives them a light brown color. Lightly roasted coffee is the most suitable type for drinking with milk.

Medium With a more pronounced flavor and smell, this roast results in coffee that is good for breakfast drinking with milk. It also makes good after-lunch or -dinner coffee, which may be drunk without milk.

Dark This roast gives the beans a deep color and a glossy finish. It provides a strong flavor and aroma, and is best for drinking black after dinner.

Continental A very dark roast, full of strong smoky flavors, this is the preferred roast of those who like a powerful coffee.

Continental roast

Dark roast

Medium roast

Pale roast

GRINDERS

There is a wide selection of electrical, mechanical, modern, and antique grinders. Choose one that has a means of controlling the degree of grind and ensure that it produces an even grind every time.

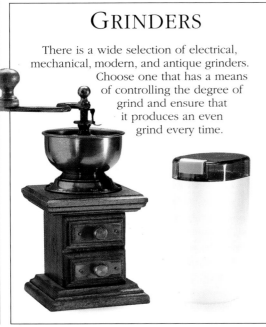

TYPES OF GRINDS

The coarseness or the fineness of the grind determines the surface area of the coffee that will come into contact with the water. Because some brewing methods have a very long, or very short, contact period between grounds and water, they must always be matched with a suitable grind. For example, in espresso machines, the water spends very little time in contact with the grounds, so they must be very fine to ensure that the flavor is passed to the water.

With a coffee grinder on hand, the beans can be ground to order. If not, buy ground in small quantities and store in an airtight container kept in the refrigerator. The flavor of coffee depends on its highly volatile oils, so it is best to buy freshly roasted beans in small quantities.

Coarse Grind It is possible to obtain this grind only at home. It may be used for the jug method and for percolators and will produce a lighter brew than medium grind.

Medium Grind The most versatile grind, this is suitable for use in jugs, percolators, cafetières, and Neapolitan flip pots. Use a fine strainer with jugs and percolators.

Fine Grind For coffee made by the filter or drip method, this is the grind to choose. It produces a large surface area of coffee that allows the water filtering through to take up the maximum flavor. The coffee will be strong because the fineness of the grind prevents the water from filtering through too fast, thereby lengthening the contact time between coffee and water.

Espresso Grind An especially fine grind, this is designed specifically for use in espresso machines and moka espresso pots.

Pulverized Sometimes known as powdered coffee, this is finest grind available. The heat generated during the grinding process contributes to the distinctive flavor.

Coarse grind

Percolators

As the brewing begins, boiling water is forced through ground coffee held in a basket. The disadvantage is that the same boiling liquid circulates continuously. With good temperature control, percolators can make good coffee, although coffee experts tend to frown on percolators because the coffee can become overheated and "stewed."

Medium grind

Cafetière

This is a refinement of the old-fashioned jug method. After the boiling water has been poured over the coffee, cover with the special lid, and allow to infuse for a short while. Then slowly push down the plunger, forcing the coffee grounds to the bottom of the pot. Use only coarse or medium grinds or the coffee will be cloudy.

Medium-fine grind

Neapolitan Flip Pots

Fill the bottom of the pot with cold water. Place the filter on top and fill with ground coffee to form a mound. Screw on the top and snap the upper pot into position. Place over a medium heat until steam starts to escape, then flip the pot over to allow the water to flow through the coffee grounds.

Espresso grind

Moka Espresso Pots

These are similar to the Neapolitan pots, but the hot water is forced through the filter by pressure into the upper chamber, so that the pot does not have to be turned over. A gurgling sound indicates that the coffee is ready; pour immediately or the coffee may burn. Use a fine grind for a good strong cup of coffee.

Fine grind

Filter

This method can be used for any style of coffee and any roast. Place the filter paper in the holder and place over a pot. Very slowly pour in the water, in time with the coffee dripping through. Keep the pot warm, over very low heat or an electric hotplate, and do not allow the coffee to boil.

Pulverized

Ibrik

Turkish coffee is traditionally made in a long-handled ibrik. To prepare, allow 1 heaped teaspoon each of coffee and sugar to each small cup. Bring to a boil, stir to dissolve the sugar, and return to a boil. Remove from the heat, let stand, then return to a boil. Leave to settle; pour without straining.

Coffees of the World

Coffee is an international beverage, with universal popularity, but it is drunk by people with divergent tastes, cultures, and traditions. As a result, each country has developed its own ways of coffee making, serving, and drinking. Most European countries start the day with a version of *café au lait* and then move on to stronger cups of black coffee, usually after meals. Americans like to drink black coffee throughout the day as well as during and after meals. In the Middle East, coffee is drunk quite strong, and strict rules of etiquette dictate the service.

The French morning ritual of coffee and croissants is copied throughout the world. Parisian cafés offer large mugs of frothy white coffee, called *grand crème*, while the more modest provincial establishments call it *café au lait*, and it may be served in deep bowls, as is done in most homes. It tastes quite different from the "milky" coffee made in America or Britain.

Later in the day, consumption continues with the smaller demitasse (literally half-cup), holding a little more than $1/3$ cup (100 ml) of strong black coffee. The French prefer a bitter, dark roast coffee. In homes and offices, the filter or drip method is most prevalent, but it is also customary to step out, at any time of day, for an *express* at the local café.

The Italians, too, are a nation of dedicated coffee drinkers, and they have different tastes for different times of the day. Mornings usually start with *caffe latte*, a rich roast espresso that is made by blending the coffee with about three times as much hot milk. After lunch and dinner (and for some, throughout the day), the traditional strong, black espresso served in a demitasse is the preferred drink. This is made in special machines that force hot water through tightly packed, finely ground espresso coffee. It is often served with a twist of lemon.

Like the French, the Italians feel that coffee with milk is difficult to digest after a meal, and the well-loved *cappuccino* is most often drunk in-between meals. In principle, café au lait and cappuccino are similar, but the French and Italian versions never taste the same. Cappuccino is made with espresso coffee that is blended with steamed milk, often topped with a sprinkling of cinnamon or cocoa powder, and sometimes a dollop of cream as well. It is said to owe its name to its color, which is similar to the mocha-colored robes of the Cappuccine monks.

Strong black coffee is also popular in Spain and Portugal, where it is known as *café solo*. In Germany, there are tiny stores or booths where standing customers can consume small cups of strong, but not very bitter, black coffee.

In the coffeehouses of Vienna, coffee is meant to be drunk with rich, cream-laden cakes, and the liking for this combination is echoed throughout Eastern Europe. The Austrians spend their *jause*, the equivalent of the British teatime, in a coffeehouse or, failing that, at home in the company of

Café Brûlot

To prepare, place 1 tbsp brown sugar, 5 whole cloves, a long strip each of lemon peel and orange peel, $1/2$ cinnamon stick, $1/2$ vanilla bean and $2/3$ cup (150 ml) brandy in a saucepan. Heat gently until the sugar dissolves and the brandy is warm. Ignite with a long match and allow to burn for about 30 seconds. Pour into 4 cups that are three-quarters full of hot, strong coffee.

An international favorite
Appreciated morning, noon, and night, coffee is a universal beverage that is served in a variety of ways.

Café au lait

Espresso

Viennese coffee

Turkish coffee

friends. As an additional flourish, the strong coffee, which is sometimes flavored with dried figs, is often topped by a dollop of whipped cream that is sprinkled with ground cinnamon or nutmeg.

In Britain, coffee drinking is fast catching on and, although tea is still the most popular breakfast beverage, coffee takes over at midmorning and after meals. Both the British and the Americans prefer a softer, milder brew than the Continentals, but Americans do like their coffee black.

Iced coffee is popular on hot days in both America and Europe. It is made by brewing coffee strong, sweetening it, and then chilling it. This is served with either ice water or milk. *Café frappé* is the French version, made frothy by vigorously shaking the coffee with ice cubes until chilled.

As could be expected, coffee is practically the national drink in Brazil, where the average consumption is estimated to be 20 tiny cups per person, per day. Unlike Europeans, however, the Brazilians drink their coffee quite sweet. The morning black coffee is sugared heavily, while for the *cafézinho* drunk throughout the day, the cup seems to be almost filled with brown sugar before the coffee even goes in.

Coffee drinking in Greece, Turkey, and the Middle East is much more than a refreshing pause; it is often a ritual. Service can be elaborate, and there is a formal ceremony

Irish coffee *is an after-dinner drink made with Irish whiskey and hot coffee topped with a layer of cream*

that dictates that the oldest and most respected guest is served first. The cups are never filled up to the brim, because this shows disrespect, and guests should take care not to drink the coffee to the last drop. Not only is this seen as bad manners, but the grounds settle into an unpalatably thick, sludgelike deposit at the bottom. Often, coffee will be flavored with cinnamon sticks, vanilla beans, ginger, or cardamom (see page 83). Sometimes orange-flower water is added. In Sudan, cloves are a popular flavoring, and in Morocco, peppercorns are favored.

AFTER-DINNER COFFEE
Combinations of strong coffee, cream, and spirits or liqueurs offer a satisfying alternative to heavy desserts. For festive occasions, they can be made in tall glasses to show off the contrasting layers of coffee and cream.

Heatproof glasses with handles are especially made for this purpose.

To prepare an after-dinner coffee, place a heaped teaspoon of brown sugar in a warmed glass with two tablespoons of liquor. Some of the more popular choices are: brandy, whisky, rum, vodka, crème de cacao, or almond- or coffee-flavored liqueurs. Pour on a strong, medium roast coffee. Stir well to dissolve the sugar. Rest the spoon against the rim of the glass and pour lightly whipped cream over the back and into the glass. If sufficient sugar has been used, the cream will float in a thick layer on the top.

COFFEE SUBSTITUTES AND FLAVORINGS
Roasted chicory root is a popular coffee extender in Europe. During the Civil War, when food was scarce, chicory was first added to coffee in the United States. The roots impart a characteristic bitter taste that is unpleasant to some. Dandelion root is toasted for a drink similar to coffee that is sold in health-food stores as dandelion coffee. Toasted barley is used to produce a drink called *malted coffee*. Spices and floral waters are often added in the Middle East, while in Austria, ground, dried figs are added for a thick, sweet flavor. Some coffees are sprayed with flavorings, such as oil of amaretto or vanilla.

MAKING COFFEE GRANITA

This refreshing iced drink may be flavored with brandy or rum and served with a spoonful of sweetened whipped cream.

1 Heat 1 cup (250 ml) water and ¾ cup (175 g) sugar, stir and boil for 1 minute. Add 1 cup (250 ml) coffee and leave to cool.

2 Place in a shallow pan and freeze for 1 hour. Stir and return to the freezer. Continue to stir and freeze for 2 hours.

TEA

One of the world's oldest beverages, tea was discovered by the Chinese—a more arduous task than it sounds, because they must have worked their way through a great number of indigenous plants before coming across the *Camelia sinensis*, or tea plant. It then took many centuries to perfect the art of tea production, resulting in the variety of types available today. First adopted by the Japanese, and then by Europeans looking for cash crops to grow in their tropical colonies, tea is now cultivated most widely in India, Sri Lanka, Africa, Georgia, and Japan, as well as in China. Tea was finally imported to Europe in the seventeenth century, and in its early days, it was a highly prized luxury item. Nonetheless, it caught on quickly in many countries on the Continent, although it is most often thought of as Britain's national drink. Today, Indian tea has overtaken China tea as the favorite.

GROWING TEA

The tea bush is an evergreen tropical plant with stiff, pointed, shiny green leaves. In order to flourish, it requires a wet, warm climate with at least 2 ft (60 cm) of rain a year. The bushes are planted in vast tea gardens at heights varying from 300–7,000 ft (100 meters–2 km) above sea level. At higher, cooler altitudes, tea bushes grow more slowly and produce smaller crops. For this reason, the flavor and characteristics of high-altitude teas are different from the faster-growing bushes on the lower slopes. In the cooler areas, such as Northern India, the harvest is seasonal, but elsewhere picking, or "plucking," carries on all year.

Young, soft shoots produce the finest tea, and only the top two leaves and bud are plucked. This work is done mainly by women and demands great skill. A good plucker can gather about 60–70 lb (30–35 kg) of leaf in a day, which will yield only about one-quarter to one-third that amount of tea after manufacture. An estimated 9,100 million bushes are required to meet the world's demand for tea.

Legend has it that tea was discovered by the Chinese emperor Shen Nung around 2750 B.C. One day, while boiling drinking water, some leaves from an overhanging tree fell into the pot. The resulting beverage was a pleasant infusion that tasted good and stimulated the senses, and a tradition was born. Tea drinking remained an essentially Chinese custom until about A.D. 800, when the beverage was introduced in Japan.

In the seventeenth century, when tea was finally introduced in Europe, the tea trade centered on Japan. But when Japan closed its borders to Europeans, China became the principal source of supply.

At first, tea was taken primarily as a tonic for the relief of a large number of maladies. One Dutch doctor advocated the drinking

Green tea

Black tea

Oolong tea

of at least forty cups a day, but he was an employee of the East India Company. Tea drinking really took off in Britain when Catherine of Braganza married Charles II in 1662 and brought a chest of tea as part of her dowry. Once it had the royal seal of approval, tea was able to move out of the smoky din of coffeehouses and into the drawing rooms of the wealthy. It soon became equally popular with the urban and rural working classes, who bought small quantities of the cheapest tea and brewed it weak. *Sligo*, an especially popular brand at the time, was advertised as being strong enough to endure as many as three or four changes of water.

The government of the day soon saw the value of instituting a tax on tea. This started off fairly low, but when it was increased to 100 percent, housewives found it prudent to keep their supplies of tea under lock and key in special boxes called *caddies*. When this tax was extended to cover tea imports to the colonies, hundreds of Bostonians threw the first shipments of taxed tea into the harbor. This historical act is known as the Boston Tea Party, and it was one of the first rumblings that set the scene for the American Revolutionary War.

The tea clipper was introduced to Europe in the 1850s to keep supply in pace with the demands of the burgeoning tea trade. Prior to this development, the return trip from London to the Canton River could last almost a year. These huge, three-masted ships, of American design, cut the sailing time by more than half, and captains would race each other to be the first to reach home port.

Meanwhile, the days of the East India Company's monopoly on trade with China were numbered, and the search began for alternative sources. Tea had been found growing wild in Northern India, and culti-

Tea caddies *were a protective as well as decorative means of storage when heavy taxes made tea a valuable commodity*

vation began first in Assam and Darjeeling and later in Sri Lanka. Tastes have evolved along the lines of supply, and by the turn of this century, Indian tea had overtaken Chinese tea as the preferred drink in North America and Britain.

PRODUCTION

The Chinese learned that by cultivating tea in different areas they could produce very different flavors of tea. They also developed and perfected a variety of production methods, which resulted in three quite different types of tea.

Green Tea As soon as these leaves are picked, they are left to wither until there is no moisture left. The whole leaves are then steamed and rolled, resulting in green-gray balls. By processing whole, the leaves are able to retain the enzymes that prevent them from oxidizing, hence losing color and flavor. The result is a pale, yellow-green

tea with a distinctly unusual flavor. The name Gunpowder Green was given to this tea by the first British colonists in China, who named it for its likeness in form and color to lead ball shot.

Oolong Tea This tea comes mainly from the southeast coasts of China and Taiwan. After harvesting, the leaves are left to wither for a few hours to remove some of the moisture. They are then rolled by machine to release the juices, followed by a short fermentation period prior to oven firing. After processing, the color of the leaves changes to copper, and the flavor is mild, falling midway between green tea and black tea.

Black Tea Produced in India as well as in China, these leaves are withered and rolled like oolong. The fermentation period, however, is considerably longer, which breaks down the enzymes, producing a varnish that coats the leaf. The leaves are then dried, and caramelized sugars are added to impart the color, aroma, and characteristic flavor of these teas.

GRADING TEA

Size and appearance are the criteria for tea grading. The two main grades—whole-leaf and broken-leaf—are used for black tea and are subdivided within each category.

Whole-leaf teas are classified as flowery orange pekoe, orange pekoe, or pekoe. The broken-leaf grades are further classified by particle size. Broken-leaf is largest, followed by another series that includes fannings, orange fannings, and dust, which is most commonly used for tea bags.

The flavor of all teas coming onto the market is judged by highly skilled tea tasters. They evaluate the flavor and aroma of the brewed tea, as well as the appearance and aroma of the fresh and dry leaves.

SMOKED TEA
The smoky, tarry flavor of *Lapsang Souchong* comes from the smoking process to which it is subjected during drying. According to legend, the practice of smoking tea developed out of a desire for better profits. Chinese tea producers realized that if drying time was reduced, production would increase— as would profits. In those days, tea was left to dry in the sun. Smoking increased the heat, causing the tea to dry faster. Rope is said to have been the original source of smoke, but today wood chips are used. Smoked tea is something of an acquired taste, and it is rarely served in China; nearly all Chinese smoked tea goes for export.

Black tea *is categorized according to leaf size, ranging from whole-leaf grades to dust, which is used in tea bags*

The largest of all the tea grades, this requires longer brewing to release the flavor

This is the best all-purpose tea because the size of the leaves reduces the brewing time

The finest grade of tea, this is used primarily for tea bags

Whole-leaf tea   **Broken-leaf tea**   **Small-leaf tea**

TEA TYPES

Just like grapes and wines, the taste of tea is dependent on where and how it is grown. The altitude, the soil, and the climate all have a marked effect on the flavor. Teas grown at the highest altitudes, for example, mature more slowly and have a lower yield, resulting in a higher quality. The main tea-producing countries are China, India, and Japan; however, there are a few other regions worthy of mention. Kenya is home to some very fine teas, particularly those cultivated east of the Great Rift Valley, where some of the tea gardens are at altitudes of 1¼ miles (2 km) above sea level. The teas are all black, with a brisk flavor. In Georgia, tea is grown on the slopes of the Caucasus Mountains, and the leaves are fermented to produce black tea that gives a very mellow brew.

The way in which tea is harvested, dried, and processed will affect the flavor of the brew: Indian tea tastes quite different to that from China or Ceylon, and teas from Assam in Northern India differ in flavor to those from Nilgiri in the South. Some teas are blended according to special recipes.

Chinese Green Teas Most familiar as the tea served in Chinese restaurants, these teas are all mild, with a pleasant fruity flavor.

Gunpowder Green This is a classic tea that uses tightly rolled, unfermented leaves. It yields a very pale drink with a light flavor.

Chinese Oolong Teas In general, these teas are stronger than green teas, but milder than black teas.

Taiwan (Formosa) Oolong Considered by some experts to be one of the finest of teas, this has a natural fruity flavor that is not too strong.

Formosa Oolong Peach Blossom This tea does not contain peach blossom—it takes its name from its unique peachy flavor that is found only in the best-quality teas.

Chinese Black Teas These teas range in flavor from mild, to smoked, to strong.

Keemum A delicate and aromatic tea from Northern China, this is low in tannins with a deep, rich flavor.

Lapsang Souchong A large-leaf tea that is rich and full-bodied, this has a very distinctive but delicate smoky, tarry flavor.

Yunnan Western A tea containing a high proportion of the youngest leaves, this has a sweet taste and a light golden color.

Indian Teas All of the teas produced in this country are black teas.

Assam One of the classic Indian teas, this is grown in the Brahmaputra Valley in northeast India. The taste is strong and malty. The best quality Assam teas contain the "tips," or unopened buds, from the bushes and are known as Tippy Assam.

Darjeeling Another popular tea from Northern India, this type is noted for its distinctive, delicate flavor. The small, broken-leaf grade

BLENDED TEAS

Most packages of commerical tea are made up of a blend of fifteen or more leaves from different areas. There are also some rather special traditional teas that are blended.

English Breakfast Tea is a blend of strong Indian teas that gives a full-bodied and fragrant drink.

Earl Grey Tea is a blend of Keemun and Darjeeling teas flavored with oil of bee balm. The recipe was given to the diplomat Earl Grey by a Chinese mandarin, and the earl took the recipe back with him to England.

Russian Caravan Tea is a blend of fine teas from China, Taiwan, and India. It was originally transported to Russia from India via camel caravan; hence its name.

produces a light, golden drink with a subtle flavor. Bushes from the highest tea gardens in the foothills of the Himalayas have large leaves that produce teas with a unique "muscatel" flavor of perfumed grapes. The most notable of all the various Darjeelings is Darjeeling Broken Orange Pekoe, which is sometimes called the champagne of tea.

Ceylon Teas The teas produced in Sri Lanka (formerly Ceylon) are all black teas.

Dimbula Grown at altitudes reaching 1¼ miles (2 km) and over, this tea has a fine quality and, like most Ceylon tea, a rich color and flavor. Orange pekoe and broken orange pekoe are the usual leaf grades, resulting in a drink with an aromatic fragrance and a delicate, fresh taste.

Kandy This tea is noted for its full-bodied quality and strength, appealing particularly to those who like a robust beverage.

Nuwara Eliya A light, "bright" tea with a fragrant flavor, this is excellent when served with lemon wedges.

Uva This is a fine-flavored tea from the eastern slopes of the central mountains.

Japanese Green Teas These are quite different from Chinese green teas because the flavor of some can be decidedly strong.

Sencha These long, green leaves make a light, bright easy-to-drink tea that is good for everyday drinking.

Sencha Brancha This is a combination of tea leaves and rice that results in a drink with a nutty flavor.

FLAVORED TEA

In addition to the many types of teas that vary in taste, there is also a wide range of flavored teas. They are flavored with flowers or fruits or with extracts such as chocolate, mint, or brandy. Many teas are flavored naturally with dried fruit, flowers, and spices; some are flavored artificially. The Chinese have long been flavoring their teas with flowers, and each region has its

Passion fruit tea

Rose-violet tea

Orange blossom tea

Chrysanthemum tea

Apricot tea

Coconut tea

Jasmine tea

Rose tea

own traditional blend. The flowers are dried with the tea so that the delicate flavor permeates throughout.

Jasmine Tea Traditionally served with dim sum dishes, this is a classic Chinese tea. It is a green tea, exotically scented with the addition of real jasmine flowers.

Rose Pouchong Tea From the province of Guangdong, this is made by interspersing flower petals with the tea leaves during drying. It makes a pale, soothing tea. *Rose Congou* is another rose-scented tea.

Chrysanthemum Tea This is medium-strength black China tea blended with chrysanthemum flowers.

Orchid Tea This is obtained by blending a semifermented oolong tea with crushed orchid flowers. It makes a light, delicate, and fragrant brew, considered to be the tea of connoisseurs.

Lychee Tea This is a traditional Chinese blend that is perfumed with the husks of the lychee fruit.

Fruit Tea Modern blends are produced using varied fruits: apricots, black currants, apples, wild cherries, passion fruit, oranges, lemons, and mangoes. The producers of fruit teas carefully blend their own mixtures of China, Indian, and Ceylon teas to go with the chosen fruit.

Fruit and flower teas are best appreciated on their own, without milk, lemon, and sometimes even sugar

271

TEAS AROUND THE WORLD

Tea is drunk in many countries of the world, and each one has its own particular ways for preparation and service. The Chinese always drink tea black, the Tibetans lace it with yak butter, and the Moroccans flavor theirs with mint or sage. In Europe, there is a choice of milk and lemon, while in Russia, they might add jam. The containers used to brew the tea, along with the bowls, cups, and mugs in which to serve it are equally variable. Tea can be served hot or cold, or it can be the base for other drinks such as punches. It is even used to impart flavor and color to foods. Although tea is an everyday drink, it is often associated with hospitality, and every country has its own special customs and ceremonies, which range from the simple to the elaborate.

The Chinese were the first to document the etiquette of tea. The third volume of a book, published in A.D. 780 by the writer Lu Yu, set out the various ways in which each type of tea should be prepared and served. It also included detailed instructions on the implements to be used and even how these should be made.

The teapot and the tea bowl are both Chinese inventions. The latter had no handles, and the first European teacups were very similar. Handles were soon found to be an advantage, although the two styles were in production simultaneously for some years. Saucers followed, and even the handleless cup was given a deep saucer from which the tea could also be drunk. The first European teapots were made of ceramic or fine porcelain china, but silver eventually took over. By the mid-1800s, ornate silver tea services, with huge tea urns on swivel stands, were much in demand. Other equipment included lacqueur trays to carry the tea services, strainers and caddy spoons, sugar bowls, small milk jugs and slop bowls, and tea cozies made of quilted silk or velvet.

At first, tea was served at any time of the day. But in Britain, the seventh Duchess of Bedford founded the very English habit of serving afternoon tea. According to the footnotes of history, the duchess was prone to light bouts of hunger in the afternoon. One day she ordered a pot of tea and some snacks to be brought to her room. She so enjoyed the experience that she began to invite guests to accompany her in the new

MAKING TEA

Proper brewing is essential for good flavor. Use freshly drawn water from the cold faucet and bring to a rolling boil. Warm the teapot with hot water, empty out the water, and add the tea. Pour on the water, stir, and leave to stand for 3–5 minutes. Stir again before serving.

Iced tea is very popular in North America and in Europe. It is made by doubling the quantity of tea brewed to allow for the addition of ice, which dilutes it. Tall glasses with plenty of crushed ice are commonly used for serving; garnish with a slice of lemon and a sprig of fresh mint. Cold tea also serves as a versatile base for both alcoholic and non-alcoholic punches.

Customs and ceremonies
In many countries, tea is more than just a drink, it is the focus of ceremonies that can be steeped in tradition or simply a pretext for gathering with friends.

Moroccan mint tea

European tea

Chinese tea

Japanese tea

Iced tea

Brew tea extra strong as the addition of ice cubes will dilute the taste.

repast. Soon all London was sipping tea and nibbling little sandwiches in the middle of the afternoon.

Serving tea is also associated with hospitality in many Arab countries, and guests are offered steaming cups of special-flavored tea to sip with candies and other delicacies.

In Japan, there is a very formal ceremony attached to tea service. There are two stages of the ceremony, named for the types of tea served: *koicha* is a thick and bitter tea, *ususha* is a much thinner tea. *Koicha* takes place in a special tearoom. The host makes the tea and acts as servant to his guests. The principal guest is the first to drink from the bowl and he then passes it on to the other guests. There are also strict rules that govern the topic of conversation, and at this stage it is most polite to discuss the tea-making equipment. *Ususha* is held in another room, where guests may chat in a more relaxed atmosphere.

FLAVORINGS

The Chinese and the Japanese have always believed that tea should be allowed to show off its aroma and flavor without any additions. But even in those countries, all kinds of flavorings may be added.

In Western countries, tea is often served with milk, a habit that dates from the eighteenth century in Britain. In those days, it was thought that pouring boiling tea into a delicate china tea bowl would break it, so the milk was added first. Modern experts agree that the milk should go first, but for different reasons. Research has shown that milk poured in after the tea is likely to form a fatty layer on the top. Sugar is frowned upon by the experts because it denatures the flavor. The Russians, however, take sugar in their lemon tea, and the Anatolians drink tea through a cube of sugar held in the mouth.

In Arab countries, herbs such as mint, sage, and basil are popular. Black tea is drunk strong, often with the addition of a stick of cinnamon, some cardamom pods, or a mixture of aniseed and chopped walnuts. Moroccan mint tea is made by infusing sweetened green tea with fresh or dried mint leaves. Lemon verbena or scarlet geranium can also be added.

One of the most exotically flavored teas is Kashmiri tea, which is a blend of green and Darjeeling tea flavored with a mix of crushed green cardamoms, cinnamon, cloves, chopped almonds and pine nuts.

COOK'S CHOICE
TEA PUNCH

Serves 10–12

2¹/₂ cups (600 ml) freshly made double-strength Ceylon tea
1 cup (250 ml) Amontillado sherry
1 cup (250 ml) rum
Juice of 1 lemon
2 tbsp lime juice
Sugar
2¹/₂ cups (600 ml) crushed ice (or more ice cubes)
Orange and lemon slices for garnish

Mix the hot tea with the sherry, rum, lemon juice, and lime juice. Add sugar to taste and stir until it dissolves. Allow the mixture to cool. Transfer to a punch bowl. Add the ice and allow to stand again until about half the ice has melted. Stir, float slices of orange and lemon on the top, and serve.

COOK'S CHOICE
HOT TODDY

Serves 4

1¹/₄ cups (300 ml) freshly made Darjeeling tea
¹/₄ cup (50 ml) whiskey
¹/₄ cup (50 ml) ginger wine
4 cloves
1 cinnamon stick

In a saucepan, combine the tea, whiskey, wine, cloves, and cinnamon. Warm over gentle heat; do not boil. Allow to infuse for 3–5 minutes. Strain into mugs and serve immediately.

TEA SMOKING

In parts of China, tea smoking is used to color and flavor foods such as duck and chicken. Peking duck was originally smoked with camphor wood, but this is not widely available and tea is now used instead. Unlike the Western technique of hot smoking, this process does not cook the food.

To proceed, mix a few tablespoons of loose black tea with brown sugar and herbs or spices, such as aniseed. Rice or flour could also be added for more smoke. Line a heavy wok and its lid with aluminum foil, place the smoking mixture in the base of the wok, and place a rack or several crossed chopsticks over the top. Place the food to be smoked on the rack (or chopsticks) and replace the lid. Place the wok over very high heat and leave to smoke for about 15 minutes. Care should be taken to open the kitchen windows because the room is likely to fill with smoke. Turn off the heat and allow to stand for 10 minutes longer. The food is now ready to cook as required.

Tea smoking adds color and a smoky flavor, but it does not cook foods

TISANES

Herbal infusions have been used through the ages for their medicinal properties. Indeed, the word *tisane* comes from the Greek for medicinal brew. Tisanes contain none of the tannin and caffeine found in conventional teas and many herbal mixtures make refreshing beverages that can be drunk either hot or cold. In Europe, tisanes have never gone out of fashion, and they are gaining renewed popularity in many other countries.

Tisanes are made by infusing the leaves, fruit, and flowers of almost any edible plant. Infusions can be chosen for their stimulating or relaxing properties, and advocates of homeopathic remedies recommend tisanes for their healing properties.

Tisanes are made in very much the same way as ordinary tea but usually in smaller quantities; allow 1/2 oz (15 g) dried herbs or 1 oz (30 g) fresh herbs for every 2 1/2 cups (600 ml) boiling water. Lemon juice and honey have an affinity for many hot tisanes, or they can be served ice-cold with a sprig of the fresh herb for garnish.

Leaves Most of the well-known culinary herbs also have medicinal properties. Rosemary makes a strongly flavored tea that stimulates the circulation and can help ease migraines. Sage is said to be good for sore throats, and thyme sweetened with honey makes a soothing cough mixture. Mint—with its 200 varieties—is valued as an aid to digestion and combines well with other herbs; it is especially refreshing with lime blossom. Spearmint and peppermint tea make good revitalizing drinks, especially when served iced. The menthol in hot peppermint tea can be useful for clearing head colds. Less well-known leaves include comfrey, verbena, lemon verbena, and raspberry leaves. Lemon balm, sometimes known as *melissa*, makes a very fragrant tea with a calming effect on the nerves; it is also good for the digestion.

Fruits and Flowers Chamomile flowers have a pungent, grassy flavor when infused and the tea is good for the digestive system, calming the nerves, and aiding sleep. In Italy, it is frequently used to calm nursing mothers and their babies.

An infusion of lavender will soothe and relax, while elderflowers and elderberries have long been used in tisanes to calm the nerves and reduce insomnia and migraines. They remain a popular remedy for soothing inflamed throats, coughing, and other symptoms of headcolds. Rose petals and violets, sweetened with honey, also produce a tisane to soothe a cough.

Rich in vitamin C, hibiscus lends a sharp, fruity taste and crimson color to herbal mixtures. Only the red petals are used in tisanes. Rosehips, also rich in vitamin C, come from the dog rose. Its stimulating properties are quite potent, so always use in moderate doses. The sharp, fruity flavor combines particularly well with hibiscus.

Very fine or crushed leaves should be infused with a fine-mesh strainer

Infusing mugs have strainer baskets to hold the tea and lids to keep the liquid hot

Infusing mug

Infusers
Infusing spoons and balls can be used to make individual cups of herbal teas.

Spoon-sized strainers allow for the proper dosage of leaves for a single cup

REVIVING MORNING TISANE

Tisanes made with selected ingredients result in an invigorating brew for the morning—or any time of day—that can be drunk instead of coffee or tea. Herbs and fruits with invigorating properties include fresh or dried nettles, black currant and blackberry leaves, peppermint, rosemary, angelica, sweet cicely, borage, lemon verbena, hibiscus blossoms, rosehips, and roses.

Combine 2 teaspoons each lemon verbena, peppermint, dried roses, hibiscus, nettle, and rosehip (for extra color and flavor, add more rosehip). Pour some boiling water in the teapot, swirl it around to warm, then discard. Place the mixture in the teapot and pour 2 cups (500 ml) boiling water over. Allow to infuse for 5 minutes. Strain before serving and sweeten to taste.

Rosehip

Lemon verbena

Dried roses

Nettle

Hibiscus

Peppermint

Orange peel

Hops

Skullcap

Chamomile

Lemon balm

Lime flower

RELAXING EVENING TISANE

After a heavy meal or an exhausting day, a soothing tisane is most welcome. Herbs with calming and sedative properties include basil, bee balm, lavender, anise leaves, marjoram, violet flowers and leaves, mallow flowers, fennel, dill, and all the ingredients listed below.

Mix together ¹/₂ teaspoon each of chamomile, lime flower, lemon balm, vervain, skullcap, hops, and dried orange peel. Crush half a licorice stick and add to the herbs. Pour some boiling water in the teapot, swirl it around to warm, then discard. Place the mixture in the teapot and pour 2 cups (500 ml) boiling water over. Allow to infuse for 5 minutes. Strain before serving and sweeten with honey to taste.

NONALCOHOLIC DRINKS

Fruit and vegetable juices are delicious on their own, but they can also be combined and flavored with herbs and spices for refreshing and unusual drinks. Dairy products such as milk, yogurt, and buttermilk can also be used for flavorful drinks. Another pleasant preparation involves the addition of yeast to herbal infusions or juices, resulting in a light, naturally sparkling drink. All of these beverages are easily prepared at home, offering a wide variety of satisfying alternatives to traditional alcoholic cocktails. The possibilities for mixed drinks are almost endless, limited only by individual taste. It is easy to build up a repertoire of interesting and unusual nonalcoholic drinks, coolers, and cocktails. Start by mixing two familiar drinks and then go on to experiment with more unusual flavor combinations, sweetening with sugar or honey and herbs and spices to taste.

HERBS FOR DRINKS

Fresh herbs can be used both to flavor and decorate non-alcoholic drinks. Mint is the most widely used herb with fruit drinks, but borage, parsley, lemon balm, thyme, basil, and dill all work well. Stronger herbs such as chives, cilantro, and tarragon are better with vegetable juices.

A refreshing pause
Use a variety of fresh herbs and spices to flavor fruit and vegetable juices or milk-based drinks.

Lemon verbena

Ginger mint

Salad burnet

Pineapple sage

Fruit and vegetable juices and dairy drinks

COOK'S CHOICE
CITRUS CUP

Serves 4

10 tbsp sugar
Grated zest and juice of 2 oranges
Sparkling water
Juice of 1 lemon
Fresh lemon balm and lemon slices for garnish

In a saucepan, combine the sugar with 2½ cups (600 ml) water over medium heat, stirring until the sugar dissolves. Add the orange zest and juice, lemon juice, and a sprig of lemon balm and allow to cool. Add the sparkling water. Chill for at least 3 hours before serving. Garnish each glass with a small sprig of lemon balm and a slice of lemon.

COOK'S CHOICE
LASSI

Serves 4

1 cup (250 ml) natural yogurt
½ tsp salt
1–2 sprigs mint, leaves only
½ tsp dry-roasted cumin seeds
Freshly ground black pepper
Fresh mint sprigs for garnish

In a blender, combine the yogurt, salt, mint, and 2½ cups (600 ml) water, and process until smooth. Chill for at least 3 hours. Pour into tall glasses and sprinkle with the cumin and pepper to taste. Garnish with sprigs of mint.

The juice of citrus fruits lends itself very well to drinks. Orange and grapefruit juice are the quintessential breakfast juices, and freshly squeezed lemon juice mixed with sugar and water is lemonade to some, *citron presse* to others. However, there is no need to stick to single-juice mixtures.

The tartness of lemon juice can be deliciously subdued with orange juice and a spoonful of honey. Grapefruit juice can be blended with orange juice and a sprig of fresh herbs can be added for flavor and eye appeal: lemon balm, sweet cicely, and peppermint are all suitable.

Herb flowers, such as borage and lemon thyme, make beautiful garnishes for fruit drinks. For festive occasions, remove the thorns and leaves from untreated long-stem roses and place the flowers in tall glasses filled with grapefruit juice, cranberry juice, and a squeeze of fresh lime.

More elaborate fruit punches and coolers are made by mixing a variety of bottled and home-pressed fruit juices together. Try apple with strawberry juice, peach with tangerine juice, or pineapple with mango juice. Some of these mixtures need the acidity of lemon, lime, or grapefruit juice to balance the sweetness. Top up with sparkling water or ginger beer, add ice cubes, and decorate with sliced fruit and sprigs of fresh herbs.

Fresh fruit juices also have an affinity for fruit syrups (see page 204). Tart fruit juices, such as lime and grapefruit, work best since the syrups are sugar based. Floral syrups (see page 213) can be blended to great effect with delicate fruits such as strawberry.

Almost all vegetables can be processed for their juice, but carrot, tomato, and cucumber are the most appropriate. Use an electric or hand-operated juicer. For extra flavor, add basil, lovage, or parsley to tomato juice, dill or chives to cucumber juice, and tarragon or mint to carrot juice.

A refreshing drink can be made from a borscht-like combination of beets, cucumber, and apple. Likewise, carrot and cilantro are natural partners in the soup pot, and the addition of orange juice helps in the transition from bowl to glass.

Tangy buttermilk is ideal for drinks. It can be used alone or subdued with milk or yogurt. Strawberries, bananas, and honey mixed in a blender with some chilled buttermilk make a delicious and wholesome summertime drink, with an appealing froth on the top. Serve in tall glasses, garnished with fresh mint sprigs.

Flavored milk is a familiar drink base, generally made with cocoa powder or fruit syrups such as strawberry. Drinking yogurt is becoming increasingly popular, though in the East, yogurt has long been the base of refreshing drinks. Lassi, the traditional Indian yogurt drink, can be either sweet—flavored with mint or rose water—or savory, flavored with cumin and cardamom. Lassi is meant to tame the fire of spicy curries, but lassis are refreshing drinks in their own right.

Releasing citrus juices
Before squeezing citrus fruits, roll on the worktop, pressing down, to help release a maximum of juice.

COOK'S CHOICE
CARROT-GAZPACHO COCKTAIL

Serves 4

1¼ cups (300 ml) carrot juice
1¼ cups (300 ml) tomato juice
1 3-in (7.5 cm) cucumber, grated
2 tbsp chopped fresh cilantro, basil, or dill
Salt
Freshly ground black pepper
Ice cubes

Mix the juices in a large pitcher and chill for 1 hour. Stir in the remaining ingredients. Pour into glasses and serve garnished with sprigs of the chosen herb.

MAKING GINGER BEER

Ginger beer is a traditional British drink, somewhat old-fashioned, but delicious and refreshing nonetheless. Serve chilled in tall glasses.

1 With the flat edge of a knife, crush 1 oz (30 g) peeled gingerroot. Add to a bowl with 2½ cups (500 g) sugar, 5 quarts (5 liters) boiling water and the juice of 2 lemons.

2 In a small bowl, dissolve 1 package dried beer yeast in tepid water. Leave to stand for 3-4 minutes so the yeast develops, then stir with a spoon.

3 Add the yeast to the ginger mixture, stir to blend, and leave for 24 hours. Strain then pour into clean bottles and seal or cork (see page 233), leaving about 1 in (2.5 cm) at the top.

ALCOHOLIC DRINKS

As long as alcoholic drinks have been made, they have served as the basis for warming and soothing spiced drinks; sometimes they were thickened with egg yolks, sometimes they were sweetened with raisins, honey, or sugar. Mulled wine and beer used to be heated with a red-hot poker, though today, specialties like glühwein and punch are more likely to be steeped on the stove. Punch originated in India, where it was made with a locally produced spirit. It became the custom to use five ingredients in the mix, and since the Indian word for five was *pānch*, this soon became anglicized to *punch*.

Mulled wines and punches are festive and flavorful uses for ordinary bottles of still or sparkling wine. They can be enhanced with spirits or liqueurs, teas or tisanes, and fruit or floral syrups (see Index). Flavorings that have an affinity for alcoholic drinks include citrus fruits and spices, such as cinnamon and cloves. Beer and lager feature less frequently in mixed drinks; the exception is Black Velvet, which is a mixture of Champagne and Guinness stout. There are many ways to enjoy flavored alcoholic drinks: from a simple blend of rum, hot water, honey, and lemon, to a more elaborate punch blending several spirits with fruits and spices.

COOK'S CHOICE
TOASTED ALE PUNCH

Serves 6

$^1/_3$ cup (60 g) light brown sugar
1 lemon, sliced
$^1/_4$ tsp ground cloves
$^1/_4$ tsp ground cinnamon
$^2/_3$ cup (150 ml) brandy
2$^1/_2$ cups (600 ml) light ale
1 slice white bread, toasted and cut into small shapes
Freshly grated nutmeg

In a large bowl, combine the sugar and 1$^1/_4$ cups (300 ml) water and stir to dissolve. Add the lemon, cloves, cinnamon, brandy, and ale. Stir to blend and add the bread shapes. Sprinkle with grated nutmeg and serve.

Flavoring drinks
The addition of herbs and spices adds greatly to alcoholic drinks, both warmed and chilled.

Mulling spices

Mulled drinks and punches

COOK'S CHOICE
WHITE WINE COOLER

Serves 8–10

2 bottles dry white wine
$^1/_2$ bottle dry sherry
Juice of 2 lemons
1 in (2.5 cm) gingerroot, peeled
Sparkling water
Sugar
Ice cubes
Cucumber slices for garnish

Mix together the wine, sherry, lemon juice, and ginger and chill for 2 hours. To serve, remove the ginger, transfer to glasses, add soda water to taste and sweeten if desired. Add cucumber and serve.

COOK'S CHOICE
MADEIRA EGGNOG

Serves 6

1 egg
5 cups (1.25 liters) milk
10 tbsp sugar
1$^1/_4$ cups (300 ml) Madeira
$^2/_3$ cup (150 ml) brandy
Freshly grated nutmeg

Whisk together the egg and $^2/_3$ cup (150 ml) of the milk. In a saucepan, bring the remaining milk and sugar to a boil. Whisk a little of the hot milk into the egg mixture, then return all to the saucepan. Whisk in the Madeira and brandy; do not boil. When frothy, pour into mugs, sprinkle with grated nutmeg, and serve.

MAKING MULLED WINE

Mulled wine is a traditional festive drink in many parts of the world, but this delicious and warming wine is suitable for any cold winter evening. Mulled beer can be made in the same way, but without the sugar and lemon.

1 In a pan, combine 1 sliced lemon, 4 bottles red wine, 2¹/₂ cups (600 ml) water, and ³/₄ cup (175 ml) brandy. Add a cinnamon stick, several allspice berries, and 2–3 cloves. Bring just to a boil; taste and add sugar if desired.

2 Cover and leave to infuse for at least 30 minutes. Just before serving, return to the heat to warm, but do not allow to boil. Strain into a heated bowl or individual mugs, and serve with slices of lemon.

Warm, spiced drinks such as toddies, nogs and grogs were all the rage in the eighteenth century, although they are somewhat less popular today.

Hot toddies are easy-to-make drinks for cold winter nights. Pour a measure of whiskey, rum, or brandy into a tall, heatproof glass. Add a teaspoon of sugar, a pinch of spice, and fill with boiling water. Good flavor combinations include brandy with allspice or nutmeg and rum with cloves or cinnamon. For a Tam O'Shanter, mix two parts Scotch and one part brandy, sweeten with brown sugar, and sprinkle with allspice. To transform this drink into a nog, whisk together brown sugar, to taste and one egg and pour on some boiling milk. Whisk the mixture over low heat until thick and frothy, but do not boil or the eggs will curdle. Divide the same amount of whiskey and brandy among coffee mugs and pour on the hot milk mixture to fill.

Grog refers to a mix of rum, lemon juice, brown sugar, cinnamon, and golden raisins. The name comes from the slang for the water-diluted rum, instigated by a naval Admiral, nicknamed Old Grog, that was allotted to British sailors.

The original five ingredients in Punch were spirits, tea, sugar, fruit juice, and water. Nowadays, punches have fallen from favor, being replaced by mulled wines that combine red wine, rum or brandy, sugar, lemon, and a variety of spices.

Coolers are lighter, more refreshing drinks than punches, the spirits being replaced with wine, sherry, or vermouth. Flavorings include fresh fruit or juice and perhaps a sprig of mint.

Sangria is a familiar wine-based drink traditionally made by adding sugar and ice to Spanish red wine. The recipe can be more elaborate, including brandy or even orange liqueur. The Spanish also make a hot red wine punch with nutmeg and lemon called *bollam*. The German, Swiss, and Austrian *glühwein* is similar, but has a more elaborate mix of spices.

Frosted glasses
To frost a glass, dip the rim into a saucer of diluted gum arabic and then into a saucer of superfine sugar and leave to dry.

FLAVORING LIQUEUR

Flavored liqueurs can easily be made at home by steeping fresh fruits in a mixture of alcohol and sugar syrup. Fruits to choose include whole oranges or just the zest, pears, peaches, raspberries, or plums. Large fruit should be sliced; small fruit should be pricked all over to help release the flavorful juices. Simply place the fruit in a clean jar and cover with a mixture of three parts alcohol —gin, rum, brandy, or vodka —to one part sugar syrup (see page 196). Spices, herbs, citrus peel, and even coffee beans can be added for flavor.

1 To make an unusual orange and coffee bean liqueur, cut three slits down the side of an orange and insert some coffee beans in each of the incisions.

2 Place the orange in a jar and add a handful of coffee beans. Pour on a mixture of one-third sugar syrup to two-thirds tequila and seal. Chill for 3 months before using.

INDEX

BIBLIOGRAPHY

Arasaki, Seibin and Teruko. *Vegetables from the Sea*. New York: Japan Publications, 1983.

Bonar, Ann. *The Macmillan Treasury of Herbs*. New York: Macmillan, 1985.

Boxer, Arabella. *The Herb Book*. New York: W.H.Smith, 1989.

Bremness, Lesley. *The Complete Book of Herbs: A Practical Guide to Growing and Using Herbs*. New York: Viking Penguin, 1988.

Brennan, Georgeanne and Glenn, Charlotte. *Peppers Hot and Chile*. Aris Publishers.

Cavage, Betty. *The Elegant Onion*. Storey Communications.

Clifton, Claire. *Edible Flowers*. New York: McGraw-Hill, 1984.

Cost, Bruce. *Bruce Cost's Asian Ingredients*. New York: Morrow, 1988.

David, Elizabeth. *A Book of Mediterranean Food*. New York: Penguin, 1988.

David, Elizabeth. *French Provincial Cooking*. New York: Penguin, 1987.

Garland, Sarah. *The Herb Garden*. New York: Penguin, 1985.

Garland, Sarah. *The Good Housekeeping Complete Book of Preserving*. New York: Morrow, 1991.

Grant, Rosamund. *Caribbean and African Cookery*. London: Grub Street Publications, 1990.

Grieve, Mrs. M. *A Modern Herbal: The Medicinal, Culinary, Cosmetic and Economic Properties, Cultivation and Folklore of Herbs, Grasses, Fungi, Shrubs and Trees*. Two volumes. New York: Dover Publications, 1971.

Gubser, Mary. *America's Bread Book: The Best Breads from Home Bakers All Across the Country*. New York: Morrow, 1985.

Hallgarten, Peter. *Spirits and Liqueurs*. London; Faber and Faber, 1983.

Hazan, Marcella. *The Classic Italian Cookbook*. New York: Knopf, 1976.

Hillier, Malcom. *The Complete Book of Dried Flowers*. New York: Simon and Schuster, 1987.

Jaffrey, Madhur. *An Invitation to Indian Cooking*. New York: Knopf, 1976.

Kennedy, Diana. *The Art of Mexican Cooking*. New York: Knopf, 1989.

Leyel, C.F. *Herbal Delights*. London: Faber and Faber, 1987.

Lowenfeld, Claire and Black, P. *The Complete Book of Herbs and Spices*. Newton Abbot: David & Charles, 1974.

Miloradovich, Milo. *Cooking with Herbs and Spices*. New York: Dover, 1990.

Mulherin, Jennifer. *The Macmillan Treasury of Spices and Natural Flavorings*. New York: Macmillan, 1988.

Norman, Jill. *The Complete Book of Spices*. New York: Viking, 1991.

Ortiz, Elisabeth. *The Book of Latin American Cooking*. New York: Knopf, 1980.

Ortiz, Elisabeth. *The Complete Book of Caribbean Cooking*. New York: Ballantine, 1986.

Ortiz, Elisabeth. *The Complete Book of Mexican Cooking*. New York: M. Evans, 1967.

Ortiz, Elisabeth. *The Food of Spain and Portugal*. New York: Macmillan, 1989.

Phillips, Roger and Foy, Nicky. *The Random House Book of Herbs*. New York: Random House, 1990.

Prudhomme, Paul. *Chef Paul Prudhomme's Louisiana Kitchen*. New York: Morrow, 1984.

Rinzler, Carol. *The Complete Book of Herbs, Spices, and Condiments*. New York: Facts on File, 1990.

Roden, Claudia. *A Book of Middle Eastern Food*. New York: Knopf, 1974.

Roden, Claudia. *Mediterranean Cookery*. New York: Knopf, 1987.

Rosso, Julee and Lukins, Sheila. *The New Basics*. New York: Workman, 1989.

Sahni, Julie. *Classic Indian Cooking*. New York: Morrow, 1980.

Simon, Andre L. and Howe, Robin. *A Dictionary of Gastronomy*. Overlook Press, 1978.

Stobart, Tom. *Herbs, Spices, and Flavorings*. Overlook Press, 1982.

Time-Life Books: *Foods of the World Series*. Alexandria, Virginia, 1968.

Time-Life Book: *The Good Cook Series*. Alexandria, Virginia, 1979.

Tolley, Emilie and Mead, Chris. *Herbs: Gardens, Decorations, and Recipes*. New York: Crown, 1985.

Willan, Anne. *La Varenne Pratique*. New York: Crown, 1989.

Wolfert, Paula. *The Cooking of South-West France*. New York: Harper & Row, 1988.

Wolfert, Paula. *Couscous and Other Good Foods from Morocco*. New York: Harper & Row, 1987.

Wolfert, Paula. *Mediterranean Cooking*. New York: Ecco Press, 1985.

Wolfert, Paula. *Paula Wolfert's World of Food*. New York: Harper & Row, 1988.

ACKNOWLEDGMENTS

The editors would particularly like to thank **Vanessa Kramer,** whose advice, research, and hard work made a large contribution to the scholarship of this book.

The following authors contributed text:
Angelika Duval
Fergus Fleming
Christopher Middleton
Judy Ridgway
Elizabeth Wolf-Cohen

Editorial Assistants:
Judy Bastyra, Elizabeth Godfray, Rosie Kindersley, Beverly LeBlanc, Sally Poole, Madeline Weston, Ian Wood

Photographer's Assistant:
Jules Selmes

Home Economists:
Sandra Baddeley
Elizabeth Burkwood
Annie Nichols

Additional Typesetting:
Rowena Feeny, Debbie Rhodes

U.S. edition prepared by:
Jeanette Mall, Christine M. Benton, Deslie Lawrence

For information and fact-finding, the editors wish to thank the following individuals and organizations:

Bui Xuan Khoa, Second Secretary of the Vietnamese Embassy; Coffee News Information Centre; Deborah Gillat and Zeba Mirza at the Ministry of Agriculture, Fisheries and Food; Terril Jones; Korea National Tourism Corporation; Melody Meade; Jill Norman; Royal Thai Embassy; Alan Wylie at Peacock Salt Ltd; Sarah Wynter

For their help, advice, and supply of herbs, spices, and flavorings for photography, many thanks to the following:

Rosemary Titterington
Iden Croft Herbs Ltd.
Frittenden Road
Staplehurst
Kent TN12 0DH

Nathalie Lopez
A Touch of Spice Ltd.
21 The Highlands
Bexhill-on-Sea
East Sussex TN39 5HL

Charles Carey
The Oil Merchant
47 Ashchurch Grove
London W12 9BU

Angelika Duval
Thyme Cottage
87 World's End Lane
Green Street Green
Kent BR6 6AE